CIO
Survival
Guide

The Roles and Responsibilities
of the Chief Information Officer

KARL D. SCHUBERT

WILEY

John Wiley & Sons, Inc.

For general information on our other products and services, or technical support, please contact our
Customer Care Department within the United States at 800-762-2974, outside the United States at 317-
572-3993 or fax 317-572-4002.

Wiley also publishes its books in a variety of electronic formats. Some content that appears in print may
not be available in electronic books.

For more information about Wiley products, visit our web site at www.wiley.com.

Library of Congress Cataloging-in-Publication Data:

Schubert, Karl D.
   CIO survival guide : the roles and responsibilities of the chief
information officer / Karl D. Schubert.
      p.   cm.
Includes index.
   ISBN 0-471-45793-0 (CLOTH)
   1. Chief information officers.   2. Information technology—Management.
3. Information resources management.   4. Management.   I. Title.
HD30.2   .S34   2004
658.4'038—dc22

                                                                    2003026694

Printed in the United States of America.

10 9 8 7 6 5 4 3 2 1

*To my wonderful, understanding, and supportive family: wife June,
son and daughter, David and Karin, my parents and sister.
Also to Joe and Catherine Stenzel and those kind souls who
have encouraged and supported me along the way.*

Acknowledgments

I want to thank Joe and Catherine Stenzel for suggesting that I write this book and for their constant encouragement and suggestions throughout the process. I had the great pleasure of getting to know them over the past five years and to have shared many discussions on a wide variety of topics. I am indebted to Joe for his editing, suggestions, understanding, and unfettered cajoling. Ruth Chiego Turner provided invaluable assistance in literature searching. Finally, it has been a true pleasure working with Tim Burgard, our partner at John Wiley, and with Kerstin Nasdeo and Janice Borzendowski, from whom I benefited tremendously in book production and the English language, respectively.

Twenty years ago, my early career mentor, Fred Springer, advised me to write down on a piece of paper what I wanted to be doing professionally in 1, 2, 5, and 10 years, and ultimately what I wanted to have accomplished by the time I retired. He told me that I would find this useful as both an educational exercise and as a way of focusing on what I ultimately wanted to do (a 20-year objective). Amazingly, I still have that piece of paper and still keep in touch with Fred. That focus helped me to achieve those goals, benefiting professionally from doing so, and (most of the time) greatly enjoying the work behind those achievements along the way. I am honored and immensely pleased to have had Fred as a friend and advisor all these years.

Over the past nearly 30 years, I have had the great honor of meeting and working with and for some very talented and inspiring people—regrettably too many to name individually. You know who you are, though, and I look forward to the opportunity of working with you again some time in the future.

And I would like to acknowledge and thank my parents, Dave and Ruth, for their quiet but always-there support, and my sister, Carol, for her encouragement and academic insights. Finally, I would like to thank June for her support and understanding during the time I have been writing this book. It has been an exhilarating experience watching our children, David and Karin, finding out who they are and learning what it means to be responsible young adults. Hopefully, they will also come to see the wisdom of having a plan for their life and their careers—it's a jungle out there, and it sure is a lot safer if you have a survival guide to assist you along the way. I hope this one helps.

Contents

PREFACE   XI

CHAPTER 1   **What We Were, Who We Are, and Who We
             Are Becoming**   1
             Brief Genealogy of the IT Profession   1
             State of the Profession   5
             What CEOs Really Want in Their CIOs   10
             Ten Questions the CIO Must Ask the CEO   13
             Notes   19

CHAPTER 2   **A Fork in the Road: Business or Technology?**   21
             Designing the Work   22
             Setting Up Shop   24
             The Fork in the Road   25
             Creating the IT Internal Partnership Network   26
             Maximizing the Partnership Network   32
             Evolving CIO Expectations: Technologist
                 or Businologist?   45
             CIO and CTO Relationships   49
             Ten Questions the CIO Should Ask
                 Network Partners   51
             Profile of Success   59
             Notes   60

CHAPTER 3   **A Unified Competency Profile**   65
             Technical Skills   67
             Business Acumen   83
             Leadership Competence and Vision   94
             Profiles of Success   101
             Ten Questions the CIO Should Ask Outsourced
                 Service Providers   102
             Notes   113

CHAPTER 4   **Connecting IT to Value Creation**   115
             The Language of the Industry   116
             Embracing the "Perfect" External Customer, or
                 Managing Customer Relationship Value   118
             Enterprisewide Strategic Planning   127
             Continuous and Discontinuous Process Improvement   130

The CIO and Practical Strategic Planning: More
  Than Just IT   135
Planning the Future without Disrupting the Present   138
IT as a Value Center   149
Ten Questions the CIO Should Ask the Entire
  Executive Team during Joint Strategic
  Planning Activities   150
Notes   170

CHAPTER 5   **Focus and Prioritization**   **173**
CIO Risk Profile Assessment   177
Aligning IT Resources to Your Organization's Strategy   184
Proper Provisioning: Resource Allocation to IT   192
Adaptive Systems: If We Haven't Started It Yet, It Costs
  Nothing to Change It!   200
Charting the Journey Milestones: IT Program
  Management   202
Ten Questions the CEO Should Ask the CIO
  for Successful Alignment   206
Notes   230

CHAPTER 6   **Final Preparations**   **235**
The Trek into (Un)Known Territory: Barriers to Success   236
Nirvana Accelerators   245
Decisions a CIO Should Not Make Alone   252
Distant Horizon   263
Creating the Horizon   269
Ten Questions the CIO Must Ask about
  Future Horizons   271
Notes   273

GLOSSARY   **275**

INDEX   **285**

Preface

Their budgets have been cut, their work's been outsourced, their staff's been down-sized, and they've been pushed off the executive team. Their status within the enterprise has suffered. That's dumb. And for CIOs, not fighting back would be dumber.

—Stephanie Overby[1]

It is a matter of survival. Survival of the fittest and survival of the prepared. It's a jungle out there, and there are a lot of natural and unnatural hazards you'll encounter on your path as a CIO or an aspiring CIO. Making your way through the jungle can be challenging, dangerous, exhilarating, and rewarding—sometimes all at the same time. A lot depends on how well prepared you are for the endeavor.

Few professions are more challenging and more challenged than that of the CIO: enabler, peer and partner, business executive with technical know-how, and technical executive with business know-how. Responsible to everyone; and master of so little. There's no other position in the company like it. The CIO is the "go-to" person for all things IT. With all these expectations and responsibilities, how does a CIO chart a course through the jungle?

The *CIO Survival Guide* is written to help you do just that. Whether you are currently a CIO, an aspiring CIO, work for the CIO, or the CIO works for you, there is much to do to get prepared, succeed, and provision against failure. The *Guide* concentrates many people's years of experience, interactions, and discussions with people at all levels in the information technology industry—especially with senior IT operations and product development executives and managers. It integrates diverse experiences, observations, discussions, and research of many experts in and about the field. Particularly, the *Guide* focuses heavily on the role of the CIO and what it takes to be a successful CIO who also enjoys *being* a CIO.

It has been incredibly exhilarating being involved in the evolution of information technology during my professional lifetime. Surprisingly, it has become increasing more complex to accomplish the bottom-line deliverable of our professional community: *to make things simpler*. As a result, a gap of understanding between those creating the solutions and those needing the solutions (or paying for them) has been opened and continues to widen dramatically. To the rescue comes the CIO who translates this complex world of information technology into a readily understandable set of ideas and solutions in a business context that focuses on creating value for each person in the company, and thereby for the company itself.

This skill is essential to a CIO's success relative to the use of technology in the business world: the ability to translate the complexities of information technology and information systems into something everyone else can understand. Just because someone *uses* IT does not mean he or she is interested in how IT *works*. Just because someone *depends on* IT does not mean that he or she knows IT or will come to know it if IT is explained in IT terms. In fact, it's just the opposite. Non-technicians either flee in frenzy or develop that blank-eyed, comatose stare before the technician has completed the first explanatory sentence. While it may be hard to believe that not everyone is as interested in information technology as you are, the fact is that (incredibly!) they are not. So the challenge is to translate the technology and the need into what might be considered a modicum of "coolness" and a solution for a real problem—or at least a solution that makes life easier or better for the poor sod. This same person, by the way, can be a great weather vane for whether or not one of your fascinating ideas *is* a solution to a real live, actual problem.

Enter June, my wife of more than 25 years and mother of our two children. June has been surrounded by technology and computers the entire time we have been together, and she is fairly proficient using them. At the same time, she has absolutely zero interest in knowing *how* they work. The two best ways I know to induce sleep is to start talking "letters and numbers" to her or to turn on sci-fi or a science program. That said, she is a daily user of e-mail and an avid researcher of information on the Web. She pays our bills online, buys things online, and recently has even begun to use online instant messaging to communicate with our son at college. (Turns out she also uses it to communicate with my daughter and me when we're in different rooms and she wants to ask or tell us something.)

Because of June's technology profile, I have sometimes called her a Luddite or technophobe; she regularly corrects me on the latter. She is not *afraid* of technology; so she says she is a "technogynist," because when it comes to technology she just doesn't *like* it. Why should she have to understand the technology behind an automobile engine to drive it? Fact is, she shouldn't have to, but that is the way that most companies and senior executives feel about IT—both the information technology and the IT organization. That's also why it is so important for the CIO to be able to translate the technobabble into something that has meaning to those who can benefit from it.

Beyond how information technology works, in order to be able to actually create value, you have to know what needs to be done and then convince those who will benefit and those who will pay for it. At times, I have used my own personal sounding board, my resident Luddite, as a reality test of my own beliefs and ability to communicate them. For example, back when interactive TV was the rage, there seemed to be one major sticking point: the cost of the set-top box. At the time, it looked as though it was going to require a computer workstation dressed-up to look like a set-top box to do the job. Consequently, this set-top box would run about $5,000, maybe more. While I thought this would be a cool thing to have at home (being able to decide what to watch and when to watch it), something told me I'd better get a second opinion.

The verdict was in well before I got to the $5,000 punch line: Given a choice, she wouldn't even fool around with a set-top box, let alone an expensive and (she was intuitively certain) a more complex one. Fast-forward nearly 10 years and my question comes up again, this time in terms of a personal digital video recorder (e.g., TiVo or Replay). Again, no interest, even though the $300 price tag made it less staggering. Circumstances, however, intervened and I was able to rationalize (a true rationalization) the purchase of one for my commuting apartment, and within two days of a family visit they were hooked on it. No amount of description ahead of time could convince, but actually seeing it and *using* it made the difference. Again, absolutely zero interest in how it worked, why it worked, or anything like that. But once they saw it in use, the value became visible. It freed everyone from being slaves of TV schedules (and from watching as many mediocre programs just because they were next on the station).

This is not to say that your nontechnical peers and partners are Luddites, but it does illustrate that your success as a CIO is tied to your ability to translate and demonstrate the information technology world of possibilities into meaningful value creation for them and for your company. Just because something seems "cool" does not mean it's of any practical use or benefit.

The subject of the *Guide* came up recently with an acquaintance who works as a *BusinessWeek* correspondent. I told him that it was about the roles, responsibilities, needs, and challenges for CIOs. He asked if the main message was how to make a quick exit or if it was prescriptive. I told him it was prescriptive. On reflection, it was most interesting that his first thought reflected how difficult a role he obviously saw it to be. Perhaps because my career in this arena started in IT, I have always felt an affinity to the employees, managers, and executives in IT and the incredible tactical and strategic challenges before them—trying to hang on with both hands as their customers (internal and external) take them in one direction and then another. For instance, consider the anarchy created by personal digital assistants (PDAs). This problem rivals the initial problems companies had trying to keep people from bringing their own coffeepots into the office. What do you do when all levels of your employees get them as gifts or buy them under the firm belief that they need to do so to survive (productivity improvement). You can't manage what you can't control and there is no way to control the ownership and use of PDAs. As the old saying goes, "If you can't beat 'em, join 'em."

I have spent the majority of my professional life building and leading groups and building solutions to help CIOs solve problems and create value for their companies. A guiding principle has been could I see myself using or needing the particular solution for IT—and bouncing that off the many CIOs, senior technology executives, and managers and architects I know, the objective being to avoid producing a solution that is looking for a problem, or producing a solution that is ahead of its time.

Being the senior information technology executive is not a job for everybody, and it is not a job that is anywhere near as generalized as the other "C"-level positions in the company (CEO or CFO, for instance). It is a real jungle, and no intelligent person would go into the jungle without a guide. So for you CIOs, aspiring CIOs, or those of you who are challenged with managing a CIO, here's yours: the *CIO Survival Guide*.

Karl D. Schubert
Austin, Texas
February 2004

NOTE

1. Stephanie Overby, "The CIO Role: The Incredible Shrinking CIO," *CIO Magazine*, (October 15, 2003), www.cio.com/archive/101503/shrinking.html, accessed October 18, 2003.

Publisher's note: A partner volume, the *CFO Survival Guide,* written by Joe and Catherine Stenzel, is available from John Wiley & Sons.

CHAPTER 1

What We Were, Who We Are, and Who We Are Becoming

[S]ince time is all one substance, one is able to use the experience of the past and the observation of the present to decipher the language in which information about the future is conveyed.

—Kristen Lippincott[1]

BRIEF GENEALOGY OF THE IT PROFESSION

The exact time and place that the IT profession began is impossible to determine. Depending on one's frame of reference, information and technology gradually move from tablets and hammers and chisels to bits stored on computer media. *Information* is the very substance of human communication, and, consequently, the history of information *technology* tracks the ways that people have applied scientific innovations to commercial, industrial, and artistic information communication applications. In ancient times, the great historians used teams of people to index, organize, write, and translate a permanent chronology of human events using the most advanced *information technology* of their day—paper. "Most advanced" is always a highly relative term in any discussion of information technology. Western information technology had not discovered pagination by the time of Johannes Gutenberg (1397–1478). With the advent of the printing press in the 1450s, Gutenberg and his thirteenth-century partners were using the most advanced information technology available.

Naturally, the definition of the information technology *professional* followed the career most associated with innovative technology. Those who were compensated in some form or fashion for their information communication expertise were the IT professionals of their day. It may seem like a long technological reach from paper to the advent of electronic tabulation and computation devices, but consider how quickly these devices have become an indispensable, ever more specialized human technology; consider the exponential acceleration of information technology innovation. Now imagine how long it might take at this pace before some form of biomechanical interface technology relegates today's state of the art into the history books.

Because electronic tabulation and computation remain the domain of our most pressing, current professional responsibilities for the foreseeable, budgetable future, a review of the electronic history of human communication illustrates the ever increasing importance of the professional as technology specialist and information manager. The IT profession began with Herman Hollerith (1859–1929) and his work with the 1890 census.[2] Hollerith invented the *punched card* and the tabulating machines used to *read* the cards for that historic record-keeping innovation. Like so many innovators throughout history, Hollerith was a savvy entrepreneur who founded the Tabulating Machine Company in 1896, which he subsequently sold to the Computing-Tabulating-Recording Company (CTR) in 1911. CTR was created when International Time Recording Company merged with Computing Scale Company to specialize in clocks and grocery weights and measure information technology products. The IT organizational genealogy becomes more familiar to twenty-first century professionals when, in 1924, the combined companies were renamed to International Business Machines, IBM (see Exhibit 1.1).

Hollerith not only invented the machines and the media, but he seems to have been a regular fixture at the census bureau, watching over, managing, and fixing the machines and working with the people to keep the census work going, thereby placing the inception of the modern-day IT profession around 1890. This earliest expression of the profession was, of course, highly mechanical and highly supervisory (and probably not very professional).

The next major milestone in the IT profession was the development of one of the earliest computers built that was worthy of the name "data center": the Colossus. Using more than a thousand state-of-the-art vacuum tubes, this computer, designed and built in 1943 by a team headed up by Alan Turing[3] was used to decipher German messages. It is considered to be the first all-electronic calculating device. While the details about what it took to manage this computer on a daily basis remain undocumented, it's not difficult to imagine, based on just a photographic comparison with a modern-day computer. A close analogy would be a comparison between early automobiles and today's cars: The ancestors in the IT innovation genealogy were less complicated but needed more minute-to-minute care and

EXHIBIT 1.1   GENEALOGY OF INFORMATION TECHNOLOGY

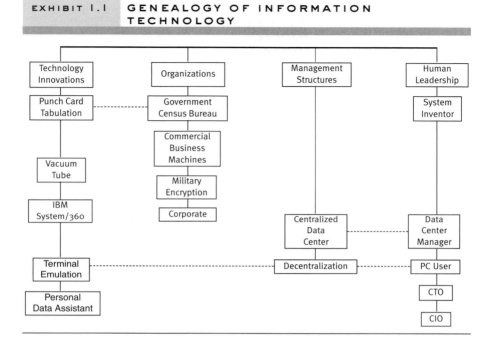

feeding while the present-day descendents are significantly more complicated but require much less constant attention.

Following World War II, and the classified examples like the Colossus that provide little information about actual IT management focuses, the pace of technology development and management increased, qualitatively speaking, exponentially. Interestingly, compared with today's IT environment, this same period is historically distinguished by a lack of interest in the development of the computer business in terms of the customers and companies that bought computers.[4] Working from available records, including collections of personal experiences and anecdotes, the common wisdom suggests that the starting point in large-scale commercial computing was inaugurated by IBM's announcement and introduction of its System/360 product family in 1964 and 1965. This innovative product line forced all other computing companies in the market to follow suit.

Moving from the IT production industry to the IT function implications within computer-dependant organizations, this same generation of products introduced the facility concepts of the *data center* or the *data processing center*— also known as the *raised floor*—with all the significant attendant implications for the future of IT management.[5] Along with this new technology facility structure came the *data center manager,* or the *DP manager.* And as the expectations, responsibilities, budget, and scope of the person in this role increased over the years, the functional leadership position evolved from that of technician to manager to technology manager to production manager to business manager to executive to senior executive.

The 1970s were dominated by these large mainframe computers and everything associated with them. Computer system operation and management were dominated by *centralization* paradigms; that is, all decisions, funding, management, operation, and even "most use" was channeled through a central IT authority. The 1980s witnessed the rise of so-called smart terminals and personal computers that acted like smart terminals (also known as *terminal emulation*). At the same time, a new dominant IT focus entered the genealogical picture: the computer user. The burgeoning number of computer users found that it was more and more difficult to get what *they* needed done by their IT organizations (functions) working to address their own provincial priorities in the same time frame. As it turned out, the cost of the personal computers became affordable within departmental budgetary limits—and this did not escape the notice of the end users.

Driven by a marketplace influenced by a new generation of users, the 1980s also saw the dispersion, or decentralization, of IT business solution decision making, acquisition, and application development. In other words, IT lost control, and the end users were ecstatic about finally being in control of their own destinies. Going into the 1990s, like the slowing of a pendulum, IT organizations made some movement back toward centralization, but they were not able to make up all the ground that they had lost. They found a more balanced point at which the end users still retained a modicum of control and independence but the IT organization reestablished its leadership responsibilities according to the new interdependencies in the emerging dynamics of the overall IT genealogy. Looking back, it was predestined. The costs of providing a dedicated IT support person (officially or unofficially, by assignments, short straw, or personal interest) must be measured and calculated in terms of degree of difficulty, dollars, efficiency, and efficacy, to name a few, all in a discipline where few users have the time, inclination, or expertise to do it themselves.

Entering the 2000s, IT professionals and their users almost had the pendulum balanced, until a new technology changed the dynamics of their relationship once again: the personal digital assistant (PDA). This new technology on the genealogy followed the same dispersion dynamics as its predecessors: At first, only a few people had them; then everyone wanted one; then many got one; then anarchy broke loose with the support problems they created; then they were forbidden (but people bought them on their own); then companies decided they had to deal with them (many senior executives got one as a holiday gift); soon they will reach an IT management equilibrium within most information systems. Heading toward the 2010s, one thing will be certain: IT organizations and their leadership will experi-

EXHIBIT 1.2   CIO CITATION IN THE PROFESSIONAL
LITERATURE

1988	135
1987	88
1986	33
1985	33
1984	15
1983	5
1982	2
1981	1
1980	1

Source: Penrod, et al., *The Chief Information Officer in Higher Education*, 1990.

ence several more swings of the centralize/decentralize IT pendulum relative to the eventual equilibrium point at which, in the end, specialists and users learn how to integrate a new technology so that everyone is better off.

This discussion has focused on the extremely rapid rate of development in the technology lineage of the overall IT genealogy, so one might assume that the professional management lineage has matured with equal rapidity. One would be wrong to do so. Humans simply aren't so easy to build or program. A major academic study conducted in the early 1990s traced the origin of the *chief information officer* title to a conference presentation quoted in a 1980 *Computerworld* article on information resource management.[6] Following this article, the term CIO finally reached 100-plus citations in the professional literature in 1988 (see Exhibit 1.2). In short, while this leadership role has been evolving alongside an applied organizational technology more than 100 years old, it is really only in the last 10 years that the term CIO has become a matter of human awareness—let alone a subject of extensive management or functional leadership experience.

STATE OF THE PROFESSION

The state of the information technology leadership profession is no different from any other profession in its earliest stages: It is evolving. The difference between a positive and negative perspective on the IT profession depends largely on when you last took a look.

From an organizational context, because all companies work at a unique level of IT management maturity, the responsibilities of the person at the top of the IT organization follow those same idiosyncratic centralization cycles and respond to influences that the prevailing business climate has from the standpoint of overall organizational maturity. Amidst all this flux, CIOs can count on one consistency from organization to organization at all levels of IT maturity: the horizontal *reach* of and expectations put on the CIO are significantly greater than they were 10 years ago. Whether the CIO reports to the chief executive officer (CEO), the CIO is expected to be more businessperson than technologist; he or she is expected to lead and manage directly, by means of influence, or through a combination of both. Within this same context of greater horizontal reach, the organization may or may not expect the CIO to perform as a key member of the senior executive team directly participating in the development of key company strategies, tactics, and initiatives. No, this lack of clarity is not a mistake. Depending on the company, the culture, and the CEO in particular, the CIO either holds a key executive position with all its obligate leadership responsibilities or works as the head manager of the company's IT utility.

In the context of the significant economic and technological growth periods and significant economic downturns, more enlightened senior executive teams look to the CIO in times of growth to help them maximize the opportunities for the company and its employees to benefit from that growth: to gain significant competitive advantage. Similarly, those same enlightened senior executive teams look to the CIO in times of downturn to help them make the most of what they have, find ways to leverage any advantage against the competition, provide the technology to get the greatest productivity from their workforce, and, of course, to find ways to get more for less throughout the company.

For example, human resources (HR) now occupy a central position in the strategic management of a company's human capital. HR executives need the high-level perspective and experience of senior IT executives so that each can contribute to a solution that gives the employees and the company their money's worth for their IT dollars.[7] Clearly, the senior HR executive who has an effective relationship with the senior IT executive will be well positioned to work to realign the resources so that they are spent most effectively.

Looking at the CIO in the context of organizational authority, it is interesting to look at the range of CIO reporting responsibilities. In an *InformationWeek* survey, 26 percent of 500 of the Fortune 1000 had CIOs who reported to the CEO, chairperson, or president, with the remainder reporting to lower-level executives. In the same survey, the 30 percent of the 100 CIOs in the top-ranked companies reported directly to the highest executive.[8] In another survey by the executive recruiting firm Heidrick & Struggles, 34.3 percent of the senior IT executives reported to the CEO, 37.2 percent reported to the chief operating officer (COO), 16.7 percent reported to the chief financial officer (CFO), and the remaining 11.8 percent reported to lower-level executives.[9] In a survey, by Giga Information Group, 33 percent of the CIOs reported to the CEO, 29 percent reported to the

COOs, 20 percent reported to the CFOs, 2 percent reported to the senior marketing executive and 16 percent reported to "other."[10] In a similar survey by *CIO Magazine*, 51 percent of the CIOs reported to the CEO, 12 percent reported to the COO, 11 percent reported to the CFO, 4 percent reported to a corporate CIO, and 22 percent responded "other."[11] Exhibit 1.3 shows a typical distribution pattern for CIO reporting.

These results will vary depending upon the competitive maturity of the companies surveyed. However, focusing on recent trends, successful, high-performance companies have begun to increasingly value the competitive advantages of a well-run, strategically aligned IT function led by a person who participates as a peer with other senior executives to determine how IT can address short- and long-term priorities.

Chapter 2 discusses the practical importance of the CIO's reporting relationships in greater detail. For now, these studies suggest two important factors that determine the effectiveness of the CIO's reporting relationship in organizations of all competitive profiles: One, the CIO needs the commitment of whichever CXO (i.e., CEO, COO, CTO, CFO, etc.) has been designated for reporting purposes; two, the CEO must formally recognize the CIO and the IT function as a key organizational asset for business planning and strategic development in front of all company employees.

EXHIBIT 1.3   CIO REPORTING PATTERNS

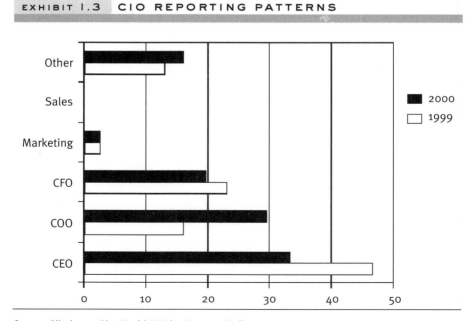

Source: Gliedman, *GigaWorld IT Value Program Poll*, 2002.

The inconsistency of CIO reporting relationships betrays how new this corporate management identity remains in the eyes of most executives and executive teams. In short, "What are we going to call it?" To make matters worse, as companies evolve into an organizational structure that captures more and more IT value, they change their understanding of the CIO accordingly. No one doubts the work identity and role responsibilities of the CEO and CFO. Like the behavioral dynamics of any club, the merit and status of the new member must be proven and stand the test of time before "full membership privileges" are granted.

What about the work identity and role responsibilities of the CTO relative to the CIO? The CTO acronym is probably more immediately recognizable than CIO, probably because it has been around for a lot longer and there are many more of them. For example, would you expect a technology-based company to be *without* a CTO? As the chief *technology* officer, the CTO is expected to be the senior-level technologist in the company or in the function. In the case where there are separate CTOs for individual business units, and perhaps one for the company as a whole, the CTOs may very well (and most probably do) have different areas of expertise, and all, some, or even none of those areas may be associated with the IT function.

This was the case while I was the CTO for the server and storage product group at Dell. There was also a CTO for the desktop and portables product group, a CTO for the CIO, and a CTO for the corporation as a whole (who doubled as the senior vice president for the portables and desktop product group). Each of us had different roles and responsibilities and areas of expertise. Of these CTOs, only one was responsible for technology related to IT: the CTO reporting to the CIO. Consider, also, that Dell was an interesting example because its IT organization at the time was larger than the entire product group. It makes sense when you think about it, because the IT group created *significant* value in Dell's ordering process, inventory management, manufacturing process, and service and support. IT is one of the key core competencies at Dell and is a major factor in its success as a company in being the low-cost producer. The CTOs for the product groups had many significant responsibilities, such as: (1) directing the product and system architectures of the product group, (2) leading the product architects for the specific areas within the product group, (3) identifying new technologies relevant to their specific product groups, (4) evaluating potential partners with whom to develop that technology, (5) identifying when that technology would apply, (6) watching for signs of an impending *innovator's dilemma*, and (7) being the *credible threat* for the product group senior vice president (SVP). (*Credible threat* was the term one of them used to mean that the CTO for a product group was expected to have development, engineering, and management experience, in addition to architecture and technology experience, and could thereby provide a counterbalancing second opinion to the SVP on critical areas of assertion and risk related to the product group's engineering, test, service and support, and marketing functions.)

And, of course, the product group CTO was in high demand for customer technical and executive briefings and for participation on technology advisory boards and standards and industry association boards. The CTO in the IT function, reporting to the CIO, has a completely different set of responsibilities although the role is similar. The IT CTO is responsible for the product and system architectures of the IT function, leading the application architects for the specific areas within the IT group, identifying new technologies relevant to the products and applications used by the IT groups, evaluating potential partners with whom to develop those technologies, identifying when a technology would apply, watching for signs of an impending innovator's dilemma, and being the credible threat to the IT groups for the CIO. Often, as a product group CTO, we would find ourselves working with the CTO of the IT function, as he or she was quite interested in what we would be doing next and whether it would apply to that group and its needs. And, similarly, we were very interested in understanding the IT function CTO's needs because they were not unlike those of similar customers. Of course, if you are in a company where your IT function would not likely be a customer of your product group's products—for example, a chemical company—this interaction is much less likely to occur. With either type of CTO, though, the emphasis is on *technology*; and even though we were expected to be able to work through the costs and business aspects, it was from a feasibility point of view rather than a commit-the-business point of view. So the distinction is very clear between the two in practice: the *CIO's* emphasis is on *business* and the CTO's emphasis is on *technology*.

A *CIO Magazine* analysis found that information technology was generally a key element of strategic planning and received attention at the board of directors level.[12] Another analysis also concluded that a consensus had not been reached on the use of a particular title for the senior information technology head.[13] Another interesting perspective on CIO identity comes from the accounting profession. In a book on the history of the accounting profession, an entire chapter was dedicated to "Information Technology and the Accountancy Profession."[14] The chapter is fascinating reading for the history, the relationship between IT and accounting, the accountant's perspective, and particularly for the accounting author's conclusion that the accounting profession has continually missed opportunities to assume responsibility for (in other words, *take control of*) the IT profession. The author also implies that the evolution of the IT profession and its responsibilities would function more smoothly and consistently if it were managed according to accountancy principles. The important relationship between the IT information engineers and the accounting information brokers is detailed in Chapter 5. For now, suffice it to say that the accounting profession has not progressed any farther along the path in viewing the IT profession as a true profession than any other function represented on the senior executive team. Biased by the fact that they control the form and distribution of information in its decision-making form, many accounting and finance function personnel, all the way up to the CFO, still regard the IT profession as if it were some kind of public utility: a lot of work, a lot of people, a lot of money (read: *cost*), a *lot* of technical complexity, and hard to quantify in terms of ROI.

In summary, it is very early on the genealogical timeline for the CIO profession compared to the other CXOs (CEO, COO, CTO, CFO) and their professions. As new and disruptive technologies push organizational IT applications and business planning through the predictable cycles of centralization strategies, the CIO will face the same challenges of changing identity that the CTO knows all too well. Thus, part of what we will be working through in this book will be to help you get to the point of doing what you want to be doing. By doing so, you will also advance the status of the profession for all your peers.

Managing IT in the Fourth Dimension

One more important context puts a final spin on the challenges of CIOs as IT leaders: time. Consider some of the realities of managing the infrastructure of knowledge for an entire organization in terms of the competitive realities and disruptive technological innovations of this age of knowledge. For example, CIOs and their executive peers need to understand the half-life of relevant knowledge in each of the knowledge arenas they make decisions. Exhibit 1.4 profiles the useful, relevant half-life for knowledge for four conventional learning environments. Consider the implications for long-term IT investments and strategic planning. Executive teams that manage an organization's IT knowledge without taking full advantage of a peer IT specialist do so at their own peril.

The dynamics of knowledge relevance become bleaker when considering the growing complexity of cataloguing and managing the accessibility of the exponential increase in all forms of information. This paradox of the knowledge age is graphically summarized in Exhibit 1.5. Organizations and their leaders simply need more time to figure out the most appropriate solution to any problem because of the increasing work required to sort out information environment complexities in terms of organizational priorities. At the same time, these same executive teams need to react faster in the face of extremely short knowledge relevance half-lives. Simply put, by the time many teams finally discover a solution, the solution will no longer be timely. Who needs a CIO? Well, that depends.

WHAT CEOS REALLY WANT IN THEIR CIOS

What *do* CEOs really want from their CIOs? This will be a continual theme throughout our journey together, so this section lays a foundation for further

EXHIBIT 1.4 KNOWLEDGE RELEVANCE HALF-LIFE

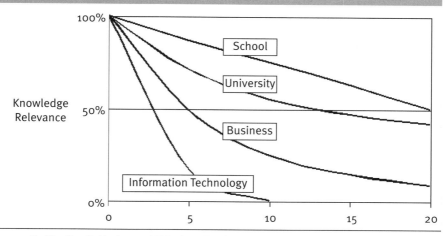

Source: M. Charlier, R. Henke, and F. Rother, "Medien für die Weiterbildung: Scheibe statt Flug," *Wirtschaftswoche* 49, (1994) 120–122.

analysis. Part of the problem is discovering the difference between *want* and *need*. Answering this question is straightforward, but not simple, because the answer for this very young profession must be pieced together from a collection of studies, conversations, and experience, all from a variety of perspectives, including the practitioner, the academic, and different management professions. Some of the most important focuses include what the CEOs *want* (and/or *need*) from their perspec-

EXHIBIT 1.5 PARADOX OF THE KNOWLEDGE AGE

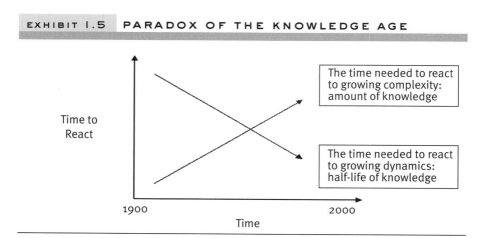

Source: K. Bleicher, *Das Konzept Integriertes Management*, 2nd Ed., (Frankfurt: Campus, 1992) 26.

tive, from the CIO's perspective, and from the CIO's peers' perspective. In the end, the most important question becomes what should *you* as the CIO be certain that you *give* your CEO?

CEOs really want a technical advisor who is a strategic business partner; they *want* and *need* this. Even if they do not know they want it, they need it. Of course, CEOs do not always know that they need. In a *Computerworld* interview, when asked about the new role of the CIO, Scott McNealy, chairman and CEO of Sun, replied:

> Sun's Bill Howard is an example of a new-wave CIO. He understands that his job is not managing data centers or the network for us. The CIO shouldn't be worried about assembling computers, or running data centers, or managing the network, or getting the printing stuff to work. So what does he spend all his time doing? He's building a world-class, LDAP directory registry implementation that will have every employee, customer, reseller, shareholder, and piece of equipment in the Sun community in a directory with a profile for each one, across all our business processes. That job alone will keep every CIO on the planet solely focused on being chief information officer. The old-style CIOs were all mechanics. They tended to buy their 10-speed bicycles and pay extra to have them unassembled. [15]

From this, it would appear that McNealy views his CIO as more of a technician and service developer than strategist and technology advisor. Along the same lines, Jack Brennan, chairman and CEO for the Vanguard Group, emphasized his view of the CIO's strategic importance. "It's our view at Vanguard that the business management team should be taking the lead on business technology projects, looking to IT for facilitation but not leadership."[16]

Contrast these views with the insights of two CIOs who work for forward-looking companies (and probably CEOs): John J. Ciulla, CIO of Vignette, and Monte Ford, CIO of American Airlines. Ciulla says CIOs today are expected to operate at the same business, strategic, and professional levels as their CXO-level peers.[17] Ford said that American's former CEO Don Carty looked to him to get them into the leading technology position in their industry because Carty saw technology as the key driver for their business over time.[18]

And, in the same quarter, marketing expert Regis McKenna and former Dell CIO Jerry Gregoire both favor giving CIOs additional responsibilities. McKenna asserts that the CIOs are well-positioned to take on several of the responsibilities formerly held by marketing: customer strategy and outreach.[19] He bases his belief on the view that the CIO is the person who has the infrastructure for the Web center and the call center—the primary points of contact by customers with a company. Gregoire proposes that there should be a CIO or former CIO on the board of directors of every company to help companies regain investor confidence by providing experience-based and customer-experience-based input on development and spending alternatives.[20]

In short, people hold a multichotomy of CIO expectations—multiple and contradictory. As part of our journey together, we will analyze the multichotomy from different value perspectives and work together to identify the optimal approach for you using a set of parameters that acknowledge who you are, where you are, and who you want to be. Along the way, we will look at "pictures of success," or profiles of people who are or have been successful with the particular perspective, idea, or approach this book explores.

TEN QUESTIONS THE CIO MUST ASK THE CEO

The CIO's relationship with the CEO is unique, regardless of any other CIO direct reporting responsibilities. The CIO and CEO each bear unique communication responsibilities in this relationship. As the senior IT executive, the CEO expects the CIO to understand and communicate important company business strategies, IT organization focuses, and executive peer/partnership values relative to information technology. The CEO also frequently calls on the CIO to work with external customers on behalf of the company.

Regardless of when you do so, there are 10 (at least) questions you must ask your CEO. Be prepared to either reconcile yourself to the CEO's responses or advocate for your own (or an alternative) point of view. These questions accomplish much more than simple information acquisition. They establish the foundation of a long-term relationship of two people with the expertise the organization needs to flourish. Accept your expertise fully before engaging your CEO in a discussion of these questions; and remember, if your CEO or anyone else in the organization knew what you know, you would not be the CIO. Simply by asking these questions, you demonstrate how you intend to partner with the CEO to guide and create value for the company. If you believe that Paul A. Strassmann has it right when he defines the CIO as "Commanding Impossible Operations"[21] and the IRM (an equivalent position in government and nonprofits) as "Impossible Relationships to Manage"[22] then it is even more important to ask these questions as soon as you possibly can.

1. What does my being the CIO mean to you?
2. What are you looking for from your Information Technology group?
3. As CIO, am I a member of your C-level Executive team?
4. As CIO, am I a member of your Corporate Strategic Planning team?
5. As CIO, am I a staff Executive or a line Executive or both? Will/Can that change?
6. As CIO, am I the *final signature* on IT-related investments?

7. As CIO, why do I report to <the person> rather than to you, the CEO? (assuming that you do not report to the CEO)

8. Are you getting the value you want and need from your IT investment?

9. Do you see the IT group as a cost center, profit center, or do you have a different business model in mind?

10. Looking ahead, what would you like to see in 1 month, 3 months, 6 months, and a year from now?

Number 1: What Does My Being the CIO Mean to You?

This is a fundamental question when taking on any new position, and especially a C-level position. This question takes top priority because the answer ensures that you can match your understanding of the CIO role with your CEO's understanding. If you report to someone who reports to the CEO on your behalf, this same question holds equal importance for your boss to understand.

Because this is an open-ended question, the variations on type of answer you can get are endless. How the CEO responds with posture, voice, and other nonverbal cues can be as informative as the words used to answer the question. Look for any information that gives insight into how this person thinks. Naturally, if the CEO talks about any problems with the company, the CIO has some immediate priorities if the problems are in any way IT-related. Beyond the role and its responsibilities, look for information about the CEO's opinion of you as a person. If the CEO talks only about the job, use a follow-up question to elicit this information by adding ". . . me in particular." Use a similar technique if the CEO focuses on you and does not address the role and its responsibilities.

Number 2: What Are You Looking for from Your Information Technology Group?

The answer to this question gives the CIO insights into the CEO's vision (a view from the top) of IT and its relationship to the rest of the company. Listen for words and phrases that suggest (or do not suggest) that IT is an integral part of the CEO's vision for company business and competitive advantage. In addition, listen for suggestions that the CEO looks to the CIO and IT to *lead the way* to the next level of business competitiveness. Every IT organization needs to maintain a balance between stretch goals and reality, so this might be your first opportunity to learn how realistic the CEO's expectation of IT really is. Also listen for words and phrases that the CEO uses to indicate expectations that your group can help integrate the company's other groups and divisions and become a unifying force in the workplace. Once again, carefully examine these expectations in terms of the realities of your own experience.

Number 3: As CIO, Am I a Member of Your C-Level Executive Team?

The CEO's answer to this question is going to give you insights into whether the CIO role is a position of leadership. If it is, then the CIO can expect to be included in the discussions and decision-making process for the key planning and strategy activities by the company's senior management team as led by the CEO. While you can expect to be accorded the respect and consideration due in such a senior-level, responsible position, expect to be held to the same higher level of performance and leadership expectations by your CEO and your executive peers and partners. Conversely, if your CEO hesitates, declines to comment, or answers no, then the C and the O are titles only and you need to examine the long-term opportunities while waiting for the company leadership to develop greater respect for IT as a value creation partner.

Number 4: As CIO, Am I a Member of Your Strategic Planning Team?

The CEO's answer to this question provides insights into whether the CEO sees IT as a key component to the company's strategic future, or if instead the IT organization serves the company merely as a utility or supporting function to everything else. The answer also indicates whether the CEO plans to use your planning skills and can see your skills as transferable across the senior executive team. If you are new to the company, this provides an opportunity for people to get to know you. If your CEO's response affirms the CIO as a key strategic role, you will be in an excellent position to enable and support your peers, partners, and company. If the CEO's response does not reaffirm a strategic role, continue to regularly inquire because expectations may change over time as the company looks more closely at its competitive position and cost effectiveness. Remain in a position from which you can step in and help at any time.

Number 5: As CIO, Am I a Staff Executive, a Line Executive, or Both? Will/Can That Change?

The CEO's answer to this question is going to give you insights into how directly responsible and empowered you are to provide leadership and resources for taking strategy to plan to reality. As a true line executive, the CIO is also likely to be re-sponsible for the company's overall IT budget. In either role, you are likely to be responsible for working with executive peers and partners to establish overall IT directions and enable them to realize the benefits of those directions. Your job as the CIO is much easier and more straightforward—particularly the accountability part of it—if you have the line responsibilities for IT.

If, however, you prefer a staff role, then you are responsible for obtaining direc-tions and assisting your peers and partners in getting the IT resources they need to achieve their goals. In this case, the CIO is also responsible for helping them retain the appropriate focus on doing so (as IT is not likely to be their primary responsi-bility). The CIO in this position frequently acts as a go-between and mediator as-sisting peers and partners to work together and integrate their IT solutions.

Number 6: As CIO, Am I the Final Signature on IT-Related Investments?

The CEO's answer to this question provides insights into whether the CIO can re-ally set and control directions for the IT organization—particularly where there are budget dollars involved. "Follow the money" almost always applies. When it comes to strategic planning for the IT organization, it is important to see that money fol-lows the implementation. Strategic or implementation funding deviations happen for good reasons, and all such changes can be justified against a long-term vision for the IT organization and the company.

If the final signature comes from the person to whom CIO reports, the CIO still has the opportunity to influence the ways that executive leadership strategically in-tegrates the IT organization. Diligently prepare your boss for each key upcoming strategic expenditure in terms of the specific needs of each of the company's im-portant organizations and their relationship to the overall strategic direction.

When the final signature and the sign-off authority is dispersed throughout the organization, the CIO has to make sure that all of the most senior executives un-derstand the limitations of the IT senior executive position. Specifically, the CIO can influence but not actually ensure, control, or manage adherence to the strate-gic direction or funding inconsistencies.

Number 7: Where I, as CIO, Do Not Report to the CEO, Why Not?

The CEO's answer to this question reveals three separate important insights:

- A rationalization about the importance of the CIO role

- How involved the CEO expects to be with the CIO on a daily basis
- The slant or perspective from which your CEO sees the IT function and the CIOs role based on which executive the CIO reports to

For example, when the CIO reports to the chief operating officer, a considerable portion of the CIO's time will likely also be involved in day-to-day operations of the IT functions and supporting partners and peers in meeting their operational objectives. This is not necessarily a bad thing; when you are directly involved in making money for your company, you have an easier time identifying the value of your work and the work of your organization.

If the CIO reports to the chief financial officer, a significant portion of the CIO's role will likely be related to the costs and investments in the IT organization and to the projections for future costs and investments in terms of the ways they are expected to create value for the company. This is not necessarily bad, either. Costs and investments justified with your CFO sail more smoothly through the approval process because you have more insight into the strategic financial objectives than your nonfinance-based peers and partners.

If the CIO reports to the chief technology officer, the CIO role is likely to be more technical and tactical and with less concentration on the business side. In general, this is not a particularly good place for a CIO to report. Your role should be a strong combination of business with technical understanding if you are to be in a good position to create value for the business.

If the CIO reports to the vice president of operations (who often reports to the COO) a significant portion of the CIO's efforts will likely be directed at the day-to-day business of the IT group and enabling your peers and partners on a more tactical basis. As this reporting structure places the CIO another layer deeper than the preceding structures, you may not have the access you need to the senior-most management and power base in your company required for leading, managing, enabling, and controlling (as opposed to influencing).

Number 8: Are You Getting the Value You Want and Need from Your IT Investment?

The CEO's answer to this question demonstrates whether you are expected to take the IT group to its next level of development or are going to be expected to be more of a caretaker for an area that is performing "acceptably." If you were hired to replace someone who is due for retirement or who is leaving because of some other normal (noncompany-generated) reason, then it may well be that your CEO is looking for someone to continue the efforts of your predecessor. If, however, you were hired to replace a CIO who left under other circumstances, the answer to this question is likely to also help you understand your CEO's IT priorities and view of the monies and effort the CEO intents to invest in IT to make the company more successful. If you are the first CIO at your company, then undoubtedly one of the reasons for the creation of this position was that the CEO does not believe that your company is getting enough value from the IT organization.

Number 9: Do You See the IT Group as a Cost Center or Profit Center, or Other?

The CEO's answer to this question suggests the approaches the CIO is going to need to take with developing, setting, and implementing IT strategies and plans. If the IT group is treated as a cost center, the CIO can work to justify needed expenses and investments on their merits; once agreement is reached, those costs are budgeted and/or apportioned to the parts of the company's business as appropriate. The downside for the CIO and the IT group is that the rest of the company will look at the IT budget with a jaundiced eye if IT does not deliver on its commitments as an enabler and partner to the CIO's peers.

If the IT group is treated as a profit center, the CIO works to justify all expenditures and investments based on the additional revenue they bring to your company; once agreement is reached, those costs will be budgeted and released to IT. However, along the way, the CIO is expected to show (as are your business group peers and partners) how IT tracks profit commitments for expenditures and investments. The downside for the CIO and the IT group is that the rest of the company may look at the IT budget and become dissatisfied with the ways IT spends on areas they care about—especially if IT has not worked on a pet project because its return on investment did not meet IT's operating hurdle.

This is a tough one: The reputation for cost-based groups is that they get sloppy in their cost management and exude entitlement; the reputation for profit-based groups is that they only work on projects that maximize profit as they are measured rather than maximizing profits of business units or the company. Does the CEO expect you to minimize or optimize expense and investment? Does the CEO expect you to maximize or optimize profit or return? In either case, does the CEO expect you to work on a companywide basis, a business-unitwide basis, or your business-unit-only basis? The answers to these questions are critical to CIO's success and to the CIO's ability to enable success for peers and partners, too.

Number 10: What Would You Like to See in One Month, Three Months, Six Months, and a Year from Now?

The CEO's answer to this question is going to give you insights into whether your CEO has given thought to IT's tactical and strategic needs. A very tactically focused CEO may expect the CIO to be strategically focused so that the company is not driving in the dark. It could mean that company leadership does not pay much attention to anything much beyond the current quarter's shareholder earnings; if that is the case, and you are strategically inclined, you either have an opportunity or a career death wish.

The very strategically focused CEO is the best of all worlds because as the chief information officer, your greatest value lies in the strategic area. Consequently, you need to align your strategy for IT with the CEO's strategy for the company. This is how you ensure value creation that matters.

NOTES

1. Kristen Lippincott, *The Story of Time*, (London: Merrell Holberton, 1999): 272.
2. Martin Campbell-Kelly and William Aspray, *Computer: A History of the Information Machine* (New York: HarperCollins, 1996): 20–28.
3. Lippincott, *Story of Time*, 25.
4. William Aspray, "The History of Computing within the History of Information Technology," *History and Technology* 11 (1994): 7–19.
5. The rooms containing the large mainframe computers were called *raised floors* because the floors the computer equipment actually stood on was a second floor approximately a foot higher than the building floor. This raised floor consisted of square tiles supported by a metal frame of posts and braces. The cables that connected the various computer pieces together ran through the spaces between the raised floor and the building floor to keep the cables out of harm's way. Air conditioning and pipes with cooling water for the processors were also routed through the raised-floor spaces.
6. James I. Penrod, Michael G. Dolence, and Judith V. Douglas, *The Chief Information Officer in Higher Education* (Boulder, CO: The Association for the Management of Information Technology in Higher Education, 1990): 3.
7. David Stein, "Measuring the Impact of HR Technology on Your Business," *Benefits & Compensation Solutions* 25, no. 9, (2002): 34–36.
8. Richard Layne, "The Best, the Biggest and the Debate," *InformationWeek* (September 18, 1989): 6–12.
9. Heidrick and Struggles, Inc., *Health Care Chief Information Officers* (Chicago: Healthcare Information and Management Society of the American Hospital Association (1988): 1.
10. Chip Gliedman, *GigaWorld IT Value Program Poll—Still a Long Way to Go* (Cambridge, MA: Giga Information Group, RPA-062000-00026 (June 26, 2000): 2.
11. Editorial survey, "The State of the CIO: Survey Results," *CIO Magazine,* www.cio.com/archive/030102/survey_results_content.html (accessed March 1, 2002).
12. Mark Gordon, "Hot Seat: How to Succeed in Strategic Planning," *CIO Magazine,* www.cio.com/archive/031502/hs_succeed.html (accessed March 15, 2002).
13. Heidrick and Struggles, *Health Care Chief Information Officers.*
14. T.A. Lee, A. Bishop, and R.H. Parker, *Accounting History from the Renaissance to the Present: A Remembrance of Luca Pacioli* (New York: Garland Publishing, 1996): 195–229.
15. Maryfran Johnson and Jaikumar Vijayan, "Q&A: Sun's McNealy on Company Plans, Role of CIOs," *Computerworld* (February 11, 2003): 44, available at: www.computerworld.com/hardwaretopics/hardware/story/0,10801,78443,00.html.

16. Jack Brennan, "CXO Perspectives: Show Me the Value," *CIO Magazine* (May 1, 2002): 45–49.

17. John J. Ciulla, "Step Up and Lead," *CIO Magazine* (November 1, 2002): 48–50.

18. Todd Datz, "Can America Keep Flying?" *CIO Magazine* (November 1, 2002): 56–66.

19. Regis McKenna, "The Job Just Got Bigger," *CIO Magazine* (October 1, 2002): 32.

20. Jerry Gregoire, in Regis McKenna, "The Job Just Got Bigger—Q&A," *CIO Magazine* (October 1, 2002): 44–46.

21. Paul A. Strassmann, *The Business Value of Computers: An Executive's Guide* (New Canaan, CT: The Information Economics Press, 1990): 298.

22. Ibid., p. 316.

CHAPTER 2

A Fork in the Road: Business or Technology?

Perhaps our abilities to make sense of the present depend not only on what we have accomplished in the past, but also what we are committed to accomplish in the future.

—Fred Alan Wolf[1]

In light of the soft and shifting management, professional, knowledge, and technology ground beneath the feet of CIOs everywhere, professional survival techniques require entirely different approaches from the typical survival priorities used by a person marooned alone on a desert island or stranded in the mountainous wastelands deep in the heart of Iowa. Many sections of the *CIO Survival Guide* focus on hard technical applications and the difficult skills needed to make them work. To create a balanced survival perspective for a profession still in its infancy, the *Guide* also digs deep into the "soft" side of organizational leadership as it pertains to the many responsibilities of the CIO. Daniel Goleman, author of *Emotional Intelligence* and *Primal Leadership: Realizing the Power of Emotional Intelligence* uses more than 25 years of research to validate what so many veteran executives already know: Skills and job experience look great on a resume, but there would be many more great leaders if that's all it took. People recognize great leaders for characteristics that until recently have been call "intangibles"—empathy, inspiration, influence, change catalyst, conflict manager, and team builder to name a few. Goleman and the researchers at the Consortium for Research on Emotional Intelligence in

Organizations discovered that not only can these intangibles be measured, they can be learned.[2]

CIOs naturally do well with the hard technology side. The great CIO also knows the nature of business as a social science. Hard sciences like physics and chemistry deal with easily managed mechanical relationships between physical components. Social sciences deal with people working in relationships according to their own free will, even when they share a common goal. Knowing the machines is not enough for this job. The great CIO knows how to listen, articulate, motivate, tell the truth, and mentor the distinct groups of people who authorize, maintain, and use the machines. A keen sense of self-awareness and social awareness lies at the foundation of emotionally intelligent leadership. This chapter carefully examines the self- and social awareness focuses critical to the unique leadership responsibilities of the CIO. As such, the soft side proves to be the most challenging (really hard) frontier for CIO professional development, and consequently, the *Guide* puts the soft side front and center.

The analysis of the profession from Chapter 1 indicated that the career path of virtually every CIO in any organization is still evolving. This is even truer for CIOs with complementary business and finance backgrounds. The good news is that the CIO has many perspectives from which to chart a professional career, and as different people exercise different personal options, they all collectively affect the evolution of the entire profession. More good news: Regardless of your current particular path or career trajectory, you can choose to change course a number of times throughout your career as your interests evolve in the context of the ever more certain responsibilities that will evolve for the CIO role.

DESIGNING THE WORK

Given the state of professional flux, current or aspiring chief information officers make career decisions in terms of personal interests, professional competencies, and work environment opportunities and barriers rather than predetermined professional definitions and expectations. Can you clearly define what it means to be your company's CIO? How can anyone be expected to excel at a job that has no commonly accepted definition, much less tangible activity boundaries and roles codified in the HR manual for all to see? Well, there are several ways to start, including: Ask your boss, ask your peers, ask your subordinates, ask someone else who has the role; or define the role as you would like to do it. How a CIO gets started defining the job significantly shapes the outcome. Many CIOs start in a professional identity void and never learn how the people in the organization really need their services. This section takes a practical approach to creating a custom-designed CIO role based on how companies value other traditionally well-established leadership positions in light of IT's most important contributions to organizational performance.

By the very nature of the job, a CIO works as an enabler whose success depends upon the success of people throughout the organization who use IT services as much as it does on the success of the people providing those same IT services. The IT provider and the IT user exist in an interdependent service relationship enabled by the CIO. The CIO is an enabler because information technology for the vast majority of companies is not the end product; IT is a business tool and can be a competitive advantage for the company and for those who create its end product.

The CIO's contribution to a company's success can be (and should be) on the three performance levels expected of more traditionally defined, well-established executive specialties like the CEO or the CFO: strategic partner, tactical executor, and reactive supporter. As a *strategic partner*, the CIO works as a member of the management team reporting to the company or divisional chief executive officer or the chief operating officer. Executive peers recognize the strategic use of information systems and information technology for competitive advantage. Organizations in the knowledge age need an IT perspective in their strategic planning processes. As an active participant in the company's strategic evolution, the executive team comes to see the CIO as an indispensable asset for directing strategic evolution.[3]

The CIO as strategic partner may be the goal for many people, but the challenge is to determine the starting point and the best path for getting there. As an evolving role in most organizations, the CIO depends on the input of many while educating everyone about the values of centralized, strategic IT leadership. As a strategic partner, the CIO works on an equal footing with the CEO, COO, CFO, VP of marketing and sales, VP of operations, CTO, perhaps some additional senior people at the VP level, and their staffs. In the most strategically mature companies, strategies are reviewed and revised for IT relevance at least quarterly based on information from the board of directors, customers, sales and marketing, the industry, the general economic climate, and the company's operational and financial performance.

As a *tactical executor*, the CIO works as a member of a senior management team where *management* is a verb. The senior management team puts tactical plans into place that support strategic goal achievement. As tactical executors, the entire team works together cross-functionally as enablers who assist in the tactical plan development and subsequently support its implementation. There is no better way for a CIO to demonstrate the strategic value of the IT organization to the company.

As a *reactive supporter*, the CIO demonstrates the ability to see the needs of a customer, the CEO, a peer, or any employee, as *they* perceive their needs. For example, as a senior executive, the CIO appropriately maintains a primary focus on strategic business and technology solutions issues. In contrast, as the senior business-oriented technology executive, when a business emergency or crisis rears its ugly head, the CIO will be asked to help or will simply volunteer to help. Because the work of the CIO is customer-based (even if they are only primarily internal customers), customer-interaction skills are very likely to be in high demand by the CEO, executive peers, and customers during stressful events. Similarly, the CIO is often called upon to address a crisis already in progress and for which the abilities of a competent reactive supporter could make the difference for a peer executive between a satisfied customer and a bad reputation.

People who naturally enjoy helping someone in need become good CIOs. Remaining ready to enable the performance of other people in the organization reinforces the practical and strategic importance of the IT organization. As such, the CIO's ability to act across this spectrum of performance levels—strategic, tactical, and reactive—can be strong reinforcement of IT's value and the CIO's contribution as a strategic business partner and technical specialist member of the senior management team.

SETTING UP SHOP

Having characterized some of the important elements of CIO performance in terms of executive responsibilities, the trick becomes developing existing professional and organizational competencies and conditions into a more successful functional relationship so that all people in the organization—executive peers, IT staff, and employees—benefit from the enabling resources of the CIO. Setting up this kind of shop starts with the answers to some intimate questions. How do you *feel* about this level and these types of contributions? How do you *feel* about being an enabler? What does your gut tell you about how well you like this role—how you *feel* about it?

Whether a person in a leadership position works on professional development from the emotional intelligence framework or some other model, great leaders eventually develop a personalized vocabulary for articulating gut intuition and other notions of self-awareness. For example, in her book *Finding Your Own North Star*, Harvard Business School researcher and executive coach Martha Beck characterizes leadership in terms of two selves: an *essential self* and a *social self*. The essential self is the base personality or who you are: "It's the personality you got from your genes: your characteristic desires, preferences, emotional reactions, and involuntary physiological responses, bound together by an overall sense of identity."[4] The social self is based on the pressures created by those around you reflecting the culture of your upbringing and surroundings. The job of the social self is "to know when desires will upset other people and to help override natural inclinations that aren't socially acceptable."[5] Anyone who has ever worked with an unhappy boss knows that this distinction clearly matters in the context of leadership development.

In another model of the relationship between personal well-being and work, professor and former chairman of the Department of Psychology at the University of Chicago, Mihaly Csikszentmihalyi, and a team of research associates around the world found that people experience some of their most valued life experiences while working. In his book, *Flow: The Psychology of Optimal Experience,* the key element of such experiences from the assembly line to the boardroom seems to depend on the emotional freedom to attentively focus on the work and immerse oneself to the point that work activities flow in a selfless manner.[6]

These different ways of looking at self-awareness and work point in the same direction. Enabling activities make up the greatest portion of the CIO's responsibilities, so successful CIOs draw a significant amount of satisfaction from what they accomplish by enabling others to perform more successfully. CIOs who achieve this state are on the way to achieving our profession's own brand of flow. People who can't find ways to feel comfortable performing the kinds of enabling activities essential to the performance responsibilities of the CIO had best look for another job.

THE FORK IN THE ROAD

> *Successful strategies flow like water; they are shaped by the circumstances of the conflict. When water flows, it avoids the high ground and seeks the low ground. Successful strategies likewise avoid difficult methods and find easy ones.*
> —Donald G. Krause[7]

What's it going to be, business or technology? One area that every CIO must continually evaluate in terms of the very personal context of the preceding discussion is the working balance between business and technology focuses. The technology is fairly straightforward: The machine breaks, you fix it; you enable the user; and everybody's happy. The business equation is a little more complicated. Can you develop the business leadership competencies you need to feel comfortable and satisfied enabling the work of an organization full of needy machines, people, departments, executives, and shareholders who all have their own ideas about how you should be doing your job?

The variations on these two themes become endless. "I practice with an extremely competent business orientation, but I wonder if I shouldn't learn how to use my PalmPilot on our system," or "I can reassemble the mainframe in total darkness good as new, but I really wish I knew more about this strategy stuff." Somewhere between these two extremes every CIO repeatedly comes to the same fork in the road in a single career.

This book recommends the Yogi Berra Solution.[8] Over the span of a CIO's career, the technology/business debate is not an either/or proposition. CIOs need to know both domains and how the domains interact so they can suggest CIO leadership priorities. However, during a single career, business and technology environments change so quickly that a CIO must learn to identify which of the two domains needs the most attention in the context of leadership responsibilities and professional competencies. With time and a growing number of new business and technological learning experiences, CIOs become more proficient at deciding which way to go when they reach the fork. People also discover that these kind of professional leadership development decisions clarify one's sense of self and one's relationships with others—actual versus ideal.

At any given time in a professional career, how does the CIO sort out immediate priorities between these two activity domains? With the help of people who can see your enabling responsibilities in terms of the support they need from you to get their work done. The most useful way to get this help is through cultivating a network of internal relationships and internal partnerships. A circle of confidants and advisors can most objectively articulate practical examples of your professional strengths and weaknesses so that you can see yourself through their eyes.

Creating internal partnerships is essential for maintaining a current set of balanced professional competencies when the job carries competing agendas such as business versus technical focuses. How these partnerships are formed and what directions they take depend on the person, organizational roles, and job expectations. The higher a person climbs on the conventional organizational chart, the fewer the peer-review resources. Astute CIOs create internal partnership communities with executive peers so that the insights of all members complement one another. The next section looks at the internal partnerships that a CIO needs to create and maintain to be successful.

CREATING THE IT INTERNAL PARTNERSHIP NETWORK

As with any senior-level executive, a CIO's success significantly depends on the ability to create, nurture, strengthen, and expand a network of partnerships with peer executives and other key employees in the organization. People working in enabling roles like the CIO rise and fall by their abilities to effectively work in an almost countless number of relationships, each with its own unique set of expectations. No other senior executive has more incentives to form partnerships with peers. Those CIOs who do not directly manage the IT function should also add the IT/IS executives to their partnership network.

Forming organizational relationships means cultivating an active network of relationships inside and outside the organization so that the CIO can relate well to both key colleagues and partners while maintaining regular connections with IT and company employees at all levels. Think of the four points on the compass in Exhibit 2.1: boss (north), executive peers (east), IT employees (west), and company employees (south). Flexible senior IT executives realize that, depending on the circumstances, many work relationships move between the four cardinal directions—employees in the southwest or southeast and bosses in the northwest or northeast.

Forming successful workplace relationships in this kind of shifting context demands that the CIO learn, practice, and become proficient with a set of personal skills and leadership competencies that guide leadership behavior relationship by relationship. They are:

1. Cultivate a broad network to exchange ideas and rally collaborative support.
2. Stay in touch with people at all levels of your organization—vertically and horizontally.
3. Continuously investigate what managers and higher-level management need from you and the IT organization.
4. Continuously rearticulate what you need from direct reports so that they understand you precisely.

EXHIBIT 2.1   KEY CIO NETWORK RELATIONSHIP GROUPS

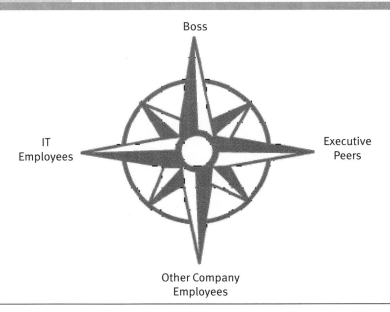

Boss

IT
Employees

Executive
Peers

Other Company
Employees

5. Continuously clarify what your peers and colleagues need from you and what you need from them.

6. Respect and openly acknowledge the individuals on your team.

7. Recognize and respond to the needs and concerns of others.

8. Adapt your interpersonal style to align with the strengths and shortcomings of other's styles.

9. Act to preserve relationships, even under difficult stress or heated emotional circumstances.

10. Promote collaboration and remove obstacles to teamwork across the organization.

Cultivating a broad network establishes the foundation for each of the following practices. The next section details network cultivation practices, and the remaining chapters of the *Survival Guide* characterize the other practices that build on the CIO's partnership network.

Cultivating a Broad Network

Great CIOs cultivate a broad network for exchanging ideas and rallying support for key objectives, resources, and goals. Trends suggest that the number of management levels in 2010 will be half the 1990 levels, therefore *broad* networks become increasingly important.[9] Cultivating a broad network is not as difficult as it may seem. As you assemble your own personal "board of directors" counselors repeat the same sequence over and over again: identify, build, expand, communicate, maintain, reevaluate, and repeat.

Identify   First, identify the existing network—which may be difficult when starting from scratch. One simple but effective network identification method starts with a list of the two or three people who are trustworthy and easy to talk to whether they come from a new job or old jobs. CIOs in new positions obviously have to cultivate network membership internally. Add to the list selectively, but create challenging relationships as your network expands. Next, add two or three people you are most uncomfortable talking to or communicating with and who are key relationships for the CIO role.

As CIOs gain experience cultivating their partnership networks, they begin to design the network architecture in ways that correspond with the workplace environment and structure. Some networking approaches follow an architecture of *concentric zones of influence* with four or five concentric circles of relationship priorities. CIOs use this model to deliberately structure and guide their network building practices zone by zone. Other CIOs work in organizational environments that favor a more *hierarchical* approach that follows the organization chart and the four cardinal points of the compass already discussed (see Exhibit 2.2). Many CIOs prefer the concentric zones approach because they have greater degrees of freedom for prioritizing network membership, rather than being constrained by the landscape of the org chart. The risk of the concentric zones approach is padding the list with too many "nice" people.

All network identification methods have to take into consideration personal needs, the needs of the organization, the needs of the network members, the needs

EXHIBIT 2.2   CONCENTRIC AND HIERARCHICAL
NETWORK BUILDING

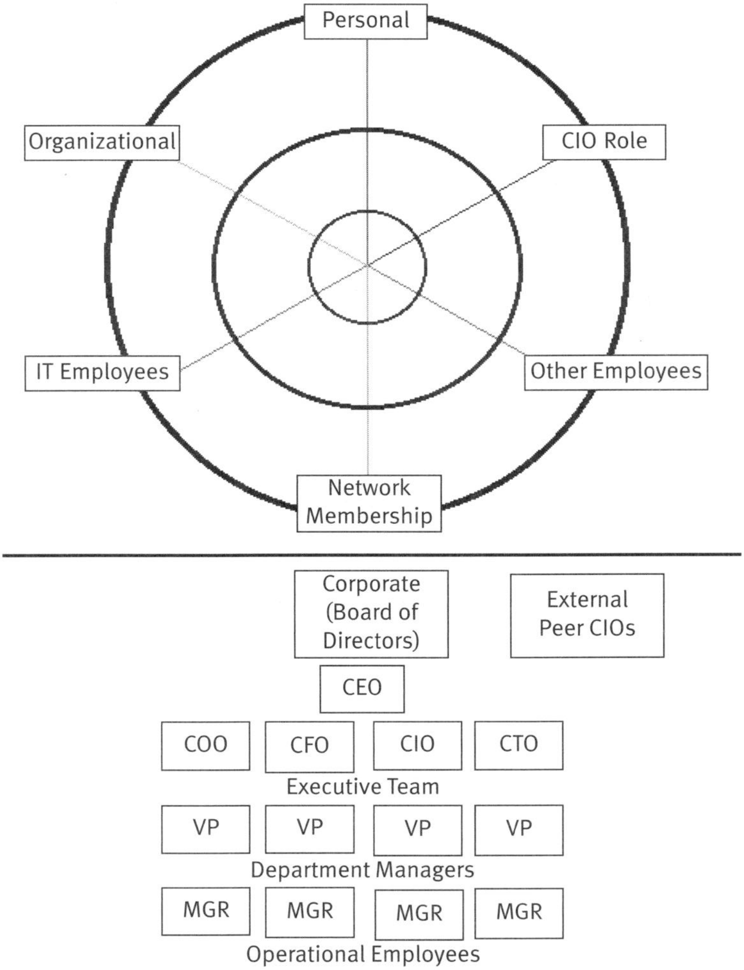

of the job and role, the needs of the IT employees, and the needs of other employee groups. Each area should have some representation in the relationship network. Of course, CIOs in a significantly hierarchical organization may be better off starting with the hierarchical approach to get early buy-in, then switch to the concentric zones approach after establishing a firm base from which to operate. Some CIOs prefer to blend concentric zone and hierarchical features into a hybrid approach. When it comes to choosing a method for identifying key network partnerships, choose a model that feels most comfortable, but choose some uncomfortable people to keep you honest.

Build and Expand   Building an internal partnership network is a continuous activity. While building an internal partnership network for the first time, most CIOs are quite surprised at the number of people who are interested—and actually have a vested interest—in seeing and supporting successful performance. After all, the CIO enables their successful performance. First contact attempts with potential internal network members take several working realities of the partnership into account. How can you demonstrate that participation in your internal network will be mutually beneficial and worth the person's investment of time and effort? Some internal network relationships will have only short-term benefits for the participant, so benefits must be tangible.

Keep in mind the importance of honesty and candor in the success of these partnerships. Honesty and candor depend on some level of comfort and intimacy. When other people in the organization cannot open doors for new introductions, move slowly and impersonally at first; for example, send a short e-mail or find some other way to give people a chance to think and ask questions on their own terms before they have to react in person. If the impersonal approach gets no initial response, follow up by phone or look for an opportunity to stop in for a visit simply to set up a meeting in an informal, neutral environment. Most people feel more relaxed about giving more intimate, meaningful advice and feedback in such settings. This also gives you a chance to learn about one another in a different environment. And, lo and behold, a real person shows up!

Keep the first meeting to well under an hour. Plan the agenda well in advance, look to see if the person can actually provide meaningful feedback, and save time to talk about mutual improvement insights. Always remember to be an *active listener* in networking partnerships and—to paraphrase the carpenter's rule—think twice/speak once. Set up another meeting within the next month to keep the dialog going. Move slowly with people of great potential value to the relationship network who may sign on reluctantly. A few more contacts will demonstrate how much you value the connection. Remember, virtually everyone in the organization has a vested interest in the CIO's success. All reasons not to participate in a CIO network fall into the shortsighted and personal chemistry categories.

People who expand their internal networks without a deliberate plan like the concentric or hierarchical approaches run the risk of either moving too quickly or forgetting to expand altogether. While establishing relationships with the people identified in the first step, remain alert to unanticipated new referrals from people who choose to participate in the network. Encourage current participants to set up introductions. Prioritizing the identification list can help control the rate of network growth. Capture the most important relationships one by one.

Communicate   The first several meetings should be oriented toward establishing an open partnership and dialog and the ground rules of the relationship. Keep in mind that the purpose of the network is to comfortably exchange ideas and gain support when necessary. Ideally, networking partners will feel the same, and this will evolve into mutually beneficial relationships. However, be patient if the partnership starts less cordially; some networking partners see the relationship as a monolog rather than a dialog. This type of person almost never asks for advice and counsel, but may well provide vital information available nowhere else. As long as such people are willing to continue to do so, they provide a significant benefit (and what you really asked for, too!).

The best way to start any new professional partnership is to share backgrounds and to look for common threads; this establishes the foundation for common language, vocabulary, and understanding. Then move to getting to know the person in greater detail. To draw out this kind of personal detail, begin by talking about yourself on the level you expect from your internal networking partner. For instance, favorite books, music, or hobbies are subjects that begin to build a level of professional intimacy necessary between trusted advisors.

Similarly, while a good dialog depends on both talking and listening, plan on being mostly in the listener role in the first few encounters. This sets the stage for those times that a CIO really needs an internal networking partner who knows what it feels like to have someone who listens. The people who are willing to talk meaningfully are also the ones more likely to listen. And, of course, when it is time to rally support for something you really need to accomplish, networking partners who have experienced the give and take of a good listening relationship are more inclined to support your objectives.

In the course of working with internal network participants, work to "iteratively improve" professional justifications, responses to professional objectives, and all the ways you articulate professional plans. Most people continue to value this kind of partnership even when their advice is not followed precisely every single time. However, it is important to take the time to explain alternative choices to internal network participants and how their input was important to your decision.

Maintain, Reevaluate, and Repeat   Think of the performer on the old *Ed Sullivan Show* who spun plates on long rods; he had to keep running to respin the plates before they fell off the rod; and as he put more plates into motion, he had more running around to do. Get the picture? Maintaining networking relationships is often more difficult and less visible—but maintenance activities are clearly just as important to CIO success as it is to the plate-spinner's.

Maintaining the network can take many forms: formal and informal visits, phone calls, e-mails, favorite comic strips. Even the smallest interactions go a long way toward maintaining the partnership and keeping the communications lines open. Naturally, some times are harder than others—and not just because of the workload. Some of the most important relationships in the network are the uncomfortable ones. Their importance stems from the conflicts they generate and the new perspectives that emerge from healthy conflict. Uncomfortable relationships are, however, the most difficult to maintain simply because they are not as much fun. Last, but not least, some relationships run their course over the career of a CIO. Let old, unproductive internal network relationships go, but find and maintain more productive replacements.

In the course of a job or a career, the CIO must also take a look at active internal network partnerships beyond the unproductive ones easily managed by attrition. Which partnerships require work to maintain but have become unimportant? Which important partnerships need greater attention? Are the partnerships receiving the proper level of attention or are some being taken for granted? Does the partnership network still have a balanced, comprehensive representation from key positions within the company? Does the relationship give my network partners as much value as it gives to me?

Networking work is all done now, right? Wrong. Time to go back to start over with the *identify* step. Obviously, roles and responsibilities evolve, needs change, and partnerships shift. Networks are a never-ending source of insight and support for the enabling CIO. They must change and develop to match the needs and emerging responsibilities of the office and the person.

MAXIMIZING THE PARTNERSHIP NETWORK

In the same way they need a deliberate method for identifying key network partnerships, leaders who manage as many key network partnerships in the workplace as the CIO need a personal system for reliably understanding people's strengths and weaknesses. Several well-tested tools serve to guide how the CIO understands the mix of self and others.

First, the Myers–Briggs Type Indicator (MBTI) is a tool for better self-awareness that also helps people in leadership positions understand the *different ways* that other people in the company approach the *same problems* and how to use these differences to everyone's advantage. The MBTI is based on a theory of personality types originally defined by psychiatrist Carl Jung. Jung believed that people have natural preferences for their common interactions with other people. Myers and Briggs refined Jung's ideas and categorized people's range of behaviors into 16 distinct types based on four pairs of fundamental preference dyads:

- Extraversion/Introversion (E/I)
- Sensing/Intuition (S/N)
- Thinking/Feeling (T/F)
- Judging/Perceiving (J/P)

Each of the 16 MBTI personality types results from the combination of one of each of the four preferences (hence the 16 possibilities). Exhibit 2.3 shows some examples of common representational behavior patterns for each of the 16 combinations.[10]

Temperament Theory[11] is a complementary four-quadrant personality framework to gauge people's performance profiles commonly used in combination with MBTI to more intuitively (and perhaps quickly) understand preferences, motivations, and behavior patterns that leaders can then anticipate. (In this context, the term "temperament" refers to that which moves people to strive for whatever it is that they *really* desire.) The four temperaments are the *Rationals*, the *Guardians*, the *Artisans*, and the *Idealists*. A matrix of Temperament Theory and Myers-Briggs personality types appears in Exhibit 2.4.

Understand Yourself

Knowing and understanding personal strengths and weakness is the basis for understanding how to interact with others.[12] CIOs who understand their own personal motivations and preferences in their work, communication, and action styles learn to manage their affairs with greater awareness. After all, like oil and water, some personality types mix with great difficulty and only after a lot of agitation. Self-awareness allows the CIO to anticipate relationship management challenges with other people with a greater degree of accuracy.

These same self-awareness tools and techniques give the CIO a more conscious and empathetic approach to the perspectives held by other people and thereby result in better work relationship outcomes. The better you understand these interactions, the more successful your relationships. With repetition, you will be able to anticipate behaviors, communicate more effectively, and thereby minimize overreactions in areas where there are strong feelings by those involved (including yourself).

To illustrate how CIOs can apply these personality tools in their professional relationships, the next section uses a set of likely roles and personality types as

EXHIBIT 2.3   MYERS-BRIGGS PERSONALITY TYPES

ISTJ	ISFJ	INFJ	INTJ
Life's Natural Organizers	Committed to Getting the Job Done	An Inspiring Leader and Follower	Life's Independent Thinkers
ISTP	ISFP	INFP	INTP
Just Do It	Action Speaks Louder than Words	Making Life Kinder and Gentler	Life's Problem Solvers
ESTP	ESFP	ENFP	ENTP
Making the Most of the Moment	Let's Make Work Fun	People Are the Product	Progress Is the Product
ESTJ	ESFJ	ENFJ	ENTJ
Life's Natural Administrators	Everyone's Trusted Friend	Smooth-Talking Persuaders	Life's Natural Leaders

Source: Keirsey and Bates, Please Understand Me, 1978.

EXHIBIT 2.4 TEMPERAMENT THEORY: MYERS-BRIGGS MATRIX

Rationals		Guardians
ENTJ Fieldmarshal Greenspan	**INTJ** Mastermind Eisenhower	**ISTJ** Inspector Rockefeller
ENTP Inventor Edison	**INTP** Architect Einstein	**ISFP** Protector Mother Teresa
ENFJ Teacher Gorbachev	**INFJ** Counselor Gandhi	**ISTP** Crafter Michael Jordan
ENFP Champion Thomas Paine	**INFP** Healer Schweitzer	**ISFP** Composer Mozart
	ESTJ Supervisor J.P. Morgan	
	ESFJ Provider Brezhnev	
	ESTP Promoter Churchill	
	ESFP Performer Elvis	
Idealists		Artisans

Source: Keirsey and Bates, *Please Understand Me,* 1978.

practical examples of relationship interdynamics in terms superiors, reports, and peers. Consider how the following set of people might interact.

- CIO: Intuition and Thinking (NT)
- CFO: Sensing and Thinking (ST)
- CTO: Intuition and Thinking (NT)
- VP of Marketing and Sales: Intuition and Feeling (NF)
- Director of Customer Service and Support: Sensing and Feeling (SF)

In this scenario, the CIO and the director of customer service and support are meeting with the CFO to get approval and support (executive and financial) for expanding a customer call center. The CIO invites the CTO to join the presentation team for technical support and the VP of marketing and sales as a networking partner with vested interests in the success of the proposal. The CTO has been a part of the work leading up to the presentation and is fully informed. The VP of marketing and sales has not been involved directly and has not been fully briefed on the specifics of the proposal.

The CIO and CTO have put together a proposal that they believe is necessary to expand the customer call center from its current "banker's hours," Monday to Friday coverage in the United States, to provide 24/7 availability worldwide. The CIO has carefully developed a presentation that starts with the problem, details the need, and contains justification testimonials from the VP of marketing and sales, the director of customer service and support, and several key global customers. The presentation walks through two alternatives—in-house and outsourcing—their associated costs, advantages and disadvantages, timeline effects, and wraps up with a summary recommending outsourcing as the better alternative. In total, the CIO has about 30 minutes worth of presentation materials, and everything's ready. Or, is it?

Based on some of the personality profiles involved in this scenario, a person who recognizes the importance of personality interdynamics sees some obvious difficulties in this presentation plan. As an Intuition/Thinking (NT) personality type, such a CIO naturally *conceptualizes* the entire proposal; that is, fairly easily sees the bigger picture, various alternatives, the implications of the alternatives from several points of view, and probably the best path to a solution. Conceptually gifted NT personality types arrive at solutions through a logical and analytical approach and have little or no difficulty designing the precise changes needed to get to the solution—in this case, the expanded customer call center. In working with teams, NT personality types like this scenario's CIO enjoy the challenge and the process of getting there. Other people with NT personalities would follow right along with the CIO's thinking and proposed solution (and they would significantly enjoy bantering words and ideas along the way).

All this is very good planning for a presentation to an audience of NT personality types. In this case, however, the CIO has to reach a CFO with a Sensing/Thinking (ST) personality to approve the proposal, a VP of marketing and sales with a Sensing/Feeling (SF) personality to become the proposal's customer, and the director of customer service and support (another SF) to implement the proposal. Buy-in and approval for the proposal depends just as much or more on what the people in the audience can see and hear from the presentation, which gives them what they need to understand and accept the new idea from their own perspectives. The CIO may have arrived at the right answer to the problem, but the presentation does not *communicate* what the other personality types need to align with the idea. Moral: The onus of ensuring understanding is on the speaker, not the listener! An enabling CIO has to understand three important listening groups: management, reports, and peers.

Understand Management

Understanding management is critical to professional success—and survival! The more you know about your boss, the better you will be able to communicate (two-way) and the more effective you will be in your job. For example, as the CIO's boss in the example scenario, the CFO's Sensing/Thinking preferences manifest with a predominately *practical* decision style. As a significant difference from the CIO's Intuition/Thinking preference, this CFO will want to get heavily into the details—*very* heavily—consistent with the Sensing preference. The CIO should expect to be asked to provide concrete examples to demonstrate that any information related to physical resources have been fully investigated. A CFO with this personality profile will likely ask the CIO to systematically clarify current actual performance and the performance gains that the new proposal will create. Importantly, the CIO should expect to be challenged on all discrepancies in the presentation.

The original flow of the presentation as described earlier works better for the CFO's personality if the CIO uses an *answers-first* focus in the first few minutes. Simply put the problems on the table and recommend direct solutions, which at the very least, saves significant time and effort in cases of total disagreement so that key problems can be discussed up-front. This kind of restructuring appeals to the CFO's Thinking preference by getting the purpose out in the open quickly. Thinking preference personality types find logical flow helpful in following detailed proposals. Be expected to have objective sources for all presentation information, with sufficient data and solid justification that the problem's cause-and-effect relationships point to the proposed solution. During the discussion, expect skepticism regarding the interpretation of the information and data available; this is a part of the process of those with Thinking preferences, so don't take it personally. It is not a matter of questioning you personally; rather, it is a matter of understanding the thought process and analysis going from the information to the conclusions.

For an N/T like the CIO, this may very well seem to be a tedious and overly burdensome process. Nevertheless, people who know how to think and speak in the language of the person giving approval stand a significantly better chance of success. Senior executives who learn how to exchange information so that each person can bring the fullest level of understanding and special expertise to bear on the decision act in the best interests of everyone in the company.

Of course, it is likely that other people in the room will have something to add according to their own personality perspectives—whether invited or not—and their preferences will mix with one another to shape (and/or derail) the outcome if their needs and insights are not anticipated. These additional people shape the outcome based on their personality preferences, how they see the boss react, whether they were included in the presentation process and/or briefed earlier, and their relationship with the presenter and the boss. Let's take a look at the next participant: the director of customer service and support, who represents the CIO's subordinates.

Understand Direct Reports

The director of customer service and support was not only involved in creating the proposal but has also been one of the primary people pulling it together since he is the one who will be charged with implementation. As a Sensing and Feeling personality type, he works on the same general Sensing wavelength as the CFO, from a details and information point of view; and he brings a new perspective: Feeling. This CIO is very fortunate to have a Sensing and Feeling personality type heading up this crucial area because the director is naturally into the details *and* can empathize with customer problems.

Leaders who learn to recognize and apply personality typing tools use the gifts of people like the director to anticipate the needs of the CFO in ways that the CIO could never see. Typical S/F personality type skills include soliciting people's opinions, identifying obstacles elsewhere in the company, obtaining supportive testimonials for the proposal, and gaining practical work experience with a number of customers and the marketing and sales teams on prioritizing the implementation phases. So, even when an N/T CIO neglects to brief a key supporter such as the VP of marketing and sales, a teammate like the director would naturally apply his Feeling traits and bring the VP up to speed. So be forewarned: Feeling team members act like an information sealant by noticing and closing critical gaps in communication that other personality types do not naturally see.

The combination of these two personality types, the Intuition/Thinking CIO and the Sensing/Feeling director ensure that they cover the expectations of the Sensing/Thinking CFO—*if they work together to build the presentation.* What a difference this can make in your communicating common, complementary points and making a better case. Viva la difference! Other members of a team may be able to add to this complementary dynamic as you come to understand, become comfortable with, and apply their different perspectives to build a more effective platform for communication for large audiences. More people will understand you more easily so that when you communicate with people throughout your organization you will find an easier time of *connecting* and delivering a message of some meaning for everyone: communicating so all can hear. Another of the many positive outcomes of learning about and working with personality types is learning to structure communications that appeal to the full spectrum of people in your organization.

Enabling CIOs can also use these personality awareness models to strengthen new or existing relationships. Consider the challenges faced by the director in this scenario while performing other typical duties in his relationship with the CIO. The CIO and director work with opposite temperaments. Reports or proposals designed by the director for the CIO to match his *own* expectations miss the mark for the CIO. Alternatively, if the director designed a report or proposal to meet *only* the expectations of the CIO, important information would be missing, and the CIO might not even be able to recognize missing elements. This poses a significant challenge to people working alone: Do you put together a proposal that includes something for everyone, or do you put together proposals targeted at key members of the audience? Do whatever you can to find a complementary person to match your own personality and build a presentation for the widest possible audience. This is why CIOs need those relationship networks.

This discussion does not, however, suggest that anyone change the *facts*. Rather, these relationship science models suggest that knowing the audience is key to success and tailoring the proposal *style* and *information* to maximize communication effectiveness just make plain good business sense. Additional, time-consuming, unnecessary, work? That depends on how much time you have to repeat and reformat presentations to get your message across. It's kind of like the old adage, "You can pay me now (front-end good communication) or pay me later (repetitious, presentations where people seem to nod off right in the middle)."

The Intuition/Thinking CIO and the Sensing/Feeling director have the Sensing/Thinking CFO boss covered, so the presentation should be complete. Well done! Whoops! Not done, yet. The CIO still has to consider the proposal presentation in terms of the needs of peers: the Intuition/Thinking CTO and the Intuition/Feeling VP of marketing and sales. Being peers, the CIO cannot manage them in the same way as the director. In addition to the challenges of managing relationships with peers, a new personality type enters the mix: Intuition/Feeling through the VP of marketing and sales.

Understand Peers

Your peers are, of course, also among your customers as the CIO. In fact, you are probably the only senior executive in the company or in your division whose peers are *all* your customers and customers of your organization. And, again, this is because the CIO and the IT team are *enablers* to the entire company. The VP of marketing and sales was not directly involved with creating the proposal but, thankfully, the director of customer service saw to it that she was up to speed. It is important to have this peer onboard because she has the responsibility for facing the customer, keeping existing customers, expanding their purchases, and getting new customers, which are all affected by the level and quality of service and support. This peer shares the Intuition trait with the CIO and the Feeling trait with the director of customer service. As an Intuition/Feeling personality type, she works on the same general intuition wavelength as the CIO in terms of seeing the big picture and connecting the ideas with the facts of the system overall. Combining this with the Feeling personality type gives this executive the right combination for helping customers understand the bigger picture and, at the same time, being sensitive to their wants and needs. These are the focus points when this executive interacts with current and potential customers. In contrast, the director of customer service customer interactions generally focus on specifics.

This VP of marketing's Feeling personality type profile complements the CIO's Thinking personality type. As an N/F personality type, she excels at relationships, generating enthusiasm for change, and maintaining high morale. As a result, she would make an excellent spokesperson for the proposal. While the CIO almost missed this partnership opportunity, the director again helped by getting her VP onboard so she could be the spokesperson at the meetings. This Feeling personality type team member will naturally apply her gifts to bring others onboard and fill communications gaps. As a N/F personality type, she sees many possibilities, and fortunately for the CIO, she was brought up to speed before the approval meeting. If the CIO had brought her onboard for earlier planning meetings, she would have been able to proactively identify stories and analogies to support the desired meeting outcome. Importantly, when the Feeling personality type is excluded from any participation in the planning process, they often withhold any support and respond with animosity.

The CTO, another peer and Intuition/Thinking personality type, likely works on the same data and communication wavelength as the CIO—*as long as the two are in agreement*. Specifically, similar personality types like the CTO and CIO are likely to see things and think along the same lines because of their particular types; how-ever, it is just as likely that they will not reach agreement unless they both start from the same perspective or until each determines that the *other* gets it. It is im-portant that these two get together early to discuss the proposal one on one. Of all the personality types, they consider many interesting alternatives and possibilities while coming to agreement, and idea sifting should occur before the final pitch. A peer who suggests multiple alternative ideas to a complex proposal only under-mines the likelihood of acceptance.

A balanced variety of different personality types supports a stronger IT organi-zation. Your approach and actions relative to the personality types of peers, subor-dinates, and superiors affects the outcome and the success of all that you do. While you cannot change how others approach day-to-day work challenges, knowing the variables allows you as a enabling team leader to modify your approaches and be-haviors to support effective individual participation and overall team performance. The enabling CIO can use five leadership postures for honoring diversity of the partnership network team.

Respect and Appreciate   As you learn more about the personality types and management techniques, one message comes through over and over: Respecting the opinions and feelings of others is key to CIO success in an enabling workplace. Showing respect is not just a matter of etiquette and common courtesies; it en-compasses a whole way of interacting with people. For instance, it sometimes means listening more and talking less. There is a pertinent saying in the personal-ity types discussion, "If you don't know what an extrovert is thinking, you haven't been listening; and if you don't know what an introvert is thinking, then you haven't asked." Another key demonstration of leadership respect keeps disagree-ments on the level of *ideas,* making sure that disagreements never settle on the *per-son*. Our differences are the source of our diversity, and diversity is the source of durability and creativity. By respecting differences and differences of opinion, you gain other perspectives that can make the difference between leadership failure and success. As before: Viva la difference!

Recognize and Respond   A superior and enabling CIO learns to recognize peers, subordinates, and superiors in need and respond in a timely and professional manner. These messages come in verbal and nonverbal forms. One particular per-sonality type is a revealing model for consistent CIO attentiveness. The Intuitive rarely uses direct channels to communicate the need for help in work-related problems that focus on culture, pride, or overwork. However, like any other per-sonality type, barriers to asking for help break down when these people witness consistent behaviors from people in leadership positions. Recognizing a need and responding as an enabler will be remembered positively and will help your peer and yourself.

Adapt   A person who knows how to recognize and respect different personality types can affect the outcome of a conversation by adapting the way messages are delivered to the needs of the listener. In the case of the CIO as speaker, the communication responsibility is one of aligning the message with the needs of the listener. Conversely, in the case of the CIO as listener, different postures and levels of participation draw more and different kinds of information from certain personality types. This kind of communication adaptation does not mean giving up your own distinctive styles, it leverages your best communication skills in ways that enhance skills of different personality types.

Reminiscent of the old proverb, "walk a mile in their shoes," the better you understand someone else, the more successfully you can communicate and work together. This is particularly important for those people who have communication needs that fall within the blind spots of your personality type. For example, the CIO working with the director of customer service wants to ensure he has approached their project and communications in a way that respects the director's Feeling personality type. This includes giving the director an opportunity to see how facts and ideas relate to people and to allow the director to participate in the prioritization of the work so he can identify with and act on the values and personal priorities.

For communicating with the CFO, a Sensing personality type, the CIO wants to ensure that the proposal has step-by-step information and explanations, uses concrete examples and applications, and gives special attention to the use of realistic assumptions and data. In contrast to the Sensing CFO, the CIO's Intuition personality profile, prefers to see the proposal in terms of an overall framework with a system-level view that provides opportunities for suggesting different potential approaches. While perfectly natural for an Intuitive personality type, the CIO's preferred approach would be received poorly by a Sensor; the presentation would likely be viewed as off the wall, out of bounds, or, more simply, impractical.

These principles create tremendous advantage and help the CIO communicate more effectively with peers, direct reports, and superiors. Becoming an adaptive communicator does not guarantee that you will win every argument or get everything to go the way that you believe it should, but you will be less frequently misunderstood and fellow employees will feel a greater level of personal participation in your way of seeing the IT organization.

Actively Preserve Relationships   To be a successful executive, the CIO must actively work to preserve relationships. The CIO, in particular, pays attention to this because it is part and parcel of the enabler role. The CIO accomplishes this by working to discover what peers need to be successful. The work of relationship-preserving activities takes a number of forms for the CIO.

An executive new to the CIO role may find that it seems difficult or even impossible to establish, much less actively preserve, relationships in the face of the demands of learning the new business and the place IT occupies in the work lives of its many constituents. Some personality types find this relationship maintenance work tedious, tiresome, time-consuming, or unnecessary: "I feel way behind and nothing's changing, so why bother?" Productivity is part of the long-term relationship management equation, and eventually you will catch up and become familiar with your new responsibilities. By that time, what will your peers think of you? Relationship work is important for the CIO personally and professionally.

As a strategic enabler, the CIO builds information technology value from a good understanding of the needs of peers. The CIO with this understanding stands ready to assist them through an awareness of the network of long-term peer functional strategies and how they align with those of the IT organization and the company. Because business conditions change the CIO works to stay in touch with the business unit heads to ensure that their changing IT needs are collectively accommodated and efficiently enabled in terms of company resources and priorities. Actively preserving the relationships is the best way to do this; use any means at your disposal. Rather than limiting yourself to on-site formal meetings, early-morning coffee, breakfast, lunch, a round of golf, and other less formal venues provide opportunities that do not impinge on the workday.

Promote Collaboration and Remove Obstacles   One of the advantages of actively preserving a network of strategic relationships is in the way opportunities arise for collaboration between the CIO and peers. Enablers create value through collaborative efforts. It is somewhat analogous to the story about the chicken and the pig: When it comes to bacon and eggs, the chicken may be involved, but the pig is committed. The collaborative CIO prefers to enable and work with committed partners who contribute something of themselves rather than those who prefer tokens of involvement regarding the outcomes of projects, tactics, and strategies. Truth be known, those who willingly accept and participate in the enabling resources of the CIO and IT function are far more likely to get what they want and need by collaborating than those who prefer the purely passive customer/provider service relationship. This helps avoid many of the service-related problems illustrated in Exhibit 2.5.

In the scenario characterized by this exhibit, the communications relationship between the people who wanted a service, their "expert" representatives, the service planners, and the service implementers lacked precision. Collaborative communications coordinated by someone in a leadership position familiar with each step of this relationship process would certainly have made a difference. In some company cultures, serious obstacles prevent the communication channels required for such an effort. Left unresolved, those obstacles can be more than just humorous; they can be devastating to the company and to the IT function. The CIO stands in the best position to arbitrate and reconcile these obstacles.

Major obstacles like these are rooted in one of two areas: executive interests or

EXHIBIT 2.5   COLLABORATION OBSTACLE OUTCOMES

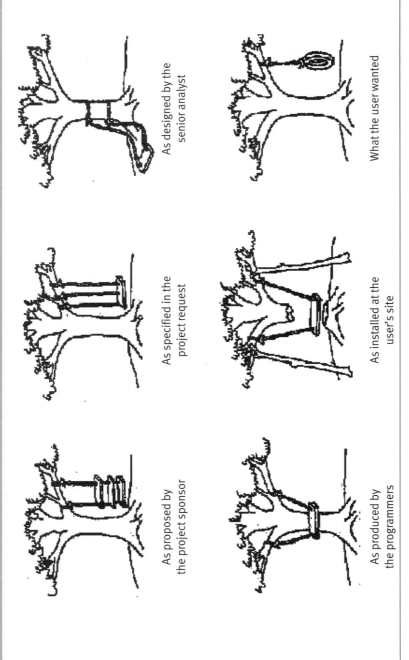

As proposed by
the project sponsor

As specified in the
project request

As designed by the
senior analyst

As produced by
the programmers

As installed at the
user's site

What the user wanted

Source: From Fred Tepfer, www.uoregon.edu/~ftepfer/SchlFacilities/TireSwingtable.html, accessed May 27, 2003.

personality differences. Based on the discussion of personality types and their importance in a CIO's awareness of partnership network relationship management, personality differences can be addressed with the techniques already described. Executive interests or executive "agendas" are often more difficult to address. Paul Strassmann observes that:

> New resistance to maintaining the historically high rates of investment in computers stems from the incompatibility between the technology and executive agendas. Executive interests have remained remarkably the same for over thirty years, while technology fads have come and gone in seven-year cycles. . . . Executives are unwilling to fund yet another cycle of information technology conversions and investments, regardless of how attractively they are advertised, unless their perceptions of assured gains improve. The only way to do that is to place the executive agendas ahead of the technology agendas.[13]

As companies look more and more at the IT function as an enabling function, there is greater interest in having the business-line executives engaged and in agreement with the CIO's technology strategy and agenda. In many companies, IT's budget comes directly from the business lines, and this same allocation approach may be used for new projects. With legacy projects allocated according to older methods (usually the apportioned tax method) the CIO accompanies the business-line executive who is the receiver of the new project to justify the business value brought to this peer organization and the company. This is another example of why it is so important for the CIO to create and maintain relationships, to understand and work through obstacles on the way to professional, organizational, and company success. Of course, it is not reasonable to expect to know the basis for the relationships without knowing who you are and who you are expected to be and who you are needed to be.

EVOLVING CIO EXPECTATIONS: TECHNOLOGIST OR BUSINOLOGIST?

To illustrate this question, let's take a look at some representative definitions over the past nearly 20 years. From the perspective of the 1970s,[14] the *job* of the CIO was management of the information systems (IS) function. Similar to the roles of other top-level managers, the *role* of the CIO was defined in terms of 10 leadership activities: leader, figurehead, liaison, monitor, disseminator, spokesperson, entrepreneur, disturbance handler, resource allocator, and negotiator.[15] In other words, there was no real concentration on job expertise or the role of the CIO/senior IT manager during the 1970s. The serious study of the role of expertise managers had only just begun.

From the evolving perspective of the early 1980s, the *job* of the CIO was to be responsible for the information infrastructure, but application development responsibilities (and local hardware) were decentralized to divisions and departments. The job of the CIO formally included staff orientation, utilizing communication, education, performance standards, and other indirect controls to facilitate integrative and gatekeeper roles for new business technologies. Additionally, the CIO job became an integral part of the top management team, including corporatewide responsibility for information resource policy and strategy.[16] At the same time, the *role* of the CIO was shaped by external trends directed at the general managerial environment. However, top management realized that not only does the CIO role evolve, but "the exact role of a particular CIO in a particular company at a particular point is contingent" upon other factors such as the company's size and organizational design.[17]

By the late 1980s the situation changed yet again. John Hammitt, VP of information for Pillsbury of Minneapolis, who then functioned as the food giant's CIO, put it this way: "The idea that we're some 'elite' that controls information is totally false and misleading. We don't control information, we help make it flow."[18] Hammitt is one of many top information managers who believe that the CIO moniker (and mythology) is not only misleading, but also harmful. "It's pompous and self-serving, and obscures the issues. It confers [on us] an authority we don't have. We're servants of the corporation. We empower others to succeed."[19]

During this same period of rapid technology management evolution, the CIO role within the organization underwent further redefinition. "Confusion over just what constitutes a CIO is rampant," says John Highbarger, then Coopers & Lybrand partner for information systems and in charge of his organization's survey of the 400 top IS executives across the nation. "Fifty nine percent of respondents thought of themselves as CIOs, yet only 27 percent reported directly to the top of the company." A direct pipeline to the top, he notes, is a prerequisite for the job. As planner of long-term strategies uniting the business and technology sides of the "house," the CIO must be part of the inner circle of top officers to have any influence at all.[20] At that time, the conclusions seemed straightforward.

As we all know, job and role definitions are redefined at increasingly frequent intervals. As Paul Strassmann describes, the *job* is one of "assuring the lowest costs for information-handling technologies that meet the firm's competitive needs . . . to set information resources management policies."[21] Similarly, he describes the CIO's role with similar precision: "Chief Information Officers will not qualify for promotion into top executive positions unless they move out of servicing internal organizations into jobs where they deliver direct contributions to profit."[22]

Very soon after, in a 1997 survey in *Financial Executive,* the CIO *job* was described in the following terms.[23]

> Successful CIOs are those who have technical ability, can communicate well internally and externally, can leverage information technology, and have ex-

perience in such areas as outsourcing, reengineering, total quality management, electronic data interchange, and the Internet. In line with the evolving expectations of the CIO's job, staff change expectations emerged, as well. The typical CIO's staff changes to accommodate new business ideas.

Accordingly, the "typical CIO's staff is changing to accommodate new business ideas. In the past, large staffs connoted power for the CIO. Today, a smaller staff that's heavily outsourced allows the CIO to get rid of the mundane and become more of a business partner, and, thus, a survivor. But outsourcing shrinks the traditional kingdom of the CIO, and the danger here is that the information-technology area can become merely the keeper of the infrastructure."[24]

During this same period in the late 1990s, the CIO *role* became one of a strategic business partner. By this time, fellow executives expected that the ideal CIO should be able to envision the best way to leverage information technology in terms of the company's weaknesses, strengths, competition, and opportunities. Such a CIO should be able to communicate inside and outside the company with anyone, from a board member to the custodial staff. On the technical side, companies began to particularly value information executives with experience in outsourcing, the Internet, reengineering, cycle time management, electronic data interchange (EDI), client/server systems, and legacy system management.

The person filling the CIO role was also expected to focus on ways to help peer executives achieve their goals. As such, the CIO needed to establish business credibility among peers, in addition to maintaining the required technical expertise, but was frequently placed in an isolated decision-making position. Colleagues frequently misunderstand the nuances of technical matters; and when the CIO addresses important highly technical aspects of certain processes with nontechnical peers, the peers commonly suspect that the CIO is overly attracted to the technology and weak on broader business perspectives.

On an ever increasing acceleration curve, by 2000, companies began to see the CIO's *job* in terms of value creation.[25] Nontechnical executives found that they had no good way to concretely measure the return on their IT investments, and they consequently saw IT as a function that consumed significant resources but offered little evidence of value. These same executives had no way to measure IT value, and had not learned to see IT as a strategic companywide asset, thus they were able to see IT only in terms of the line managers, who assumed more and more responsibility for planning, building, and running the information systems that affected their operations. In this context, CIOs worked to build relationships with line managers and assume new and more strategic roles to respond to business and technological changes.

Naturally, the CIO *role* varied significantly from company to company in terms of the senior technology executive's ability to assume a strategic role and the willingness of peer executives to allow the CIO to do so. Importantly, the CIO is concerned with a wider group of strategic customer issues than most managers. "As a manager of people, the CIO faces the usual human resource roles of recruiting, staff training, and retention, and the financial roles of budget determination, forecasting, and authorization. As the provider of technological services to user departments, there remains a significant amount of work in publicity, promotion, and internal relations with user management."[26]

And from one of the more recent analyses of the CIO's rapidly evolving job and role, the CIO *job* begins to take on some strategic clarity within the company as peer executives find ways to actually measure the IT function's return on investment against strategic IT objectives. In this value measurement insight, the CIO's *job* involves "planning and implementation for an enterprise resource planning (ERP) system [and] work to expand Web-based services, improve decision making through access to timely and accurate information, and enhance productivity with technology tools."[27]

Along with these same focuses on measurable value, the CIO *role* becomes one that can assemble, mentor, and maintain a skilled and knowledgeable staff—in other words, an executive team player and a technology team builder. In this kind of role, the CIO and the IT staff members know which questions to ask and how to evaluate the answers they hear, rather than taking the posture of someone who already has all the answers.[28]

The evolution from more technical-based to more business-based to a balance of technical and business basis is easy to see in this progression of jobs and roles. This progression will definitely affect the CIO's job and role and, therefore, what companies and peer executives expect from you.

In this evolving context of CIO job and role definitions from the highest perspective on this senior executive position, every CIO needs to interpret this professional evolution in terms of the needs of the specific place of current employment. What does this company need and want from its CIO? At several points in the career of every CIO, priorities change from a technology focus to a business focus. Making this choice can be difficult.

If you happen to be a believer in the many-worlds interpretation or in parallel universes, you have made both choices, and perhaps even more.[29] And because your reality is the result of the choices that you (remember, *you*) have made, you have to live them. That said, this should open up the possibility that if you change your mind, the world will not (necessarily) come to an end. You may, however, join that other timeline a little later than you could have.

So, if at the fork in the road you made the decision to become a CIO along a technical path, it probably seemed like an either/or decision at the time. Greater experience usually suggests otherwise. As you interpret your own personal version of the evolution of the job and role of the CIO, remember that the increasing pressures for greater knowledge of the business and strategic partnerships with peer executives have become basic definitions of the CIO. Since technology expertise and business knowledge are both required of the CIO, but with different emphasis at different times, take the fork in the road that the company demands: If the expectation is more business-related, take the business fork in the road; if the expectation is more technology-related, take the technology fork in the road. Depending on personal preference for one or the other, most CIOs need not worry when they find themselves on the less comfortable fork.

The 1980s emphasized CIOs who came from the business side (see *InfoWeek, Computerworld, CIO Magazine*), but at that time, the CIO as strategic business partner was an emerging concept. These articles concluded that when the business-background executive became the CIO he/she came away with a greater appreciation of the challenges of the IT organization and its people; the IT people better understood the business(es) they were employed to support and advance; and more mingling, mixing, and cooperation between IT and the rest of the company became the norm. This same bias showed in conclusions drawn about the situation when the technical-background executive became the CIO. These CIOs came away with a greater appreciation for their true mission: enabling and supporting the business that employed them and a far greater understanding of the real business(es) of their company and how important it was for the entire IT organization to understand and act on this. In both cases, internal partnerships were reported as being key to success.

Of course, there are those who believe that within the next 10 years or so the CIO or senior IT executive position will become obsolete.[30] This belief is based on an assertion that the senior executives and managers across a business will find ways to manage technology directly without an intermediate expert. This laudable goal is not unlike the search for the holy grail. As these first two chapters have demonstrated, the life cycle of the technology solutions, uses, and evolution in the company is too young and too rapidly evolving to expect any credible management predictability in terms of future leadership directions. The complexity of IT management in a companywide context is simply too complex and time-consuming for all nontechnological managers. Given this state of the art, it is not yet clear that it would be cost- and resource-effective to fully disperse this responsibility fully.

CIO AND CTO RELATIONSHIPS

Many CIOs have the good fortune to work with a chief technology officer, specifically, a CTO who is associated with the IT function; or, if the company is an IT-related company, a CTO whose areas of technology coverage included IT by nature of background, role, and responsibility. The CTO gives added leadership options to the CIO profile by concentrating the responsibilities of the senior *technology* executive and the senior *information management* executive in two entirely different people.

CIO with CTO

As presented in this chapter, the trend over the past 20 years has seen the CIO role become more and more business-oriented. Yes, there remains an assumption that the CIO is technically savvy, but trends demonstrate an even greater assumption that the CIO is business savvy—specifically in terms of the business of the company and how the IT function contributes to the overall value of the company. An industry executive recruiter describes it this way: "The CIO is more about strategy while the CTO is more hands-on technology. The CIO is 99.9 percent leadership, applying technology to solve business problems. The CTO focuses on technology more so than strategy and vision."[31] In a State of the CIO survey referenced in the same article, *CIO Magazine* found that only 18 percent of CIOs shared responsibility with a CTO.

The vast majority of the IT senior management needs and directions are covered by the significant synergy of a CIO/CTO team. The CIO typically makes sure that the CTO understands the business and then delegates the responsibility for identifying potential areas for evolution and revolution to the CTO. The CTO can then evaluate potential technology improvements and advancements based on the intersection of the two. The CTO can also work with the CIO's peers and their staffs to understand their requirements. Then, working with the CIO, the CTO works to translate customer requirements into business values and service-level priorities to ensure the optimal enablement of the CIO's peers and partners. The CIO/CTO partnership is a work of beauty—when it works.

CTO as CIO

The person who, as a *true* CTO, has been unexpectedly asked to take on the role of the CIO deserves everyone's sympathy. While the good CTO has some sense of the business, people generally first choose to become a chief *technical* officer based on a strong preference for work with a technical focus. At the same time, the chief *information* officer role evolved from this same technology focus to include and emphasize the business focus. This being the case, a CTO who is not very strong on the business elements works at a significant disadvantage in terms of understanding the needs of the other senior executives and of the CEO. As both CTO and

CIO, the senior information executive faces multiple, often contradictory challenges. The strategic importance of information technology as an companywide resource justifies both roles *and* a different person to fill each role in companies of significant complexity or sophistication: "The CTO, as the right hand of the CIO, provides the company with an executive-level subject matter expert on the issues surrounding the technologies that the CIO must employ in order to achieve the company's strategic objectives."[32]

TEN QUESTIONS THE CIO SHOULD ASK NETWORK PARTNERS

There is no adequate defense, except stupidity, against the impact of a new idea.
—Percy W. Bridgman[33]

A significant theme of this chapter is networking with peers, so this "10 questions" feature is designed to disclose the IT needs of the CIO's network partners. This set of questions has two temporal focuses: concerns and interests at the beginning of a network partnership, and ongoing, periodic relationship redefinition. Use the second focus of each of these 10 questions for network partners to keep your understanding of their IT needs current by reviewing them at least once a year with each network partner.

1. When you sense a need for critical IT support in your work, are you comfortable asking me for help?
2. From your point of view, what are my blind spots?
3. One of my key goals is to be an enabler for your work; am I enabling your most important work priorities?
4. What can I do to remove obstacles to our mutual success?
5. In your opinion, what is my primary role and job definition as CIO?
6. Am I working with a proper balance on tactical issues relative to strategic issues?
7. Am I spending the right amount of time on business issues relative to technical issues?
8. In light of my last two questions, do you believe it is more effective to have IT report to me directly or would it be more effective to my role if operations management reported indirectly?
9. Do you see IT as an expense or an investment?
10. What do you believe the CEO is looking for from me?

Number 1: Are You Comfortable Asking Me for Help?

This is the fundamental question for you with your networked peers. The successful CIO views his/her peers as *partners,* and views their relationship as a partnership: "a relationship between individuals or groups that is characterized by mutual cooperation and responsibility,"[34] and each descriptor is important for your relationship to be a successful one for you and your partners. Your partners need to know they can count on your cooperation and assistance and on your providing and/or supporting an atmosphere of shared responsibility. You want to be the person they come to when they have business-critical problems or needs. When others come to you for help, they do so in the hopes that you can help them. In the case of a critical need, your best efforts hold up your portion of the partnership.

It is important for the CIO to learn how comfortable his/her network partners and associates are with asking for help in times of need, and the best way to find this out is to ask them one by one. The specific approach with any particular individual varies but the message, the intent, and the result should be consistent. The message: "As CIO, I genuinely want to help you resolve your IT-related business problems, *especially* in times of critical need. Do not hesitate to call on me." After emphasizing this commitment, attempt to determine whether your partners really believe you. If they do not, then you will want to work with them to identify why they do not, and work to address what may be holding them back. Trust has to be earned in the early stages of most network partnerships, and the CIO builds trust in network partners by demonstrating prudent relationship resource management skills.

Think of a "favor bank" as a metaphor for managing relationship resources prudently and building network partnership trust. The favor bank is the place where all the people in the partnership network deposit and withdraw favors. People make deposits when they do someone a favor, and they make a withdrawal when they ask someone for a favor. Similarly, when helping someone in times of critical need, a person makes a significant deposit in the bank. As with any savings plan, the more you deposit over time, the more rewarding you will find it over a period of time. The successful CIO has many accounts in the bank and is generally known as an excellent depositor and saver, who makes frugal withdrawals. Of course, avoid thinking of this metaphor as a "they owe me" bank; rather, think of it as a way to build mutual trust, confidence, cooperation, and responsibility. Your associates will naturally want to help you in times of critical need if you have done the same. As the CIO leads this kind of relationship-building process, people become more comfortable with one another and can begin to use the same processes outside the CIO's network.

Number 2: What Are My Blind Spots?

Everyone has blind spots. There are many ways to get at your blind spots—to find out what they are and to do something about them. For example, you can use such tools as the Myers-Briggs Type Indicator. In fact, you should ask about your blind spots from your networking partners regardless of the use of tools. Each networking partner sees a slightly different *you,* and the one each person sees depends on how you have structured your personal and professional relationship with them. If you have worked together over a period of years, it may well be that you know each other's personal *and* professional blind spots. Hearing about blind spots may be difficult, but addressing them in your day-to-day duties allows you to be more effective with your partners and your job.

One of the most common blind spot examples for all professional specialties is that experts often assume that other professionals know what they know. Think of a doctor describing a complicated disease using advanced medical terms to an adult patient with an eighth-grade education. It is easy to assume that everyone knows what you know at the same depth that you know it. The practical results of this misunderstanding are almost always negative and sometimes disastrous. The remedy requires a persistent awareness that each member of the executive team needs careful guidance outside his or her own specialties; and simpler, more thorough, and adaptive explanations of IT services and functions prevents the misunderstanding that nontechnical professionals often experience with the IT organization. The positive consequences of discovering blind spots often turn out to be as simple as rethinking how to establish better two-way communication with nontechnical executive peers—who have their own specialization blind spots. Making use of this two-way feedback can have immediate results for the entire executive team.

Number 3: Am I Enabling Your Most Important Work Priorities?

Be prepared to hear two answers to this question. The first answer addresses the IT *organization* and this partner's views of how well the organization enables him/her. You may have to repeat the question to hear an answer related to *you* specifically. This perceptive dichotomy often exists regardless of whether the CIO is new to the position or has worked in the position for a long time. Naturally, you want to hear the answers to both perspectives. However, it is important to avoid being sidetracked by debates that focus exclusively on the IT organization and its relationship with the network partner who is giving performance feedback.

Water flows down hill, and if the CIO does not work in an enabling fashion, neither will the IT organization. Conversely, if the CIO *is* enabling the company, then either the IT organization follows suit or is hopefully being transformed into an enabling mode by the example of the CIO's leadership. If pressured to talk about the IT organization as a whole before talking about you in particular, go ahead and do so. Just be certain to listen, take notes, and ask for clarifications while carefully avoiding debate about whether your network partner's perceptions are correct. As perceptions, they *are* correct in the eyes of the network partner. The input will be useful and worthy of follow-up.

Just be certain to steer back to *your* performance as an enabler. By sincerely doing so, you will be rewarded with honest feedback that addresses specific ways you can continue and improve in this capacity. Don't be surprised if you are asked what you mean by *enabler* or *enabling* when you use these terms the first time with a network partner. A clear, proactive response is, "I see IT as a key business tool that should give you a competitive edge, and I see my role as enabling you to leverage this tool to realize that competitive edge." This response should elicit an interest and willingness to work with you.

Number 4: How Can I Remove Obstacles to Our Mutual Success?

Much of being an enabling manager or executive deals with removing obstacles and finding solutions to problems that prevent others from making progress toward their goals. Experience suggests that many such obstacles and limits are self-imposed. That is not to say that they are not real to those who experience them. However, some people in leadership positions *perceive* obstacles that are not apparent to others. Another viewpoint may help remove either the obstacles or perception of obstacles.

As a senior executive, the CIO's success depends on the success of the other senior company executives, and as the senior executive for a service organization (in contrast to an end-product organization) the CIO's performance has a material affect on the success of the company's other senior executives and a material affect on the success of the company as a whole. Therefore, clearing performance obstacles—whether real or perceived—can have a material affect on everyone's success. The manner in which this question is asked helps shape the answer. To illustrate, consider the difference between these two ways of offering to help:

- Is there anything I can do to help remove obstacles you have?
- What can I do to remove obstacles to your, and therefore our, success?

The first question sounds like a polite offer, but one that does not explicitly express a strong desire to help; the implied polite answer is, "No, thank you very much." The second question is more proactive. It assumes that the network partner currently or eventually will need help, and the question focuses the network partner on concrete obstacles. The difference is significant, and the enabling CIO recognizes the importance of helping others remove obstacles to mutual success.

Importantly, clearing performance obstacles works best when the method is compatible with the preferences and expectations of the person being served. Lawn mowing offers a good analogy. When someone is kind enough to offer to mow a neighbor's lawn in times of hardship, the person accepting the offer generally uses personal experience and technique to project a picture of the outcome. As an enabling CIO who learns to become aware of the preferences of network partners, seek to discover how they think their lawns should be mowed. Without a clear understanding of network partner expectations, misapplied good intentions can quickly lead to a grudge. Consequently, get into the habit of checking in along the way to ensure that the lawn is being mowed consistent with your network partner's expectations. In short, make certain that you are in agreement on what the obstacle is and on how to go about removing it.

Number 5: What Is My Primary Role and Job Definition as CIO?

This question appeared in the Chapter 1 "10 Questions" section for the CEO. It is an important question for all key network partners. Experienced CIOs usually ask this question during the interview process, but interviews have a limited exposure to key company leaders. Experienced CIOs also quickly learn that the answers evolve after the job is secured and people become more at ease with the new senior IT executive. This question reveals where you fall in the spectrum, from glorified data processing (DP) manager to top company IT and business executive in the eyes of each network partner.

If you persist, you may also find out to what degree you are or will be seen as major contributor to company leadership from a business perspective. The answer regarding the job definition reveals the network partner's specific biases on two important themes: where you should be spending your time, and a current snapshot of your job focus in the context of existing business strategic priorities. You might also get a sense of which business areas require greater focus from you and the IT organization. The change in IT focus may require broad redefinition in terms of strategy, tactics, or some of both. That said, network partners may focus exclusively on specific IT staff or line roles that offer them an unexpected strategic advantage. Always ask about ways that the IT organization itself (and its leader) become an operational or strategic burden.

If there is a consistent major discrepancy between what you believe your role and job definition to be compared to what you hear from your partners, discuss your concerns with your boss. Hopefully, your views will align with your boss and the CEO. In that case your challenge is to find ways to revise your partners' expectations so that they understand the role and job definition as the job has been assigned to you. Your boss and the CEO should become allies in this important redefinition process.

Number 6: Am I Balancing Tactical Issues Relative to Strategic Issues?

As a senior executive, the CIO is generally expected to spend more time on strategic than on tactical issues, but the tactical issues cannot be ignored. For instance, critical customer situations (internal or external) commonly demand CIO-level attention. And if a network partner has an unexpected critical tactical fire and asks for help, the enabling CIO would certainly want to pitch in to assist. However, most tactical issues can be delegated to a capable assistant and followed indirectly, whereas it is unwise to delegate most strategic topics and issues. Strategic work is leadership work, and only a CIO is informed to lead the way within the usually pressing strategic time frame.

Asking network partners about strategic/tactical balance helps the CIO calibrate a more accurate view of where to spend time and effort more efficiently. In looking for better balance, adjust the points of view from each network partner. When talking to someone who has a very tactical role, he or she is likely to overemphasize strategic issues and directions. Conversely, when talking to people with very strategic roles, they are likely to value the importance of the CIO's tactical obligations. You may find then that some people view you as too strategic and others may view you as too tactical, and this might be a reflection of a well-balanced distribution of work priorities between strategic and tactical activities. Once you learn to see your network partners' answers through lenses with appropriate attitude filters, you can adjust your activities with those partners according to their needs and the responsibilities of your companywide role. Those network partners who are not really in tune with the company's need for a strategically focused CIO need to see some concrete demonstrations of the value you add by paying attention to strategic issues and the opportunities that the company misses when you do not.

Number 7: Am I Spending the Right Amount of Time on Business Issues Relative to Technical Issues?

While this is analogous to the strategic/tactical balance in number 6, it carries important tacit distinctions. Similar to the ways a CIO can balance strategic/tactical activities, much of the detailed technical decision making can be reasonably delegated to capable assistants. But as the senior IT executive, you will be expected to be on top of your business and your business' contribution to the profitability of your partners' businesses. Delegation of the business leadership aspects may add time for technical activities, but in most companies this places the CIO more in the CTO ranks.

Of course, you will have to apply the same filters to the feedback you hear to this question based on its source. In the technology/business balance debate, however, the technology concentration can be of two types: high-level professional interpretation of the technical details or technical direction/technical strategy to address the ongoing IT needs of company business (the "nitty-gritty" type); and the translation of unintelligible IT mumbo-jumbo into something meaningful for the other senior executives (the not "nitty-gritty" type). In any case, leave the "rooting around" in the technical details to the technologists. Once you learn to put on the properly filtering lenses, you can see the input from an appropriate perspective and adjust your business/technology-balancing activities accordingly.

Number 8: Is it More Effective for IT to Report to Me Directly or Should Operations Management Report Indirectly?

Why open this can of worms? Well, some of the most practical information from this question comes in the form of "why or why not" answers, and a CIO is far better off knowing what network partners currently think in this commonly cyclic area of CIO leadership responsibility. Regardless of where the company is in the cycle, remain attentive to this question and learn to anticipate changes in the cycle as they occur. At any given time there may be a series of events and forces that could cause the cycle to shift.

If IT reports directly to the CIO today, it may be divided up into pieces and parceled out to each of the business units tomorrow. And if the IT presence is primarily distributed in the business units today, it might very well be consolidated and brought under the CIO tomorrow. The common thinking suggests that lack of responsiveness and attention to the needs of company businesses causes each of the businesses to lobby for its own sub-IT groups; and, before long, most of the businesses' IT decisions are being made at the business unit level (with the budgets following). The common thinking also suggests the converse IT reporting structure under different circumstances. Duplication of effort, inefficiencies, cross-business incompatibilities of business operations, and more time spent on IT issues than on the businesses' goals and objectives cause the senior-level executives in the company to insist that the IT organizations be consolidated and centralized to regain the necessary efficiencies.

By discovering network partner views on this important issue, the astute CIO learns directly whether the business executives believe IT is fulfilling their mission relative to the business unit (or if there is significant unrest). The astute CIO also indirectly learns whether the business executives believe they are appropriately working with their business units to provide them with the support they expect. Importantly, ask this question often—the needle can swing quickly from one direction to the other, and the CIO has to be ready to manage it, or to prevent it, depending on personal preferences and the specific role and job definition.

Number 9: Is IT an Expense or an Investment?

Experienced CIOs know that though the previous question was a hot one, this question can be even touchier. This question provides some of the most important feedback that a successful CIO needs in order to understand how each of his/her partners see the IT function: Is it a drain on the company? Is it a black hole? Is it a necessary evil? Or, is it a value-add to the company? Is it a value multiplier? Is it a competitive edge? Does it provide the business units with greater insight into their sales and operations and costs? Does the IT function create value by making it possible or easier for business units to create their own form of value? Remember to ask follow-up questions that allow the network partners to specify why they answer as they do.

The CIO must recognize these subtle shades of value perception because if IT is indeed seen as an expense without real business value, the opinion must be characterized as endemic or merely the view of a select few of network partners. If the "expense" answer is endemic, there is comprehensive companywide work to be done, because the tide has come in unexpectedly. If it is an isolated view, then you are presented with a golden opportunity to work with those network partners to find a way to use IT to enhance the value of their business and to increase their profits—a goal all senior executives can agree on!

Number 10: What Is the CEO Looking for from Me?

While you will be regularly asking this of your boss and, hopefully, of the CEO directly, the successful CIO realizes the value of triangulating on this topic with the perspectives of network partners. Proactive investigation only makes good sense because they are probably providing their viewpoints to the CEO already. Knowing their opinions can help the CIO work to address any perceived shortcomings, and may also provide some excellent topics to explore when talking with the CEO directly. Whether the CEO actively elicits or even knows of your network partners' perspectives, network partner input is valuable because it points the way to the value you and your IT function can add for the company through the CEO as seen through the eyes of one of your peers—a very powerful and very useful set of information.

There is a saying that you should not ask a question to which you do not wish to know the answer. However, in the case of the "10 Questions" feature, the objective is for you to get to that point, because if you do not ask, it is not certain that your peers will tell you—even though you really *need* to know!

PROFILE OF SUCCESS

Chapters 1 and 2 have established an almost inconceivable array of business, technical, and leadership competencies commonly expected of the CIO. Can anyone fill such shoes? Yes. Any number of fine CIOs currently manifest many of these competencies. This new and rapidly changing executive position did not emerge from nothingness, and some of today's finest CIOs have participated in shaping the roles of the senior technology executive by trial and error as they worked to keep pace with the changing IT needs of their businesses. In a running feature, this book profiles the experience and wisdom of one such success, Dr. C. Bruce Kavan.

Kavan provides both business strategy and technology leadership to The CMI Group based on his extensive industry and academic backgrounds. While on leave as the Bank of America Professor of Information Technology at the University of North Florida, Kavan served The CMI Group as executive vice president and chief operating officer. CMI was organized in 1985 to fill a void in the area of credit management and debt collection for the cable television industry. Previously, he has worked for Dun & Bradstreet Corporation, and has over 18 years experience in managing technology, having held such positions as vice president, information services, and chief technologist for its Receivable Management Services division. He has "retired" three times from Dun & Bradstreet, each time to return to academia. He has coauthored more than 15 textbooks and monographs and has almost 50 journal articles to his credit. Kavan often addresses both academic and business conferences on the strategic use of technology and IT leadership. The subsequent chapters include what he considers to be some of his most important experiences and "lessons learned" for current and aspiring CIOs.

Exhibit 2.6 is part of a system that Kavan developed to assess and review the performance of The CMI Group's senior IT executive, who goes by the title of chief technologist. While talking with Kavan, he emphasized the following points regarding his company's CIO equivalent:

- The senior IT executive is a key member of the senior executive team charged with the responsibility for the formulation and implementation of

EXHIBIT 2.6   IT EXECUTIVE JOB DESCRIPTION

JOB DESCRIPTION

JOB TITLE: Chief Technologist	**TYPE OF ACTION:** (Circle one) New Position Reevaluation
REPORTS TO: CEO	**APPROVAL:**

BASIC FUNCTION

This individual is the chief technologist for The CMI Group. The incumbent is a key member of the senior Vital Factors Management team that is charged with the responsibility for the formulation and implementation of the CMI strategic direction. This position has organizational responsibility for the alignment of information technology in support of the CMI business strategic direction. This individual will provide the technology vision and leadership for developing and implementing information technology initiatives that create and maintain leadership for CMI in a constantly changing and intensely competitive marketplace. This is accomplished through the creation of an information technology architecture and infrastructure that enables technology transfer. Other significant responsibilities include managing strategic partnerships with CMI departments, customer satisfaction (both internal and external clients), business technology planning, applications development, and coordination to meet CMI objectives, as well as active participation in creation of company policy.

MAJOR JOB DUTIES/RESPONSIBILITIES	PERCENT OF TIME
Strategic Management • Facilitate strategic development process to ensure information technology actionable outcomes. • Align information technology in support of the strategic direction through the development of an IT infrastructure and architecture (e.g., computers, applications, databases, and networks). This internal CMI Group alignment process occurs in conjunction with other departments and their budgeting processes to ensure ongoing investments are made in support of the CMI Group direction. • Responsible for the technology planning process in a collaborative fashion with other vital factor areas. **Measurement** will be through managerial feedback.	25%
IT Management • Responsible for defining the application development processes to ensure system and data integrity while maintaining total system integration of all components. This process includes the sourcing decision (e.g., make versus buy), requirements, validation and translation, monitoring, testing, implementation, and integration. These activities are required to ensure system interity, as well as accurate and timely product fulfillment.	25%

- Manage departmental relationships within the CMI Group to ensure that needs are handled in a manner consistent with the strategic direction in the most cost-effective manner possible.

Measurement will be through the team review feedback survey.

Technology Transfer Management - Establish and maintain communications mechanisms to distribute information technology update information to all stakeholders within The CMI Group in order to improve understanding and management expectation. - Establish, maintain, and communicate technology policy and procedures through reference manuals, training materials, and correspondence to ensure system integrity and consistent service levels. - Establish and maintain communications mechanisms for information technology management and control in order to ensure timely implementations of specified functionality within budget. **Measurement** will be through managerial feedback.	25%
Customer (Internal and External) Satisfaction - Coach and maintain highly technical staff with superior communications skills in order to manage and deliver high levels of customer satisfaction. - Implement and maintain procedures for continuous process improvement in systems and service in order to raise product quality, customer satisfaction, and productivity while maintaining cost-effectiveness. **Measurement** will be through a functional area survey to measure satisfaction.	25%

QUALIFICATIONS (Education, Training, Knowledge, Skills, Abilities, and Experience)

MBA in Management, Management Information Systems, or Strategic Use of Technology.

The ideal candidate will:

- Demonstrate strategic planning skills to formulate appropriate strategies and architecture with corresponding implementation tactics.

- Have a strong business orientation (broad experience in industry).

- Have strong analytical skills and a 10-year record of successful system implementations.

- Demonstrate ability to bring the benefits of IT to solve business issues while also managing costs and risks. He or she will also have the ability to conceptualize and translate into system design and develop appropriate business case and with corresponding ROI.

- Be skilled at identifying and evaluating new technological developments and gauging their appropriateness for the business.

- Have the ability to communicate (written and verbal) with and understand the needs of nontechnical internal/external customers.

EXHIBIT 2.6 (CONTINUED)

- Possess strong organizational and significant facilitation skills.
- Be able to mesh well with the existing management team by being a good listener, a team builder, and an articulate advocate of their IT vision.
- Be dedicated to outstanding customer service.

WORK BEHAVIORS

The major challenge for this position is managing the information technology efforts of The CMI Group while balancing technological and operational needs with financial and marketing needs. This is to be accomplished with the use of computer and communication technology that support both self-generated growth and growth through acquisition of new business lines and services. Seamless integration of data and information from the customer through settlement (i.e., the debt cycle) with appropriate management and customer reporting is one of the primary challenges of this position. This requires considerable negotiation skills in order to obtain the appropriate level of buy-in by all stakeholders to ensure successful implementation.

This position requires time management skills in directing a variety of projects, in addition to an understanding of the ways in which information technology can be applied within The CMI Group. The position requires supervisory/management experience and the flexibility to deal with people at a variety of organizational levels, both internally and externally, who possess varying levels of technological understanding.

WORKING CONDITIONS

(Rotating Shifts, Overtime, Weekend Work, Travel, 10-Hour Workdays, etc.)

Normal business hours. Individual must have good work ethic and set a good example.

Source: C. Bruce Kavan, Ph.D., Executive Consultant, June 24, 2003.

the strategic direction and the alignment of information technology resources in support of the company's business strategic direction.

- The senior IT executive provides the technology vision and leadership for developing and implementing information technology initiatives that create and maintain leadership for his/her company in a constantly changing and intensely competitive marketplace.
- The senior IT executive needs to demonstrate the ability to: (1) bring the benefits of IT to solve business issues while also managing costs and risks, and (2) conceptualize and translate the appropriate business case and with corresponding ROI into system design and development.

- The senior IT executive must be able to mesh well with the existing management team by being a good listener, a team builder, and an articulate advocate of his/her IT vision.

- The major challenge for the senior IT executive is managing the information technology efforts of the company while balancing technological and operational needs with financial and marketing needs. This requires considerable negotiation skills in order to obtain the appropriate level of buy-in by all stakeholders to ensure successful implementation.

This is practical information. It's one thing to read one author's perspectives; it's quite another to have those perspectives substantiated by experienced, practicing CIOs. After all, good ideas must be able to be put into action in concrete ways. That's what survival is all about.

NOTES

1. Fred Alan Wolf, *Parallel Universes: The Search for Other Worlds* (New York: Simon and Schuster, 1988): 308.
2. Daniel Goleman, *Emotional Intelligence* (New York: Bantam Books, 1997); and Daniel Goleman, Annie Mckee, and Richard E. Boyatzis, *Primal Leadership: Realizing the Power of Emotional Intelligence* (Cambridge, MA: Harvard Business School Press, 2002).
3. Charles Wiseman, "Final Word: Two Questions Differentiate Potential and Actual CIOs," *Information Week* (May 25, 1987): 48.
4. Martha Beck, *Finding Your Own North Star* (New York: Three Rivers Press, 2001): 4.
5. Ibid., p. 5.
6. Mihaly Csikszentmihalyi, *Flow: The Psychology of Optimal Experience* (New York: Harper-Perennial, 1991).
7. Donald G. Krause, *The Art of War for Executives* (New York: Penguin Putnum, Inc, 1995): 51.
8. "When you come to a fork in the road, take it." From Yogi Berra, *The Yogi Book: I Really Didn't Say Everything I Said.* (New York: Hyperion Press, 2002).
9. Marvin J. Cetron and Owen Davies, "Trends Shaping the Future: Technological, Workplace, Management, and Institutional Trends," *Futurist* (March/April 2003): 30–43.
10. Otto Kroeger with Janet M. Thuesen, *The Workplace Profiles* (Bethesda, MD: USA Otto Kroeger Associates, 1992).
11. A good introductory treatment is available in David Keirsey and Marilyn Bates, *Please Understand Me: Character & Temperament Types* (Del Mar, CA: Prometheus Nemesis Books, 1978): 210. This book includes a questionnaire that can be self-administered to help you identify your type. You may also learn some pointers that could be useful for understanding and improving your personal relationships along the way. See also Isabel Briggs Myers, *Introduction to Type* (Palo Alto, CA: Consulting Psychologists Press, 1998): 34.
12. One of the most useful books on this subject is Paul D. Tieger and Barbara Barron-Tieger's book *Do What You Are: Discover the Perfect Career for You Through the Secrets of Personality Types* (New York: Little, Brown & Company, 2001).
13. Paul G. Strassmann, *The Politics of Information Management*, (New Canaan, CT: The Information Economics Press, 1995): 170.

14. Paulette S. Alexander and Prashant Palvia, Ph.D., "The Roles of Chief Information Officers in Domestic and International Corporations," http://hsb.baylor.edu/ramsower/acis/papers/alexandr.htm (accessed May 24, 2003).

15. Henry Mintzberg, "Managerial Work: Analysis from Observation," *Management Science,* 18 (October 1971): B97–B110.

16. Carol V. Brown, "The Successful CIO: Integrating Organizational and Individual Perspectives," Proceedings of the 1993 Conference on Computer Personnel Research (St. Louis, MO: ACM Press, 1993).

17. Quoted in Alexander and Palvia, "Rules of Chief Information Officers."

18. Quoted in Ralph Emmett Carlyle, "CIO: Misfit or Misnomer?" *Datamation* 34, no. 15 (1988): 50.

19. Ibid., p. 53.

20. Ibid., p. 52.

21. Paul A. Strassmann, *The Business Value of Computers: An Executive's Guide* (New Canaan, CT: The Information Economics Press, 1990): 300–301.

22. Carlyle, "CIO: Misfit or Misnomer?" p. 52.

23. David Palmlund, "In Search of the Ideal CIO," *Financial Executive* 13, no. 3 (1997): 37.

24. Ibid., p. 38.

25. Petter Gotschalk and Nolan J. Taylor, "Strategic Management in IS/IT Functions," Proceedings of the 33rd Hawaii International Conference on System Sciences (2000).

26. Palmund, "In Search of the Ideal CIO."

27. Carol A. Cartwright, "Today's CIO: Leader, Manager, and Member of the 'Executive Orchestra,'" *EDUCAUSE Review,* (January/February 2002): 6.

28. Gotschalk and Taylor, "Strategic Management."

29. The hypothesis of parallel universes, also known as *multiverses,* states that with each choice we could make there is a unique associated time line. Your reality (the reality *this instance* of you knows) is based on the choice(s) you remember having made.

30. C.J. Prince, *Will the CIO Role Be Obsolete?* (New York: The Chief Executive Group L.P.), www.chiefexecutive.net/mag/146/article3.htm (accessed May 24, 2003).

31. Lorraine Cosgrove Ware, "Trendlines: Whatever Happened to the CTO," *CIO Magazine,* www.cio.com/archive/080102/tl_role_content.html (accessed May 26, 2003).

32. Scott P. Mullins, "Defining the Roles of CTO and CIO" *ZDNet-Australia,* www.zdnet.com.au/jobs/features/story/0,2000038309,20273846,00.htm (accessed May 26, 2003).

33. Quoted in Charles P. Curtis, Jr. and Ferris, Greenslet, ed., "What Is Truth," *The Practical Cogitator: The Thinker's Anthology* (Boston: Houghton Mifflin, 1962): 44.

34. Editors of the American Heritage Dictionaries, *The American Heritage Dictionary of the English Language,* 4th ed. (New York: Houghton Mifflin, 2000) http://dictionary.reference.com/search?q=partnership (accessed June 15, 2003).

CHAPTER 3

A Unified Competency Profile

Management is a set of processes that can keep a complicated system of people and technology running smoothly. . . . Leadership defines what the future should look like, aligns people with that vision, and inspires them to make it happen despite the obstacles.

—John P. Kotter[1]

Successful strategies flow like water; they are shaped by the circumstances of the conflict. When water flows, it avoids the high ground and seeks the low ground. Successful strategies likewise avoid difficult methods and find easy ones.

—Donald G. Krause[2]

When asking a successful executive about the key to his or her success, expect a two-part answer. The first answer is likely to be a one-liner, and it may not necessarily be the most important. People usually first talk either about what comes naturally or their greatest challenges. Wait a while longer and you are likely to hear the three or four components that have truly been most important. Whatever the second response, it is sure to include some mix of technical skills, business acumen, management expertise, and leadership competence and vision. "The ideal CIO needs to be a marketer, a strategist, a technologist, a leader, an organizational behaviorist—all these things," says Pete DeLisi, academic dean of the Information Technology Leadership Program at Santa Clara University, California. "That's what makes the job so difficult."[3] And Randy Mott, Dell's CIO, says "There is far too much focus on technical skills. In order, we invest in business knowledge, leadership, technical skills—which can be learned and developed faster than most people think they can."[4] The willingness and ability to work on developing these four key areas determines the degree of leadership success for the CIO as well, so each deserves a closer look.

Technical Skills

People expect you, as the chief information officer, to have a level of technical skills sufficient to meet the requirements of the role, the company, the technical skills levels of your peers, the technical skills levels of your staff (CTO included), and the technical skills level of your boss and the CEO (they may be the same). CIOs who also work as the company's CTO probably already have an abundance of technical skills, and this is not an issue. (You may, in fact, have the problem of being *too* technically skilled, and you may need to emphasize the other skills to compensate.) People at all levels frequently expect you, the CIO, to be the *senior business technologist* for the company, that is, your partners will look to you to be their sounding board and advisor on technology, regardless of specific goals and projects.

Business Acumen

More than any other leader in the organization, the CIO needs business acumen—a quick, accurate, keen sense of business judgment. CIOs, in particular, need this kind of savvy awareness because, as a partner and supporter, your value and the value of your team depend on your ability to leverage investments in people and capital. As an organizational enabling role, a CIO's business acumen helps everyone in the organization achieve their business objectives. As a leadership competency for a leadership role, business acumen is more important than technical skills for the CIO. The ability of the CIO to leverage and articulate technology and information for the benefit of the business is a critical measure of leadership competency.

Management Expertise

As discussed in Chapter 2 and throughout this book, CIOs need to travel both directions of the fork in the road: technology and management expertise. In this context, CIO management expertise includes not only direct management abilities but also expertise in managing when not directly in charge (even more so for companies organized such that the CIO resides in an IT staff function and the IT organization reports elsewhere). In all reporting scenarios, remember the C-level expectations that come with the title. People expect the CIO to be able to articulate a common IT vision that aligns, influences, and shows people the way to leverage IT for themselves. The CIO needs this kind of management expertise to successfully lead and manage the IT team and the company for expected areas of technical IT responsibilities.

Leadership Competence and Vision

As a leadership position, leadership competencies determine the success of the CIO. People expect peer executives at the C-level to work in partnership and show the way for their own areas of responsibility and the entire organization. As the head of IT, the CIO must be a competent leader, to attract and keep competent people (success breeds success). Importantly, CIOs who show the way must know the way. That is, a leader works from a *vision*; its one of the basic elements people expect from a leader. Do you see yourself as a leader? Do others see you as a leader? Are leaders born, created, or some combination of these two origins? Do you have a vision? Find a way to answer affirmatively to all these questions.

TECHNICAL SKILLS

Over the past 20 years or so—for as long as there has been a discussion of who and what defines the need and responsibilities of a chief information officer—there has also been debate over what level of technical skills a CIO needs. One of the reasons that this question remains unresolved is that there is still no such thing as a typical CIO. More than any other senior executive, the CIO's responsibilities depend on the needs of each company as a unique organizational entity. It would be simply incorrect for the *Survival Guide* to suggest otherwise.

In fact, because the question has become so common, yet remains unresolved, it has been documented on the *Darwin* magazine Web site, excerpted here:

> **Question:** Does a CIO require any technical skills?
> **Answer:** It sometimes takes a while for a CIO, regardless of background, to accept that the people in the IT organization know more than the boss about any given subject. Even so, without a reasonable level of technical knowledge, it is very difficult for a CIO to recognize the consequences of the decisions that he or she will be making. Putting it another way, CIOs need to know enough so that they can ask relevant questions, understand the answers, and determine how much confidence to have in what they hear.[5]

Surveys such as one published in *CIO Magazine* put the need for technical acumen lowest on the list of key skills (see Exhibit 3.1). More in-depth research corroborates the opinions in this survey. In its CIO Influence Project, researchers at the School of Business Administration at Dayton, Ohio, concluded that influential CIO behaviors "vary in accordance with the peer's background."[6] Apart from interactions with IT organization staff members, most of the CIO's relationships were with nontechnically trained peers, and the more influential CIOs were those that could adapt to a nontechnical communication approach. The successful CIO communicates in technical terms for those who are technology-oriented and in business terms for those who are business-oriented. The low technical skills requirement expectations should not be a surprise. The CIO has a *technical* job over a *technology* function; any CIO should expect that people assume a high level of technical acumen. Therefore, the *requirement* will appear low because the *assumptions* will be high! The assumption that the CIO has *some* level of technical competence as the overseer of the information technology function should not really come as a surprise.

All that said, the role of the CIO depends on the application of technical skills in the context of increasingly complex business management skills. A CIO has to integrate a set of highly specialized technical skills into the ways the company manages the business in terms of vision, strategy, goals, and objectives. The *Survival Guide* suggests two ways that aspiring and working CIOs can assess their technical skills: the baseline fundamentals and advanced skills in context. Consider the baseline fundamental skill set of entry-level requirements for any CIO position. The advanced skills in context characterize CIO skill sets by some of the most common types of organizations now employing CIOs as strategic business partners; that is, leaders with technical IT expertise who know how to apply that expertise to achieve specific goals.

EXHIBIT 3.1   SKILLS MOST IMPORTANT FOR CIO SUCCESS

Effective communication	70%
Understanding business processes and operations	58%
Strategic thinking and planning	46%
Thorough knowledge of technology options	31%
Negotiation skills	19%
Ability to influence/salesmanship	17%
Technical proficiency	10%

Source: Adapted from Edward Prewitt, "The State of the CIO," *CIO Magazine*, March 1, 2002.

Basic Technical Fundamentals

The baseline fundamental skills are a set of entry-level requirements for any CIO position. These entry-level requirements are what everyone around you will expect you to know. Of course, you are not expected to be the worldwide expert in each of these skills, but you are expected to be conversant in all and expert in several. The key basic technical fundamentals are:

- Computer systems architectures, implementations, and vendors
- Computer networking architectures, implementations, and vendors
- Application solution designs, implementations, and vendors
- Outsourcing and insourcing viability
- Help Desk and problem management designs, implementations, and vendors
- Translating "technobabble" to something meaningful to the listener

Computer Systems Architectures, Implementations, and Vendors   Because computer systems are the underpinning of the information technology solution, it is absolutely essential that a CIO understand computer systems fundamentals. This will continue to be true for a very long time to come. *Computer system architecture* refers to the underlying organization of the computer systems and how they do their job; *computer system implementation* refers to how the various components of the architecture are combined to make solutions; and *computer system vendors* refers to the companies that make or sell the computer systems and computer system components that are used to build IT solutions. Exhibit 3.2 lists some typical examples of contrasting computer system architectures, implementations, and vendors.

The point is that, as the senior IT executive, the CIO must understand the issues involved from the point of view of where IT is today and where IT needs to be tomorrow. These many technologies are the vocabulary and knowledge base that the CIO uses to meet the company's IT-related business needs.

Computer Networking Architectures, Implementations, and Vendors
Because computer networking is the underpinning for connecting the elements of the information technology solution, it is absolutely essential that a CIO understand computer networking fundamentals. *Computer networking architecture* refers to the underlying organization of the communications systems and how they do their job; *computer networking implementation* refers to the way the various components of the architecture are combined to make solutions; and *computer networking vendors* refers to the companies that make or sell the computer networking systems and computer networking components that are used to build IT solutions.

Contrasting examples of computer networking architectures include TCP/IP

EXHIBIT 3.2 **TECHNICAL FUNDAMENTALS: ARCHITECTURES, IMPLEMENTATIONS, VENDORS**

Computer System Architectures

Shared memory versus partitioned memory

Internal disks versus external disk systems

RAID versus non-RAID

Single processor versus multiprocessors

Busses versus switched

Host-based versus client/server-based

Centralized versus distributed

Local versus networked

Reduced instruction set computing versus complex instruction set computing

Single tasking versus multitasking versus parallel tasking

Relational database versus index sequential database versus object-oriented database

Computer System Implementations

Batch versus interactive

Mainframe versus LAN server

i960 versus Strong ARM

Single-disk versus parity-based RAID

Internal RAID versus external RAID storage controllers

IDE versus ATA versus SATA versus SCSI versus FC disk technologies

Ethernet versus Token Ring

MVS versus VM versus Windows

HP-UX versus AIX versus Solaris versus Linux

COBOL versus FORTRAN versus C versus Assembler language

Oracle versus DB2 versus IMS versus MS-SQL versus MySQL

Novell Netware versus Windows Server

Netscape versus Internet Explorer

Sabre versus Galileo

Laptop versus desktop computer

Object-oriented programming versus procedural programming

Computer System Vendors

Sun versus Hewlett-Packard

IBM versus Dell versus Legend

Cisco versus Nortel; Microsoft versus Novell

Intel versus AMD

Hitachi versus NEC

Bull versus Siemens versus ICL

EMC versus LSI Logic

IBM Global Services versus EDS

versus SNA, ADSL versus Digital Cable Modem versus ISDN, LAN versus WAN versus SAN versus wireless, and Ring versus Star. Contrasting examples of computer networking implementations include AppleTalk versus Ethernet, iSCSI versus FC, SAN versus iSCSI, SAN versus NAS, SNA versus VTAM, and ATM versus Frame Relay. Contrasting examples of computer networking vendors include Nortel versus Cisco versus Alcatel, QLogic versus Emulex, Vixel versus Brocade, 3Com versus Intel versus Broadcom. As with computer systems, the CIO has to be conversant in this basic vocabulary and the operating characteristics of these computer networking choices in terms of the company's current and future needs. This is part of the knowledge base for today's CIOs. (Nontechnically trained senior executives can use the Glossary at the back of this book as a quick reference to the many acronyms used here.)

Application Solution Designs, Implementations, and Vendors Because application solutions are the actual means by which the IT solutions are put to work, it is absolutely essential that a CIO understand fundamental application solutions. *Application solution design* refers to the underlying decision and processing flow of the applications themselves and how they do their job; *application solution implementation* refers to the way the various components of the application are combined according to the design to make solutions for end users; and *application solution vendors* refers to the companies that make or sell the application solutions and application components that are used to build IT solutions.

Contrasting examples of application solution designs include batch versus interactive, local versus remote, character/line mode versus GUI, single-entry versus workflow, and query/response versus OLTP. Contrasting examples of application solution implementations include RYO versus shrink-wrapped software and vertically integrated single-vendor application components versus separate application components integrated by IT. Complementary examples of application solution implementations include advanced planning and scheduling, enterprise asset management, business intelligence, enterprise application integration, enterprise resource management, quality management, customer relationship management (CRM), financials, demand forecasting and planning, human resources, supply chain management, e-business, international trade logistics, transportation management, inventory management, warehouse management, engineering development and change control and configuration management, and manufacturing execution systems.

Examples of application solution vendors include SAP, PeopleSoft, SPSS, SAS, Trillium, J.D. Edwards, E_piphany, Oracle, Alventive, Freemarkets, Plumtree, SeeCommerce, and an almost endless list of startup companies. Most IT functions will be using one or more of these solutions; regardless, the CIO must be familiar with the vendors and their applications. Whether the company uses an established vendor or a startup, the CIO is expected to know the benefits and risks of continuing to use the current vendor's applications versus the potential lost opportunity of not going to a startup company's product that is in tune with today's markets and needs.

Outsourcing and Insourcing Viability   As technology evolves and the profession matures, the CIO is expected to know what *can* be outsourced and what *should* be outsourced and *when*. The converse is also true: The CIO is expected to know when it's right to bring something back in-house that has been outsourced. Bringing something back in-house does not necessarily mean that the outsourcing relationship was unsuccessful or a bad decision; rather, it signals that the economics or the rationale for the outsourcing has changed and that bringing it back in-house now makes more sense. No such decision is permanent; it is important to maintain the flexibility to adapt to the needs of the business and to the market economy. Outsourcing has become such an important subject for companies and CIOs that entire issues of *CIO Magazine* have been focused on different options. Similarly, that publication devotes an entire section of its Web site to the topic of outsourcing.[7] There are entire Web sites devoted to outsourcing, forums for discussions for those who are or who are thinking about outsourcing, and forums for those who want to outsource to find those who will do it for them. Just how prevalent is outsourcing? A survey by *CIO Insight* magazine found that more than 75 percent of the CIOs surveyed had outsourced functions or applications in the previous 12 months, and they were considering outsourcing for both operations management and network installation and management in the future.[8] When asked what they were most likely to outsource next year, the CIOs surveyed put business-to-business e-commerce at the top of their list. In the same survey, CIOs were even considering outsourcing those functions that have been slow to be outsourced: those that directly face the customer and those that are directly connected to revenue production (see Exhibit 3.3).

The what-to-outsource question seems to be tied to CIO motivations for outsourcing. In a major outsourcing survey by *CIO Insight,* the most common reason CIOs cited for outsourcing was to reduce costs; to focus on core competencies, lack of internal expertise, and lack of internal staff were other common reasons.[9] However, in the same survey, the most commonly outsourced IT functions were application development (54 percent of respondents), Web site hosting (44 percent of respondents), and Web site development (39 percent) followed by application hosting, network management, network design, and the Help Desk. As the CIO, the choice of what to outsource will be dependent both on your motivations and your specific environment.

Even armed with all these data, the CIO's choices of what and when to outsource are going to be influenced by situational and financial, cultural, risk, and personnel factors. Success factors in outsourcing are many and varied. For a CIO

EXHIBIT 3.3 OUTSOURCING CANDIDATES

Candidates for Increased Outsourcing	2000	2001
Business-to-Business E-commerce	22	32
Customer Relationship Management	22	30
Supply Chain Management	8	14
Business-to-Consumer E-commerce	17	22
Human Resources Applications	14	20
Applications Hosting	26	30

Source: Perkowski, "Research: Outsourcing," May 1, 2001.

with no experience in outsourcing, the most common recommendation is to communicate with industry peers to learn of their experiences—both positive and negative—and perhaps find an industry mentor who can advise and coach step by step along the way. In looking through the experiential and anecdotal evidence there are several common themes to being successful at outsourcing partnerships.[10]

- *Understand each other's business.* Strive toward a shared understanding of important goals and policies.

- *Set short- and long-term goals.* Prioritize to accomplish intermediate goals without losing the long-term focus.

- *Define realistic expectations clearly.* Set reasonable expectations and anticipate a learning curve. No partnership is perfect on the first day.

- *Share benefits and risks.* Establish explicit articulation and agreement on the benefits and risks. Good performance should be rewarded, while a bad situation should be addressed together.

- *Develop performance standards.* Define, agree, and communicate clear and measurable standards of performance.

- *Expect changes and revisions.* Improvement and growth come from revision and refinement.

- *Prepare for the unexpected.* Try to identify potential problems by playing out what-if scenarios and discussing options.

- *Nurture the relationship.* Like any relationship, a successful partnership requires continual maintenance to increase its value.

The inverse of outsourcing is coming to be known as *insourcing.* Research has found that the focus on insourcing has been wanting in terms of ensuring there is a good business balance in the decision-making process for outsourcing. The current IT sourcing research covers the motivations and consequences of out-sourcing, but has neglected the important option of insourcing, the practice of evaluating the outsourcing option, but confirming the continued use of internal IT resources to achieve the same objectives of outsourcing. Insourcing must be fully explored to complement the growing body of outsourcing research; only by un-derstanding the processes and outcomes of both outsourcing and insourcing can a comprehensive understanding of IT sourcing result.[11]

The research showed that the success or failure of outsourcing or insourcing was in the eyes of the beholder:

- Senior management's expectations of IT performance is on *minimizing costs.*
- Users' view of IT performance is of *service excellence.*
- IT managers' view is caught in the middle.

The researchers said it very succinctly:

> [S]enior executives were demanding cost cuts while users were demanding service excellence. IT managers were expected to perform the near impossi-ble: provide a Rolls Royce service at a Chevrolet price in order to be super-stars. IT managers could not simultaneously satisfy both stakeholder groups because the best practices associated with one objective are in direct conflict with the best practices prescribed for the other objective. In general, the dif-ferentiator quadrant calls for decentralization, customization, and encouraged user demand. The commodity quadrant calls for centralization, standardiza-tion, and curtailed user demand. The result: neither stakeholder group was sat-isfied and began to perceive that IT provided poor service that cost too much. IT was a Black Hole.[12]

In today's world, CIOs spend a significant amount of time deciding exactly what and when to outsource. So, it is clear that outsourcing will be a consideration and this is part of the knowledge base for today's CIOs.

Help Desk and Problem Management Designs, Implementations, and Vendors   Why put the help desk on a list of CIO basic technical skills? *CIO Magazine* asked its readership whether their help desk staff had the necessary train-ing to be effective with their company's end users. The results: 30 percent said yes and 70 percent said no, leaving little doubt about the high-level attention this serv-ice requires. All too often, the help desk caller attitudes define the poor service management standards. Even though callers lack technical training, they usually be-lieve that they know more about their problem than the help desk service special-ist. When the person working at the help desk takes a careful, deliberate diagnostic history, the impatient, all-knowing callers become frustrated customers who sub-sequently rarely use the service to their full advantage. Rather than placing the help desk in the "lost cause" management category, the CIO has to be ready to spend some time understanding and delivering the value of this important, basic, technical skill area.

The help desk is one of the few directly customer-facing IT functions. As the saying goes, a little bit of love (to your end users) can go a long way! When *CIO Magazine* surveyed its readership, it found that "roughly 20 percent of the respondents described the user/IT staff relationship as negative. The reasons most frequently listed for IT's poor image were: setting incorrect or inappropriate service-level agreements, poor response times, poor communications, and a lack of clear technical support procedures."[13] Because the help desk is the front line for the IT function, the CIO must know not only that it exists but what it was designed to do, what it is doing today, where it needs to be tomorrow, and some idea of how to get it where it needs to be. In this case, as in many others, the customers have all the answers—whether they are internal or external customers. As the senior IT executive, you must come across as technically competent and knowledgeable about your company's IT infrastructure and applications in order to lend credibility to your help desk.

Is it within the realm of reasonableness for a (perceived to be) nontechnical CIO to have a technically qualified help desk? Yes. Is it likely? No. Is it within the realm of reasonableness for a (perceived to be) technical CIO to have a technically qualified help desk? Yes. Is it likely? Absolutely! Whether this is the reality, it is the customer perception. The CIO's credibility can certainly affect the credibility of the rest of the IT function. And with the help desk, it is most definitely the case. Many CIOs have taken the time to sit in with the customer support group and actually field calls; those who have done so have walked away with a better understanding of the work protocols and the trials and tribulations of the help desk personnel. The fact is that it's even more valuable for the CIO's understanding of the problems and tribulations of the *end users*. This way, the CIO eliminates the "middle man" between the customer feedback, so there is no real opportunity for the message to become muddled on its way to the senior IT executive.

Translating Technobabble   Whatis.com defines *technobabble* as:

> In information technology and other specialized areas, technobabble is the use of technical or "insider" terms that, to the uninitiated, have no meaning. Technobabble can be divided into (1) technical terms with some formal standing in language such as new transmission or computer communication protocols, especially in their abbreviated or acronym forms, (2) marketing terms in which terms with prior meaning are given new missions (for example, *industrial strength*), and (3) informal, colloquial, or jargon terms (of which *technobabble* itself would seem to be an example).
>
> Although this term primarily connotes words that discourage understanding, it is not always used in a negative sense, but often in the sense that "here is some technical information expressed in the terms that have been

invented for it." Closely related terms include: neologism, technospeak, and geekspeak.[14]

The fact that many people actually use this as a real word might itself be considered justification for many companies to have a CIO. As the senior IT executive, the CIO is expected to have both technical and business acumen and, therefore, is expected to be able to make the translation *intelligible* for the "mere mortals" in the rest of the senior executive team—including and especially the CEO. When performing this act of "mercy," the successful and effective CIO remembers that it is important that the listener understand the material, and that if the listener does not understand, it is not the listener's fault—the onus is on the speaker to ensure that the listener understands (recognizing the difference between listening and hearing). CIOs who translate effectively are in high demand and held in high regard by the senior executive team—especially the CEO.

Advanced Technical Skills in Context

The advanced skills in context characterize CIO skill sets by some of the most common types of organizations now employing CIOs as strategic business partners—that is, leaders with technical IT expertise who know how to apply that expertise to achieve specific business and company goals. Advanced technical skills in this context include technology evaluations of potential suppliers, technologies specific to the CIO's industry, and the ability to "mix it up" with the IT function's employees when necessary. The key advanced technical skills in context are:

- Environment-specific designs, implementations, and vendors
- Outsourcing and insourcing viability
- Development project planning and cost estimation
- Key technologies evolution

Environment-Specific Designs, Implementations, and Vendors   The CIO must also have knowledge of the requirements and implementations that are specific to the company environment. Although it is unreasonable to expect a new CIO coming from another industry to know the environment's specific requirements and implementations on the first day, it is reasonable to expect that the same CIO will have become quite familiar with the needs of the business within 30 days. For example, if a company in the chemical industry were to hire a CIO from the airline industry, that CIO would not be expected to know all the environment-specific aspects immediately; there would be an acceptable grace period for learning those specifics. In contrast, if that chemical industry company were to hire a CIO with chemical industry experience, the new CIO would be expected to be immediately conversant in the nuances of the chemical company's environment. Environment-specific applications in the chemical industry use products for chemical plant design, chemical plant simulation, and hazardous chemicals management, whereas environment-specific applications in the airline industry use products for aircraft management and routing, crew scheduling and management, weather advising, and yield management. There are analogies across industries, but the actual applications and how they are used may very well be quite different. The successful CIO quickly comes up to speed on the environment-specific applications as part of his or her expected base technical skills. Employers assume as much, and their peers and employees expect it.

Outsourcing and Insourcing   The advanced arts of outsourcing and insourcing are quite contextual and are therefore treated in significant depth in Chapter 5 as they relate to aligning IT with your company's strategies.

Development Project Planning and Cost Estimation   One of the CIO's greatest challenges is estimating the cost and length of time it will take to complete a project. Mountains of articles and books have been written on this subject. The key skill for the CIO in this area is to employ qualified people who can see that work is completed correctly. One of the best treatises on this subject is by Tom DeMarco in *Controlling Software Projects*.[15] Among his many pearls of wisdom is an effective method for measuring (and therefore compensating) the program management people on your team. Exhibit 3.4 gives a graphic representation of this "Area Under the Curve" method.

Estimates become easier and more accurate as a project approaches completion, even for those miserable projects that come in years past the original estimate. It is

EXHIBIT 3.4   MEASURING PROJECT PLANS ESTIMATES REALISTICALLY

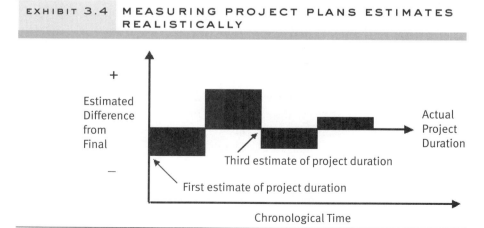

Source: Thomas DeMarco, *Controlling Software Projects*, 1982.

simply unrealistic to hold a project management team to an estimated completion date for complex projects (especially projects heavy in software development and user interaction). However, it is critical that the project/program management team zero in on the actual completion date as the project evolves. At each significant project interval, the area under (and over) the actual duration line in Exhibit 3.4 becomes smaller and smaller. This measurement method discourages wild shifts of optimism and pessimism and casual or frequent changes in projecting the schedule. By quickly and accurately zeroing in on actual progress toward project completion, duration becomes a more measurable and tangible goal.

As the senior IT executive, this kind of visible project management tool helps the IT organization complete its work efficiently and effectively, while greatly enhancing the reputation of your IT employees. Its value to your customers and peers and your company and the business are obvious. Importantly, your management team and project managers can appreciate the fairness of this open-book progress report approach to project management. To a great degree, one of the truisms of development is that those dependent on its completion are more interested in an accurate reporting of *what* they will get and *when* they will get it than getting something unknown later than expected.

It is important to maintain a focus on being realistic. The successful CIO will be continually closing the loop between pessimism and optimism and desire and reality by repeatedly asking three project management questions:

- How did we think this would turn out?
- How is it turning out?
- How is it likely to finish up?

To be successful in development and project planning it is necessary to have a handle on technology, marketing, and finance perspectives. *Architects* and *technologists* provide the means for addressing workplace needs, *marketing* identifies the needs of greatest interest, and *finance* translates the solutions to business value. In the end, the relevance of any IT project is a function of need, timeliness, technical capability, and financial viability. The CIO coordinates how the company and IT organization addresses each of these essential elements. As a corollary, it is a key responsibility of the CIO's architecture team to understand and translate *interesting* technology to *relevant* technology—all on a *meaningful* timetable.

Successful project oversight and management focuses on more than just the project management team. Project success also depends on managing strategic commitments with partners, people, products, customers, and revenue. For instance, the CIO still hears about the many, many things that people will want done after project completion gives them new levels of IT capacity. The challenge at hand is one of all the things that *could* be done versus those that *should* be done. Another challenge in the earliest days of any project is getting from interesting to relevant without being ahead of the times or falling behind the times. Simply stated, the CIO and the IT organization are expected to deliver relevant solutions to relevant needs in a manner that is timely, cost-effective, and revenue-effective. As complex as this expectation seems, project management remains one of the key basic technical skills of the CIO.

Key Technologies Evolution

> *If we begin with certainties, we shall end in doubts;*
> *but, if we begin with doubts, and are patient in them,*
> *we shall end in certainties.*
>
> —Francis Bacon, 1561–1626[16]

Bacon's words apply perfectly to technology evolution. Because technologies evolve at uneven and unpredictable paces, it is extremely difficult to predict when the next technology breakthrough or discontinuity will occur. For this reason, it is prudent to manage the technology deployment within the IT organization through a combination of commercial off-the-shelf (COTS) products, partnerships, and internal R&D (which, of course, could be outsourced). Over the past 20 years, technology sources and deployment methodologies have evolved to an ecosystem (see Exhibit 3.5). This ecosystem provides a balance of time-to-market and original research and development with strategic investments and partnerships and mass customization through technology standardization. The ultimate result of this ecosystem is that strategic R&D investments drive rapid deployment of industry-standard platforms.

Selecting the key technologies important to the company involves a combination of innovation, continuation, and regression. Innovation is essential for survival, and the CIO is expected to select the best—most appropriate—IT-related technologies for the company. This selection is crucial and could mean the difference between success and failure—for IT and for the company. For instance, some years back there was a pin-on button created by some IBM customers that read "Braniff ran JES3"; the implied message was bankruptcy (like Braniff Airlines) followed on the heels of IBM's JES3 product. Of course, the CIO is also expected to show technology leadership, and you can do so through well-managed creativity. If it is important for your business to be in a technology leadership position, you must manage that process by holding the development groups accountable, manage them to on-time delivery, and keep them within their budgets.

Where key technologies are concerned, ensure that everyone understands the difference between *research* and *development*. One means of doing so is to reaffirm that the IT function and its products should not be regarded as nonrevenue-generating, *and* that they should not be considered a cost overhead. Instead, IT plays a major part in the current and future company success. The CIO's role in managing through key technologies evolution is as much a management issue as it

EXHIBIT 3.5   STRATEGIC INFORMATION TECHNOLOGY R&D INVESTMENTS

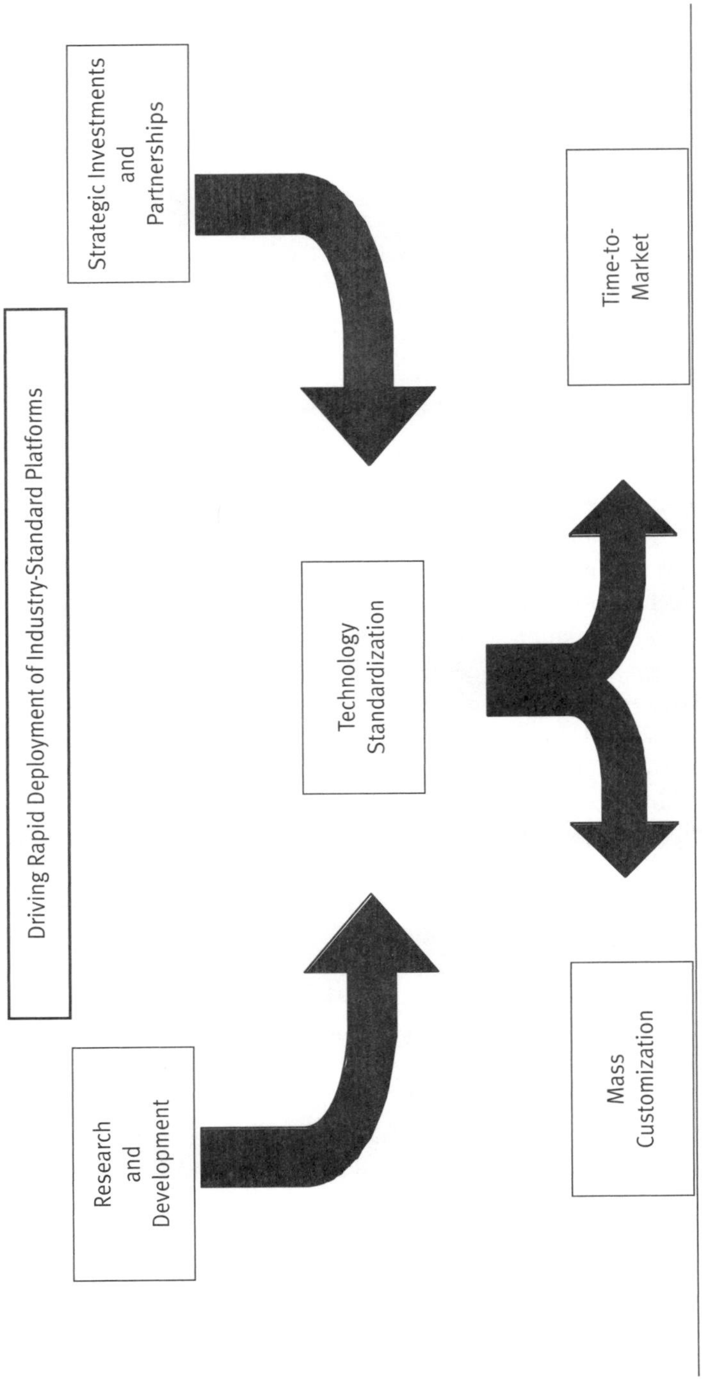

Strategic Investments and Partnerships

Driving Rapid Deployment of Industry-Standard Platforms

Research and Development

Technology Standardization

Time-to-Market

Mass Customization

is a technology issue. Key technologies are key *only* if they are necessary to providing products or services customers want today and will be happy to buy (for internal use) tomorrow.

Technology evolutions and discontinuities provide an opportunity to create breakout products—products that create a "Wow!" kind of reaction. These are typically products that commercially exploit a technology in a new way for a new purpose. These breakouts have risk/reward factors that are much greater than the expense of development. In fact, not exploiting the opportunity might prove to be a greater risk than the risks associated with deploying the new technology. Therefore, as the senior IT executive you need to manage such resources very closely, manage the time scales more closely, and manage the specifications *extremely* closely.

As a CIO, many new technologies and evolutionary technologies cross your path. Therefore, it is important to keep in mind not only the *what* (and the "coolness factor") but the *when* (and the *probability* and *relevance* factors). A study by the Australian Institute for Commercialization reported that for every 3,000 to 4,000 raw ideas, somewhere between one and two actually make it past launch. The point is that just because a technology appears to be cool or interesting does not mean that it is relevant; it may not be commercial, it may be ahead of its time, and/or it may not really be feasible. Once the IT function is committed to a technology, evolutionary success is not yet a certainty. In fact, though you may be tempted to gauge the probability of success of a project by taking the current temperature of the development team, it is not guaranteed to be a good measure of the final outcome. Exhibit 3.6 captures only one sequence of innovation process experiences, but the up and down pattern is characteristic of such efforts. This roller-coaster progression is normal for technology evolution, and the challenge for the CIO and for the IT senior management staff is to recognize where they are on the chart to ensure they are making the right decisions at the right time and for the right reasons.

Drawing Up Your Own Approach   Two questions help shape one's personal approach for many people regarding technical skill set competencies:

- Do the *better* CIOs rise through the technical ranks or through the business ranks?

- Do the *more successful* CIOs rise through the technical ranks or through the business ranks?

That is, the question comes in two flavors: technical or business, better or more successful.

The answer boils down to a matter of learning and preference. Some people prefer the technical so strongly that they never spend enough time learning about

EXHIBIT 3.6   IT INNOVATION AWARENESS

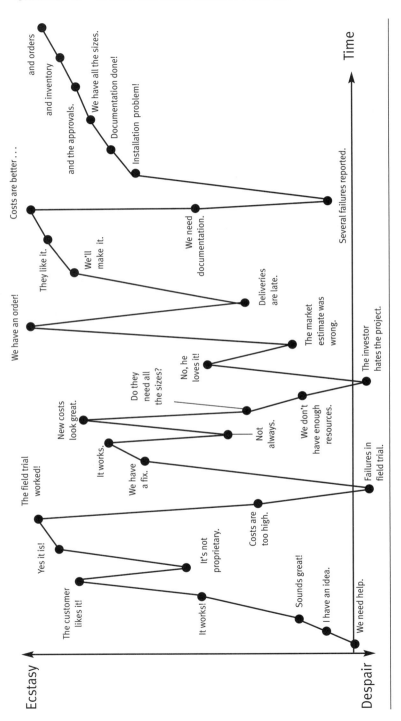

Source: Adapted from R. J. Saldich, "Genesis of an Innovation," accessed at www.tuta.hut.fi/studies/Courses_and_Schedules/lsib/TU-91.123/slides/Kuhn-color.pdf, July 1, 2003.

becoming a better businessperson. Conversely, some people find some disciplines so difficult that they learn very slowly. That said, given the capacity for learning a new discipline, it seems more likely that a technically trained executive can learn business than the other way around. What really matters, of course, is that a person evolves as a CIO or as an aspiring CIO to be able to understand, work, and lead from both a technical and a business point of view. And it is important to learn which circumstances demand one more than the other.

The most challenging CIO responsibilities come in the business applications of the technical skills, and that is what the *Guide* is all about. A CIO with all the technical skills on the planet does not serve the company unless those same skills can be applied in the world of business—the world of people and machines working according to ever changing rules of a very strange and unpredictable behavioral science: management science. By all means, discover and master essential and emerging technical skills as a routine practice throughout your career, and learn how your fellow employees can help you create value from what you know. But be aware that, as the CIO, your technical acumen is *assumed* and your business acumen is to be proven.

BUSINESS ACUMEN

In a survey by *CIO Magazine,* 58 percent of the responding 500 CIOs reported that understanding the business is a pivotal skill for CIO success—a skill that falls well outside any classic set of technical skills.[17] Understanding the business is part of the CIO's business acumen. While every CIO works to discover the unique ways the company executes its vision, mission, and goals, some general principles guide this discovery process. Interestingly, the United States government's Office of Personnel Management defines *business acumen* as the:

> Ability to acquire and administer human, financial, material, and information resources in a manner that instills public trust and accomplishes the organization's mission, and the ability to use new technology to enhance decision making.[18]

The Office of Personnel Management also provides an excellent list of the six key characteristics of business acumen:

1. Assessing current and future staffing needs based on organizational goals and budget realities; applying merit principles to develop, select, and manage a diverse workforce.

2. Managing the budgetary process, including preparing and justifying a budget and operating the budget under organizational and congressional procedures; understanding the marketing expertise necessary to ensure appropriate funding levels.

3. Overseeing the allocation of financial resources; identifying cost-effective approaches; establishing and assuring the use of internal controls for financial systems.

4. Overseeing procurement and contracting procedures and processes.

5. Integrating and coordinating logistical operations.

6. Ensuring the efficient and cost-effective development and utilization of management information systems and other technological resources that meet the organization's needs; understanding the impact of technological changes on the organization.[19]

CIOs in the commercial sector can just as easily translate the government sector focus to their analogous environment with lines of business, corporate organizations, and boards of directors.

This set of responsibilities is much more complex than the learning and applying of the technical skills required of the CIO role. Business acumen is a form of experiential learning defined by the rich context of company dynamics. Technical skill learning and application is formulaic compared to business acumen abilities, so a CIO's business acumen can be measured in terms of time on the job and the number of management experiences the job demands. If part of your CIO responsibilities includes managing all or a significant amount of the IT organization, you probably recognize and manage many of these areas. Conversely, these same areas may not seem important to the CIO who leads a staff function. Think again. As an enabling role, the CIO works in a partnership relationship with other divisional or company senior executives. While certain CIO positions do not demand the direct application of a broad range of business acumen abilities, these abilities help the CIO to understand the needs of partnership peers and better enable their productivity and success. They expect nothing less from a person in a leadership role. So, let's take a look at each one of the areas, in turn.

Personnel Staffing and Management

> Assessing current and future staffing needs based on organizational goals and budget realities; applying merit principles to develop, select, and manage a diverse workforce.

As a senior executive—and an executive with leadership and vision—you, the CIO, have a responsibility to the IT organization, and to the company, to recruit and retain a diverse workforce of the right size and with the right skill mix and skill complementarity. Successful CIOs apply a holistic approach to their recruiting and retention activities. Just like peers in other leadership positions, you have the vision; only you know who you need to help you implement that vision.

Experienced CIOs assess the IT staff *at least* every quarter, which makes it clear that getting to know the staff members and completing a full staff assessment should top the business acumen agenda of a new CIO. Remember, you are only as good as your team. Making staffing a top priority also establishes and maintains the level of respect and confidence a CIO needs from the people who implement his or her IT vision. Importantly, a careful early and ongoing assessment of IT staff skills, strengths, and weaknesses allows the CIO to balance the performance reports given by peers and partners. And it is important to move the assessment process right down through the direct reports of your direct reports. This helps you get to know more staff members and gives additional insights into your direct report staff. Using an iterative business acumen management process, staff management sets a good example for direct reports and all members of the staff for managing their own relationships and teams. Staff management interactions give the CIO yet another opportunity to reinforce the IT vision and identify who's still onboard.

Mature business acumen practices suggest that successful CIOs integrate staffing assessment activities with future visions of the IT organization, for several reasons. First, the CIO can use the IT vision as a visible model for demonstrating the required skill sets for various stages of the vision to IT staff, peers, and partners. Skill sets need to change and adapt at certain specific points in any long-term vision for the IT organization, and people have the chance to prepare their own skill sets as the vision evolves. You may need a different skills mix now from those currently available, and seeing the vision helps people understand the reasons behind your staffing priorities.

Second, in light of today's competitive IT job market, the CIO can use IT vision and staff assessment activities to anticipate key hires as important new phases of the IT function vision draw closer. The CIO can identify important *interception points*—points in the development of the vision that require new staff skills—and have people with the right skills onboard just when they are needed. In some cases, new hires are unnecessary when current staff members deliberately grow their existing skill sets to meet clearly identified future needs.

Knowing the right mix of skills and diversity over time to achieve the IT vision is not an easy task, but it is a critical one. Living and mechanical systems that work smoothly over the long term have certain redundancies incorporated into their designs. Work to build and maintain an IT staff with at least one person who can demonstrate mastery in each specific area of key business acumen for the IT organization. These kinds of staff members not only support and complement each other, they carry the CIO's leadership and vision throughout the company. Start by mapping out key areas of business acumen for your IT organization and create a matrix that identifies which IT staff members address your needs. Then start filling in any gaps—and don't forget to adapt the matrix as the IT vision evolves.

Clearly, developing the IT organization staff is critical to the CIO's overall success. One practical way to approach staff development is to begin your own success. One practical way to approach staff development is to begin your own success. One practical way to approach staff development is to begin your own success cession planning from within your existing staff. This is another iterative management approach that keeps the CIO focused on a vital resource. Staff development includes managers and employees and employs didactic instruction, new experiential learning opportunities, and mentoring. All staff development efforts should prepare people for their places in the IT vision and the directions of the company. Doing so not only prepares staff members to contribute to their fullest but it also helps them meet their own career vision, goals, and objectives. For both those reasons, it is cost-justified and cost-effective to do so.

Similarly, peers, partners, and bosses regularly call on the senior information technology executive to provide development opportunities to those outside the IT organization, who, nevertheless, need to be have better-than-average knowledge or skills in the information technology area. CIOs who have invested in staff development can turn these learning opportunities over to IT staff members and give them opportunities to practice mentoring skills with those outside the IT organization.

This section has underscored the importance of workforce diversity as an extremely valuable asset for any team, regardless of legal requirements. It goes beyond the important ethical realities; diverse workforces are more effective. Monocultures cannot survive over the long term because they make such easy targets for single-weapon invaders. Unfortunately, both the general business and IT management communities fall prey to silver-bullet fads and can easily be distracted or be caused to forget to deliberately maintain balance and diversity in their ideas, approaches, methods, and people. Diversity by its very nature has a positive effect on a team and on the organization in innumerable ways—including perspective and insight. With the increasingly global pluralism of today's workforce, few companies or IT organizations can claim that diversity is not available. Remember that the IT staff comprises a team of enablers. Who would dare turn a service team of lookalike act-alikes loose in a world of increasingly shrewd customers?

Budget Management

Managing the budgetary process, including preparing and justifying a budget and operating the budget under organizational and congressional procedures; understanding the marketing expertise necessary to ensure appropriate funding levels.

The budget management area in a product-based company is often referred to as financial planning and analysis (FP&A), but organizations in the government sector, from schools to the military, have no real "finance" equivalent—that is, the stock market and shareholders—so the budget replaces performance measurement

and incentive systems as the primary means of internal control. Remember that the sayings, "the devil's in the details," "follow the money," and "show me the money" apply to good fiscal management. The senior IT executive manages money, people, and information technology. Managing IT's portion of the money is all about managing the IT budget so that it positively and appropriately influences the budgets of peers and partners. Together, executive peers can realize individual goals and objectives on behalf of the company. As an enabler of organizational performance, the CIO stands in the best position to model and orchestrate the ways to align individual budgets with the company's overall vision and budget. More visibly than any other function, IT has a finger in everybody's piece of pie.

Specifically, the person (the CIO) responsible for a commonly owned organizational asset (IT) works directly and indirectly with many different budget managers throughout the company. The challenge (and art) in working with indirect budget relationships comes with the accountability of expertly justifying what others need to perform their work. To do that requires that you learn to focus direct and indirect budget justifications on the common good: those areas that will help ensure the company's vision, goals, and objectives. All mature C-level executives are expected to work across functional boundaries in this way. This ability comes naturally to the enabling CIO who builds partnership networks to create IT value for the company.

The CIO might receive the IT budget along one of several common paths. Depending on the company's maturity, some CIOs get the budget from the boss in an unmarked brown paper envelope by some mysterious courier, as in *Mission Impossible*. Inside the envelope, the "impossible" budget is written in stone and resembles the Ten Commandment tablets. In a more mature approach, the CIO sits down several times a year with the boss, an executive team, or other group that represents a wide range of interdependent company interests to discuss how the common pool of resources can be distributed to best achieve the company's overall vision and immediate goals. Somewhere in the middle of these two levels of budgeting maturity are CIOs who find themselves creating an IT budget in relative isolation according to a complex set of rules in an environment of parochial posturing from fellow senior executives.

Versatile CIOs follow some commonsense guidelines as their organizations grow into more mature budgeting practices: (1) When in doubt, earlier is better. Submit your IT budget ahead of time because many companies simply give IT a high priority and almost every other function gets their budgets in late. (2) Remember that the budget process is all about distributing finite resources, and one of those resources is IT. Consequently, the CIO again stands in a unique position as change agent to guide the company to greater budget management maturity. Demonstrate the advantages of working together with your peers by going to them first. It's an old kid's game: "I'll show you mine if you show me yours." Well, show yours first. Your peers will quickly see how this kind of practice works to everyone's advantage. Similarly, if you find yourself in an organization with a yearly budget cycle, begin to review projected against actual with your peer executives and functional leaders—especially when performance drops away from that demanded by the vision, strategy, and shareholders.

Budget Management and the IT Staff Whether it was developed bottom-up with staff and peers or given top-down by the boss, it is essential that the CIO next discuss the budget and its related IT management expectations throughout the IT organization. The CIO can use the budget as an internal control for the entire IT organization and as a learning experience for direct reports. In an excellent example of open-book management, give direct reports full access to the budget and delegate full budgetary responsibility and spending authority for those parts of the budget that each report owns. Encourage direct reports to use the same type of open-book access and responsibility management approaches with their own subordinates.

When introducing direct reports to budget management responsibilities, emphasize that, when managing monies (and making spending commitments), they do so with funds that have been entrusted to you and that you now entrust to them. By accepting this trust, they explicitly agree to use the budgetary resources to accomplish IT's objectives and vision. This kind of responsibility carries certain duties and safeguards. Inform direct reports in advance that planned versus actual expenditures for type and timing will be reviewed each month. Frequent reviews sharpen a budget manager's awareness of how to identify and anticipate variances.

The CIO wants the entire IT staff to learn to identify variances as quickly as possible: spending faster than expected might indicate a project that is actually completing ahead of schedule; spending slower than expected might indicate that project targets or milestones designed to trigger the next stage of spending have not been met. To accelerate this learning curve, the CIO can request that the IT FP&A administrator work locally, attend IT staff meetings, receive IT staff distribution lists, and be treated by all IT staff as another IT team enabler. In this same way, encourage the IT FP&A administrator to immediately come forward with new insights and issues.

When reviewing budget outlooks with direct reports, consciously choose to concentrate on variances and exceptions rather than absolutes and "met plan." Managing budget reviews this way sends two important messages to the IT staff: first, that budget management is an important activity; second, that budgets should be managed within *reasonable* tolerances. Moreover, budget reviews give direct reports an opportunity to learn what "reasonable" means in this context. During budget reviews, make it clear that you want to understand the decision environments of direct reports and how IT staff members think for themselves as they interpret the IT vision through their spending decisions.

This gives the CIO an excellent opportunity to mentor direct reports to manage those inevitable exceptions and wide variances that occur everywhere from time to time. Another budget management mentoring technique gives direct reports the opportunity to help each other if they are having a financial problem. For example, if one of your reports comes up short and others can help out by giving some monies, this helps foster teamwork, mutual support, and recognition within the team. This not only helps the CIO understand that not everything works out as planned, but reinforces the view that as long as reports can meet the overall objectives and budget, they can work together and expect the support of their leader. In another example, where one month is overbudget and the previous month was underbudget, emphasize the long-term results rather than slight variances. Remember to bring your FP&A administrator onboard for this approach to teach, guide, and monitor the team from period to period.

Let's look, now, at direct mandates—the "I am in charge" approach. Direct mandates may work more quickly, but undermine the opportunities for IT staff to grow. After all, a good IT staff makes the CIO look good; and an IT staff that learns to autonomously make resource spending decisions that align with the IT vision makes the entire organization look good. This kind of leadership demonstrates *excellence by example*. On a practical level, as you learn more about the spending thought processes your direct reports use to make their decisions, you become more knowledgeable about where the monies are going.

Once again, the success of a person functioning in an enabling role like that of the CIO depends on how people throughout the IT organization and the company come onboard with the CIO's vision. This way, as people make their day-to-day IT spending decisions, they can gauge those decisions in light of the IT vision. This is important because, from a practical point of view, the CIO cannot review every IT-related decision and every purchase order. Even if you could, it's not your job; senior executives should delegate as much operational tactical management to direct reports as possible because executive attention belongs elsewhere: on strategic goals and objectives. Address tactical issues on an *exception* basis and allow your direct reports to do their jobs.

Financial Management

> Overseeing the allocation of financial resources; identifying cost-effective approaches; establishing and assuring the use of internal controls for financial systems.

CIOs who entered the game during the economic "bubble" may think that financial management and budget management are synonymous. More seasoned veterans know better. Financial management focuses on the external financial deliverables and measures of the business—a macro view of the business for invest-ment analysts and shareholders. Budget management focuses on the internal plan-ning, spending, and analysis of "plan versus actual," the aforementioned FP&A, financial planning and analysis. To some degree, the difference will appear to be the contrasting viewpoints of the accountant (financial management) and the plan-ner/analyst (budget management).

As a senior executive, the CIO has a fiduciary responsibility to ensure that the company prudently and cost-effectively spends IT monies on behalf of all stake-holders. CIOs with financial management acumen ensure the efficient and effec-tive use of IT financial resources by means of internal controls. In many cases, the senior information technology executive frequently oversees what, for many com-panies, is the one of the single largest expenses: the IT capital budget.

This kind of CIO wears two hats: accountant and planner/analyst. Even when the CIO bears an indirect responsibility for the IT budget—as when the actual budget for each division is held by a peer or partner who heads up a particular di-vision—the CIO directly serves as a reviewer and approver for IT-related spending to ensure that the expenses fall in line with the company's strategy and IT's overall vision, goals, and objectives. Because of the technical expertise involved in such an analysis, the CIO's superiors and the CFO also expect the CIO to shoulder the same financial management responsibilities.

In short, financial management experience plays a key role in the business acu-men of any CIO role that carries significant leadership responsibilities. If you lack this experience, find some classes, programs, and seminars to fill this gap. If you al-ready have some financial management experience, stay on top of your game and continue to learn more. Accountants are always coming up with "better" ways to track costs. Some of these new systems—for example, activity-based costing (ABC)—actually do make spending habits more visible in some organizations. When it comes to the significant IT capital investment decisions and depreciation budgets that organizations must manage to keep the company competitive, the CIO has important long-term fiduciary responsibilities that affect the business for years to come. When the boss is the CFO, financial management competency ex-pectations automatically increase.

As a C-level executive, the financial focus includes a company-level view of the performance measurements for which the CIO, peers, and partners are responsible. Executive teams link performance measurement systems with incentive systems as a means of internal control to focus employees on key organizational priorities. Ex-ecutive teams use performance measurements to track decision making in terms of performance outcomes; they expect the CIO to understand how spending choices affect performance. To complicate matters, the CEO also expects the CIO to re-main aware of his/her top-level commitments established by the board of directors so that IT spending choices, decisions, and actions support those expectations.

These kinds of financial management business acumen priorities for the CIO increasingly focus on lagging financial outcome measures rather than on leading operational performance measures. Specifically, senior executives and shareholders want the CIO and the IT organization to show a good ROI. As the sole senior executive with the expertise and experience to see the short- and long-term needs of the IT vision, your peers, partners, and superiors in all shapes and sizes expect you, the CIO, to show them how to create IT ROI. The IT recommendations and decisions made by the CIO in many cases lead to years of planning and development, related continual improvement and maintenance activities, and significant effort and expense to adapt when new technologies evolve. The CIO's resource investment decisions—your investment decisions—create long-term, sustainable value from these kinds of expenses and commitments.

Very few other areas of business management have such wide-ranging organizational potential and result in a long-lasting risk/benefit ratio profile. This is why it is important for you, as a CIO or an aspiring CIO, to become very comfortable with the business side—the financial side—of your business.

Procurement and Contract Management

Overseeing procurement and contracting procedures and processes.

At first glance, this area might seem like it falls outside the context of the chief information officer's standard business acumen expectations, but capital investments in equipment generate CIO responsibilities in terms of executing and managing contracts for services and supplies. Based on this kind of experience, peers and partners may ask the CIO to perform the same function for their IT-related investments. Some things cannot be delegated, and it is in the CIO's own best interest to help negotiate terms and approve certain procurements or contracts within the allowable limits of the company's financial control processes.

Two of the most visible, high-profile areas of procurement and contract management are *outsourcing* and *capital equipment*. The experienced CIO's business acumen in both areas is highly sought after; it can account for significant expenditures and future commitments of funds, and may either lead the IT organization, peers, partners, and the company to success or put you all out of business. (We will take an in-depth look at the outsourcing and insourcing issues in Chapter 5.)

Aspiring CIOs who have not had the opportunity to be involved in procurement and contracts should look for every opportunity to do so. Dealing with the details of contracts and the negotiations "at ground level" will be invaluable later. As CIO, you may well be expected to pass judgment on the acceptability of the terms and conditions of a contract or procurement. Certainly, advice from the IT team is necessary and helpful, but personal experience is more important because of the potential conflict management skills involved in the learning curve of this management process. Also, look for an expert in your company who can boil down the key elements, and work with that person (whether directly in your management responsibilities or not) as one of your network partners.

Operations Management

Integrating and coordinating logistical operations.

The CIO may be responsible for at least two important operational areas: IT operations and IT technology and equipment. Collectively referred to as "IT," newcomers to IT operations management discover the entirely different and challenging experience of leading a company within a company. As one of the more important responsibilities of this operations management business acumen, the CIO becomes the senior customer support executive to IT "customers" of all kinds, including executive peers and partners. The IT organization within the company looks very much like a product-based company with a product (application) architecture, product development and test, and product rollout, and subsequent (internal) customer support, procurement, and capital equipment management. Operational management is an excellent assignment for a competent direct report. IT operations is the CIO's *execution task force;* they are the group through which the CIO implements the IT vision, goals, and objectives for the company.

Operations management is important to the company because it is, in the end, the operations side of the "house" that makes things happen and makes things work on a day-to-day and hour-to-hour and minute-to-minute basis. Many companies use the auspices of operations management to match organic and inorganic resources (such as drivers with trucks) and to optimally map out resource flow paths (such as minimizing the amount of travel required to make all deliveries). Operations management and logistical control are used by many companies and IT organizations to manage the timely delivery of products to their customers,[20] and in some industries, such as the airline industry, customers to their product. This is a very immediate task and focus for the CIO.

In attempting to balance the immediate needs of day-to-day operations management with the requirement for the CIO to function strategically, a number of companies have reexamined their organizational model, and many have settled on a two-person CIO approach. Three successful approaches are the *Office of the CIO* model, a *Federated* model, and a *Co-CIO* model.[21] Some companies and government agencies have reached the conclusion that a single CIO cannot realistically fulfill both the strategic role and the tactical (operations) role. The rationale for why this is different for every organization, but two factors are significant in choosing this kind of model:

- Strategic roles and responsibilities require significant thinking and consulting time devoted to peer needs.

- Tactical roles and responsibilities arise unexpectedly and demand rapid response times—more action, less thought.

Jerry Gregoire describes a common CIO experience in terms of fellow senior executive expectations of the IT chief. "Every year they all say they plan to spend 75 percent of their time on strategy and 25 percent of their time on operations, and then they end up having to do it the other way around."[22] Having a deputy or co-CIO can help address this problem. By focusing the deputy on the area where the CIO is weakest (strategic or tactical/operations) the result is a greater than "two plus two" result because they are so complementary. Many of those who have tried it have liked it—particularly in cases where the personality types are also complementary. For this to work, of course, the CIO must cede some of the decision making to the deputy or co-CIO. Although this is not always easy to do, it is necessary for the approach to be successful. To make the leadership team approach work, you as the CIO have to figure out which approach best matches the needs of the company culture, find compatible people to make the commitment to team-lead the IT organization, and to then make the move. It may even require that you move your desk into the middle of the operations group so you can understand the *buzz* and *flow* of that kind of work. This not only helps you to gather real-time information; it will also positively affect the morale of the teams involved.

Information Technology Management

> Ensuring the efficient and cost-effective development and utilization of management information systems and other technological resources that meet the organization's needs; understanding the impact of technological changes on the organization.

Clearly associated with the responsibilities of the chief information officer, this business acumen management area essentially defines the job of the CIO, and all the preceding management areas in this section have characterized information technology management. In this context, the CIO is *the* corporate executive responsible for IT across all business lines and all levels of the company. These responsibilities include all key executive interrelationships where the CIO integrates vision and strategy to leverage information systems and technology evolution and information systems and technology management for the benefit of the company. Just as technical skills pave the way to practical applications in terms of business acumen and management skills, a CIO capable of integrating vision and strategy to leverage IT resources into a valuable company commodity needs to develop some specific areas of management expertise, leadership competencies, and leadership vision.

LEADERSHIP COMPETENCE AND VISION

Leadership competence and vision go hand in hand. In a sense, vision guides leadership in all phases of its practical expression and bridges the gap between current and future conditions. Virtually everyone claims to be able to recognize a leader, but few can define what it takes to become one. Leadership depends on context, and with so many organizational leadership contexts—employees, customers, products, strategies, stakeholders, resources, and competition to name a few—there is no single all-purpose definition for what a leader *is* and what a leader *does* outside specific context. CIOs work in a profession of rapidly changing context, and they need to understand how organizational context shapes personal leadership expectations and responsibilities.

Competence

The word "competence" comes from the Latin *competere*—to be fit, proper, and qualified. In this context, CIO leadership competence refers to a combination of skills, abilities, and experience that enable a person in this role to meet the IT needs of the organization and its people. As an enabling role, the CIO leadership competence can be judged in terms of two elements of CIO performance: how others see it and what actually gets done. People judge CIO performance in terms of credibility based on past performance experiences with the CIO and each new CIO vision. Credibility requires constant attention. While working to implement any given vision, people extend credibility to the degree that the CIO achieves milestones along the path to completion. Accomplishment builds an even greater level of credibility and confidence in those who follow and work to support the competent CIO's vision. Coming full circle, competent accomplishments lend credibility to the new visions that the CIO generates for the IT organization. Those you are leading "must believe in your ability to move them toward what you envision, and they must believe that they can help to bring the vision closer to reality."[23]

Because leadership is so difficult to define without specific context, a more productive approach for understanding leadership characterizes the leadership competencies by contrasting them with another easily defined and well-studied role—the manager. How do people and organizations usually distinguish the basic identity and competency activities of the leader and the manager? The work of Geoffrey M. Bellman compares and contrasts leading and managing, as summarized in Exhibit 3.7.[24]

This perspective does not gauge the relative merits of leaders and managers; it contrasts these equally important but very different competency activities within the organization—not unlike the responsibilities of a team of CIOs—one strategic and the other operational. As such, each CIO works to achieve the correct balance of each activity set to address the needs and expectations of the company and its people, sometimes leading, sometimes managing. The generally accepted view of the relationship between leadership competency and vision has changed significantly over the last 50 years. Exhibit 3.8 shows the evolution of this changing perspective decade by decade.

Looking at the visioning trends in the first years of the twenty-first century, this decade might be known for leadership competencies in "management by business reality." Consistent with this trend, companies increasingly recognize the need to articulate the strategic plan in such a way that all members of the management team have no choice but to identify the truly strategic issues for achieving a common vision and generating a sense of urgent purpose. Leaders capable of articulating the vision behind the strategic plan consistently demonstrate the leadership competencies summarized in Exhibit 3.9.

Vision

During the interview process, people ask an applicant for the CIO position about vision because it's a basic expectation for any position of leadership. Depending on the interviewer, applicants can be asked about IT visions for department sections,

---

EXHIBIT 3.7 CONTRASTING LEADERSHIP AND MANAGEMENT COMPETENCY ACTIVITIES

Leading Activities	Managing Activities
Expand boundaries.	Work within boundaries.
Influence others.	Control others.
Create a vision of a possible future.	Plan to reach goals.
Commit totally to work completion.	Contract time and method of work completion.
Emphasize how intuition and feelings support cognition.	Emphasize reason and logic supported by intuition.
Make current decisions based on a vision of the future.	Make current decisions based on the past and precedent.
Pursue data to make a decision now.	Wait for all relevant data before deciding.
Assess accomplishments against vision.	Measure performance against plans.

Source: Bellman, *Getting Things Done*, 1992.

EXHIBIT 3.8 EVOLUTION OF VISIONARY LEADERSHIP COMPETENCY

Leadership Competency Focus	
1950s	Management by Control
1960s	People Management
1970s	Management by Leadership
1980s	Management by Creativity
1990s	Management by Innovation and Entrepreneurship

Source: Kenneth Primozic, Edward Primozic, and Joe Leben, *Strategic Choices: Supremacy, Survival, or Sayonara* (New York: McGraw-Hill), 1991.

the IT organization, the entire company, and just about any other areas that relate to IT performance. At one point in my career, a friend gave me a definition of vision that has stayed with me through the years:

> An executive is a person who can envision a future for the organization and then inspire colleagues to join in building that future.

During an interview soon after he became CEO of IBM, Lou Gerstner was asked about his vision and strategy for the company. He answered that the company needed to focus on what it was doing and learn to do it well—not on vision and strategy. People began referring to this notion as "the vision thing" debate. For IBM, at that place and time, it was undoubtedly the right focus (although many in the company may not have agreed at the time). However, in the broadest sense of my definition of vision, Lou Gerstner had a vision for IBM, and he spent the next

EXHIBIT 3.9 BUSINESS REALITY LEADERSHIP COMPETENCIES

Visualize the interrelationships among strategic market forces.
Restructure and revitalize the organization to think and act strategically.
Perform strategic planning and prioritize winning projects.
Implement projects by leveraging organizational skills and resources.
Innovate and take necessary risks.
Network functions within an organization and build network alliances.
Possess good communication skills and have a dynamic personality.
Accept change and technology as a way of life and be proactive in exploiting it.
Lead teams that execute the vision.

Source: Primozic, et al., *Strategic Choices*, 1991.

several years inspiring his team to join him in building that future. Those not interested or incapable of doing so were encouraged to move on; those who were interested were given more opportunities.

As the senior-most information technology executive, the CIO can significantly enhance the value and probability of achieving an IT vision by working with all levels of the company to ensure that people at those levels hear and understand the IT vision in terms of how it relates to them as a shared picture of a mutually beneficial destination. This shared understanding inspires people to help the CIO achieve it because it empowers them through the experience of participation. In this way, "working a vision" enlists the help of all stakeholders to ensure accomplishments that lead to competitive advantages for the entire organization. "An empowering vision meets the following three criteria: a *focus* on your strategic advantages, the *inspiration* to deliver those advantages consistently, and *clarity* to be used as a decision-making criterion."[25]

The competency perspectives in each of the three preceding exhibits demonstrate how a CIO articulates and focuses all leadership activities and goals in terms of the steps required to achieve a specific vision of IT value creation for the company. Competent CIOs establish visions for their work that meet certain essential criteria:

- The CIO must be able to articulate the vision to a wide range of people.
- The person in an IT leadership position must actually believe in the importance of the vision and actually work to achieve it.
- The vision must be important to the organization's basic values, mission, and strategy.
- The vision must be reasonable in terms of available resources: people, skills, time, and capital, to name a few.

Leadership competencies rely on the ability to articulate a vision to others, therefore, the CIO assesses personal vision in terms of the different relationship perspectives that come with the role. For example, all CIOs report to someone in a superior role, but some superiors lead with little or no sense of vision; and because the CIO works from a position of leadership, it is important that he or she be able to recognize poor leadership competencies and lack of vision in working relationships with superiors. That means when you can sincerely align with the leadership vision of a superior, follow the superior's vision and look for ways to integrate it with your own. When you cannot sincerely align with the leadership vision of your superior and that superior is someone other than the CEO, look for a higher version of the company's vision and integrate your vision for IT with that higher authority. When you find yourself unable to align with the vision of the CEO, you need to determine whether your CEO is a true leader. CIOs face a different brand of leadership challenges from the subordinate relationship perspective.

In this case, the CIO's leadership competency and vision go on trial according to the same criteria.

The CIO redefines leadership competency and vision relationships with both superiors and subordinates according to several organizational cycles. For example, the company reorganizes and the CIO ends up in a different reporting structure with different goals and objectives. Alternatively, the company makes a significant change in its business model and product set in an attempt to keep up with the competition and changing market conditions. In another increasingly common cycle, the visions of a new CEO, CFO, or COO change the entire company's approach to business as usual.

Closer to home, as you analyze your own leadership competency in terms of essential visionary criteria, how highly do short-term priorities like money, position, power, location, or prestige figure into your current leadership success (or lack thereof)? When a CIO overemphasizes any of these short-term priorities as personal goals for taking or keeping a job, peers, IT staff members, and other important company relationships easily detect a short-term vision incongruent with competent leadership. How do they know? Consider your own professional relationships with such "leaders." They broadcast their inability to see and articulate a common leadership vision with their verbal and body languages. When it comes to articulating a common vision for the organization, such "leaders" appear as though they either have no vision or choose not to get onboard for the company's official common vision.

Looking carefully at your own posture in terms of how genuinely you articulate a leadership vision, can you provide a deliberately reasoned offensive and defensive argument for the ways that you see IT creating value for your company? Can you articulate cogent analogies to help others understand your own, peer, CEO, or companywide visions for IT and its role in creating value for your company? If you can't even sell *yourself* on any of these visions, good luck selling anyone else!

A leader without a vision is like a boat without a rudder, and with the increasing importance of the IT function for all aspects of company performance, mature CEOs and other superiors look to the CIO as an IT leader—someone who can function as a leadership peer in the context of how IT can best leverage their companywide vision. They depend on the CIO to create and articulate a vision for IT that aligns with the overall vision that these superiors have for the entire company. In this case, the org chart rank-ordered distinctions begin to blur and the executive team members work together as a collective of specialists, each member representing a different specialty with a vital piece of the overall vision.

In order to be a leader, there must be followers, and in the work of the CIO, followers come in two forms: direct and indirect. Direct followers such as IT staff members work to implement the CIO's vision. Indirect followers depend on IT resources and the ways that the CIO's vision for IT improves their performance and productivity. In each case, followers insist on leadership competency at the before, during, and after stages of each new CIO vision for IT. Let's take a look at an example with two cases: one where you have signed up for the vision and one where you have not (really) signed up for the vision. Or, alternatively, the case where you have a leadership role and you have a vision and the case where you have a leadership role and you do not have a vision or have a version that you have not really internalized.

The Onboard Scenario   Anyone can spot a leader who truly believes in the importance of his or her vision. Such a leader peddles the vision to everyone, everywhere, at every opportunity. This person's positive mood generates an infectious aura. This kind of CIO wakes up in the morning looking forward to the day's challenges, and often stays late because the work is enjoyable. Based on a firm belief in the importance of the vision, this kind of CIO applies the same energy to problems and obstacles as they arise for any member of the team. As other employees learn to see personal advantages in the CIO's vision, they sign up for the vision and everyone begins to click. As everyone participating in the vision begins to feel a sense of accomplishment, the CIO's aura changes from that of avid promoter to visionary leader.

The Rudderless Scenario   People are equally capable of spotting a CIO in a position of leadership without a vision for IT. There are a number of signs that betray a passive person taking up space in a position of leadership—just read the converse of the signed-up scenario. Showing up late, leaving early, this listless CIO rarely moves around the company unless called into service, and seldom speaks of IT in any other terms than the day-to-day routines that employees expect from a utility service. For these reasons, superiors and peers wouldn't dream of asking this kind of CIO to represent the company. Aura? There's a Yiddish term for a kind of person who enters a room and people feel like someone just left. In a ship with no rudder, fellow employees hope they can stay out of the way.

Looking back between these two extremes, can you recognize which one fits the way you embrace the active interrelationship between leadership and vision? To get a clearer view of this interrelationship and its impact on employees, customers, products, strategies, stakeholders, resources, the competition, and other key focuses you may wish to include, take the leadership vision assessment in Exhibit 3.10. For each of the focuses in the left-hand column, identify the way you formulate and articulate your vision for the IT organization as either onboard or rudderless as characterized in the two scenarios. It may also help to add an adjective such as "begin" or "end" to each focus in recognition that something may have changed from the time you took your current job to the present day. This would not be unusual.

EXHIBIT 3.IO LEADERSHIP VISION ASSESSMENT

Key CIO Focuses	Onboard	Rudderless
Employees		
Customers		
Products		
Strategies		
Stakeholders		
Resources		
Competition		
Other		

After completing the assessment—with a spirit of ruthless honesty—test your assessment in terms of how fellow employees or customers at different levels of the company might fill out the assessment based on their experience of your performance. When in doubt, ask them. This same assessment can be applied to former jobs so that you can begin to identify patterns in your leadership focuses and priorities. Almost everyone takes at least one job or assumes one role based on a sense of career-building obligations. Similarly, almost every person has at least one important leadership focus that consistently lacks visionary integration. Pay attention to these gaps as they surface during this leadership assessment. CIOs need to be able to identify where vision is important and where it is not. Geoffrey Bellman elegantly encapsulates the valid differences that every leader faces when working to distinguish between leadership and management activities: "Leading has more to do with visualizing what could be than sorting out what is."[26] The successful CIO looks for ways to clarify which focuses require visionary leadership or simple commonsense management.

The Reluctant CIO

So, as CIO, you are (or are going to be) looked upon by your peers and partners, your organization, and the person to whom you report as *the* person with the competence to lead the way and leverage the best value and competitive advantage from information technology in your company. Feel up to it? If you feel able to lead but somewhat uncomfortable in the role, then perhaps you are a *reluctant leader*. Some reluctant CIOs find themselves in their roles thanks to happenstance situations—unforeseen promotions or interim service requests. Sometimes it's an opportunity; sometimes it's misfortune. Other reluctant CIOs were attracted to the trappings of the role before completely understanding the full set of expectations and responsibilities that come with the job.

The *Survival Guide* would be incomplete if it did not repeat the words of Hippocrates at least once:"First, do no harm." Reluctant leaders harm themselves, their fellow employees, and their organizations until they identify the cause of their reluctance. The challenges of leadership may actually encourage such a person to identify the causes of the reluctance and achieve his/her full potential as a CIO. People in this situation are again referred to Martha Beck's *Finding Your Own North Star.*[27] This is the first work of the reluctant leader. Worried about the loss of power and prestige? Most people prefer finding the door on their own accord rather than having it shown to them.

PROFILES OF SUCCESS

As amply demonstrated in Chapters 1 and 2, there are many ways an IT professional can find just the right job to match his or her personality profile and work interests. All too often, the professional IT literature attempts to cut IT executive leadership profiles from the same cloth in a one-size-fits-all pattern. As but one example of the many paths that a senior IT executive can follow, this section highlights the experiences of John Valente, a former colleague at Dell, who now serves as vice president of operations and engineering (IS) for Best Buy, a Fortune 100 Company and North America's number-one specialty retailer of consumer electronics, personal computers, entertainment software, and major appliances. In his role, Valente reports to Best Buy's CIO and is responsible for the engineering, design, deployment, and operations of Best Buy's technical infrastructure, which includes voice and data networks, e-mail, computing platforms, Help Desk, global information protection, and data center operations. Valente joined Best Buy in 2002, with more than 20 years of information technology experience in banking, consumer goods, and technology companies.

In moving to Best Buy, Valente gave serious thought to whether he wanted to be a CIO, and in the end he decided that he did *not,* based on personal preferences and his work experiences of the past 10 years. In his experience, the CIO's job had become significantly concentrated on the business, not the technical, side of IT. In many cases, the budgets given to the CIOs are top-down—here it is; live with it. While some of Valente's Best Buy peers want to be CIO some day, he has looked over his past, his successes, and where he has most enjoyed work within the IT organization. He has come to the conclusion that a CIO's role would take him too far way from execution and from the technical aspects of IT—the work he loves and the work at which he excels.

In his role as the VP of IS at Best Buy, Valente characterizes himself as the "guy in the middle who can see everything: why IT decisions are made, how IT decisions pay off, and whether IT decisions meet the company's TCO objectives." From his point of view, especially in today's environment, the CIO's job is a thankless one, and he feels that he has been most successful and felt the most productive and happy when he works in roles that are execution- and technology-based. He knows enough about himself (because he has taken the time to learn and has used various self-analysis tools) to recognize that his talents lead to organizing, problem solving, and execution. This has been a key factor for Valente's sense of well-being and his excellent performance as a senior IT executive: He has not specialized in *business;* he has specialized in *execution.* In this career so suited to native skills and personal work interests, Valente hints at one of the secrets to his success: "I had to learn how to flex my style to manage large teams. I had to let go of how I wanted to get something done and flex my style to get consensus—to coach my team to succeed."

Knowing who you are, and working to improve that, are keys to success, and Valente is most definitely a success. Beware the one-size-fits-all approach to senior IT executive leadership. Get your fantasy from a good science fiction book.

TEN QUESTIONS THE CIO SHOULD ASK OUTSOURCED SERVICE PROVIDERS

> *In the early years, we all thought outsourcing was about saving money, but then we discovered the truth: Outsourcing is not only about saving money, it's about rerouting money from noncore to core activities.*
>
> —Steve Andriole[28]

A significant portion of this chapter discusses outsourcing and working with outsourced service providers so it seems appropriate to focus these 10 questions on outsourced service providers. There are two ways to approach the questions for this unique CIO relationship:

- As a new *outsourcing relationship* or a new CIO learning for the first time about an existing company relationship with an outsourced service provider
- As routine maintenance of an existing relationship with an outsourced service provider

For convenience, each question is phrased in both ways, as appropriate.

  1. **New:** Why are you attracted to this relationship?
     Existing: If, when we negotiated our relationship, you knew then what you know today, would you have still done it?
  2. **New:** From your perspective, what we are looking for from you in simple, easy-to-understand, terms?

Existing: Looking at our agreement, do you find that it has matched what we have actually done and what we are currently doing?

3. **New:** What makes for a highly successful win–win outsourcing relationship? Are you committed to executing that?
   Existing: What can we do better, together, to ensure we have a win–win outsourcing relationship? Can you commit to doing that?

4. **New:** Are there areas we should consider that we have not outsourced and to which you believe you bring unique value? Conversely, are there areas we are looking to outsource to you in which you have no expertise? Will that continue to be true?
   Existing: Same. Also, where could we work better together? Conversely, are there areas we have outsourced to you for which you cannot provide expert or optimal service and that we should consider reinsourcing?

5. **New:** Is ours the first firm in this market/business for which you are taking on an outsourcing role?
   Existing: Since our relationship began, for which other firm(s) in our market/business have you taken on an outsourcing role?

6. **New:** Based on your experience with others companies, what key core competency or competencies should not be outsourced to you or to anyone else?
   Existing: As you have learned more about our operation, what key core competency or competencies should not be outsourced to you or to anyone else?

7. **New:** If situations change, do we have the ability to reinsource or to move to another vendor without significant penalties?
   Existing: If we found some areas we would like to reinsource, and at the same time found some new areas that we would like to outsource, would you be amenable to that?

8. **New:** How do you internally measure your quality of delivery to our agreement?
   Existing: What do your own internal measurements of quality tell you about us?

9. **New:** What will make for a successful, regular performance review?
   Existing: How often do you internally review your performance? How often do we review your performance together? What can we do together to make these reviews more effective?

10. **New:** What is your view of, and how do you handle, new and possibly risky technologies and companies?
    Existing: If the IT team identifies a new and possibly risky technology or company with which to work, would you be willing to do so?

Number 1: Why Are You Attracted to This Relationship?

Outsourced service providers perform work for other companies that fulfill the service provider's company charter. This obvious connection is not a bad reason for forming a business relationship, but it is seldom the only or even the key reason. The outsourced service provider ideally uses one of several key drivers for pursuing a relationship with any business:

- Good match with its skills, experience, and industry focus
- Good match for its business model
- Good match with a new industry focus area for its expansion
- Good match geographically, for leverage
- Defensive or offensive move relative to its competition

Because outsourcing is more about *business* than *technology*, the CIO who outsources successfully must know what it is that has made his/her company attractive to the outsourced service provider. If the facts support a relationship based on a good match to skills, experience, and industry focus, or for its business model, then there is an equal likelihood of a good match in terms of genuine interest and willingness to succeed. Conversely, if the same two drivers are not well matched, the answers probably support a relationship that was initially driven by industry focus area expansion, geographical leverage, or a defensive or offensive move relative to the outsourced service provider's competitors. In this latter case, the longevity and flexibility in the relationship over time may not match the provider's posture going into the relationship. While some aspects of the first two relationship drivers may be secondarily important, they are unlikely to move the relationship on solid ground over the long term, unless they are of primary importance.

For an existing relationship, the value of this question comes in comparing today's answer to tomorrow's answer. If the relationship began as a speculative venture for the outsourced service provider, sooner or later the CIO can expect to hear some variation on the following response: "Well, with business evolution and changing business conditions, we might not choose this particular relationship over other opportunities today, but since we are in the relationship . . . " How soon an outsourced service provider gives this response depends on how speculative the provider was at the beginning of the relationship. Once two companies reach this point in the outsourcing relationship, the mismatch in mutual goals becomes steadily more apparent. It is the CIO's responsibility to decide whether the company risks any *business* disadvantage in maintaining the relationship.

If, however, outsourced service providers indicate that they would indeed engage the contract again, it is highly likely that the match was based on the first two relationship drivers: a good match to skills, experience, and industry focus, or for their business model. As CIO, the primary responsibility for a successful outsourcing strategy and execution of the strategy rests with you; your *business sense* is key, and your relationships with your peers at the outsourced service companies keeps this business sense on track.

Number 2: What Are We Looking for from You?

As a child, you may have played a game called telephone, where you sat in a circle and someone started the relay by whispering something to the person next to him or her. That person did the same, and the process repeated until it came full circle back to the originator. The fun of the game was to see how different the message ended up from the first telling. Adults in business seem to also experience significant gaps between what someone says and what someone else hears. This challenge does *not* change with age, and experience suggests that the CIO should directly and repeatedly ask what might otherwise sound like a dumb question of outsourced service providers: "What are we saying we are looking for from you?" And, equally important from a business executive's point of view, "in simple, easy-to-understand terms."

The CIO's first and foremost responsibility is creating and bringing business value to the company through IT. In choosing to outsource a portion of any area of IT responsibility, it is critical to have a crystal-clear understanding of service expectations (not only in writing) with the outsourced services provider. Moreover, the provider should be able to repeat this understanding back to the CIO without ambiguity. Only then can the senior IT executive validate all service activities, progress, and quality in regular update meetings with the provider against this common understanding. By taking this approach, the CIO begins each key engagement with the supplier at the appropriate executive level, from a business point of view, and uses an *answer-first* approach to know right away that things are well, or what is to be done when they are not well.

A new CIO working to understand an existing relationship also benefits from asking this question and then using it as the basis for a second clause: "Is it as we agreed it would be?" Over time, it is very easy for work activities to drift away from the original intent (or officially amended intent) due to any number of reasons. Regardless of the reasons, it is important to discover such drift and recognize how it undermines the interests of your company. By keeping the relationship focused on the current best business intentions—or getting it back to the original intent if that is really appropriate—the CIO may be able to avoid having to be among the 78 percent of senior IT executives who end up terminating their outsourcing relationship early.[29] The successful CIO carefully manages the service relationship either by holding it to the original intent or quickly and regularly renegotiating it over time to a predetermined point that matches the *needs of the business*. Without attention to one or the other, early termination of the relationship is inevitable. In point of fact, the CIO should use this as the same expectation for direct reports and their organizations as they work to fulfill their commitments and execution responsibilities. The successful CIO expects nothing less of the outsourced service provider, and knows that even more careful monitoring and management is required because the outsourced service provider's employees work for his or her *company*, not him or her.

Number 3: What Makes for a Highly Successful Outsourcing Relationship?

For a relationship to be win–win, the CIO and the CIO's outsourced service provider counterpart have to believe that each of the service objectives is being met or exceeded. Fortunately, earlier questions have identified mutual expectations and performance against those expectations so that with this question the CIO and service provider are in a position to decide together whether the existing relationship is win–win. Those in a win–win situation are probably in that minority 22 percent who do not end up terminating their outsourcing relationship early.[30] However, if you find yourself in the majority, you want to convert your outsourcing relationships to a win–win situation rather than prematurely terminating the relationship.

First things first. The CIO must draw up a win list for the company and then sit down with the outsourced service provider to reconcile discrepancies into a final win–win form. Once you do, the critical final question becomes, "Are you committing to executing that?" If yes, then you have a new expectations baseline; if no, it's back to a lose–win and another premature outsourced relationship closure. There are many opinions about what makes for a successful outsourcing experience. Several of the most time-tested, commonsense practices include:

- Focus the outsourced service provider on using its expertise to manage commodity tasks.
- Be sure there is a good cultural fit between your company and the outsourced service provider; this is all about people.
- Ensure that the costs of outsourcing are lower than the costs of insourcing—also taking into account the lower number of employees likely to be needed onboard.
- Take an active role in overseeing the outsourcing for strategy, planning, and execution.

- Retain the responsibility (i.e., do not abdicate it to the outsourced service provider) for the overall IT strategy and directions that meet the requirements of your company partners.

- The intellectual capital of the IT group is systems integration, and for this reason do not delegate it to the outsourced service provider.

- Ensure ahead of time that you have the support *and sponsorship* of your boss and the support of your executive peers.

- Remember that the lowest bid for your business is probably the lowest for a good reason.

- Develop win-win metrics and establish an agreement in writing to review them against service execution at regularly scheduled intervals.

- If the relationship is not what it should be, do something about it, *today*.

The CIO is ultimately responsible for service outcomes even though the outsourced service provider relationship management responsibilities have been delegated to someone else. As the senior IT executive, it is absolutely necessary that you put in the time and effort to overseeing the relationship and ensuring that the results are no less effective than if the work were insourced.

Number 4: Are There Areas We Have Not Outsourced That We Should Consider?

When looking to enter a relationship with an outsourced service provider, recognize that although you may have already decided what to outsource, the perspective provider may have additional unexplored specialties that complement IT strategy. While being careful not to outsource the company's core business, it makes sense to leverage a provider's expertise that you might not otherwise have considered when doing so fits your IT strategy. This could come in the form of reduced expenses or improved service to internal or external customers.

The question is no less important to discuss for an existing relationship. Over time, as two companies come to know each other and work well together, the CIO can use the outsourced service provider as a means for offloading mundane activities and allocate the new and interesting work to company employees, thereby creating good opportunities for their professional growth and career advancement. This creates a win-win-win scenario and a real opportunity to free the IT staff for creative and value-generating projects.

At the same time, as overseer of IT strategy, planning, and execution, the CIO evaluates the outsourced service provider relationship, carefully watching the outsourced services performance metrics and execution statistics. The service provider may not be expert or motivated in those areas that are not performed to negotiated standards and expectations. If appreciable improvement does not come after several reviews, the CIO has a signal to act—perhaps reinsourcing that particular activity and exchanging another one for outsourcing, or reducing the total outsource by the amount the particular activity represented. This can be done when you have a good relationship with the peer executive at the outsourced service provider company. And be aware, you will have to start the conversation for it to happen.

Number 5: Is Ours the First Firm for Which You Are Taking on an Outsourcing Role?

Does it make sense for a CIO to pay an outsourced service provider to learn about the company's business focus area and your market? I don't think so! The domain of knowledge and experience counts among the most important factors for choosing between different providers. The CIO is expected to know the difference between amateurs and pros, and a provider that does not have domain expertise must be considered an amateur. To pay an outsourcer to become knowledgeable and experienced puts the CIO at risk financially and in terms of service execution, and counts as one of the few times that the service provider gets paid while making mistakes of omission and commission with the customer's full knowledge. That's just not good business for you and is a significant risk for your company. Sometimes a CIO has previous experience with a particular outsourced service provider in another industry and therefore believes the provider can adapt to the current business and future needs, and at the same time develop the domain experience and knowledge required to be fully effective. If so, just make certain that you are realistic about the learning curve and the costs and risks.

For an existing relationship, regular review meetings with the service provider should include information about any additional outsourcing relationships that the provider maintains (or loses) in your market focus area. This provides more evidence for reassurance, or cause for concern, based on your relationship and its current focus. For example, if the provider has just won a large, visible contract in the same domain area, they may well take some of their better staff off your work and put it onto the newly acquired relationship. Similarly, if the provider has lost a contract in the domain area, it may well transfer some good people from that contract and reassign them to your situation. Knowing an outsourced service provider's evolving profile is important because it is all about people.

Number 6: What Key Core Competencies Should Not Be Outsourced?

This is a question potential outsourced service providers should *expect* from a CIO, as it reveals at least two things about potential outsourcing partners: how honest and forthright they will be and in which areas they do not excel. A good partner does not take on more than they should or take on activities that should be retained to ensure business objectives are met. At the very least, the outsourced service provider should respond that the IT strategy, objectives, architecture, and execution commitments to and on behalf of the senior executive team should *not* be outsourced. An astute outsourced services provider also suggests that if your underlying objective is to delegate what might be considered some of the more tricky management or procedural issues in IT—such as uniform deployment of applications—outsourcing is not the answer because it would be clear abdication of responsibility and authority as the CIO. Taking responsibility and showing clear leadership and strength of will based on professional convictions is the CIO's responsibility.

Number 7: Can We Reinsource or Move to Another Vendor without Significant Penalties?

This is a real test of the potential outsourced service provider and their level of confidence in their ability to satisfy their customer on a long-term basis. Flexibility is unquestionably important in today's business environment. The CIO has to be able to position the organization for flexibility and avoid becoming locked in to a proprietary set of solutions from an outsourced service provider. One of the best ways to flush out such a *lock-in* plan is to ask whether outsourcing relationships can be moved to others (including reinsourcing) should the justification arise. If the potential service provider is expecting to create lock-ins, they appear as additional costs such as licensing when transferred or as functional losses when moving the outsourcing relationship to a different service provider. Some providers assure that implementing with their specific and proprietary tool(s) is the most cost-effective and efficient approach, but your business sense should tell you that this is unlikely to be true in the long run.

The second question for determining service provider flexibility is whether outsourced areas can be exchanged for one another. This situation commonly occurs as businesses evolve and develop new capacities. From the perspective of the CIO, when all functions are insourced, there is no problem reallocating resources (dealing, of course, with the skills and personnel-related issues of moving people from project to project) based on changing business priorities. Realizing that a contract with an outsourced service provider creates a commitment and legal contract, it is in the CIO's best interests to manage this as closely as if the activity were insourced.

One way of achieving that flexibility while creating a potential win–win situation and keeping the outsource service provider "whole" is to establish or negotiate the ability to trade or exchange outsourcing scopes of work with the objective of being able to reinsource some key element of your strategy and do so by outsourcing some less important element for that period. The scope of the two services need to be similar, or for some combination of reinsourcing and outsourcing be roughly equivalent, to make both the IT function and the service provider whole. This flexibility is important for enduring the many changes that commonly occur before the end of most outsourcing contracts. Otherwise, the relationship will not evolve as the business evolves—like the piece of wood that does not have the flexibility to change with the load—and the predictable result is a broken relationship and another company and CIO in the 78 percent of early termination outsourcing agreements club. It is in the best interests of both the CIO and the (potential) outsourced service provider to agree to this approach. The CIO should feel comfortable insisting that it be so and, conversely, feel very *uncomfortable* if it is not!

Number 8: How Do You Measure Quality of Delivery?

The senior IT executive can create a set of outsourced service goals and measures and/or use a set previously established by peers and the CIO's boss. Subordinates use these goals and measures to help meet company goals for the outsourced service. Many of these performance measures apply just as they would for insourced services: to direct work priorities, monitor outcomes, and create incentives. In addition, the CIO uses a subset of specific measures to track the progress, problems, and successes associated with an external provider. These may or may not correspond to the service quality measurements that the outsourced service provider uses to measure themselves and report internally to their senior executives.

The CIO makes reasonable efforts to discover the outsourced service provider's set of performance drivers and measures and contrast them with company measures of the relationship. This practice stems from Schubert's First Law of Performance Measurement: You get what you measure. If the outsourced provider's measurement set causes operational results that are not aligned with the CIO's operational expectations, the divergence quickly manifests as a significant cause of business and relationship instability. Some outsourced service providers are reluctant to share this kind of information in new relationships. If that is the case, simply explain the obvious good business sense behind mutually sharing this kind of information: Performance measurements allow each partner to address the ongoing, changing needs of the relationship more efficiently and effectively; the information probably holds some value for the outsourced service provider's relationships with other companies.

Measuring service quality can also affect service charges. The more resources you take due to poor quality of interactions, the higher the costs are going to be to you. Knowing how outsourced service providers evaluate your performance gives you a tremendous advantage at no cost within your company. What do you have to lose? What do you have to gain?

Number 9: What Will Make for a Successful, Regular Performance Review?

When entering into a new relationship with a particular outsourced service provider, it is worthwhile learning from them what has worked in their successful relationships. Because outsourcing oversight is one of the CIO's key responsibilities, this is not a task to be delegated. However, as the senior executive, be careful to not make this a full-time job. Work with the outsourced service provider by means of regular performance reviews. At a minimum, schedule reviews on a quarterly basis to address key objectives met (and not), mitigations, and service contingencies from the perspective of both your team and the service provider's team. Ideally, the two teams share most of their information with each other ahead of time so that there are no true negative surprises. Each team should prepare a formal report of their service relationship experiences—the home team and the away team. In this way, both teams have the opportunity to highlight and resolve problems by speaking and listening to each other's experiences in turn.

A regularly scheduled performance review structure creates other efficiencies for the CIO. The CIO and his/her peer from the outsourced service provider can get together alone before or after the teams meet to manage those issues that involve strategic or directional decision making. By assuming a progress-review posture, the CIO can keep the longer-range view and focus on maintaining the service relationship's overall direction and preventing endless changes and expansion of scope—also known as *creeping elegance*. This kind of vigilance can dramatically decrease cost and risk and preserve the primary value of the outsourced service relationship.

Last but not least, every regularly scheduled performance review gives the CIO and the outsourced service provider peer an opportunity to identify relationship management process improvements for greater time and resource efficiency. In a matter of only a few meetings, this approach shows itself to be invaluable at all levels because it makes more effective use of senior executives' time and the time of all involved employees and parties. Do not let yourself get trapped in endlessly repetitive meetings. Review, improve, and iterate with each encounter so that you have a successively and iteratively improved performance review. Your effectiveness will not go unnoticed.

Number 10: What Is Your View of, and How Do You Handle, New and Possibly Risky Technologies and Companies?

As the senior IT executive, the CIO must be aware of how much risk each key IT area can tolerate. Such risk management assessments naturally reflect the CIO's own risk profile, but they must also acknowledge the risk-readiness profiles of peers, the boss, and the company from a competitive standpoint. Similarly, it is the CIO's responsibility to ensure that the entire IT organization understands the tolerable level of risk as it applies to their daily work. This applies to the outsourced service provider, too: Avoid being taken too far to the technological edge but also avoid being left behind. The responsibilities are no different from managing IT activities within the organization. The CIO has to ensure that the service provider understands the company risk profile.

As a thorough risk manager, the CIO independently looks for new technology solutions; new discoveries take the outsourced service relationship to new levels. Is the outsourced service provider flexible enough to work with the CIO and the IT organization in a new technology assessment for use in the company environment? Inflexible outsourced service providers and those that do not regularly explore new technologies cannot be expected to remain competitive or maintain a long-term service relationship. With an approximately 18- to 24-month cycle on technology-based products, the CIO expects to move to new technologies in no more than 24 months. If the product is not ready, the competitive edge is lost and the CIO and IT organization spend all their time playing catch-up. Again, as CIO, you have the responsibility of setting the direction and overseeing its realization; delegating this (implicitly or explicitly) to an outsourced service provider is abdication of responsibility and must be guarded against. *Just say no!*

Marcus Aurelius said it well in his *Meditations*: "Cast no side-glance at the instincts governing other men, but keep your eyes fixed on the goal."[31] This is especially true when outsourcing is involved. Generally, the best interests of the outsourcing partner and the outsourced partner (you) are not the same; they may be similar, but they are not the same. So it is paramount that you be involved in *what* gets outsourced and *why* and that you stay directly involved in the outsourcing relationship to ensure that your company's best interests are not superceded by your outsourced service provider's best interests. Your success is in your own hands! As you ponder this, give some thought to additional questions for your outsourced service providers:

1. **New:** What savings or time-to-market improvement or (something else) will we achieve yearly?

   Existing: What savings or time-to-market or (something else) have we achieved yearly, and what are the going-forward projected savings versus the original projected savings for the remainder of the current agreement?

2. **New:** What is your equipment/technology depreciation schedule and how does it compare to ours, today?

   Existing: Same.

3. **New:** What safeguards are there to keep us from ending up with a hodge-podge of applications across the company as you are responsive to the requirements and needs of the various business units?

   Existing: Same.

NOTES

1. John P. Kotter, *Leading Change* (Boston: Harvard Business School Press, 1996): 25.
2. Donald G. Krause, *The Art of War for Executives* (New York: Penguin Putnum, Inc., 1995).
3. Mary Kwak, "INFORMATION TECHNOLOGY: Technical Skills, People Skills: It's Not Either/Or," *MIT Sloan Management Review* 42, no. 3 (2001): 16, available at: http://mit-smr.com/past/2001/smr4231f.html.
4. Tony Hallet and Randy Mott, "Dell's CIO on Strategy, Skills, Microsoft and More: One of the Top IT Users in the World Opens Up to Silicon.com," *silicon.com*, www.silicon .com/news/500021/1/3769.html (accessed June 1, 2003).
5. Robert M. Rubin, "Ask Darwin: Straight Answers to Real-World Problems," *Darwin* online magazine, www2.darwinmag.com/connect/ask/answer_detail.cfm?486 (accessed June 1, 2003).
6. Harvey G. Enns, Sid L. Huff, and Brian R. Golden, *The CIO Influence Project: Reported Results* (Dayton, OH: School of Business Administration University of Dayton) www.sba .udayton.edu/CIO_influence/ (accessed June 1, 2003).
7. *CIO Magazine*, online research Web site, "Outsourcing Research Center," www.cio. com/research/outsourcing (accessed June 2, 2003).
8. Mike Perkowski, "Research: Outsourcing," *CIO Insight*, www.cioinsight.com/article2/ 0,3959,24700,00.asp (accessed June 4, 2003).
9. "OUTSOURCING Survey" *CIO Insight*, ftp://ftp.cioinsight.com/pub/cioinsight/01/13/ research.ppt (accessed June 4, 2003).
10. Jae-Nam Lee, Minh Q. Huynh, Ron Chi-Wai Kwok, and Shih-Ming Pi, "IT Outsourcing Evolution: Past, Present, and Future," *Communications of the ACM*, 46, no. 5 (2003): 84–89.
11. Rudy Hirschheim and Mary Lacity, "The Myths and Realities of Information Technology Insourcing," *Communications of the ACM*, 43, no. 2 (2000): 99–107.
12. Ibid., p. 106.
13. Editorial survey, "User Support Survey," *CIO Magazine* (December 3, 2001), www2.cio.com/research/surveyreport.cfm?id=33.
14. From Whatis.com's SearchTechTarget.com sub Web site http://whatis.techtarget.com/ definition/0,,sid9_gci213107,00.html (accessed June 5, 2003).
15. Thomas DeMarco, *Controlling Software Projects* (Englewood Cliffs, NJ: Prentice-Hall, 1982).

16. Charles P. Curtis, Jr. and Ferris Greenslet, *The Practical Cogitator: The Thinker's Anthology* (Boston: Houghton Mifflin, 1962): 41.

17. Eric Berkman, "The State of the CIO: Skills," *CIO Magazine,* www.cio.com/archive/030102/skills.html (accessed June 1, 2003).

18. Senior Executive Service: ECQ 4: "Business Acumen," (United States Office of Personnel Management), www.opm.gov/ses/ecq4.html (accessed April 19, 2003).

19. Berkman, "State of the CIO."

20. Karyl Scott, "Polishing the Dirt," *Informationweek.com,* www.informationweek.com/story/showArticle.jhtml?articleID=6502324] (accessed June 5, 2003).

21. Polly Schneider Traylor, "IT Takes Two: IS Architecture" *CIO Magazine,* http://cio.com/archive/111501/two.architecture.html (accessed June 5, 2003).

22. Ibid.

23. Geoffrey M. Bellman, *Getting Things Done When You Are Not in Charge* (San Francisco: Berrett-Koehler, 1992): 18.

24. Ibid., p. 14.

25. James A. Belasco, *Teaching the Elephant to Dance: The Manager's Guide to Empowering Change* (New York: Penguin, 1990): 99.

26. Bellman, *Getting Things Done,* p. 18.

27. Martha Beck, *Finding Your Own North Star: Claiming the Life You Were Meant to Live* (New York: Three Rivers Press, 2001).

28. Steve Andriole, "Key Questions When Considering Outsourcing," *Datamation,* http://itmanagement.earthweb.com/columns/bizalign/article.php/973091 (accessed June 5, 2003).

29. Stephanie Overby, "Bringing I.T. Back Home," *CIO Magazine* (March 20, 2003): 56.

30. Ibid.

31. Marcus Aurelius, *Meditations,* translated by Maxwell Staniforth (New York: Penguin Books, 1964): 55.

CHAPTER 4

Connecting IT to Value Creation

The primary focus of a CIO is not to program, not to operate computers, not to make technical choices. The primary job is power politics—to play several different roles simultaneously. The job is to manage conflict, to oversee the redistribution of power and to reallocate money so that information technologies may support the success of an organization.

—Paul A. Strassmann[1]

It doesn't take long before an active or aspiring IT executive career encounters a company that views the IT organization as an expense, a burden, or a necessary evil. The first three chapters examined ways to become a strategic partner, a peer, and an enabler. This chapter explores another area of generally untapped CIO potential: value creation. Because the CIO and the IT organization enable decision making throughout the company, research shows that the CIO has the potential to enable all employees to see new ways to convert basic day-to-day decisions into value-creating opportunities for the entire company. This chapter also investigates the CIO's value creation potential in light of the research results regarding the primary focus of IT value creation: the customer. Information technology is the coin of the realm for creating value in the knowledge economy. As custodian of information technology resources, the CIO who also learns the language of business becomes a steward of human and intellectual capital, enabling people in the company to create value for all stakeholders.

You, the CIO, have the unique opportunity to work with customers of both varieties: internal and external. As the senior executive of a service that virtually every employee in the company expects as a dial-tone service in their day-to-day activities, the odds suggest that the CIO is witness to many more direct interactions with unhappy customers. It's the nature of any senior-level executive work, but even more so for the CIO and IT. You may also be called on to be the "relationship executive" for one or more of your company's external customers just because it is what your company's senior executives do.

The CIO's behavior during these experiences—however painful at a particular moment—can result in several common outcomes that have a lasting effect on the company. A positive customer experience creates a customer for life; a negative experience becomes the last straw, causing a valuable customer to leave for good. Positive outcomes can also occur with unexpected results—the CIO and a customer determine that their two companies are not good matches for one another.

CIOs work with technology executives and nontechnology executives within their own companies and at other companies. As such, the CIO working as a company representative must be ready with an articulate strategic, operational, financial, and technology vocabulary. Representing the company appropriately sometimes means losing a customer. While this flies in the face of the MBA Sales and Marketing 101 course, not all sellers and customers meet each other's needs. Reasons for customer relationship mismatches range from incompatible quality standards across the customer/supplier/partner relationship to simple, incorrect assumptions about product or service utility. One way to reconcile this apparent conflict is to incorporate the concept of "the perfect customer"[2] with formal customer relationship management strategies and performance measures. As Mohanbir Sawhney points out, "Ultimately, whether you deal with external customers or internal customers, the only way to make yourself successful is to make your customers successful."[3]

THE LANGUAGE OF THE INDUSTRY

In the business of relationships, communications are of paramount importance. As technical specialists, CIOs who communicate with customers in terms of strategy, operations, and finance are not using a *different* vocabulary; they are using an *expanded* vocabulary. How a CIO expands any given facet of his or her overall vocabulary depends on the company, the customers, and the CIO's career path. CIOs who learn their jobs along the technical route need to concentrate on expanding their vocabularies in the financial, capital, service, and other business-related areas. Those who have come through the business route need to concentrate on expanding their vocabularies in the information technology, user/customer requirements, applications, development, service and support, and service-level agreement areas.

After acquiring an expanded business vocabulary to communicate with internal and external customers, as the senior executive in charge of information technology *services*, the CIO quickly learns to apply the expanded vocabulary through the structure of service-level agreements. Yes, service-level agreements. These seemingly ho–hum little exercises can give customers a first-hand perspective on what it takes to deliver the services they have come to expect: "Well, Mr. VP of marketing and sales, we can give you exactly what you've asked for in the time frame you expect, but this is what its going to cost you, item by item . . . " Handling service level agreements is one of those tactical responsibilities that the CIO can delegate to a bright, personable, confident direct report to make more time to attend to executive IT strategic business activities. When negotiated and drawn up in a vocabulary that incorporates the business language familiar to the customer in terms of the line-item technology services the IT organization provides, the service-level agreement becomes a contract and a professional lesson plan for managing both IT performance and customers' expectations.

As with any specialized branch of knowledge, the acronym becomes a significant barrier to effective communication with people outside the circle of specialists, and IT has more than its share of service-level agreement acronyms. Exhibit 4.1 lists but a few, including the king of service-level agreement acronyms: MTBF, or mean time between failures, and one thing leads to another.[4] As soon as an IT staff finds itself in the middle of managing a MTBF scenario, the MTTR scenario comes into play. And along with the king, every list has its dark lord: MT-TLTFEDBS, or mean time to listen to field engineer's disclaimer blaming software. Acronyms may be funny, but outside the specialized area they are no joke. School the IT staff to use this kind of vocabulary only among themselves by personal example.

One practical way to assess and build an expanded vocabulary takes advantage of your partnership network:

Step 1. *Arrange a relatively formal meeting with each of the people on your partnership network*. After all, they represent your most valued customers. Ask each partner about communication difficulties that arise during your business discussions. Specifically, which words or phrases do you commonly use that they have difficulty understanding? Each of your partners represents a different area of business vocabulary, so you can use them to identify where you need to expand your ability to better articulate what you want others to hear.

Step 2. *Take a look at your company's organizational chart*. Identify any significant holes that your network partners do not represent. Pay particular attention to areas that stand out as recurrent IT management "problem children," and set up a second round of meetings with representatives from these groups.

Step 3. *Take your new insights out into the professional education marketplace*. Find

EXHIBIT 4.1   SERVICE-LEVEL AGREEMENT ACRONYMS

Acronym	Meaning
MTTR	Mean Time to Repair
MTTNF	Mean Time to Notice Fault
MTTRTF	Mean Time to React to Fault
MTTLFEPN	Mean Time to Locate Field Engineer's Phone Number
MTTCFE	Mean Time to Call Field Engineer
MTAFECB	Mean Time Awaiting Field Engineer's Call Back
MTTCSC	Mean Time to Check Service Contract
MTTCFES	Mean Time to Call Field Engineer's Supervisor
MTTLTFEDBS - 1	Mean Time to Listen to FE's Disclaimer Blaming Software
MTTCA	Mean Time to Call Attorney
MTFFEA	Mean Time to Field Engineer Arrival
MTTD	Mean Time to Diagnose
MTTLTFEDBS - 2	Mean Time to Listen to FE's Disclaimer Blaming Software
MTOOSCM X M#	Mean Time Ordering/Obtaining Software/Changing Modules Multiplied by the Number of Modules
MTTRB	Mean Time to Reboot
MTTRRB	Mean Time to ReReboot
Gosub MTTD MTTR^n	Sum for the entire series, for which there are no easy convergence tests

Source: Kelly-Bootle, *The Devil's DP Dictionary*, 1981.

resources—books, courses, seminars, even degree programs—to help you build your working business vocabulary.

As the CIO, you are expected to have a facile business vocabulary equivalent to that of other C-level business executives, and at the same time be able to translate the technical vocabulary into the language of business and the language of your partners and peers. The sections that follow detail some of the most important customer relationship management responsibilities of the CIO.

EMBRACING THE "PERFECT" EXTERNAL CUSTOMER, OR MANAGING CUSTOMER RELATIONSHIP VALUE

Thinking of customers and how to attract customers is never far from the mind of a senior executive. As an enabler and service provider, the CIO's internal customers may not be paying net monies like the external customers, but they probably contribute a significant portion of the IT organization's budget. Like any other good entrepreneur, once the CIO succeeds in attracting customers, those customers need to be *retained*. In the case of the internal customer, this means a positive service record. This is common thinking: *Any* customer is a good customer; once you have a customer, do whatever it takes to keep the customer happy. While this applies to internal CIO customer relationship management practices, the common thinking does not always apply to external customers.

A concrete example of an actual company is the best way to demonstrate the many options that an enlightened CIO and executive team can use to manage customer relationships and find perfect customers for the company's strategic needs and goals. The following scenario describes a composite of actual customer relationship management efforts that a startup high-tech manufacturer used to find its first customers.

The story focuses on the start-up company's team of seasoned senior executives who each have more than 20 years of customer-related experiences to draw on as they begin to look for their company's first perfect customers. As each executive began to tell stories from thousands of actual customer relationship experiences, some common patterns emerged. While the vast majority of customers were superb—even when their needs were not fully met despite the best of efforts—every executive described a group of customers with whom they had an unsuccessful relationship despite the fact that they had clearly met the customers' own stated needs. In other words, good products and concordant follow-up support services that fulfilled these customers' requested specifications led to unhappy customers. Up to this point, each of the start-up company's senior executives believed that their companies were somehow at fault for the customer relationship failure. The consistently common experiences led them all to move forward with a single understanding: As with some people, some companies simply are not a good match for one another. The trick was to discover what makes a relationship work.

Consequently, the start-up company's executive team became extremely deliberate as they worked to identify their first (potential) customers. As members of a start-up, they could not afford to have any significant—or maybe even *any*—negative or really difficult customer relationships for at least two reasons: They would lose valuable time and other resources in a nonproductive relationship; and first customers provide invaluable information about relationship interactions that extend into new future customer relationship practices. A "wrong" first customer would not provide balanced feedback about ways the startup had to improve as it grew into the marketplace. Thus, in order to discover what makes good customer relationships work, the executive team focused their discussion on how things go wrong rather than on what makes customer relationships work well.

The approach was fruitful. According to each executive, at some point the companies they worked for all began to focus more on customer quantity than customer quality. This raised a key question, which also contained what appeared at first to be counterintuitive: Would we be more successful if we concentrated on attracting a few quality customers rather than a large number of unknown risks? In short order, the executive team began exploring ways to actually measure customer quality. They hit upon the notion of attempting to attract *only* perfect customers and passing on less-than-perfect customers. That's right: Even as a start-up without a single client, they began to pick customers carefully, actually refusing to do business unless the customer met certain criteria that naturally evolved as these new customer relationship managers gained experience. Based on their formidable combined experience, they drew up a target client list and explained their rationale to the sales force.

As the start-up's salespeople went out to visit potential customers—several in the Fortune 100 category—the executive team members began to speak of less tension and greater optimism than at any such point in similar past experiences. The differences could be huge: Acquiring less-than-perfect customers would require the start-up to spend an enormous amount of time, effort, money, and other resources on meeting the requirements of a customer that was "sold," "baited," or "snatched away" from the competition. In the process, less-than-perfect customer relationships often mature slowly, and the amount of damage control they require does not become apparent until the need becomes significant. In contrast, experience suggested that by attracting perfect customers they would end up with loyal customers—supportive customers who wanted and needed the startup to succeed.

Strategic Customer Relationship Management

The perfect customer is one whose needs perfectly fit the supplier company's mission or product. In fact, when customer needs and supplier products and services (solutions) align perfectly, positive results unfold very quickly and with little effort. This kind of "strategic synchronicity" seldom happens by accident.[5] The CIO has to take part in strategic development with other members of the executive team to tap IT's full customer relationship value. Equally important, the strategically briefed CIO has to get outside the four walls of the organization and become one of the company's foremost customer relationship representatives.

Most senior executives have experienced the immediate and exhilarating exchange of information when two well-matched business partners talk terms on a sales call. These same senior executives know short-term and long-term strategic preparation makes this kind of experience reproducible. In fact, when a company deliberately manages customer relationships as part its strategic planning cycle, it is not long before perfect customers begin to make the first move. They seek your company out because they have already heard that it stands ready to solve their problems—today.

Selectively soliciting, choosing, and sometimes firing customers flies in the face of most marketing, sales, and business objectives, which focus on acquisition of the largest possible customer base. It is quite easy to get caught in the trap of trying to figure out how to get more and more customers; in the process, companies commonly spend significant time and money trying to get the attention of less-than-perfect or even horrible customers. Strategic customer relationship management is not a practice that lends itself to economies of scale. More customers often mean more compromises. How many times can a company fiddle with features, functions, products, and pricing to satisfy a potential or existing customer before all product and service value becomes diluted? Many customers are simply too expensive. Customer relationships born from a winning-the-customer-over-to-our-solution strategy puts a heavy burden on the supplier to make good on an ever increasing number of such promises. The bottom line is very straightforward: More doesn't always mean better; both customers and suppliers do better business when they are well matched.

Perfect customer relationship management discipline depends upon deliberate strategic resolve with a focus on long-term value creation. Value creation in the knowledge economy often begins with IT products and services, therefore the CIO must perfect a strategic customer relationship management vocabulary to help other executives to leverage IT value as a means of locating the perfect customer.

As the executives in the start-up group example shared their own past experiences, they began to realize that the responsibility for poor customer relationships started with an incomplete strategic plan, and that it was *their* job to correct this shortcoming. They decided to make customer relationship management a central component of the start-up company strategy. First, they began to characterize what the company's perfect customer might look like. Second, they used this picture to help each of the executive team members articulate how their different departments and organizations fit into the picture. Third, they integrated these insights into the company's existing strategic plan and created some customer relationship management performance measurements to hold themselves accountable so that they could more easily resist the more-is-better temptation.

Think of advocating such an approach on the "pre" side of the sale—before the company has a single customer, when the sales team feels a significant amount of pressure to get to work with a traditional quota mentality. Strategic customer relationship management depends on a communication system within the company that translates this kind of strategic initiative into all appropriate employee jobs. As such, sales requires a new, more focused, strategically guided set of criteria other than the quota system.

Internal customer relationships also fall into the perfect and less-than-perfect categories. As the senior executive of an enabling service group, the strategically minded CIO approaches internal customers from a competitive marketplace perspective, one that recognizes that they could go somewhere else for their IT services and support. Unless you truly believe that you and your IT organization can be everything, everywhere, at all times to all of your internal customers, it simply makes good common strategic sense that internal customers might find their perfect supplier for some particular IT services elsewhere—and that they should be encouraged to do so when it is in the company's best interest. This does not mean that you abandon them, of course. Rather, you assist them in finding the best solution to their problem regardless of whether it comes from your group, some other group, or a provider outside your company. In the process, you have just become a more perfect supplier for a still loyal internal customer—that is, CIO as IT supplier supplier.

Chapter 3 addressed the importance of the CIO's vision for the IT organization. Just as an executive team governing a company depends on clearly articulated strategy to implement their vision for the company, the CIO also needs an IT customer relationship strategy to manifest a vision for the IT organization. Some specific strategic postures help build sound IT customer relationship strategies.

Strategic Customer Relationship Postures

Imagine what it might be like if Disney and Nike or the U.S. Marines and Greenpeace decided to work with one another in a supplier/customer partnership. Certain cultural standards and public postures apply in customer relationships. Stacy Hall and Jan Brogniez propose six customer relationship postures that CIOs can use to develop perfect customer strategies.[6]

Be On Purpose with Your Mission   This first customer relationship posture is one with which all CIOs should be familiar. It is focused on having and staying true to a mission, by:

- Becoming clear about whom it is we mean to serve.
- Hiring only people who are truly aligned with our mission.
- Ensuring our products, management practices, and organizational structures are in alignment with our mission.
- Measuring how well we achieve our mission each and every day.
- Trusting that money (revenue) is a by-product of staying true to the mission.[7]

An attractive business is one that stays true to its mission, that is, one that stands still and solid on a mission so that the most perfect customers can find their way to it over the company's lifetime.

Like Attracts Like   Who do you like? Common sense dictates that one of the basic forces that attract businesses to one another lies in the principle of reciprocity. In other words, customers generally look for supplier relationships that can provide *mutual* value, because agents in reciprocal relationships naturally look out for one another. This is another example of the importance of codifying the company's customer relationship values into a formal strategic plan. Product and service value thereby becomes more concrete for the customer and the supplier. Customers and suppliers who recognize their own value can deliberately create a clearer value profile for one another. By recognizing the value of what they do in their IT organizations and company, the CIO and the IT staff create a more attractive profile for their internal and external customers.

A CIO manages a constant (endless) stream of internal and external relationships with varying degrees of strategic alignment, or "fitness." Every once in a while the customer makes it easy and falls into that slot called the "perfect fit." Both sides experience a mutual spark of attraction and connection almost immediately. The feelings of being needed, appreciated, respected, and understood can be so strong that both sides momentarily take on a cautious posture. This kind of relationship beginning commonly signals the discovery of a nearly perfect customer.

A new CIO commonly meets with longtime customers whose relationships were established long before the company embraced strategic customer relationship management practices. These unfulfilling, unsettling, and uncomfortable meetings lack any sense of mutual communication and understanding. The customer's expectations give them away: policy exceptions, special discounts, unique terms of credit, and unwarranted future commitments. In essence, they pit their needs against yours and those of your other customers by making claims that the other customers consume resources that should be reserved for them. In the terms of the oncologist, this kind of company is a space-occupying lesion on the customer roster of any business that seeks to strategically manage its customer relationships. Call the surgeon and cut it out.

In the meantime, if you attract new customer prospects that fit this profile, take a good look for deficiencies in your own customer relationship profile in terms of explicit or implicit advertising that suggests a departure from your mission or some way that your organization or company has publicly compromised its strategic customer relationship standards. What is it about your reputation that attracts unfit customers?

Strategic customer relationship postures begin to reinforce one another. Organizations that focus on a strategic customer relationship match reinforce their mission as well. Losing focus increases the likelihood of failure; and the most common reason for loss of focus is trying to serve anybody and everybody all the time. Likewise, a focused sense of mission clarifies which customer relationships are most important. In the most attractive matches, some customer/supplier relationships result in strategic collaborations where the partnership reciprocally fills strategic gaps for the two companies.

Customers and Employees Want You to Succeed   Reciprocity works to strengthen already strong customer relationships, thus, the CIO and the people in the IT organization must demonstrate loyalty and support to their customers to receive the same in return. When a supplier resorts to gimmicks such as premiums, discounts, and special offers, these ploys only train customers to postpone purchases and demand that the value of the gimmicks constantly escalate. The communications between the CIO/IT organization and their most valuable customers need to be direct, strategic, and mutually beneficial. Which would you prefer in a relationship with your most important supplier: being plied with trinkets or working together to solve one another's problems?

> The real magic of customer loyalty is . . . when you increase it, a beneficial fly-wheel kicks in. Powered by repeat sales and referrals, revenues and market share grow. Costs fall because you don't exert excess energy foraging to replace defectors. These steady customers are also easier to serve; they understand your modus operandi and make fewer demands on employee time. Increased customer retention also drives job satisfaction among your employees, in fact job pride, which leads to higher retention. In turn, the knowledge employees acquire as they stay longer increases productivity. The very idea of customer satisfaction helps align employees behind a common goal that everyone can understand.[8]

Whether communicating with internal or external customers, the CIO who shares strategic growth and expansion plans in the context of barriers to execution draws on the feedback of a loyal, supportive ally, and in doing so, only strengthens existing strategic customer relationship bonds. Think of it from your customer's strategic point of view: It's always easier to assist a trusted, established partner who has a track record of working with your best interests at heart than to start all over again cultivating a well-matched supplier.

A parallel relationship management process works when applied to employees. In the structure of the knowledge economy, customer and employee satisfaction criteria show remarkable similarities. A CIO running a tight strategic customer relationship management ship knows that employees want the IT organization and the company to succeed because their livelihoods depend on it.

Choose Collaboration, Not Competition   Choosing a collaborative customer relationship posture can have a dramatic effect on the way an IT organization does business and how its people treat their customers. This actually happened in the start-up company example we have been discussing. The COO of this high-tech manufacturer was concerned about product service and support. The company could feasibly staff and train a team to provide service and support to the more than 35 systems to be released in the first year, but three important questions needed answering:

1. Would the team be able to meet company and customer response time and quality as the product line grew and diversified?

2. How would the company handle the situation where the customer required that service and support be supplied by a third party?

3. How would the company respond to the customer who did not want a startup providing service and support?

Clearly, an alliance or collaboration was the answer, and the executive team decided on a strategic partnership with a third-party service and support company.

To find and establish successful collaboration relationships, you apply the same strategic customer relationship management techniques discussed in this section. But in the case of strategic collaborative partners, you must also look for openness, credible skills and knowledge, integrity, honesty, commitment, and focus. Importantly, look for strategic collaborative partners that complement the needs and profiles of your best customers, because the links in this kind of supply chain become very tight.

You Have the Power to Attract Whatever You Desire   The message behind this customer relationship posture is to think in terms of abundance rather than scarcity when it comes to the potential numbers of perfect customers over time— a challenging notion for the CIO's relationship with internal customers. An optimistic outlook that seeks opportunities establishes a very different customer relationship foundation from that of the pessimistic firefighter who sees nothing but problems. Take your pick; it will rub off on the way the entire IT staff work with your customers. Optimistic outlooks described in this customer relationship posture do not mean pasting on a silly grin in the face of adversity. Optimism is a proven leadership competency that can be learned, practiced, and applied strategically.[9]

Looking at external customer relationship activities, if the CIO operated from a vantage point of good-customer scarcity, the customer immediately assumes the advantage. Drastic tactics like stealing "good customers" from the competition carries risks. First, the CIO's company might incur one of the competition's less-than-perfect customers. Second, customer-chasing activities often force companies into a bargaining process with an ever increasing list of new (and maybe even outrageous) demands that end up in a never-ending cycle of frustrating customer relationships. Like leadership optimism, companies that develop an effective customer relationship management strategy work with an attitude of good-customer abundance, and the strategy gives the company an attractive customer relationship posture.

Interestingly, internal and external customer relationship management strategy development for attracting the right customers depends on asking the right questions of the customer. Mohanbir Sawhney described a situation where a company used surveys to measure customer satisfaction. Before they were able to finish congratulating themselves on how satisfied the customer was they were notified by a senior customer executive that the project was about to be shut down. The reason? The project was not meeting the expected objectives. The surveys showed that the customers were pleased with the working relationship and that intermediate results were satisfactory; unfortunately, none of this information addressed the overall requirement that the project deliver the expected business value. To quote Sawhney:

> Customers initiate projects to drive specific operational and financial changes in their businesses. The only thing they care about is the actual business value delivered by the vendor. [The company] now measures customer success on a set of "business success metrics" established jointly with each customer. These metrics are relevant to the senior business sponsor and are designed to measure the value delivered throughout the life of the project.[10]

As a senior IT executive, you probably have seen this in your own experience with both your external customers and with some of your "captive" internal customers who have not been free to go elsewhere for their services. Envisioning the abundance of perfect customers allows the CIO and the IT organization to spend their energy and focus on those customers who truly need and want what is available today. Perfect customers are more interested in success than satisfaction; success is the leading indicator that results in a satisfied customer.

Create an Atmosphere of Accomplishment   If success breeds success, the positive reinforcement that CIO and IT team members provide one another starts the success ball rolling. Subsequently, IT organizations that work to demonstrate an employee and customer relationship posture of gratitude for one another's accomplishments keep the ball rolling. More than just a sign of good manners for family, friends, and social acquaintances, formal and informal expressions of gratitude are also appropriate and appreciated in the world of business. Expressions of gratitude reinforce a customer relationship management mind-set that focuses on abundance rather than scarcity. Don't forget that legendary accomplishments come rarely, and people actually feel more personally gratified when someone acknowledges their day-to-day performance and other "small" accomplishments.

The Perfect Customer Revisited   The so-called perfect customer mentioned over and over in this section hopefully triggers some important introspection for your—the CIO's—strategic customer relationship management practices. How do you deliberately choose and then manage your customers to align them with your company's mission, products, and business—strategically rather than tactically? What formal identification criteria do you use to accept and pass on new customers? How have you modeled a posture of strategic customer relationship management to IT organization's staff members? "IT organizations should not forget that business units aren't captive customers whose loyalty can be taken for granted. CIOs who can't satisfy end users may find their jobs on the line."[11]

It really becomes a matter of seeing a customer in terms of the root meaning of the word *perfect* from the Latin *per facio,* thoroughly done. Because customer relationship management is an ongoing practice, the strategic CIO learns to see the same customer, internal or external, from different points of view, always a work in progress. You have the opportunity to choose the way you see certain internal customers as either a captive less-than-perfect customer or a perfect customer for someone else and to find a way to get their needs satisfied elsewhere. When you can choose the best perspective in terms of the IT organization, the internal customer, and the company, you will have demonstrated yourself to be the enabler and partner you need to be as CIO. Sometimes, the role of being an IT supplier to your partners and peers is a matter of reverse engineering: You may very well need to identify what must be changed so that what *you* provide matches the customer's needs.

ENTERPRISEWIDE STRATEGIC PLANNING

> *Science has not yet mastered prophecy. We predict too much for the next year and yet far too little for the next ten.*
>
> —Neil A. Armstrong[12]

To become a truly effective business partner, the CIO needs to find a way to become involved in the company's enterprisewide strategic planning process. The functional objective of strategic planning is to have strategic thinking permeate the entire company and guide day-to-day work activities in the context of what needs to be accomplished for long-term success. If the company does not have a strategic planning process, the CIO can start with an IT strategic plan and demonstrate IT directions and investments as a model for initiating an enterprisewide strategic planning process for information access, sharing, and management.

If the company actively uses an enterprisewide strategic planning process, the CIO can be a great asset to that process and its team. As the company's strategy evolves, the CIO's role includes identifying where information technology can be used to help improve the probability of overall strategic success. Information technology can be used to track progress toward the strategic goals and objectives, gain more information about customers—current, past, and future—and provide information that will enhance the abilities of your peers and partners to make effective decisions.

IT involvement in strategy development is the second most important enabler to organizational (and career) success for senior IT executives—right behind senior executive support for IT.[13] Looking through the enablers in Exhibit 4.2, the other key enablers are topics already discussed as keys to CIO success. Enterprisewide strategic planning is the key responsibility of the senior executive team members, hence *not* an activity that should ever be delegated. Doing so is an abdication of the senior executive's single most important responsibility: setting the strategic direction for the company.

As demonstrated in Exhibit 4.3, senior executive management is a right-brained task.[14] Left-brained tasks are those logical, tactical, and data-driven activities such as cost, quality, cycle time, and productivity. Right-brained tasks are intuitive and creative and focus on innovation, design, and lateral thinking. Strategic planning should never be confused with financial planning. Strategic planning focuses on outside forces that affect overall company success. Financial planning is focused on internally relevant topics such as personnel costs, capital costs, economic forecasts, and the like.

It is not unusual for an organization to have a visionary who leads the way in establishing and selling the strategic direction. Considering the volatility of the senior executive market, when that person leaves (for a "perpetrator's walk" or for whatever reason), it is highly unlikely that a ready replacement will step in to seamlessly carry on leadership vision. In the meantime, the company management focus becomes increasingly tactical, and operations languish without strategic renewal: Strategy gives way to tactics gives way to stagnation. While this could very well be the beginning of the end, the CIO has the opportunity to at least return the company to a strategic focus by once again using IT as a model for the other senior executives.

EXHIBIT 4.2   IT SUCCESS ENABLERS AND INHIBITORS

Enablers	Inhibitors
Senior executives support IT.	IT/business lacks close relationships.
IT is involved in strategy development.	IT does not prioritize well.
IT understands the business.	IT fails to meet its commitments.
Business/IT is a partnership.	IT does not understand the business.
IT projects are well-prioritized.	Senior executives do not support IT.
IT demonstrates leadership.	IT management lacks leadership.

Source: Adapted from Jerry N. Luftman, Raymond Papp, and Tom Brier, "Enablers and Inhibitors of Business–IT Alignment," 1999.

EXHIBIT 4.3   BREAKDOWN OF IT SUCCESS ENABLERS AND INHIBITORS

	Activity	Business Objective	Types of Thinking Process	Types of Planning
Right Brain *Conceive*	Reach the customer.	Reach the customer.	Strategic planning	Form the vision.
	Enhance executive decision making.	Take strategic advantage.	Unstructured decisions	Strategic
	Enhance products and services.	Gain market share.	Management control Semistructured decisions	Tactical
Left Brain *Implement*	Leverage investments.	Control resources.	Operational control	Implementation and operations.
	Reduce costs.	Manage daily operations.		

Source: Adapted from Jerry N. Luftman, Raymond Papp, and Tom Brier, "Enablers and Inhibitors of Business–IT Alignment," 1999.

CONTINUOUS AND DISCONTINUOUS PROCESS IMPROVEMENT

> *It is not the employer who pays wages; he only handles the money.*
> *It is the product that pays wages.*
>
> —Henry Ford[15]

Because the needs of the CIO's peers and partners change with the company's strategic goals and objectives, as an enabling role, the CIO also evolves. However, as an enabler of all peers and partners in the company, the CIO manages continuous IT improvement from a more complex perspective than peer senior executives who interpret strategy for their own functions alone. Like peer senior executives, the CIO works to interpret the overall strategic plans with one eye on the IT implications. With the other eye, the CIO works to see company strategy in terms of its implications on the work of different internal IT customers, because information technology is itself a strategic resource for the entire organization. As a technical business specialty, peers and partners cannot always see the best ways to leverage IT as a strategic resource in the work their people perform. It sometimes feels like playing 10 games of chess simultaneously.

As such, the CIO quickly learns about two forms of process improvement: continuous and discontinuous—continuous in the leadership management of the IT organization and discontinuous as evolving strategic plans change IT priorities and other functions work to interpret new strategies. Another good way to characterize these two very different process improvement focuses is *evolutionary* (a continuous unbroken thread of process improvement) and *revolutionary* (a sudden, adaptive discontinuous response to unexpected, significant strategic corrections) so common to the IT environment of disruptive technologies.

Resistance to Change and the IT Culture

As the CIO looks at process improvements of any kind, it is important to remember that the IT organization is culturally resistant to change. In general, groups that perform research and development work are culturally resistant to change. How easily or in what manner change can be accomplished in any particular company is a function of a number of factors including—and especially—the culture within the technical portions of the company such as the IT organization and the R&D functions. As John Buckley explains:

> [W]ith most scientists and technologists, it is the personal/professional agenda that takes precedence over corporate aspirations, which will therefore tend to

be resisted if they happen not to coincide.... [T]he scientific fascination with detail means that technologists require analysis and study of why change is necessary and become much more change-resistant than others.[16]

This resistance to change is based on two cultural predilections: their individual pursuit of knowledge, and focus on implementation and detail. The challenge here is that even with high-level technical people, the senior management is likely to be tripped up by the pursuit of knowledge focus when the technical person works to address strategic issues. There are many ways to handle this tendency, but suffice it to say that the senior management, the CEO, and the CIO must not let the IT organization or the R&D function resist changes that are necessary for business survival and business strategy for the sake of a specialized IT knowledge focus. The R&D function and the IT organization support value creation throughout the company, so it is critical that resistance to change in these groups be reduced, eliminated, or removed at every opportunity.

Technical communities that prevent necessary business changes doom their companies to the *Darwin effect*—only the fit survive. They may be *technically* correct, but that does not mean that they are thinking correctly for the *business*. An old National Safety Commission television commercial began with two cars approaching an intersection. The one with the right-of-way took it, even though the other car was traveling at excessive speed and did not appear to see the red traffic signal. After the inevitable crash, the epilog was: "They had the right-of-way; they were right—*dead* right." Survival scenarios are based on fitness, in this case, a blend of technical and business acumen. If the technical organizations prevail by resisting business-justified change (and, in many cases, making technical directional changes for marketing reasons also apply), then although they may be right from a technology point of view, they may be *dead* right from the company's point of view—the company may not survive.

Any CIO who has difficulty implementing business-related or other performance goal changes in the IT organization toward a business or other performance goal probably has a cultural resistance problem. There are several ways this can manifest itself in a company, and this can be a particular challenge for companies and employees very early or late in their life cycles. For example, consider a young company whose senior technical people have struggled for some time to meet their objectives but have been unable to do so. The company's technical professionals have finally reached the point in their career where they are at the top of the technologists' pyramid. As individuals, they have made a significant investment in themselves, stand firmly behind their points of view, and consequently create the status of the technology status quo. However, if the *business* facts demonstrate that commitments of these same technical professionals to the company are months, quarters, or even years behind schedule (or, equivalently, overbudget), then the resistance of the technical team to changes imposed by senior management are neither warranted nor defensible. Nevertheless, they are usually culturally supported and as such are defended to the point of ruin for the company.

The influence of senior technical people can be greater than that of the business or senior executives, particularly in young and middle-aged companies. In such cases, the CEO and CIO must work together to authoritatively mandate that the technology culture adapt and change to meet the pressing needs of business. Mandates sit poorly with most professional groups, and resistance can be overt, covert, and both. Therefore, if the CEO and CIO do not persist until the technology culture adapts completely, the technical team will prevail—that is, they'll be dead right: technically prevail while the business fails. The speed at which senior executives negotiate some change initiatives may exacerbate this issue, but the responsibility to reduce resistance to change remains constant. This is particularly problematic when dealing with senior-level technical people who abruptly leave the company after spending their careers working for technical recognition because the technical directions and the recognition are now being determined by the business staff. Certainly these are some of the most difficult times in the working life of the CIO, but the survival of the business depends on how successfully he/she can reduce and eliminate resistance to technology change for sound business reasons within the IT organization and R&D function. A thorough understanding of the dynamics of continuous and discontinuous change helps the CIO accomplish this task and move the company's attention beyond survival concerns.

Selecting Process Improvement Management Perspectives

Information technology has both service and physical aspects. The service aspects relate to the CIO role (and the IT organization's assistance in fulfilling that role); the physical aspects relate to the capital equipment and associated applications. The acquisition, management, development, maintenance, and improvement aspects of IT services have very quickly evolved into a professional discipline subjected to new innovation pressures almost daily. The history of IT management has roots in both finance and engineering, so its basic processes reflect the priorities of both organizations. If you have had the opportunity to work for both groups, you have probably noticed their fundamental differences. If you have worked in one group and then moved to the other, you undoubtedly remember discovering that your existing processes and procedures were viewed as some combination of inefficient, unnecessary, inappropriate, and/or ineffective. Despite your starting point, you intuitively know that you need to have a combination of continuous and discontinuous process improvement perspectives.

The hallmark of continuous process improvement is the *iterative* approach. Continuous, evolutionary processes in nature improve over time by means of countless repetitions. Repetitions in these natural systems fail far more often than they succeed, but, then, nature has all the time in the world. In business and IT management, the CIO uses repetition but constantly works to minimize the number of iterative repetitions and the time between iterative repetitions by looking for ways that the IT organization and company can learn to improve their processes as part of day-to-day work activities.

The CIO in a valid leadership role must use both. A CIO new to an organizational group or the position has to work with the existing processes and procedures regardless of what has to be done going forward. The amount of pressure the new CIO feels from a boss and from peers and partners focuses his or her immediate priorities and pace. When the CIO is asked to take over a dysfunctional IT organization that has not met its service commitments and added business value to the company, the IT organization may not inherit effective processes. In this case, the CIO is highly pressured to make quick, significant, discontinuous changes. In this common scenario, there is risk in doing something and there is risk in doing nothing. As a leader, to be effective (and to reduce your stress and that of your organization), you have to think about this scenario from a strategic point of view. Not every step you take in the best of scenarios will meet all your continuous and discontinuous strategic objectives. The most mature CIO leadership goal is to make progress gradually toward where you need to go and succeed.

Adding the risk management factor to strategic thinking makes this balancing act more explicit, and it puts strategic thinking on a continuum, as opposed to the usual five or six strategic objectives nicely bound and sitting on a shelf collecting dust. The two strategic scenarios in Exhibit 4.4 demonstrate how risk management fits into the CIO's strategic process improvement equation: the iterative strategy on the left and the explicit strategy on the right. In the second profile, sudden explicit departures in company and IT strategy reduce the available time for the iterative, continuous process improvement approach. Accelerated delivery curves follow revolutionary changes in strategy. Iterative, continuous approaches are more safe; sudden discontinuous approaches incur risk because they are unexpected. In this case, risk is not bad; it's simply a fact of leadership life.

Pacing Process Improvement

In addition to continuous and discontinuous forms of process improvement, the third part of the equation is rate of change or rate of instigating process improvements. You, the CIO, need to address the rate question to better select approaches, combinations, and timing sequence of planned changes, additions, and improvements. Plan on experimenting how far apart the iterations are introduced based on

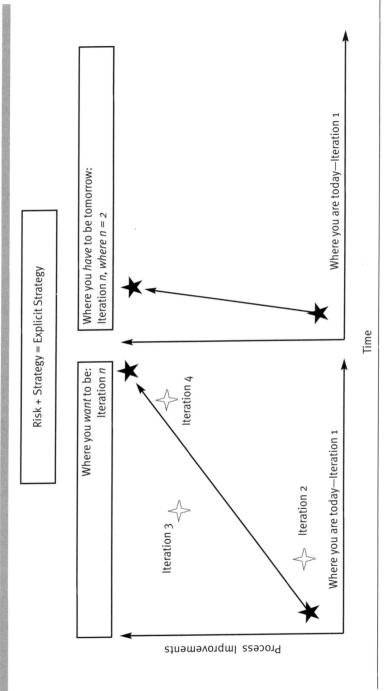

EXHIBIT 4.4 PROCESS IMPROVEMENT, RISK, AND EXPLICIT STRATEGY

the readiness and maturity of the IT organization and company. Start slowly, but look for opportunities to increase the iterative improvement pace as the IT organization and company learn to see continuous and discontinuous process improvement as part of their standard work activities.

The rate of process improvement work is also determined from an employee point of view—especially in the case of continuous, iterative process improvement. Regardless of how you start out (revolutionary or evolutionary), your long-term goal as CIO is to lead continuous, evolutionary change whenever possible. For the new CIO, everybody expects some changes, but most people also expect change to slow down after a while. Referring back to the Myers-Briggs Type Indicators, some people enjoy and even seek change opportunities, whereas others have difficulty dealing with change, hence consistently seek to avoid it. For this latter group of employees, you must work to gradually make process improvement a part of their everyday work life.

The start-up case cited earlier in this chapter demonstrated the best way to practically characterize these CIO challenges. By their very nature, start-ups manifest constantly changing strategic focuses that challenge the leadership experience of all functional veterans, but in the case of the high-tech manufacturer, especially the CIO.

THE CIO AND PRACTICAL STRATEGIC PLANNING: MORE THAN JUST IT

Over the period of its first year, the example start-up experienced a number of strategic challenges beyond the customer relationship management choices already discussed. In the first nine months, strategic changes focused on product definition, product development, and product delivery (marketing, hardware and software engineering, test engineering, and program management). Slowly but surely, strategic priorities shifted to market segmentation and market penetration (marketing and sales), and the next phase of company capital investments needed to fuel the "go to market" strategy—finance. At the very end of those first nine months, the strategic priorities shifted to operations (manufacturing readiness). In the midst of these rapidly shifting strategic and process priorities, the COO and CIO lost track of which changes were evolutionary and which were revolutionary. However, they found comfort in the fact that through rapid changes in strategic focus, each step had followed the initial business plan, and they decided that they had been working a continuous, evolutionary path all along.

With all the changes in the start-up's first-year management focus, the COO and CIO decided to bring the company's various groups together to reinforce the common goal: the urgent need to get a well-designed product out to the customers who needed it (their perfect customers). As management priorities continued to change rapidly in the next phase of their go-to-market strategy, the two senior executives worked together to bring new work teams "into the fold" by using the initial strategic plan to demonstrate shared goals, objectives, directions, deliverables, and performance metrics.

Keeping the Executive Team Sharp

Over the next six months of the second phase, the executive team hired several additional executives and senior managers to fill out its leadership team. Thanks to the CIO's partnership network, the COO and CIO discovered that not every member of the initial management leadership team was fully onboard with the company's overall goals and objectives, so they brought on new team members to replace old before the whole team suffered. In fact, the executive team eventually become concerned that the miscreants were actively sabotaging strategic goals by acting from short-term self-interests. As a result of the influx of new, committed people, this unified executive team moved forward to their next challenges with excitement and more confidence.

Nonexecutive Employees

Over the startup's first year, there were also a significant number of changing strategic focuses in terms of nonexecutive employees. As the company drew nearer to the time that its first products were projected to go to market, the executive team focused on goals, objectives, deliverables, repeatable processes (in engineering), and metrics, while bringing a repeatable processes focus to the operations function. Specifically, the COO and CIO took an employee survey to find out how successfully the executive efforts were focusing operational priorities.

In the second half of the first year before product introduction, the executive team witnessed significantly decreased employee turnover and an improved sense of teamwork in the operational employee group. Constantly reaffirming that working in a startup meant being highly flexible—from a personal and professional point of view—the COO and CIO saw production areas and assignments change, as well as new dimensions of personal growth and development open up for many operational employees. The timing and effects of the changes that resulted from the survey and direct COO/CIO involvement with this key function clearly enhanced their ability to meet the go-to-market target date. In this case, the COO and CIO introduced a timely, temporary, discontinuous parallel process to the existing strategic plan: Bring a key implementation employee group fully onboard with strategic priorities.

Looking forward, over the first six months of their second year, the executive team planned a number of significant "discontinuous" additions to a number of teams to help them adapt to the smoothly evolving strategy. In marketing and sales, they hired several experienced sales representatives and systems engineers (providing technical support to customers and sales reps). In engineering (hardware, software, and quality), they replaced unexpected departures with people who had different and new skills and who easily aligned themselves with the next several years' goals, objectives, deliverables, and metrics. In operations, they added a customer service and support engineer. The executive team used the second year to complete company staffing to achieve the right balance of product development and manufacturing, product marketing and sales, and financial and administrative support, thereby rounding out their go-to-market employee team.

Clearly, the CIO led the strategic evolutions and revolutions, with the COO, at every step of the process. In this startup company, the CEO deliberately focused on external concerns and left internal leadership to the COO. Recognizing the essential enabling function of the CIO, the COO and CIO formed an interdependent team based on decidedly different roles. The CIO used partnership network relationships to keep on top of strategic progress and specific functional needs, and the go-to-market strategy unfolded. This left the COO free to focus on high-level implementation priorities. Strategic employee management is one of the most important practical ways that the CIO's partnership network can serve the company. Everybody needs IT.

Strategic Resources: Blending Continuous and Discontinuous Methods

In the latter nine months of the second year, the executive team made another significant round of key strategic decisions including:

- A commitment to leadership and management excellence
- Renewed focus on goals, objectives, deliverables, and more precise metrics
- Definition of core values
- A commitment to formally reevaluate the validity of the overall strategic plan before another year passed

Within six months of the go-to-market target date, the executive team decided to use market segmentation to discover the best markets for the company's product debuts. They chose the first two markets, and thereby focused their beta-level product development marketing and sales efforts. In a discontinuous move, the executive team changed the engineering development and test processes to make them more efficient, predictable, and manageable. From this foundation, they used evolutionary strategic priorities and cooperatively planned the features and functions of the next product releases with the product marketing team and moved forward to begin development. Keeping an eye on the competitive environment, the CIO recommended that the company engage external counsel for its intellectual property, contracts, and other legal services. Finally, the executive team decided to engage a third-party service and support partner and, for credibility reasons as a new start-up, to be in a position to announce this partnership at first customer ship. Negotiated by the CIO, the support contract included installation, level 1/level 2 call-center support, break/fix support, and logistics management (spare parts management and dispatch from central/distributed locations). As a final step to enhance their final deployment strategy, the executive team decided to move final assembly and testing to a contract manufacturer and move preinstallation site survey and evaluation responsibilities to their own field/sales/systems engineers, thereby concentrating deployment team activities on chargeable services for complex installations and complex configurations. This complex deployment team would also serve as the first line of technical interface for difficult, complicated problems that the contracted service provider could not solve. All these major deployment strategy enhancements came from the COO/CIO working team. As an internal provider of many of the same type of enabling services addressed in the company's customer-related deployment strategy, the CIO was able to see opportunities that even the COO missed.

PLANNING THE FUTURE WITHOUT DISRUPTING THE PRESENT

> *The Seven Catastrophes of Computing: The user, the manufacturer, the model, the salesperson, the operating system, the language, and the application.*
> —Stanley Kelly-Bootle[17]

Referring back to Exhibits 1.3 and 1.4 in Chapter 1, companies hire a CIO to guide strategic development and value creation in terms of an environment of fast-paced innovation. Innovations mean value creation for customers of the IT organization; but innovations are expensive and can disrupt a company's focus on the successful present business priorities lining shareholder pockets. One day I was on an airplane seated next to one of the best executives I have ever had the pleasure of working for, and we talked about a new division we were going to create—the types of departments, what their missions would be, how they would be staffed, and the like. During the flight, we got to talking about how these groups would work with and complement each other (as partners, peers, and enablers). Then the conversation turned to considering the future and how we could implement our ideas without disrupting the present product development and sales business. As it turned out, we both had experience leading and managing separate, small groups that were isolated from the mainline product and sales groups, and we transferred our personal experiences as we created a new kind of company group that could help introduce our new division.

This small group would be chartered to focus solely on potential future innovations. One of the group's most important tasks would be to test products early in the technology cycles to give decision makers a hands-on feel for the technology's commercial readiness. We called this group the future technology evaluation team. Working from an isolated lab, its members collectively served as an effective gatekeeper of technology and product advancements. Thanks to the isolated environment that shielded the team from mainline product politics and executive enthusiasm, the team has also become very effective in separating the truthsayers from the charlatans. This same innovation-testing team concept can work for any IT organization.

Building a Technology Evaluation Team

To build a technology evaluation team from scratch, start with one or two direct reports who demonstrate specific professional aptitudes, including:

- Formal technical engineer training (software, hardware, and applications)
- Hands-on inquisitiveness (the enjoyment of getting dirty hands that comes with taking things apart and putting them back together)
- An adventurous innovation profile (Cool! You mean nobody's ever done this before?!)
- Self-confidence, to stand his or her ground against executive pressure (yours)
- Ability to engage a project without complete information (no specs, because he/she has to create them)
- Candor, to admit that first attempts will probably fail (there's always a better mousetrap)
- Self-determination, to take the time to find solutions (no clock punchers!)
- Discipline, to recognize that the work is meticulous and that test results must be carefully recorded, summarized, and interpreted for conclusions (including recommendations for next steps)

In my case, I initially started with three such people, and over the space of a couple of years the team grew to five people, covering a range of expertise including hardware, software, service and systems, applications, and networking. As a team, they learned to cover just about any new product or application area.

Setting up such a team is definitely warranted and is becoming recognized as part of the process of IT value creation. Exhibits 4.5 and 4.6 show that the more successful companies apply resources to identifying new technologies, and clearly use these resources to identify which technologies are more applicable to their environments than others.

Is building a technology evaluation team the CIO's responsibility? In the same survey, when asked who had the primary responsibility for deploying new information technologies, 38 percent of respondents cited the CIO, while the next three most-cited groups (Joint IT-business, CTO, IT systems deployment executive) together only amounted to about 34 percent. Surprisingly, only 22 percent of IT executives who indicated they were successful at meeting their strategic goals have dedicated new technology teams.[18] There is a clear correlation to improving the likelihood of successfully finding and deploying new technologies by having dedicated resources to do so.

In my case example, the team also forged an excellent relationship with two other groups in the company's IT organization that performed similar functions for back-office and client-side technologies. The team worked with the two groups and coordinated the sharing of finds, evaluations, requirements, and other process efficiencies. Although the objectives of the groups were dissimilar, their process insights were invaluable to each other. For example, all three groups were interested in looking at continuous backup and snapshot backup and restore products—each from its own perspectives: the product engineering group for its (external) customers, the back-office IT group for the mail servers (among other applications, internal customers and internal/external interactions), and the client-side group for its traveling (internal) customers. The three groups participated with each other in meetings and shared evaluation information. Ultimately, only one of the groups decided to deploy one of the technological solutions at

EXHIBIT 4.5   NEW TECHNOLOGY RESOURCE
             APPLICATION

	Mean	<1,000 Employees	>1,000 Employees
CIO Time	16.8%	19%	14.6%
IT Staff Time	9.5%	12.4%	6.6%
IT Budget	8.6%	9.9%	7.3%

Source: New Technologies Research, *CIO Insight*, 2003.

EXHIBIT 4.6	REASONS FOR ADOPTING NEW INFORMATION TECHNOLOGY		
	Mean	**‹1,000 Employees**	**›1,000 Employees**
Reducing Costs and Increasing Productivity	40.0%	36.8%	43.2%
Business Speed, Flexibiity, Agility	27.8%`	28.0%	27.6%
Increasing Revenue	11.8%	13.6%	10.0%
Improving Customer Service	11.8%	12.4%	11.2%
Providing New Products and Services	6.0%	7.2%	4.8%
Competitiveness	0.8%	0.8%	0.8%

Source: New Technologies Research, *CIO Insight*, 2003.

the time: the back-office group. The other two decided otherwise for different reasons: There was not a clear winner for the general customers of the product engineering group; and the client-side group decided to defer the decision about automatically backing up all traveling clients to a later time. The positive effect was clear to the members of each group: Meaningful interactions between such groups accelerate the process learning curve and management decision-making maturity of all individuals involved, regardless of their specialty orientation. Given that these groups looked at several hundred products a year, and selected fewer than a dozen for implementation and deployment, the value creation implications become obvious.

Of course, one of the challenges with such a team is that people working on mainline IT organization programs easily misunderstand the team's purpose. Therefore you must be very careful about what is said outside the technology evaluation team. Imagine the effects of offhand remarks heard out of context in the general mainline product work areas, where other people are using what the team is testing (and rejecting): low morale, reduced motivation, and lower productivity. Everyone wants to be a part of long-term value creation. Innovation teams can give mainline workers a feeling of performing temporary work awaiting the next version of real value.

Structuring the Innovation Evaluation Workload

Some company IT organizations work under a significant burden of new technology and product testing, and CIOs who decide to solve this problem with the creation of a technology evaluation team need to remember the scope of the task. Transferring the responsibilities to a committed workforce does not diminish the sheer quantity of evaluative work, nor decrease the relatively short amounts of time required to perform it. This scarcity dynamic becomes even more apparent because so many products and services are prematurely placed on evaluation readiness status, and the work has to be repeated.

The volume burden carries an unexpected customer relationship management challenge for some CIOs. Depending on the environment of competition between individual customers, internal or external, the CIO and the technology evaluation team become privy to a significant amount of information about products, services, and futures. Who else can learn this information? Think of a company that uses the budget as an internal control, or any company with poorly linked departments or functions that compete against one another for scarce resources. To prevent unfounded suspicions, give your technology evaluation team and your customers strict guidelines on information flow and on where and how information, test results, summaries, conclusions, and recommendations are stored.

Another technique for training new technology evaluation teams, structuring their workload for greater efficiency, and increasing the quality and comparability of their output is to establish a set of standardized tests for putting technologies and products (and companies) through their paces. In some cases, make the tests available to those being evaluated so they can pretest products and services themselves, and thereby know what to expect. Standardized methods clarify reports and other communications for both the technology evaluation team and the customer. This helps engender a cooperative relationship and provides a way to double-check work for reasonability. Whenever possible, look for out-of-the-box testing experiences to document the overall installation instructions and quality. When things go wrong, as they so often do, the documented installation gives the team the additional opportunity to test service and support.

Leading the Technology Evaluation Team

For this to be an effective strategic customer relationship management group, the CIO has to safeguard the technology evaluation team against any groups, internal or external, that might be threatened by poor evaluations and have connections to senior executive peers. One of the greatest challenges comes from within the IT organization, itself. Depending on the structure of authority in the IT organization, other senior executives or direct reports who work exclusively or predominantly in the mainline production group are placed in a conflict of interest when asked to manage the technology evaluation team as well. The CIO can work to maintain the principle of enabling IT peers working in partnership by remaining aware of some important dynamics when delegating technology evaluation team supervisory responsibilities.

This is a job best reserved for the CIO, CTO, or other senior-level technical executive. The mainline group will be concerned that successful results from the technology evaluation team might render the work of the mainline group obsolete or in need of significant overhaul. To the people working in the mainline groups, smooth operations and change are antithetical. Their day-to-day efficiency depends on familiar, predictable products and processes. However, without the information and insights from a group like the technology evaluation team, the mainline group's efficiency and productivity eventually atrophies, for at least two reasons. First, their only other ready alternatives are severely back-level solutions that fail to meet growing and evolving customer needs. Second, these same suboptimal remedies also add ever expanding costs to maintaining the tired, old technologies. Remember that the technology evaluation team is designed to facilitate strategic customer relationship management. Their work often disturbs today's customer but delights tomorrow's customers. And, tomorrow's customers do not know who to thank.

Once you have created your technology evaluation team, you will soon realize an additional benefit: They can be the counterbalance to your mainline team. By virtue of their future-oriented mission, the technology evaluation team is not encumbered by the day-to-day demands of product-related deliverables, and they are able to objectively look at the ways work is currently being performed from different angles. While these teams quickly become overly optimistic about what changes can actually be implemented, they work as an excellent catalyst for setting the bar higher for the next round of improvement attempts in the IT organization. Because of their objectivity, they can become the reasonability test for the CIO and the other areas in the organization. Before long, members of the technology evaluation team develop skills that place them in high demand because they have learned to be open to discussion and have a wide range of expertise and experiences with change. In fact, in one instance, my colleagues and I thought of this group as the *credible threat*; that is, it was staffed with people who had engineering backgrounds and whose leadership was very experienced such that, if necessary, they could lead and work in the mainline group (and had done so in the past).

All this may be well and good, but at this point, many CIOs and IT staff members from the mainline group pause thoughtfully and quietly until someone asks, "So does this team have any *real* responsibilities or deliverables?" In a word, *yes!* The senior team manager and the CIO manage the team to a set of deliverables and schedules; and it is important that they have a process and well-defined deliverables. Because of the significant but constantly changing set of responsibilities the team has in helping the CIO, the IT staff, executive peers and partners, and the company with a wide spectrum of evaluations, the team members need repeatable and predictable processes to focus their activities and support their confidence to perform this highly independent function. There will still be grousing by those who believe the resources could be better used, and who believe they should be made part of the mainline group. So what else is new? Employed properly, a technology evaluation team gives multiple returns on its investment by sorting out the expensive difficult alternatives involved in adopting information technology innovations. Like a miniature version of the IT organization, the technology evaluation team enables the work of everyone in the company, the difference is that the team's work today can't be seen or felt until tomorrow. It's enough that you know this and stand by their purpose and work.

One theme remains a constant for the success of an enabling CIO working within a profession defined by rapid, disruptive change, and it is one that can influence the strategy of the entire organization: *delivery*. Planning the future always builds on the present, and for the IT organization and its strategic internal and external customers, future planning focuses remain fairly constant: innovation, customer feedback, engineering, development, business, and (yes, it does not go away) delivery—today. In each of these focuses, IT delivery means success for peers and partners. For most people, the *transitions* between past, present, and future delivery responsibilities generate the most anxiety.

Source of All Future IT Value

As company business priorities change, the CIO often focuses almost exclusively on selective, strategic external customer acquisition and internal delivery needs. It's a lonely job deciding when to push new IT products. Does it have enough features and high enough quality? Will our customers like it (and how will we deal with the ones who don't)? What happens if this new IT product gives them ideas about things we simply can't deliver? These are all difficult questions, and all have uncertain answers. The "if" and "when" parts are determined as much by insight based on experience (which includes trial and error) as they are by hard facts. The "how" parts are something that the CIO has to experience, learn, understand, and adapt case by case; they help the IT organization develop the cross-functional teamwork that is necessary to support the evolving (and sometimes revolutionary) strategic needs of a great company.

The longer a CIO works for the same company, the more likely the past remains the strategic context for present and future focuses, and the more aware he/she realizes the context of the present moment emerges as the source of all IT value creation. This is a huge leadership step in the CIO's history with any company. Once this awareness becomes permanent, the priorities of the present moment as a context for future IT value lead all aspects of CIO decision making and strategic partnership. The present moment focus has two leadership priorities for the CIO: deliver to customers *now* and create IT value foundations *now* for work in the future.

Consider the practical IT service delivery spectrum for meeting established goals across the many possible IT responsibilities in different kinds of companies. In IT engineering, delivery means completing and shipping product. In IT architecture and marketing, delivery means completing a marketing requirements document (MRD) for future releases and planning. In IT sales, delivery means achieving the necessary number of unconditional POs to ensure you have a good valuation for your next fundraising round. In IT operations, delivery means having the supply chain ready to meet demand and working cost reductions. It may also mean transferring manufacturing from a prototyping house to a tier 1 contract manufacturer. In IT manufacturing, delivery means ensuring the production of a quality product in a timely and cost-effective manner while handling the upswings in customer demand without excessive inventory. In IT facilities, delivery means greeting all guests professionally so they think well of the organization on their first impressions. As they go through the building they see and experience a truly professional environment. In IT finance, delivery means managing monies, paying bills, rearranging loans for more attractive terms and lower expenses, and managing outside lawyers and meeting IT needs in a timely and effective manner. Delivery is a significant part of another of the CIO's key core values: results.

While delivery is vital to CIO success, so is planning for the future. Without daily work that builds toward the future, there will be nothing in the future requiring delivery! (I know this seems obvious, but you'd be surprised . . . or maybe not.)

Planning for the Future: Innovate Today!

To keep ahead of the competition, innovation becomes a daily value creation process improvement focus for the CIO. CIO success depends as much on the key features desired by the company's internal and external perfect customers as those of the competition. Today's "must have" IT feature may be yesterday's buggy whip by the time you can reliably offer it—sometimes referred to as "shooting behind the duck." At the same time, when innovating IT services, keep in mind the continued needs and trends in cost reductions, customer flexibility, and product density (in the storage world, this translates as terabytes/ft^2 and terabytes per height of rack). The CIO's number-one innovation priority is to reduce complexity for the customer.

Look for as many options as possible as you develop your own innovation philosophy. Clayton Christensen has developed an instructive innovation dynamic thesis as food for thought.[19] There are three key foundations to his thesis:

1. Technologies can progress faster than market demand.
2. Suppliers often overshoot the market for revenue, profit, or competitive reasons.
3. Today's underperforming technology may be tomorrow's competitor.

Exhibit 4.7 uses a common technology market dynamic to summarize the CIO's most important considerations when developing a personal innovation philosophy for the IT organization and the company. The solid parallel lines define the band of requirements at the low end and the high end of a particular technology market. The dashed line represents the progress of technological evolution through sustaining technologies—technological advances that are incremental and continuous, such as Texas Instrument calculator features. The dotted line represents a sudden shift in the sustaining technology to a lesser performance profile due to the introduction of a disruptive technology with a new line of incremental "sustaining technologies" that initially have *fewer* features overall when compared to the product on the dashed line.

Notice what happens as time goes on: Some competitors may continue on the dashed line while others observe and choose to use the disruptive technology and move down to the dotted line. Why does this matter? Put the influence of the disruptive technology in the context of high- and low-end performance demands. IT organizations and companies that continue to provide IT products on the dashed line not only far exceed the requirements of customers with low-end IT performance requirements, they quickly exceed the actual requirements of customers at the high end as well.

As it turns out, those working on the dashed line after the introduction of a disruptive technology get trapped in having to continue to add more features and functions than their customers need (even their high-end ones) in an attempt to maintain value, price, and customer interest. Do companies really get trapped on that dashed line? Yes, without question; and so do many CIOs. The computer industry graveyard is filled with tombstones—with appropriately negative financial epitaphs—of companies that missed one or more disruptive technology shifts and got trapped moving their way up the dashed line with no way out—companies including the BUNCH (Burroughs, Univac, NCR, CDC, Honeywell), IBM, DEC, EMC, and Auspex.

Working with the Dell Storage Division, my objective was to ensure that we never got more than half the way toward the dashed line before developing our own disruptive technology or disruptive approach to a product to ensure we could once again drop down to the dotted line. We were just fine being underfeatured

EXHIBIT 4.7 INNOVATION MANAGEMENT DYNAMICS

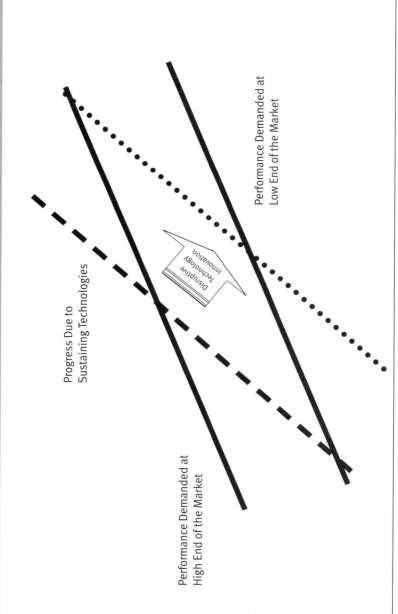

Progress Due to
Sustaining Technologies

Performance Demanded at
High End of the Market

Performance Demanded at
Low End of the Market

Disruptive
Technology
Innovation

Source: Adapted from Clayton Christensen, *The Innovator's Dilemma: When New Technologies Cause Great Firms to Fail,* 1997.

and underfunctioned relative to our competition when we would first drop from a dashed line to a dotted line. Why? Dell often led with price (our costs could support it), and that was enough for many customers to give us a try—or to buy more products from us. Remember that Dell's approach was to enter with "good enough" features and functions at exceptionally attractive prices (and unparalleled costs); and our internal goal was to be the low-cost leader.

Innovative CIOs use this kind of early adoption strategy to build a personal innovation philosophy for the IT organization and the company. These considerations are particularly important for watching IT cost while meeting internal customer needs. Internal IT customers often shop the market like teenage males looking for the ideal car stereo. The service-level agreement plays a central role in the ways that the CIO can respond to internal customer IT expectations in terms of what the customer really needs and whether the customer can actually afford those bells and whistles that often go unused and rarely create strategic value.

CIO Innovation Focuses

As technology experts, we do have to be careful about being "all dressed up with nowhere to go" or "majoring on the minors" or "overengineering because it's cool." Products provide a focus for discussing deliberate innovation, but the same principles can be applied to IT innovations for finance, manufacturing, and all other areas that have analogous themes. The same questions come up in all areas with potential for innovation:

1. What *can* we innovate?
2. What *should* we innovate?
3. How do we tell the difference?
4. *When* should we innovate?
5. *Why* should we innovate?
6. *Who* needs our innovations?

The CIO has two ways to answer these questions, which depend on internal and external customer perspectives. Externally, the CIO wants to identify the company's "perfect" customer profile and seek partnerships with other companies that fit that profile. Internally, the CIO wants to teach and guide peers and their organizations into becoming perfect customers for the IT organization in terms of company strategy and the ways that peer organizations within the company use IT to create value together.

In terms of the innovation dynamics of Exhibit 4.7, after identifying either the external or internal perfect customer profile, the next step is to discover which IT products and services fall above and below the dashed line. In other words, find out what really matters to your customers and, whenever possible, create innovative IT product and service solutions that meet essential needs at lowest cost. Note the distinction between price and cost. In engineering and manufacturing activities, IT must do its best to have the lowest costs possible so that the CIO can provide the company with the greatest possible flexibility in pricing and margins. Once the CIO discovers what those key attributes are, innovation focuses become clearer.

Where, Why, and When   Looking at IT value creation for external customer relationships, the innovative CIO starts with the marketplace. The marketing, design, and business development teams look at the various markets and learn what it takes to enter and compete in those markets with current and future products and services.

A concrete deliverable from this kind of deliberate innovation planning is a marketing requirements document (MRD) and an updated technology strategy, business strategy, and architecture. Ideally, the MRD includes all markets, customer types, usage models, and scenarios for current (and soon-to-be) perfect customers, technical feasibility assessment, and design analysis. Consider the pros and cons of entering some particular market in a disruptive manner, but talk with a lot of customers in these new markets: where they were, where they are, and where they're going. This is how the "when" comes into the picture. And customers (existing and future) like to talk about the future and about the innovative services they can expect from you.

What and How   Next you have to figure out what to innovate. No, I am not going to fall into the trap of talking about how to innovate. I believe the *how* is really about how we are going to realize the results of the innovation. It is very difficult to plan innovation; but it is possible to plan the implementation of an innovation as a follow-up activity based on the results of the MRD. This necessarily involves lead technical people—managers and designers. The product and service designers provide the bridge between the marketing requirements and how you plan to achieve them—bridging the where/why/when and the what/how. Again, circle back to validate directions with customers and marketing to ensure that the right problems are being solved.

IT AS A VALUE CENTER

> *Granted, it can work a thousand, a million times faster than the human brain, but it can't make a value judgment, it hasn't intuition, it can't think.*
>
> —James T. Kirk[20]

A 1999 online *CIO Magazine* Quick Poll asked readers if their IT department was a profit center, a cost center, or a total loss.[21] The results were interesting: 67

percent reported that their IT group was a cost center, 20 percent reported that their group was a profit center, and the remainder reported their IT group as a total loss. In another *CIO Magazine* poll conducted in early 2001, the results were not significantly different: 70 percent reported that their group was a cost center and 30 percent reported that their group was a value center.[22] Value center? Should IT be a profit center, cost center, or value center?

Although a CIO should be prepared to make any one of these work, the best solution for the IT organization is a value center orientation. As a profit center, the CIO is forced to focus on producing revenues through IT investments—to maximize revenue of the IT organization/investments. As a cost center, you, the CIO, are forced to focus on minimizing costs for IT investments, not to maximize the revenue of your company or your peers and partners. As a value center, the CIO focuses IT on providing value through IT investments to all internal and external customers. In other words, the company charges the CIO to maximize the value of the IT organization and its investments. This incidentally focuses the CIO on maximizing the revenue of the company.

In its "Measuring IT Value" poll, *CIO Magazine* asked which metrics were used to measure IT value; and return on investment and total cost of ownership represented 70 percent of the approaches. Exhibit 4.8 summarizes the answers to two important questions about IT value creation.[23]

To be measured as a value center, the key measures in this exhibit are external customer satisfaction and service-level agreements for those groups whose formalized service expectations supported customer satisfaction. The CIO should get a specific measure from each peer and partner involved in these value creation relationship areas. A *specific* measure means an IT performance dimension that the CIO's peers and partners really need to be done well to accomplish their own goals. Besides helping your peers and your company become successful, you will also help yourself and the IT organization: These same peers and partners become your strongest supporters and advocates. So, work to become (if you are not already) a value center; it is the best way to connect yourself and your company's investment in IT to value creation.

TEN QUESTIONS THE CIO SHOULD ASK THE ENTIRE EXECUTIVE TEAM DURING JOINT STRATEGIC PLANNING ACTIVITIES

> *When an organization selects a strategy it is choosing the approach it will employ to isolate its activities from those of its competitors. Strategy is the creation of a defensible competitive advantage.*
>
> —Richard A. Goodman and Michael W. Lawless[24,25]

EXHIBIT 4.8   MEASURING IT VALUE

What metrics/methodology do you use to measure IT value? (Select all that apply.)

Return on investment (ROI)	40.7%
Return on assets (ROA)	8.2%
Internal rate of return (IRR)	13.6%
Total cost of ownership (TCO)	29.1%
Other	8.4%

What do you consider in your value equation? (Select all that apply.)

Number of transactions	35.9%
Costs/expenses	85.2%
External customer satisfaction	55.5%
Productivity	66.8%
Profit	43.8%
Response time of Internet	19.9%
Revenue	44.9%
Service-level agreements	43.0%
Soft benefits	48.4%
Uptime	46.5%
Visitors to Web site	18.0%
Non-IT Web costs (PR, Marketing)	21.1%
Other	2.7%
Total Number of Responses:	1,361

Source: Adapted from "CIO Research Reports: Measuring IT Value," *CIO Magazine,* June 9, 2003.

This chapter has carefully examined the CIO's executive-level interaction and, in particular, strategic planning at both the corporate level and for the IT organization, itself. So it is appropriate to focus these 10 questions on what the CIO should ask the *entire* executive team during strategic planning activities. Thanks to so-called Internet time, many executives have started to question the value of strategic planning when by all outward appearances there does not seem to be the need for a strategy beyond a three-month horizon. This paradox is one of executive perception, not strategic execution. Some of the best thinkers and researchers in this area sharpen the focus of how the CIO can and must practice strategically. David Brooks reminds executives of the "need to actually execute and finish your strategies, rather than just develop grand visions and capitalize in earth-shaking revolutions."[26] *Good to Great* author Jim Collins characterizes what he has learned about strategic execution: "Throughout our research we were struck by the continual use of words like 'disciplined,' 'rigorous,' 'dogged,' 'determined,' 'diligent,' 'precise,' 'fastidious,' 'systematic,' 'methodical,' 'workmanlike,' 'demanding,' 'consistent,' 'focused,' 'accountable,' and 'responsible.'"[27]

If you are going to provide the greatest possible IT value to your company, you need to create value through *your* resources and *your* strategy and *your* planning and execution in the IT organization for *your* fellow senior executives and *your* company. To do so you need to ensure that you are aligned with your peers, and that means that you need to be participating in the corporate-level strategy sessions and ask some key questions of your co-senior executives.

Strategic planning is an iterative process, which means the CIO works to integrate IT strategic planning priorities into any evolving discussion of overall company strategic renewal. As an iterative process, the members of the senior executive team usually talk their way into the development of new strategic directions—team members get new ideas from one another and the final product emerges by stringing the best ideas together into a final strategic plan. Along the way, the CIO has two levels of participation: outwardly, adding to the discussion by making sure that the other senior executives understand how IT can serve as a strategic resource; and inwardly, asking the same question at each new turn in the iterative development discussion, "How does this affect my existing IT strategic plan?" At some point in the strategic planning work with the entire executive team, the CIO must ask some concrete questions to align IT resources with the company's emerging strategic priorities. The ritual of strategic planning does not guarantee that the result will be a truly strategic plan. These are questions the CIO must ask as the strategic plan emerges, not after full development.

1. Are you aware of our information technology strategic plan?

2. Should the IT strategy be an input to our company's strategic plan, or should our company's strategic plan drive our IT strategy?

3. Have we allocated and invested the resources necessary to execute the new strategic plan, and is our IT investment portfolio aligned with our company's needs?

4. Do we have appropriate measures in place to validate our execution against the strategy?

5. What IT shadows that have not been discussed might cross our short-term strategic horizon from your divisions and functions to impact our emerging plan?

The next five questions focus on specific ways that the CIO can work with the executive team to align IT and company strategies.

6. How dependent is our company's success in the strategic time frame on the successful execution of our IT strategic plan?

7. Does our IT strategic plan support our overall corporate strategic plan?

8. Is there a clear linkage between our IT strategy and our company's competitive strategy?

9. Based on our corporate strategy, can we do a SWOT of the IT portfolio?

10. Is there a difference between our intended strategies and our realized strategies?

Number 1: Are You Aware of Our Information Technology Strategic Plan?

This is a fundamental question the CIO must ask of each and every senior executive, because even though the CIO is responsible for the IT strategic plan, IT strategy really needs to be *owned* and *embraced* by the *entire* senior executive team. Of course, this assumes that there *is* an IT strategic plan. According to a survey reported in *CIO Magazine*, as many as 39 percent of companies do not have a formal IT strategy at all.[28] In contrast, *CIO Magazine* reported a dramatic change from 2002 to 2003 in the criticality of strategic thinking and planning: In 2002, less than half of the surveyed CIOs gave strategic thinking and planning as a critical skill; in 2003, 76 percent of the surveyed CIOs said this was a critical skill.[29] It is the CIO's responsibility to enable the success of each and every member of the senior executive team; and before they work with the CIO, they have to actually be aware of the IT strategic plan.

After you ask this first question, look carefully at the respondents. A blank stare is an obvious sign that one of the first orders of business is to develop a formal means for taking all the senior executives through the IT strategic plan. This kind of formal presentation gives you, the CIO, an opportunity to elicit senior executive help in the further development, evolution, and maintenance of the IT strategic plan. Naturally, you present the IT strategic plan in terms that nontechnology executives can clearly understand as a demonstration that IT is listening to their needs in many ways. Involving senior executives in the IT strategic planning process and keeping them informed about the possibilities that technology brings is considered a key requirement for CIO success.[30] The blank stare response is all too common. According to research published by *CIO Insight*, 46 percent of IT executives and 62 percent of business executives polled said their company communicated strategic mission well through their company—that is, 54 percent of IT executives and 38 percent of business executives polled said their companies communicated strategic missions only "somewhat clearly or not at all."[31]

Once the senior executives are involved and engaged in the IT strategic plan, the follow-up question is: "What needs to change in the IT strategic plan to align it with the company's new strategic plan?" Each senior executive is likely to have a different view (although hopefully not fully orthogonal or fully skewed). The CIO gets a wide range of input and sits in the rare position as one of the few senior executives who knows the individual views of all of the senior executives. A rare and most fortunate position, indeed! The particular alignment achieved by the CIO on behalf of the IT organization depends on the needs of the business executive and the business unit—from both business and technology points of view. The CIO who learns about and understands these four dimensions aligns with the business partner more quickly than one who does not make this necessary effort. The kind of CIO who can "sit on the same side of the table" with business peers becomes more empathetic and enabling. Alignment means success.

Once individual business partnership alignments are complete, the CIO can ask the entire senior executive team whether the IT strategic plan supports each of their business' strategic plans *in the context of the company's emerging strategic plan.* This follow-up question is the entrée to the essential off-line, private dialog between each individual senior executive and the CIO. These private conversations, which should take place between joint executive strategic planning sessions, have an added benefit in that they can disarm (that is, bring onboard) even an unwilling yet well-informed internal IT customer. Willingly or not, the CIO needs the input, participation, and endorsement of each member of the senior management team.

One of the most important decisions that managers make concerns investment in new technologies for products as well as processes. These decisions have enormous strategic significance, as they influence the competitive position of the firm through cost and revenue implications for many years into the future.[32] The CIO can take several definitive steps to proactively align the IT strategic plan with each of the business units:

- Enlist a business unit executive to participate in the IT strategic planning process.
- Volunteer an IT executive to participate in the business units' strategic planning processes.
- Regularly review, reaffirm, and modify the results of both strategic planning processes, as necessary.

Some senior executives already have members of their teams involved in the IT strategic planning process, but recent studies suggest that their numbers are few. In the *CIO Insight* study, only 33 percent of the polled IT and business executives reported a regularly deployed one-on-one relationship between their IT/non-IT organizations.[33] Interestingly, in a more recent *CIO Magazine* study, conducted approximately one year later than the first, only 59 percent of the polled IT executives reported such a relationship. This is amazing (and disappointing), given that, in the same survey, 72 percent said the business units have a direct say in their IT budget![34] These senior business executives and their business units are the CIO's customers and are the CIO's funding justifications; therefore, the CIO really *must* get them involved in the development of the IT strategic plan. The question to ask is: "How can we get you and your teams more involved in IT strategic planning so that we can also address your operational priorities?"

In an innovative example of how to do this, Stephen C. Finney, senior vice president and CIO for Kraft Foods North America, has created regular retreats to which he invites the senior business executives for Kraft's business units to join his senior executive team in discussion.[35] Finney uses the opportunity to have his senior IT executives hear directly from the top business executives what they are trying to achieve in their businesses and what they see as holding them back. The discussions in these sessions give the IT team an opportunity to work directly with their senior customers, to understand the *real* business problems, and, potentially, to come up with real IT solutions to help the business unit executives be successful—that is, to *enable* their success!

Number 2: Should IT Strategy Be an Input to Our Company's Strategic Plan?

From a practical point of view, the alignment of the IT strategic plan and the company's strategic plan is an iterative process (at least, it should be!). As a member of the senior executive team whose organization contributes to the success of all company activities, the CIO enables the entire senior executive team to evolve the company's strategic plan in unison with their own business unit plans. Using the important information gathered off-line from the different senior executive team members' answers to question 1, the CIO delivers IT value by creating an IT strategic plan that takes into account technology evolution, risk, business need, and requirements for operational stability, all in the context of question 1 answers. In doing so, the CIO gives the executive team an IT strategic context that serves as a foundation for companywide strategic intentions. What comes first, the chicken or the egg? The strategically minded CIO knows that any actionable strategy with any hope of execution depends upon certain resource and environmental exigencies that cannot be simply wished away by high-power executive intention; IT resources and needs are one such exigency.

Working as a strategically effective and enabling CIO includes leveraging what can and what should be executed over the strategic planning period and continuing to provide expert technology advice to the company's senior executives. In short, the CIO must develop the IT strategic plan in anticipation of the company's strategic plan. In doing so, the CIO is in a much better position to contribute to the company's strategic plan rather than just react to it. A proactive IT strategy sets the CIO apart from the competition. According to the results in the *CIO Insight* survey, "Some 47 percent of . . . CIOs and business executives say IT is a reactive problem-solver at their companies, while only 28 percent say IT has input into business strategy."[36] This is not a balance that is likely to produce a winning combination for either the CIO or the company, and moving the IT strategic plan into a secondary level of importance is likely to have negative competitive effects down the road—especially if your competitors (today's or tomorrow's) keep theirs an ongoing priority! The successful CIO heeds the strategic call and stands ready as advisor, enabler, full partner, and proactive co-participant in formulating the company's strategic plan. One of this same CIO's most important tools is an IT strategic plan (at least a first pass) that can be used as a tool and vehicle for discussion.

It is important to keep the IT strategic planning process part of the company strategic planning process because, in most companies today, there is a symbiotic relationship between the company's and IT's strategic plans—whether everyone realizes it or not (seems like the "or not" heavily outweighs, based on polls taken over the past few years, as noted earlier). There may be some academic questions as to when this relationship became fully entwined; however, with the advent of the Internet, there is no turning back. As an enabler, the integrated approach, ensures that the CIO's strategy supports the company's strategy; without the integrated approach the result is similar to two people trying to move an object in differing directions: They do not end up where either of them expected to be!

For example, the director of IT in one company was advocating (along with his senior executive) for procuring and installing a massive (read: complicated and expensive) MRP system over the next 18 months. This system would cost millions of dollars to procure and at least half a million dollars to install and train those who needed to work with it—this for a company of around 100 people that was only just getting ready to introduce its first product. The IT executive had not done an adequate job of ensuring that his strategic plan (this specific portion of the IT strategic plan) was in alignment with the corporate strategic plan. The corporate strategic plan was for the company to grow its business processes and support at a rate (cost, complexity, etc.) that matched the rate at which customers would be acquired. Bringing the IT director and the IT strategic plan into alignment with the corporate strategic plan was relatively straightforward: Refocus, to bring onboard an MRP-lite that would satisfy business needs for the next several years and cost two orders of magnitude less, yet be upgradeable to a medium-sized package without a significant amount of trouble. The IT strategic plan then fell into alignment with the company's strategic plan.

Number 3: Have We Allocated and Invested the Resources Necessary to Execute the New Strategic Plan?

How often, as a senior manager, have you felt the rush of completing a strategic planning session, then gone out and celebrated together with your team to "seal the deal?" But, after sleeping on it, you get up the next morning with a bad case of buyer's remorse, realizing that the strategic desire and intent were strong but the ability to execute is weak? This dynamic sets the senior executive team, their business units, and the company up for a monumental strategic failure. From the employees' point of view, it serves to reaffirm the apparent disconnect between the senior staff and the line management. The weakness in ability to execute can be due to a combination of any number of factors, including insufficient staff, insufficient skills, unrealistic assessments of the level of effort, and lack of clear priorities across the company and within the business units. Add to that the challenge of cross-prioritizations of business unit needs with single priorities within the IT organization and the probability of success is looking mighty low. All the while, the most significant question has not even risen to executive consciousness: "How do we pay for it?"

CIO Magazine asked its CIO readership to list their greatest challenges; their response was lack of staff and skills (40 percent) and budget shortfalls and lack of budget prioritization (37 percent) as their top two challenges.[37] These strike directly at the heart of investment and resource allocation. The adage "follow the money" practically demonstrates the most important form of strategic commitment. Strategic intention and resource allocations go hand in hand. The entire senior executive team has to keep this in mind, *especially* the CIO. Sooner or later, if the CIO does not ask the question, the CFO is likely to do so: "This all sounds grand, but how will we pay for it?" Once the CFO asks this question, it is often time to haul out the axe and the chopping block, and the current topic of discussion becomes the prime candidate for the first swing. An immediate and suffocating pall drops over the once-lively proceedings as the CFO has gone from peer and partner to executioner in a matter of seconds. Is this the only way to introduce resource allocation accountabilities into the strategic planning process? Not at all.

By working with the *entire* senior executive team beforehand, the astute CIO takes steps to understand the likely needs of the business units and the likely resource requirements to proactively match the IT organizations' skills and resources appropriately. Similarly, by working with the CFO, the CIO receives a good grounding in the company's business requirements, likely business unit prioritizations, context for the value needed to be created by the IT organization on behalf of the business units, and the available budget for realizing the strategic plan. Susan H. Cramm, a former CIO for Taco Bell, believes that to be *strategically fit* CIOs need to proactively ask themselves:

- Are the benefits articulated as well as the costs?
- Do you have an implementation plan backed up with the money and re-sources to realize it?[38]

Perspectives on expected results such as plans, actions, and deliverables become eas-ily misaligned when nobody asks these questions. The most damaging expectation misalignments occur between the CIO and the other senior executives and the CIO and the staff of the IT organization.

Another key advantage to incorporating resource allocation investigation into the IT strategic plan before going into the company's strategic planning session is that, in today's knowledge age, knowledge workers need expensive machines, plat-forms, and software to execute the *actual work* that lies between the lines of a strate-gic plan. It is therefore critical that the CIO align the IT investment portfolio with the emerging company strategic plan. In the process, the IT investment portfolio and business unit needs and expectations can be brought into similar alignment. The CIO must bring these discussions to the forefront *as the new strategic ideas emerge*, not after they are cast in concrete, to avoid significant differences in the per-ceived priorities of strategies across the business units. Different priorities among the various IT strategies, plans, and projects can only be reconciled by the entire senior executive team, including the CEO; and as the priorities go, so go the abil-ity to execute in terms of skills and resource allocations. Proactively directing the attention of the senior executive team to the matter of resources at the front end of the process is a completely legitimate role for the CIO; citing the matter of re-sources (usually lack) at the back end of the process to explain a failure is disin-genuous—whether legitimate or not.

Number 4: Do We Have Appropriate Measures to Validate Our Execution against the Strategy?

Continuing with the logic that resources fuel strategic execution, those same re-sources are consumed by people whose work needs to be aligned with strategic priorities. CIOs aware of this dynamic deliberately leverage the first law of per-formance management: You get what you measure. Like gravity, while this straight-forward law seems tacitly obvious, little more than half of top executives review IT performance relative to strategic goals and initiatives.[39] Failure to align the work-force with new strategic priorities is the second most common cause of poor strategic execution. To align employees with IT/company strategies, the CIO works together with the entire executive team *during* the strategic planning session to develop IT-related measures of strategic success that apply to technical and non-technical employee group performance. Along the way, a good executive team remembers to measure its own performance. Commitment and clarity are good places to start.

Money is one of the simplest measures of executive commitment to strategic intentions. How well do companies link their overall budget and the priorities of their IT strategic plan? Not all that well: Less than one-third of surveyed IT and business executives say that their companies link their strategic IT priorities with the overall budget. This measure of strategic commitment is measurably more poorly correlated with larger companies. While these executives commonly attribute poor linkage to the complexity of their budgets, a combination of executive shortcomings play important roles, including a failure to communicate the strategic mission within the IT function and throughout the company.[40]

Executive clarity is another important measure of strategic success. Companies can measure executive clarity by measuring how well they communicate their strategic intentions to the rest of the workforce. Well-designed, strategically aligned performance measures are some of a CIO's best means of capturing employee attention and communicating executive intention. How well do companies communicate their strategic missions? It depends on whom you ask. Research shows that 46 percent of IT executives and 62 percent of business executives report clear or adequate strategic communication within their companies.[41] These appalling figures present the CIO with a genuine opportunity to advocate for the needs of both the IT organization and business units. Perhaps though, it might be hoped, those communications that do happen are successful. Not so. Exhibit 4.9 shows how poorly understood the strategic vision is by those who are entrusted with the tactical actions to actually achieve it.[42]

Most senior executives understand their company's strategic vision, but the rate of attrition increases rapidly moving toward the general employee level. As evidence for the first law of performance management, few companies actually measure whether their people understand their strategies. You get what you measure, which means executives in these companies do not create incentives to understand strategic plans. The fact that the IT professionals more consistently believe that they clearly understand the strategy, compared with their management and nontechnical employees, is good news for the strategically minded CIO looking for ways to communicate more clearly. And because professionals from the IT organization work with every person in the company, a well-schooled IT staff can itself become a means of strategic communication for the CIO and the executive team. Given this kind of strategic reach, as a group, CIOs need to put significantly greater efforts into communicating the strategic visions and plans in terms of both the company and the IT organization. Performance measures can help the CIO and executive team determine whether they are communicating clearly.

As the leader of the IT function, the CIO has the responsibility for reviewing the performance of the IT group's contributions to the company's strategic goals.

EXHIBIT 4.9   STRATEGIC COMMUNICATIONS

	Business Executives	IT Executives	Average
Senior Executive Team	87%	83%	85%
Middle Management	78%	66%	73%
Line Management	57%	46%	52%
IT Professionals	59%	61%	60%
General Employees	33%	26%	30%

Source: "The Strategic Alignment Research Study," CIO Insight, 2002.

You get what you measure, so performance measures must be customized for every strategy and every organization. Some industry standards almost always deserve some measurement attention, but what unique measurement profiles does the current strategy demand? Exhibit 4.10 gives a range of performance measurement methodologies that companies use to assess their corporate and IT strategies. Most companies use more than one approach, and while there is general alignment, there are several outliers; especially notable is the higher incidence of formal review for IT strategies over corporate strategies, and this has been attributed to the project orientation of the IT function.[43] To help support strategic execution, performance measurement analysis also needs to happen more than once a decade. In the case of the companies polled for Exhibit 4.10, 71 percent of the corporate executive teams and 67 percent of the IT executive teams met on a monthly or quarterly basis to review performance relative to the strategic goals. Both groups were evenly split between the monthly and quarterly review intervals.[44]

All good performance management methodologies address five key questions at the CIO and executive team level:

1. Are we measuring the right things?

2. Are we measuring these things at the right frequency?

3. Are the measurement results being reviewed and appropriate course corrections being made at the right frequency?

4. Does the entire set of performance measurement and management activities comprise continuous, closed-loop process?

5. Are the measures being applied across the entire IT organization to executives, managers, technical employees, and nontechnical employees?

One very effective approach focuses specifically on the strategic implementation of IT performance measurement—an approach pioneered and advocated by Dr. C. Bruce Kavan.[45] Kavan's first premise is that the key to successful IT

EXHIBIT 4.10 STRATEGIC PERFORMANCE
MEASUREMENT METHODS

	Used to Measure IT Strategic Goals	Used to Measure IT Corporate Goals
Periodic Initiative Review	64%	57%
Gap Analysis	60%	69%
Regular Customer Analysis	50%	48%
Formal Reviews	42%	26%
Balanced Scorecard	25%	32%
Business Intelligence	24%	33%
Hypothesis Testing	19%	18%
Management Analysis	11%	12%

Source: "The Strategic Alignment Research Study," *CIO Insight*, 2002.

performance measurement is a CIO who recognizes that IT is not unique when it comes to performance measurement. There are a number of organizations within a company who have cross-business-unit responsibilities, including human resources, facilities management, finance, and IT. His second premise is that all levels and responsibility types within the IT function can have goals and objectives and can be measured across three distinct levels: the strategic level, the application development level, and the operational level. This structural framework can be very effective in tying together the disparate employee types typical in an IT organization.

Infrastructure and architecture are at the strategic level; these are the template and road map for the IT organization and are the links to the company strategy and initiatives. At the application development level is the set of individual applications that together provide the solutions that fulfill the strategy; and at the operational level is the set of measurements everyone always hears about: service-level agreements, response time, performance, uptime/downtime, "five nines" or less, and the other typical reporting metrics from an operations point of view.

Clearly, as focus shifts from the strategic level to the application development level to the operational level, it becomes less straightforward as to how to link the performance elements to the overall strategy. The successful CIO, however, works with each new strategic version to find the key measures that link back to the business strategy, thereby enabling strategic success. Once strategically aligned performance measures are in place, the business strategy can be used as the compass.

The value that comes from linking each level to the one above it, and the IT strategy to the company business strategy, is that everyone is focused on the same vision, goals, and objectives; the only differences are manifested in each individual's particular role and job responsibility—his or her piece of the "execution pie." Measurement linkage also eliminates the problem shown in Exhibit 4.9. By implementing this approach, the entire organization goes from unconnected and ill-informed to well connected and knowing where they fit in—especially at the bottom of the strategic pyramid where the day-to-day activities of the workforce are usually farthest removed from strategic management concerns.

For example, what is the best way to design performance measures for an IT lab technician? Resist the temptation to jump to the operational level of measurement. Start with the strategic level. In a company that has developed a strategic plan to move its primary presence from domestic markets to international markets, an astute CIO recognizes how this translates into an IT strategy that provides support for international operations and for international customer interactions. The IT lab technician's activities could be measured against both of these aligned strategies—company and IT. Even more important, the IT lab technician could use strategically defined expectations (measures) of his/her performance as a compass to light up the roadway to making the strategy a day-to-day work reality.

Next, moving to the application development level, the CIO could hold this IT lab technician responsible for initial procurement and installation of lab equipment and, eventually, for deployment throughout the company. A reasonable strategically aligned application performance goal would be to move the IT organization to equipment that is approved for use worldwide so that multiple suppliers and/or multiple models and part numbers would not be required for equipment fulfilling the same function. This links the applications level and the strategic goals, and the IT technician's activities cumulatively help achieve company strategy. Last, moving to the operational level, this same IT lab technician could be expected to, one, achieve these performance objectives at quarterly marks and, two, select and monitor equipment that has a good track record for uptime and stability in all the key countries required. This last set of measures is quite operational; but when held up to the light of the strategy, they clearly support strategic execution and communication. Imagine the difference in the poll results if the majority of CIOs used this approach!

Number 5: What IT Shadows Might Cross
Our Short-term Strategic Horizon?

Information technology resources can be carefully aligned with this strategic plan as the executive team understands it today, but experience suggests how quickly strategic priorities can change in a competitive environment and a cost-conscious economy. Before an executive team tests the strength of its new strategy against the challenges of the outside world, someone should at least open an inquiry about unrecognized potential problems from within: "What IT shadows might cross our short-term strategic horizon from your divisions and functions to impact our emerging plan that have not been discussed?" Let's face it. When things go bad, people commonly look for a new tool (or weapon) as the first solution, and the tools usually have something to do with IT. While we're at it, let's face another related practice regarding the human condition: Don't reveal unsuspected weakness in a group setting designed to plan for future success. The CIO should ask about areas of potential trouble for two reasons: One, it makes simple business sense to discover areas of unexpected cost and work cloaked by executive ego; two, openly asking for this information in a "public" setting establishes responsibility for the time when the fan blades need cleaning (aka, a previously secret situation becomes publicly known).

At first glance, the combination of "short-term" and "strategic" might appear incongruous, as "short-term" is typically associated with tactical activities and "long-term" is associated with strategic activities. However, being the senior IT executive, many short-term and long-term strategic priorities cross the CIO's path requiring the IT organization's immediate direct attention. As a strategic enabler, the CIO carefully aligns the IT resources with the strategic plan as it is developed in both the short-term and the long-term perspectives. In the past, many companies developed and executed a strategic plan that would remain relatively static for years, whereas today's instantaneous information gathering, analysis, and knowledge sharing in a more competitive and cost-conscious environment often forces frequent reexaminations, reevaluations, and reprioritizations of plans and actions, and altered or new strategic directions.

In this kind of environmental flux, there is every reason to believe that each member of the senior executive team is likely to experience—indeed, should *expect* to experience—some environmental backlash on the well-crafted business unit version of the overall strategic plan. The best way for the CIO to know what problems might cross peer senior executives' paths (and, subsequently, IT strategic priorities) is to ask them directly: "What IT shadows, which have not been discussed, might cross our short-term strategic horizon from your divisions and functions to impact our emerging plan?" Why should the CIO assume that things are likely to happen that would cause impact?

Common sense says that when business things go bad, people tend to turn to a new or different tool as the first solution, and such tools usually have something to do with IT. Many times in my 30 years of work as an IT professional, a peer executive approached me with a serious business challenge that the executive believed IT could resolve. Enablers know that strategic reprioritizations are part of the job description—even though they may carry implications that ripple through the rest of the strategic plan. In one case, 30 years ago, the company (actually, a university) was having problems accounting for computing time. Certain users and user groups consumed more resources than they were allocated or they could pay for, but the system could not account for user time. After the kind of tedious study that would put the corporate world to shame (many committees and committee meetings, all run by academicians) the decision was made: Get a new accounting system. Thus, it immediately became IT's priority to identify, evaluate, and recommend a new (replacement) accounting system that would solve these problems. This turned out to be a complex, multiyear effort that had the amusing side effect of causing the creation of an internal IT mantra: "All our problems will be over when we get the new accounting system installed next year." In this particular case, the new accounting system was not able to cure all evil, but it did at least allow some chargeback.

In another case, about 20 years ago, the same university was having a similar problem with its users on the now-interactive systems. The problems with accounting and resource control 10 years earlier were with batch-oriented systems fed by card readers. So, 10 years later, the same shadow "suddenly" crossed the IT strategic horizon, and the university decided it needed some means for identifying and controlling nefarious offenders who were using too much computing resources. The "opportunity" for this fell to me. Because these were tight times, the project became a highly charged issue, and the solution a top strategic priority— above all other work by the two-person systems group. The system was defined, approved, designed, implemented, tested, and ready to deploy; and it was actually turned on for a few hours. Then it was turned off when the first complaint came in. Nefarious conduct often starts with senior department heads, (good thing it had an on/off command), and that was the last anyone ever heard of the chargeback and resource utilization problem on that system (at least, while I was there).

Finally, in a case within the last year, a corporate manufacturing executive decided that the e-mail method of managing manufacturing orders, shipment, inventory, service, support, and the rest of operations would not scale into the larger management control systems. The IT people reported to him, so he gave them a new goal of identifying and evaluating a materials resource planning (MRP) system to solve the problem. This priority was grafted onto the existing IT strategy; it figured to not only consume the entire IT staff but also to require at least an order of magnitude increase in the IT workload and budget. Naturally, the familiar IT mantra structure became, "These problems will go away when we get the new MRP system installed." As it turned out, a new MRP system did help, but the one we deliberately installed was more like "MRP-Lite," which matched the needs, abilities, scope, expertise, and pocketbook of the company and the existing IT organization.

In each of these cases, the "unexpected" problems resulted in the *finding* organization looking to the IT organization for a solution; each expected IT (as an enabler) to adjust its priorities to accommodate the finder's needs. These readjustments did not blow the IT strategies completely off-course, but some cast a long shadow and had a significant effect on the priorities of IT's own short-term strategic horizon. Why didn't these needs surface in the strategic planning sessions? Certainly, many of them existed and were even known about, yet never became part of the strategic dialog. The reason is probably related to another workplace practice of the human condition: a reluctance to reveal unsuspected weakness in a group setting that plans for future success. With senior executives, this problem can be both acute and harmful to the company and its business.

In addition to revealing a weakness, many corporate executives experience a reluctance to cause conflict or divisiveness at the top for fear of being labeled a non-team player. Such cultural or social considerations leave the executive team open to "groupthink," a group dynamic that has a high correlation with monumental failures because problem solving requires some openness to healthy conflict. Groupthink refers to the behavior of people who are more concerned with avoiding conflict, animosity, or even endless debate than they are with bringing up and resolving potential problems and issues. Some corporate environments encourage executives to fear the "troublemaker" label to such an extent that the same executives can never rise to the role of problem solver. Importantly—and perhaps contrary to popular management thinking—issue-oriented conflict has been identified with superior executive performance: "[T]he evidence is also overwhelming that low conflict levels are associated with poor decision making."[46]

By asking question number 5, the CIO proactively seeks areas of potential trouble for two reasons: It makes simple business sense to discover areas of unexpected cost and work cloaked by executive ego or social concerns; and openly asking for this information in a public setting establishes responsibility for potential problems when they eventually emerge. As with many things (especially legal), ignorance of a problem (or of the law) is not an acceptable defense for a senior executive. Conversely, as an enabler of the entire company's workforce, the CIO stands as a ready target for blame, that is, the scapegoat, the poor creature upon which all the members of the entire human community purify themselves by ritually transferring their sins and misdeeds (see *Leviticus* 16: 8, 10, 26 KJV).

Number 6: How Dependent Is Our Company's Success on the Successful Execution of Our IT Strategic Plan?

For a CIO, this question hopefully falls into the category of *leading the witness*: The company's success in the strategic time frame hinges on the successful execution of the IT strategic plan. This being the case, support for the CIO's initiatives and strategies, in conjunction with the business unit executives' strategies and initiatives, should be transparent, readily achieved, and have staying power. However, if peer senior executives do not see the IT function as key to the company's strategic needs, the astute CIO either works to change this impression or moves on to a job where the IT organization's strategic plan, and its execution, is valued as a strategic contributor to the overall success of the company.

Earlier questions emphasized that, as an enabler, the CIO needs to take the initiative to include the needs of the senior executive team and their businesses in the formulation of the IT strategy. By preemptively developing the IT strategic plan, the CIO works as much as possible to include and prioritize the elements of the IT strategic plan to match the priorities of the senior executive team members for their businesses and for the company as a whole. As a result, each senior executive should be able to identify with elements in the IT strategy that are critical to that business unit or divisional success. Consequently, all peer executives should be able to see concrete ways that the overall strategic time frame depends on the execution of IT's strategic plan.

Number 7: Does Our IT Strategic Plan Support Our Overall Corporate Strategic Plan?

Just as there is—or should be—an expectation by the CEO that each of the senior executive's strategic plans for his or her business unit are (or will be) developed to support the overall corporate strategic plan, so must it be with the IT strategic plan. Intuitively, this should be the norm; the fact that it is not is both disappointing and a potential trap of executive team expectations that the CIO should avoid falling into. One survey showed that only 34 percent of senior executives believed that the priorities of the IT strategic plan were well linked to the overall corporate strategic plan; and 22 percent said that, from a practical point of view, the result was that there was not an effective or useful linkage between the two.[47] This lukewarm overall perception is not going to give the CIO a strong base from which to enable or to provide IT value. Knowing how each senior executive sees IT strategic alignment within overall strategy helps the CIO create a plan to work with each peer executive to uncover discrepancies in the IT strategic plan and to correct them. Some CIOs believe that the focus of this kind of work should be on correcting non-IT senior executive perceptions so that the nontechnical peers can understand and embrace the original version of the IT strategic plan. Experience suggests, however, that though that type of fix *might* work, it is likely to work only temporarily, until the senior executive thinks it through again.

If the IT strategic plan is to be truly linked to the corporate strategy, it must be visible to the technical and nontechnical executive alike! When it is, it will be obvious not only to the CIO as senior IT executive but also to all of the company's senior executives. Because two-thirds of senior managers report that they review the performance of IT against their company's strategic goals and initiatives, the prudent CIO addresses this concern proactively.[48] When it comes to budgeting, the strategic plans of those organizations in a company that support the overall strategic plan are certain to have an easier time gaining agreement on and approval for their budgets. This is especially true for the CIO, as the majority of the IT budget is rationalized against the needs and support of the company's business units. As before, the best way to do this is to directly work with the senior executives *before* major executive team strategic planning activities.

Number 8: Is There a Clear Linkage between Our IT Strategy and Our Company's Competitive Strategy?

Research has shown that those companies that have a high level of integration of IT strategic planning with overall corporate strategic planning clearly benefit from IT value creation for their company and for their business units.[49] John Valente, VP of information systems for Best Buy, sees this as one of his roles as a middleman between the CIO and the senior executives of Best Buy's business units. He works in a unique position that allows him to not only see why decisions are being made but also to help translate how those decisions create value and optimize the total cost of ownership (TCO). As a senior IT executive, Valente participates in strategic planning and then translates the company's strategic plan and the IT strategic plan into business, development, and technology integration points of view. Once again, the CIO and the *entire* senior executive team must be partners in all three strategic plans (corporate, business unit, and IT).

Successful companies create competitive strategies through processes that are flexible enough to allow for evolution as the competitive environment changes or as more information about the existing environment becomes available. Ensuring that the company and the IT organization are on the right path starts with taking a *strategic inventory*;[50] that is, ask these 10 questions and compare the answers between peer senior executives and the answers from the IT senior management. The quality of information and understanding from the strategic inventory are improved when the CIO also includes all levels of the IT organization for a more comprehensive picture of the health of the IT strategy and initiatives.

The competitive strategy of the company is likely to be a function of the type of company the senior executives have decided to make it. Applicable descriptive terms such as *defender, prospector, analyzer,* or *reactor* help the CIO to match up the IT strategic plan and initiatives in terms of the company's competitive style and approach. That is, if the CIO works with the senior executive of a business focused on a *defender* strategy, then the aligned IT strategic plan and initiatives might very well need to be focused similarly as they apply to this business unit. It is unlikely that the senior executive for such a business unit would advocate a *prospector* pro-file for his or her portion of the IT budget and his or her portion of the IT initia-tives. Knowing your customer is always important.

Number 9: Based on Our Corporate Strategy, Can We Do a SWOT of the IT Portfolio?

This really lays it on the line for a CIO: asking the entire senior executive team to do a strengths/weaknesses/opportunities/threats (SWOT) exercise of the IT port-folio in the context of the corporate strategy sounds like a risky proposition. It may well be as much risk for the other senior executives as for the CIO, because some IT projects favored by particular peer executives may not stand up to the scrutiny of a SWOT analysis, and the emphasis and resources of the IT organization might be reallocated based on the outcome of such an analysis.

The following matrix shows a simple representation of the SWOT concept:

Strengths	Weaknesses
Opportunities	Threats

where the executive team makes an assessment of the company's offerings versus its competitors and places each offering in the most appropriate box. Strengths and weaknesses are considered to be controllable as they are related to decisions and ac-tions by the company. Strengths and weaknesses come in two forms, the *absolute* and the *relative*. Absolute applies to many or all; relative applies to one versus the other. For example, a company with an IT infrastructure that supports real-time updating of inventory has an absolute advantage against those who do not have the ability to update inventory electronically; this would be an absolute strength. Whereas a company with an IT infrastructure that supports real-time updating of inventory electronically *may* have a relative advantage over a company that can only update its inventory on a daily basis, this would be a relative strength. In an-other example, a company that cannot track its delivery trucks has an absolute dis-advantage—weakness—against those companies that know where their trucks are at any point in time. In contrast, a company that can track trucks once a day is at a relative disadvantage—weakness—to one that can know where its trucks are in real time.

An opportunities/threats analysis usually follows the strengths/weaknesses analysis because opportunities and threats are considered to be uncontrollable; they are forces acting on the company externally. Opportunities are areas where it is possible for the company to improve its position, while threats are difficulties that will be encountered and that will need to be addressed. However, looking at competitive opportunities and threats takes a broader strategic view than strengths and weaknesses, and as such, reversing the usual order and performing an opportunity/threat analysis first can be more effective for some companies.

For example, there may be an opportunity to reduce the number of delivery trucks as the company expands the number of points of delivery each truck must make. At the same time, there may be a threat of increased delivery times and higher accident rates (both leading to higher costs of delivery) due to company expansion in areas of inclement weather. From the CIO's point of view, whether the results confirm the current strategy and initiatives or suggest significant revision *should* be irrelevant. What should matter is that the IT portfolio actually matches the corporate strategy.

Number 10: Is There a Difference between Our Intended and Our Realized Strategies?

Is it possible for a senior executive team to execute a strategic plan and an accompanying set of aligned initiatives that match their intentions while remaining aligned with a corporate strategy that does not live up to executive expectations? All too often, and usually as a result of how the strategy was created. Rather than developing the strategy from tomorrow backward, strategies that fail to live up to executive expectations are designed from today forward. In other words, rather than engaging in a strategic planning session to create *future-based intentions,* many executive teams actually only perform *incremental planning,* also known as *incrementalizing.*[51] "Strategies" designed according to an incremental plan-over-plan approach usually have incrementally *realized* results. However, a different approach is needed if the CIO and the executive team intend to design a strategy that looks back from future results goals. This kind of strategy is plotted from the future *intentions* to the present.

When the CIO asks peer senior executives if they see a difference between the intended and realized strategies, he/she may be asking a question that the execs may not be able to answer—maybe not even the CEO. Historically, the results of the company's "strategies" that were designed according to the realized approach actually were the results of incrementalizing rather than strategic planning. If strategic planning is the means by which major business achievements are envisioned by the company (to be realized by the actions and plans of the senior executive team and their employees), then it is essential that the CIO and the senior executive team are in agreement on how to create a strategic plan.

Strategically mature CIOs want to be in an organization where strategic planning is *inquisitive, demanding, confrontational, inventive, expansive, prescient,* and *inclusive.* Contrast this with an organization where strategic planning is *ritualistic, easy, positioning, reductionist, extrapolative,* and *elitist.* The latter organization is one likely filled with boundaries and where strategic planning is probably considered to be one of those necessary evils.[52] If this matches your organization, and you are not able to change that view, then it will be very difficult to be an enabler for the company and the senior executive team because the company culture does not believe in strategic planning. If the realized strategy is significantly different from the envisioned strategy, then from one point of view that could be very good: If the realized strategy is the result of enlightenment and adaptation to new information to improve the competitive position of the company, then it is good news; if the realized strategy is the result of poor execution or lack of execution, then it's bad news. Yet, if the realized strategy is the same as the envisioned strategy, and both are lame, then the lack of difference could be disastrous.

At all times, the CIO must keep in mind that strategic planning with the senior executive teams is about the alignment and future health and well-being of the corporate strategic plan, the IT strategic plan, and the senior executives' strategic plans. The CIO's responsibilities are to enable the success of the other two strategic plans by implementing an aligned IT strategic plan. Their success is your success, and your success is in enabling them to be successful.

NOTES

1. Paul A. Strassmann, *Power Politics of the CIO,* Luncheon talk at the Armed Forces Communications and Electronics Association, March 19, 2003.
2. I strongly recommend Stacy Hall and Jan Brogniez's *Attracting Perfect Customers* (San Francisco, CA: Berrett-Koehler Publishers, 2001) for every CIO serious about customer relationship management—both internal and external. What I find intriguing and universally applicable about this book is that it has some very down-to-earth and practical ideas, observations, and actions that are natural follow-ons to market segmentation, in the spirit of *Crossing the Chasm* by Geoffrey Moore. The basis for the author's approach is what they call "Creating synchronicity with perfect customers and clients," and they advocate replacing the thought "We need more customers" with the conviction "Our business now attracts perfect customers only."
3. Mohanbir Sawhney, "How to Keep Your Customers Happy," *CIO Magazine,* www.cio.com/archive/050103/netgains.html (accessed May 3, 2003).
4. Stanley Kelly-Bootle, *The Devil's DP Dictionary* (New York: McGraw-Hill, 1981): 85–86.
5. Hall and Brogniez, *Attracting Perfect Customers.*
6. Ibid., p. vii.
7. Ibid., pp. 17–24.
8. Rahul Jacob, "Why Some Customers Are More Equal Than Others," *Fortune* 130, no. 6 (1994): 220.
9. Daniel Goleman, *Emotional Intelligence* (New York: Bantam Books, 1997); and Richard E.

Boyatzis and Ellen Van Oosten, "Developing Emotionally Intelligent Organizations," Roderick Millar, ed., *International Executive Development Programmes*, 7th ed. (London: Kogan Page Publishers, 2002).

10. Sawhney, "How to Keep Your Customers Happy."

11. Ibid.

12. Ashton Applewhite, William R. Evans, III, and Andrew Frothingham, *And I Quote* (New York: St. Martin's Press, 1992): 471.

13. Jerry N. Luftman, Raymond Papp, and Tom Brier, "Enablers and Inhibitors of Business-IT Alignment," Communications of the Association for Information Systems, vol. 1, article 11 (March 1999): 16.

14. Adapted from Kenneth Primozic, Edward Primozic, and Joe Leben, *Strategic Choices: Supremacy, Survival, or Sayonara* (New York: McGraw-Hill, 1991): 110–112.

15. Applewhite, et al., p. 236.

16. John V. Buckley, *Going for Growth: Realizing the Value of Technology* (New York: McGraw-Hill, 1998): 108.

17. Stanley Kelly-Bootle, *The Devil's DP Dictionary* (New York: McGraw-Hill, 1981): 115.

18. New Technologies Research from *CIO Insight* (June 2003): 2; available at: http://common .ziffdavisinternet.com/download/0/2090/RESEARCH_0603.pdf.

19. Clayton Christensen, *The Innovator's Dilemma: When New Technologies Cause Great Firms to Fail* (Boston: Harvard Business School Press, 1997). I highly recommend this book. It is one of the best on technology, innovation, and corporate evolution I have ever read. The philosophy and observations brought to the discussion by Professor Christensen have driven my thinking for some time, and they were the basis for the philosophy of the storage division at Dell.

20. Statement made to Dr. Richard Daystrom, on the M-5 computer from Jill Sherwin, *Quotable Star Trek* (New York: Pocket Books, 1999): 257.

21. *CIO Magazine,* "CIO Quick Poll: Is your IT department a" www2.cio.com/poll/previous_h3.cfm?ID=89 (accessed June 3, 2003).

22. *CIO Magazine*, "CIO Research Reports: Measuring IT Value," www2.cio.com/research/surveyreport.cfm?id=1 (accessed June 9, 2003).

23. Ibid.

24. Richard A. Goodman and Michael W. Lawless, *Technology and Strategy* (New York: Oxford University Press, 1994): 9.

25. Ibid., p. 27.

26. David Brooks, "Essay: A Nation of Grinders," *New York Times Magazine* (June 29, 2003): 15.

27. As quoted in Ibid., p. 16.

28. Derek Slater, "Strategic Planning Don'ts (and Do's)," *CIO Magazine* (June 1, 2002): 84.

29. Lorraine Cosgrove, "CIO Research Reports: The State of the CIO 2003," *CIO.com*, www2.cio.com/research/surveyreport.cfm?id=54 (accessed March 26, 2003).

30. Brooks, "Nation of Grinders," p. 86.

31. "The Strategic Alignment Research Study: Strategy Research Results," *CIO Insight*, Special Issue 2002 (2002): 5; available at: ftp:ftp.cioinsight.com/pub/cioinsight/01/15/research_strategy.ppt

32. Suresh K. Nair, "Identifying Technology Horizons for Strategic Investment Decisions," *IEEE Transactions on Engineering Management* 44, no. 3 (1997): 227.

33. "Strategic Alignment Research Study," p. 7.

34. Cosgrove, "CIO Research Reports," p. 4.

35. Ann Therese Palmer, "How Kraft 'Primed the Pump' for Alignment," *CIO Insight* (July 1, 2002): 1.

36. Erik Sherman, "CIOs' New Choice: Get Strategic . . . Or Else!" *CIO Insight* online, www.cioinsight.com/print_article/0,3668,a=29362,00.asp (accessed May 26, 2003).

37. "CIO Research Reports: The State of the CIO 2002," *CIO.com,* www.cio.com/archive/030102/survey_results_content.html (accessed June 1, 2003).

38. Susan H. Cramm, "Leadership Agenda: Get Strategically Fit," *CIO.com,* www.cio.com/leadership/edit/la0226022_strategy.html (accessed June 24, 2003).

39. "Strategic Alignment Research Study, p. 8.

40. Ibid., p. 9.

41. Ibid., p. 6.

42. Ibid., p. 7.

43. Ibid., p. 8.

44. Ibid., p. 9.

45. Joe and Catherine Stenzel, "Implementing IT Performance Measurement: An Interview with Dr. Bruce Kavan," *Journal of Strategic Performance Measurement* 1, no. 6 (December 1997): 14–21.

46. Kathleen M. Eisenhardt, Jean L. Kahwajy, and L. J. Bourgeois III, "Conflict and Strategic Choice: How Top Management Teams Disagree," excerpted from *Navigating Change: How CEOs, Top Teams, and Boards Steer Transformation,"* by the Harvard Business School Press, in *Engineering Management* 26, no. 1 (Spring 1998): 28.

47. "Strategic Alignment Research Study," p. 13.

48. Ibid., p. 7.

49. Yash P. Gupta, Jahangir Karimi, and Toni M. Somers, "Alignment of a Firm's Competitive Strategy and Information Technology Management Sophistication: The Missing Link," *IEEE Transactions on Engineering Management* 44, no. 4 (November 1997): 404.

50. Joseph C. Picken and Gregory G. Dess, "Out of (Strategic) Control," excerpted from *Organizational Dynamics* by the American Management Association, in *Engineering Management* 26, no. 1 (Spring 1998): 48.

51. Gary Hamel, "Strategy as Revolution," Chapter 2 in *Seeing Differently: Insights on Innovation,* edited, with an introduction by John Seely Brown, (Boston: Harvard Business Review Publishing, 1997): 19–37.

52. Ibid., p. 24.

CHAPTER 5

Focus and Prioritization

[Like a laser,] a well-crafted and well-understood strategy can, through alignment and coherence of the organization's limited resources, produce a nonlinear performance breakthrough.

—Kaplan & Norton[1]

The appropriate focus of top management is on above-the-line issues that have the greatest impact on the future success of the organization.

—Primozic, Primozic, and Leben[2]

If we have not started it, it costs us nothing to change it.

—Karl D. Schubert, 1991

*F**ocus* and *prioritization* always challenge people who work in a senior executive position, especially the CIO. By the vary nature of your job, you have a strategic *and* a tactical role. Although the CIO's role is supposed to be primarily strategic, CIOs are forever associated with the IT group. Consequently, the CIO must be prepared to handle any number of tactical issues, and even projects, whether the position involves direct IT group management responsibilities. As such, the CIO is continually challenged to stay focused on achieving strategic objectives while prioritizing key personal work activities and IT organizational work activities to meet enabling commitments to peers and partners.

Specifically, the CIO works in partnership with peers to ensure that the company's organizational strategies are translated into actionable plans that the IT team can execute. The CIO demonstrates an enabling partnership relationship by visibly aligning and prioritizing IT resources with commitments made to peers. There will be times when you want to say no, but you know that you cannot. Knowing when to rearrange priorities for the good of the company, customers, or partners and peers is also important to CIO success.

Water runs downhill, and considering the CIO's strategic responsibilities, there are some focus and priority questions the CEO should be asking the CIO. The 10 Questions sections in this book have usually focused on questions the CIO can use to seek information from others. A shrewd CIO also expects similar questions to be asked of IT in return, especially from the CEO. When none are forthcoming, the CIO is wise to take some risks and find out why not. Like most strong leaders, a capable CIO knows and manages his/her own risk profile to achieve timely opportunities and gains. A personal risk profile can be characterized in terms of chain of command, timing, technology, personnel, market conditions, and other IT work variables that might pressure a CIO to lose focus or disrupt key strategic priorities. Mapping and knowing one's personal risk profile allows the CIO to anticipate and manage situations that might otherwise disrupt focus and priority work. Armed with a personal risk profile, the CIO can extend the map to individual strategies. Finally, the focus and prioritization work of the CIO must be continuously adaptive: If you haven't started something, it costs nothing to change what you might have done.

If strategy is an endpoint, then business plans are the means for realizing strategic goals. As the senior IT executive, the CIO works two levels of strategy: the company's strategy and the IT organization's strategy. The IT strategy and plans visually align with the strategic needs of the company when they are mapped together. As an enabling role, the CIO's strategic map also includes the strategies and plans of peers and partners, and they need to be able to see and buy in to the map's strategic interdependencies.

What means can the CIO use to translate strategies into actionable business plans? That depends on what needs to be done, what gets measured, and what is done with measurement information. One of the more thought-provoking authors in this area is H. Thomas Johnson, who advocates moving away from *management by results* and toward *management by means*. In his book *Profit Beyond Measure*, Johnson argues that the most commonly used measurement systems have moved businesses from an operational focus to a financial-accounting obsession.[3] The long-term implications are disastrous for both product-based companies and IT organizations in any company.

The management focus derailment has a well-documented history, but the argument is elegant and relatively transparent. The rise of financial planners and accountants has pushed business focus and priorities too far away from the most fundamental management information and insights: knowing how the business *operates* and how the work is organized. As companies became increasingly obsessed with looking good in terms of financial numbers (after all, that's how successful executives are ultimately measured and rewarded), executives had less and less incentive to focus on improving the ways that the company actually *performed* the operational work that delivered the product or service revenues. The company and its customers took a back seat to the interests of Wall Street and shareholders as executives managed lagging financial indicators rather than the value-creating leading performance measures of the company's work operations. Financial obsessions and the rise of management accounting to control operational organizations led to the stagnation and decline of businesses during the 1960s and 1970s and have visibly resurfaced with the bursting of the stock market bubble. As an operationally grounded strategic enabler, the CIO stands as one of the key senior executives who can steer company leadership back to measuring how to create value for all stakeholders, rather than only wealth for shareholders.

People with strong financial backgrounds generally become even more reactionary during bull markets and may find this logic hard to swallow. An entire layer of IBM executives in the 1980s rose on the coattails of the executives who created IBM's mainframes (the S/360 and S/370 systems and software). This new layer of executives was characterized by a lack of leadership and dearth of real knowledge about the company's products, technologies, and customers (a condition later recognized by Lou Gerstner). They successfully toadied up to the executives above them and bullied down to those below them. The result was a company where individual executive "numbers" (results) looked good, but leadership languished, products got old, and in the end, IBM nearly went bankrupt. But, as Johnson would probably observe, *they had only to understand the intricacies of financial reporting.* Of course, a more contemporary set of companies in this same financially obsessed club includes WorldCom and Enron.

Johnson reminds us that the accounting methodologies and companies that focus on them as top management priorities are getting just what they ask for—even if they do not really realize what it is that they are asking for. That is, the financial-accounting obsession causes executives to focus on meeting numerical abstractions that give a lagging, unbalanced perspective on company health. The parallels to leading and managing an IT organization are obvious. If you manage by results, you end up managing to a set of dated numbers—very quantitative. You may well succeed in meeting your "numbers" and at the same time see your company, peers, and partners fail. Understanding the business is a proven CIO success factor in the eyes of fellow IT professionals and in the eyes of IT's customers. Managing by financial numbers is a poor substitute for understanding the business and technology of the company.

Management by means is the logical focus for product-based companies, and by extension, operationally oriented IT organizations: Agree on what to do and measure how well it gets done from an operational point of view. In other words, manage resources to match customer and business needs based on what you can afford—judgment and partnership calls—and forget the by-the-numbers accounting-sheet format priorities.

More operational logic. Which is more natural: working to a set of measurements that have been artificially created to *account* and *control* or working to a set of measurements that capture the quality and efficiency of the activities and work that is actually being performed to create a service or product? In fact, in a company that manages by means there are only very small roles for financial accountants and no need for a controller. Why? Because expenditures are managed to match business, and the responsibility for this lies in the hands of senior executives. IT expenditures and deliverables against them are fully in the CIO's hands. The role of the financial planning and analysis (FP&A) administrator is reconfigured but remains important. The focus and priorities of this person also reorient to the activities and work performed in terms of what IT needs to save and spend to fulfill its strategic obligations. This is *not* an accountant; and, once you have worked with both, you will be able to spot one from another a mile (or more) away. The operationally oriented FP&A administrator sees the role as a partnership with IT to achieve *operational* goals by managing the *means* IT has to reach these goals that focus on real costs, expenditures, deliverables, revenues, and enablement.

Johnson observes that the operationally focused management-by-means approach is aligned with the ways that living systems work, and operationally oriented CIOs are very likely to feel right at home with this way of focusing IT work priorities. Efforts to maneuver this kind of CIO into abstract accountinglike approaches feel very unnatural because it becomes difficult to focus on operational enabling responsibilities while working to look good from an accounting point of view. Leading performance indicators measure the operational work that creates value; lagging financial indicators report results that can't be changed. The logic of the operational IT leadership focus is undeniable because strategic priorities are realized by shaping present work conditions to meet future goals. Like product-based companies, IT organizations have to spend money to create value, and if the CIO chooses to reduce R&D to the lowest possible number, revenue and value creation are sure to follow. The only business designed to save money itself is banking. Brian Maskell (an operationally gifted accountant) puts it very well:

> [T]he accounting and operational people really [need to] come together and face the fact that the assumptions built into a traditional accounting system, and the assumptions built into a lean, world-class operations method are different assumptions. [And] the traditional accounting methods and the newer approaches such as strategic performance measures are not just two views of the same thing but are, in fact, in conflict with each other. Then they work together to develop an approach that is meaningful to everyone within the organization.[4]

It is becoming abundantly clear that the traditional accounting-based means of measurements for product-based companies and technology-based groups fall significantly short in enabling value creation. Accounting-based methods are founded in analysis and fall short in environments where intuition, insight, qualitative (in contrast to quantitative) considerations prevail. For the most part, the nonfinance/nonaccounting community has recognized this for decades. Recently, even the finance and accounting professions have begun to realize that a change is necessary.[5]

To be a contributing member of the executive team, the CFO and his/her staff must focus not only on the analytical but must also allow—and even participate in—the strategic and operational planning and management of the corporation. The CIO has the opportunity to help the CFO evolve through such approaches as excellence by example, and both become full business and strategy partners. To do so, they release the requirement for pure facts and endless analysis and make use of intuition, common sense, and good judgment. Lack of willingness to do so ultimately has the same effect seen by those companies that worked hard early on to be Baldridge Award winners and in a short periods afterward went bankrupt: They focused solely on the *process* and *numbers*. In a recent survey, experienced professionals in a variety of roles were asked how frequently they used intuition in their work: 57 percent said they did so often or always, while 43 percent said they did sometimes, seldom, or never.[6]

CIO RISK PROFILE ASSESSMENT

One of the most interesting professional experiences is how one's risk profile changes and becomes more mature with different jobs and greater levels of responsibility because risk often clouds any person's ability to focus and prioritize. Here "risk profile" means the amount of risk that a person willingly accepts, or recommends that others accept, to achieve a predetermined goal. In the earlier years of my working life, I was a chemical engineer responsible for proposing, designing, supervising construction and startup, and bringing on-line production lines for new products. We process/project engineers were responsible for everything from start to finish because the company I worked for was very small. Because most of the chemicals we worked with were highly toxic, they all came with a level of risk (a risk profile). The level of risk I would choose in my production proposals could well affect me, my company, and many others in the chemical plant. Such risks could often be immediately life-threatening, and the consideration of risk in that environment taught me the value of evaluating levels of risk throughout my career.

As a computer industry executive, my experience in risk profile has varied through the years. With the passage of time, I accepted an increased risk profile; that is, I have become more comfortable with more risk—risk in development schedules, risk in cost estimates, risk in career choices. Certainly, you could consider substituting the word "aggressiveness" for "risk" in these situations, but the point is the same. Without significant risk, there is not the opportunity for significant gain. Some CIOs may well be responsible for an IT organization or strategy that carries similar immediate risks—a hospital, a nuclear power plant, a transportation authority—but the role carries significant first-hand or second-hand risks for partners and peers in almost all companies. This section of *The Guide* continues its focus on CIO self-awareness by exploring how risk profile assessments can improve IT executive decision making. Like most other aspects of professional development, risk profiles change with the internal and external workplace environment. An agile CIO looks at each situation to determine the proper level of risk by using personal risk profile awareness to generate a risk management strategy that takes advantage of significant opportunities. Such a CIO becomes much more comfortable using the word "yes" and less automatic about using the word "no."

Risk Profile Spectrum

The following descriptive terms are a good way of identifying and internalizing one's position on the risk profile spectrum.

- Lunatic fringe
- Bleeding-edge
- Leading-edge
- Not-on-the-edge
- Trailing-edge
- What edge?

What do these terms mean and how do they apply to risk? People commonly see themselves on different points of the spectrum than their peers do. Like the perception of risk itself, these terms are relative and the relativity is based on the perspective of the observer. With *leading-edge* in the middle position on the risk spectrum, each term characterizes a common approach to risk and its management forward and backward in terms of more and less risk.

What edge? People who work with a *what edge?* risk profile shun anything that has any risk whatsoever. When a product-related topic comes up, these people look for the reassurance (with facts) that they will be the last to deploy this product. Such people have commonly been burned one or more times by involvement in a higher risk profile project and have resolved to not get caught again taking risk.

Trailing-edge. The *trailing-edge* risk profile wants to minimize risk whenever possible. That is not to say that no risk is the only acceptable option, just that whatever little risk there is clearly mitigated with alternatives and backups. CIOs with this risk profile can commonly be found in an organization or company where IT is not treated as a strategic asset or there is not a sense of peers and partners or enabling. IT is an expense, and this person's management expects the expenses to be minimized. However, when everyone else (the majority, plus those who take on more risk than the majority) accepts a risk proposition, it becomes a valid justification for a trailing edger to accept it too.

Not-on-the-edge. People with the *not-on-the-edge* risk profile want to be sure they do what everyone else is doing. People with this profile see safety in numbers. They can only be wrong if everyone else is wrong. An old saying comes to mind: "No one ever got fired for choosing IBM." A person with this risk profile can commonly be found in an organization where IT is considered an asset and important enough to day-to-day operations. The CIO's boss, peers, and partners develop significant concerns when a major IT problem occurs or if they are not being given the competitive tools, applications, and information available to their competitors. This does not generalize into providing competitive advantages, only that this person will not be providing a trailing-edge environment.

Leading-edge. A CIO with the *leading-edge* risk profile is comfortable taking some risk, focused on providing competitive advantage for peers and partners, and cares about enabling them for success. A person with this risk profile is less concerned about safety in numbers and usually watches several companies with an equal to or greater risk profile to ensure competitive advantage. The CIO with a leading-edge risk profile also develops a comparable leading-edge budget to be in several key areas that involve major competitive issues for the company and for one or more peers and partners. If you have this risk profile, you probably have a champion or two among those peers and partners who are close to you and encourage you to take this approach. They see your value in their portion of the business.

Bleeding-edge. A person with the *bleeding-edge* risk profile thrives on risk and the balancing of risk to gain in nearly all professional endeavors. This CIO is entrepreneurial, focused on getting out in front of technology, applications, and information, and looks to ensure that the company, peers, and partners are enabled by a clear competitive advantage. The CIO with this risk profile realizes that competitive advantage could be lost to an emerging leading-edge-crowd key competitor at any time. Budgets follow this risk profile carefully; and because bleeding-edge approaches are often fraught with risk, these CIOs carry significant budgets.

The risk with a bleeding-edge profile is greatest in being too consistently "ahead of your time." People with this profile tend to believe they are woefully behind the competition, when in fact they are significantly ahead of the competition, the customers, and the technology. Conversely, the bleeding-edge risk profile can yield significant business gains that can make it difficult for the competition to replicate and catch up. Examples of this in recent times are Dell's online order taking and Wal-Mart's entire history in EDI.

Lunatic fringe. An IT executive with the *lunatic fringe* risk profile can be found either far out in front of technology or unaware of the risks and risk mitigation. People with this profile belong in an organization doing research work, or perhaps in an academic environment. Such a person commonly fails to consider the level of risk that can be absorbed by the IT organization or the company. These are the people who talk about the future as if it will happen today, and woe be to those who are susceptible to their Siren's song. Such a person is unlikely to have the right balance of technology and business savvy to be a CIO. A CTO, perhaps, but not a CIO.

Most successful CIOs have a leading-edge risk profile for most of their decisions but have the ability to be situational in their decision-making risk profile. That is, they successfully tailor a risk strategy to match a particular project, environment, time period, and/or partner and peer (even relative to their CEO when necessary and appropriate). Successful executives must be able to work with varying levels of risk; yet to make any significant progress, a self-aware CIO learns to strategically select and deploy a risk profile in terms of the actual risk, the opportunity it presents, the timing, the means, and the ends, matching risk with reward for all concerned.

Matching Risk Profiles to Strategies

An agile, forward-thinking CIO develops a risk profile for each of the company's key strategies, each of which considers a number of factors:

- The importance of that strategy to the company's overall success
- The importance of that strategy to the CIO's partners' and peers' success
- The complexity of factors in realizing that strategy
- The CIO's and the IT organization's ability to assist
- Any other factors that may be specific to the company's industry.

It may often be less important which risk profile you prefer in comparison to your ability to match the right risk profile with a particular strategy.

Imagine the permutations and combinations. Within these risk profiles—and visible through the descriptions—are the next-layer considerations. The subject of innovation and risk was the theme of an entire issue for a respected technical management journal. This journal has one of the better descriptions for a cross-reference of Probability of Failure with Consequences of Failure to form a risk matrix, as shown in Exhibit 5.1. Using this tool, the CIO, IT team, partners, and peers can place significant strategies into the appropriate column and row for risk management assessment and discussion.

The matrix becomes an objective way to begin discussing different perspectives on risk management that supports the needs of strategic intentions. It is not uncommon for a CIO to find a particular project placed in the high-risk portion of the risk matrix and be comfortable with that assessment. Peers, partners, and IT team members usually do not share the same level of comfort with this level of risk. Conversely, some strategies demonstrate a low-risk assignment on the risk matrix where peers and partners believe that the CIO is too conservative. This kind of overly cautious posture may be due to a lack of familiarity with the particular strategy area or required implementation. Alternatively, someone may convincingly believe that a significantly higher priority needs to be on the particular strategy, and the CIO becomes willing to tolerate and manage to higher risk when the overall picture has been clearly articulated.

Most people can more easily tolerate higher risk on a strategy that has a lower failure severity than the risk involved in a strategy with higher failure severity— with a few exceptions. Consider the case where the failure severity related to *no* movement in the strategy is greater than the severity of a noncatastrophic failure? In this case, the risk of no action (or progress) exceeds the risk of taking action (or progress). This is why each strategy needs to have its own risk profile matched to the business, technical, and organizational readiness, not dissimilar to a portfolio risk analysis perspective.

This is one of the major differences that distinguishes the role of CIO from that of a technical manager: It is all about business, value-add, value creation, partnership, and enabling of your peers. In matching strategies to risk, if your risk profile is too aggressive, you put yourself, your peers, and your company at risk. Conversely, if your risk profile is not aggressive enough, you put yourself, your peers and your company at risk. Interesting! In the end, the CIO can learn better decision-making focus and prioritization by becoming aware of personal risk profiles and choosing a balanced, flexible approach to risk that encompasses the needs of strategy and strategic implementation matched with the risk profiles of the technology, the business, the competition, and partners and peers.

EXHIBIT 5.1   QUANTIFYING RISK

Probability of Failure

Score	Maturity	Complexity	Dependency
Low	Existing technology	Simple design	Not limited to existing system or clients. No external or uncontrollable events are likely to impact on the project.
Moderate	Major change	Moderate increase	Moderate risk to schedule or performance due to dependence on existing system, facility, or processes. The effect on cost is moderate.
Major	State of art; research unfinished	Extremely complex	Schedule and performance are dependent on new system and process. Very high cost or schedule risk.

Consequences of Failure

Score	Cost Estimate	Schedule	Reliability	Performance
Low	Budget not exceeded	Negligible impact on program/path	Minimal or no reliability consequence.	Minimal or no performance consequence.
Moderate	Exceeded by <15%	Small slip; starting to impact critical path	Some reduction in reliability.	Some reduction in system performance May require moderate debugging.
Major	Exceeded by >50%	Large slips; system will miss client time frame	Reliability goals cannot be achieved under current plan.	Performance goals cannot be achieved. Results may not be usable.

Risk Matrix

	High	Moderate Risk	High Risk	High Risk
Severity	Medium	Low Risk	Moderate Risk	High Risk
	Low	Low Risk	Low Risk	Moderate Risk
		Low	Medium	High
			Likelihood	

Source: Jeffrey K. Pinto, "Project Management 2002," *IEEE Engineering Management Review*, vol. 31, no. 1 (First Quarter 2003); 92–106.

Knowing When to Say Yes!—Regardless of Risk

Over the past several years there has been a considerable amount of attention paid to helping leaders and managers know when to say no—a never-ending lesson. Knowing when to say yes is just as important. Saying yes is a form of commitment to partners, peers, bosses, and the company. Granted, information and circumstances may change, and while most people occasionally decide to run a risk profile greater than they normally would, the CIO must clearly understand and internalize that this simple word implies a commitment. Those to whom you have committed will undoubtedly be counting on you and your team to deliver. If the CIO answers yes to a major enabler for one of the CIO's other partners and peers, the CIO's commitment (with the appropriate risk profile) becomes part of *their* business commitments.

So, when should the CIO say yes? The strongest case for agreeing to a service commitment is when there is clear alignment of the request with the company's business strategy and goals, the CIO's understanding of the priority of the request, and the IT organization's ability to meet the requirement in the time required and with the quality expected. As CIO, it may also be necessary to recognize when your team does not want to say yes yet saying yes is the right thing to do. Certainly, if the commitment is made it will be expected to be met; however, if the commitment is not made, then significant opportunities might be missed. The latter case may not be obvious in the moment but is likely recognizable just as the moment passes (accountants call it "opportunity cost"). Once the opportune moment has passed, it often cannot be recaptured.

I had the (mis)fortune of seeing how an unwillingness to say yes can be significantly detrimental while working as one of a company's senior executives. We were in an introductory meeting with a potential partner (a major corporation) to whom we could potentially OEM our product. From my company, the chief operating officer, the VP of marketing and sales, and the chief architect attended. The director of marketing, director of sales for a specific vertical market, senior architect, and a senior engineering manager represented the potential customer's company. We later found out that the senior architect was widely known as "Dr. No," not after the James Bond character but rather after someone who demonstrates intelligence but who says no first and asks questions later (if at all).

Dr. No's presence at this meeting was ominous for us and for those who could have used our help in this other company. Even his body language said no. After the usual introductions, the other company's marketing and sales executives talked about their needs and the challenges they were facing from a competitive point of view. Once we described what it was that we were doing and how we could potentially help, it was clear to us all that we could work together to solve some of their sales gaps—all of us *except* Dr. No. The fact that their sales and marketing teams really did have a gap to be filled turned out to be unimportant to Dr. No. Rather than working to help his company solve a real problem, this senior technical expert/architect was working only to make sure that the final solution came from his organization, and if it could not be sourced from within, then it could not be done at all. He was able to do this because he was a very strong personality and was able to prevent them from either developing or finding a solution. He (and his managers) had clearly not learned when it was right to say yes for the benefit of the company, partners, peers, and (needy) customers. His managers appeared to have abdicated their responsibilities by allowing one person to stand in the way of a clear yes solution to the marketing and sales teams difficulties, even though they might not yet know all the steps in the process.

It is important for you, the CIO, and the senior IT staff to not get caught up in the wake of a Dr. No or even to generate a first reaction of no when a new need or request comes your way. Listen to yourself and to your team: Is the first reaction to requests no? If so, the reputation for "can't do" quickly follows. Corrective measures are not difficult. When preparing any response, practice the "think twice, speak once" method. Actually take the time and mental cycles to carefully evaluate the request by gathering more information for a more informed response. Peers and partners see the CIO who answers yes a bit too often in a far more favorable light than one who uses no too frequently. The same teams who risk saying yes miss far fewer opportunities. "Just say no to Dr. No!" and you and your management team are well on your way to ensuring that your organization's strategies and priorities are lined up with the needs of your company and your business.

To make this long story short, the lack of awareness regarding personal risk profile tendencies undermines the focus and judgment of any person working under the tremendous responsibilities of the senior technology executive. Focus and judgment are prerequisites of informed, balanced decision making and prioritization. When you know your own strengths and weaknesses regarding the spectrum of risks that a CIO routinely faces, you and your network partners can anticipate problem areas. One of the most important points of awareness on the risk spectrum is strategic application and alignment. Let's take a look at how the CIO can work to mitigate the associated risks and create value for all concerned.

ALIGNING IT RESOURCES TO YOUR ORGANIZATION'S STRATEGY

Chapter 4 introduced, examined, and recommended strategic alignment, which included enterprisewide strategic planning, practical strategic planning, and the importance of the CIO's involvement as a full participant in the strategic planning process and strategic resource management. Two of Chapter 4's 10 questions focused on those the CIO should ask the entire senior executive team during the strategic planning process, with an emphasis on alignment with his or her peers and partners:

1. Does our IT strategic plan support our overall corporate strategic plan?
2. Is there a clear linkage between our IT strategy and our company's competitive strategy?

Clearly, once the executive team agrees on the strategic plan, it is the CIO's responsibility to see that the IT resources are aligned with those strategies.

The CIO works to align resources to strategy on two levels: within the IT organization and its strategies, and those of the IT organization within the company as a whole. Once the strategic plan for the IT organization is in alignment with the overall company's strategic plan, the CIO aligns the IT resources to the IT organization's strategic plan and validates that alignment with the strategic plans of the peers and partners. Real alignment means that all local strategic plans support the achievement of company strategy. As an enabler of all local and global strategy, the CIO and the IT organization figure as one of the company's primary strategic resources. As Paul A. Strassmann puts it in his book *The Squandered Computer*:

> Alignment is the capacity to demonstrate a positive relationship between information technologies and accepted measures of performance. [What should be measured is] what, how, and when [information technologies support] improvements in the delivery of operating results.[7]

As a practical matter, the means by which the "wheels of motion" are put into place to realize strategic alignment and to benefit from the results of this alignment is the *allocation of resources*: actual, perceived, physical, and mental.

The word "resources" conjures up different things to different people: quantity, quality, dollars, people, mind-set, attention, meetings, e-mails, and motion, to name a few. While qualitative performance leads to profit, most people focus on the quantitative financial results of workplace performance—visibly physical aspects and the number of people aspects (all in dollars)—used to evaluate whether enough focus is being placed on what they think is of financially strategic importance. This leads to a focus where *quantity* becomes an indicator of *commitment*. Focus and prioritization are the demonstrable by-products of commitment, and all too often, this type of focus becomes misguided.

Strategic focus and prioritization are easily sidetracked. One of the most commonly used—misused and misguided—indicators of the level of commitment to the company's strategic direction is the amount of money budgeted and spent on a particular strategy and strategic initiative. Studies over the past 30 years have debated the correlation between monies budgeted or allocated to information technology and business success (although there does appear to be a correlation to monies budgeted to individual information technology projects and the rate of successful project completion). The early 1990s witnessed several comprehensive studies of this relationship—or lack thereof—and the intervening decade sees the debate rage on.

One of the earliest and most comprehensive research surveys on the subject was by well-known researcher Erik Brynjolfsson of the MIT Sloan School of Management; he coined the phrase "the productivity paradox of information technology," or "the productivity paradox" for short:

> The relationship between information technology (IT) and productivity is widely discussed but little understood. Delivered computing power in the U.S. economy has increased by more than two orders of magnitude since 1970, yet productivity . . . seems to have stagnated. [In fact, a] sharp drop in productivity roughly coincided with the rapid increase in the use of IT. Although recent productivity growth has rebounded somewhat, especially in manufacturing, the overall negative correlation between economywide productivity and the advent of computers is the basis for many of the arguments that IT has not helped U.S. productivity or even that IT investments have been counterproductive.[8]

From these generalized assertions, subsequent research "peeled the onion," looking at two industry categories: manufacturing and IT services. The results were interesting. After analyzing a half-dozen empirical studies in the manufacturing industry, the conclusion was that IT was neither a positive nor a negative factor in its capability to "measurably affect return on assets or market share."[9] In one ray of sunshine, a positive effect on productivity could be identified for transactional IT applications (e.g., ATMs, online ordering, and similar technologies). In the services industry, the results were much more polar:

> [O]n average, IT's impact was not significant, but . . . it seemed to be associated with both very high and very low performers. This finding . . . tends to reinforce existing management approaches, helping well-organized firms succeed but only further confusing managers who have not properly structured [how they are applying IT] in the first place.[10]

Interestingly, it is also plausible that improvements in productivity might not be apparent because the management team may be choosing to focus the positive effects of information technology investments on providing additional buffer or program management and project management contingency. Such an approach is usually designed to improve the probability of a project or efforts completing successfully within expected performance parameters (risk matrix, anyone?). One result of such an approach is that the key benefits may be judged more in terms of not having been considerably worse, in contrast to being definitively better through the application. Risk perception is everywhere. It is all a matter of what the baseline probability outcome would be without the investment in information technology, and whether that baseline was assumed (perhaps incorrectly).

Nearly a decade later, Brynjolfsson's follow-on findings and conclusion suggest that there has been improvement over time:

> [A] big part of the productivity resurgence that the United States has experienced since the mid-'90s can be linked quite directly to investments in information technology. [A] series of analyses . . . showed that computers were contributing quite significantly to productivity growth . . . [The] bigger benefit comes when the managers who work with it learn more about how to interface with their suppliers and their customers and understand their product line better and make decisions that build off that. You can go through lots of industries and see changes in, say, retailing with efficient consumer response and vendor-managed inventory, and in banking through a whole host of services, but each of them is different, not just by industry but even at the level of individual firms.[11]

This research concluded that the application of information technology—particularly to areas where there are direct customer interactions (whether internal or external) or value to the customer—had more positive effect than applications whose objectives were primarily cost-cutting and/or management control. Applications such as those resulting in better customer service or responsiveness or providing more product variants certainly fall into these positive categories, as do (back to the banking example) ATMs.

Interestingly, to the naysayers who note that many companies still invest heavily in information technology yet cannot show significantly improved financial performance, the results also showed that:

> [T]here were hundreds of firms that had disappointing performance despite spending heavily on IT. IT is only one factor. It's an important factor and it's one that on average is clearly [associated] with greater performance, but the individual management of the technology and the investments in the complementary organization changes are at least as important, if not more so.[12]

Risk, risk, risk. Resource alignment, resource alignment, resource alignment. Focus, focus, focus. Priorities, priorities, priorities. At the same time these academic studies were underway, another key voice in the study of information technology investments and their relation to productivity improvements belonged to the aforementioned Paul A. Strassmann, a former CIO for Xerox and, more recently, for NASA. Probably many peoples' introduction to Strassmann's work was through an *Information Week* article, which appeared shortly after publication of his seminal book *The Business Value of Computers*.[13] His findings and conclusions were controversial and thought-provoking:

Except in cases of direct cost displacement, IT has no intrinsic value and cannot be justified as an expense. However, technological advances make IT potentially the single-most efficient resource for improving a business. In this respect IT exhibits the characteristics of a miracle pharmaceutical: It can produce a rapid cure, but only if the conditions are right. Otherwise, the drug has no value and can be harmful. . . . Ultimately, the value of any action involving IT is the difference between a company's cash plans with or without a change in IT. . . . [A company has] various options for executing some plan. [It] can either advertise more, hire more accountants or more tax lobbyists, or buy some MIS.[14]

And, in a later interview, Strassmann elaborated, saying:

Spending money on IT guarantees absolutely nothing. The absence of a demonstrable relationship between profitability and IT spending should be seen as evidence that other influences, such as strategic advantages, competitive positioning, and leadership's effects are likely to be more decisive than information technologies.[15]

In the end, the choice of which one(s) to do should be decided by the value brought to the company in terms of productivity and return on investment. Over the past nearly 20 years, Strassmann's research and analyses have led him to continue to believe that there is no real correlation between information technology investments and profits. This is a view that he and others have reinforced through surveys and analyses of most of the Fortune 1000 companies.

That said, there is ample evidence to suggest that IT executives do see a correlation in information technology investment rates and profitability. When asked about their investment and spending, a group of 300 IT executives reported a range of views on the amount of monies being spent versus what they felt they needed to be successful (see Exhibit 5.2).

The fact that most reports related to IT investments are provided in terms of budgets adds to this perspective. In fact, IT budgets are often benchmarked by companies relative to their industry peers like an arms race approach. Another survey reinforced this problem: Some 30 percent of the surveyed CIOs reported they were primarily measured on "budget versus actual," while a little over 40 percent responded that they were measured on the value IT investments bring to their company.[16] This should not be a great surprise. In the same survey, only 10 percent of the respondents reported that their major projects were accompanied with business plans, including estimates of the benefit and value of that IT investment.[17]

One of the more recent academic studies on the business value of information technology investments makes an even stronger case supporting the existence of the paradox, concluding that:

[The] valuation benefits of IT spending are concave in IT spending intensity. . . . [Firm] IT spending is valued relative to IT spending by industry peers and

EXHIBIT 5.2   IT EXECUTIVE PERSPECTIVE ON
CORRELATION OF INVESTMENT RATE
AND PROFITABILITY

	Spent All or More Than Initial Budget	Spent Less Than Budget	Revised Budget Downward	Budget at Appropriate Level	Budget Too Low
IT Budget	39%	58%	43%	64%	34%

Source: Adapted from Charles Phillips and Ryan Rathman, "Morgan Stanley CIO Survey Series: Release 3.8," *Morgan Stanley Equity Research* (December 9, 2002) 3.

. . . differences in the market valuation of IT spending vary across firms based on the business role IT plays in the firms' industries.[18]

Using data from previous surveys, these researchers constructed and validated an empirical model for the business value of information technology investments. Based on their findings, they were able to construct an equation for the resulting business value made up of two terms:

- A linear component representing the cost of IT
- A concave component representing the benefits of IT

In short, their results show that increasing investments in IT lead to diminished returns on the investments and, therefore, a nonproportional increase in business value.[19] An interesting side benefit to their investigations was a look at the actual levels of IT investments with a correlation to business success. They came to a most interesting conclusion: At least 50 percent of the firms surveyed were below the optimum level of investment in information technology and, therefore, were underinvesting in new IT:

> [T]he valuation impact of IT is higher in industries where IT plays an informating or transforming role. In these industries, companies have more scope for making investments in other organizational assets that increase the returns to investing in IT. An important implication is that managers have opportunities to affect the pay-off to investing in IT by developing human resources and organization structures that enable companies to make innovative use of new IT.[20]

As these researchers point out, human and organizational effectiveness essentially makes the difference as to whether information technology investments prove effective and, therefore, whether the investments align with the business strategy. In order to know whether this is true, it is important to be able to assess and evaluate—which usually goes under the banner of "measure," where "measure" means identify, assess, and evaluate. Not surprisingly, the challenge of evaluating information technology investments has received considerable attention over the past 10 years, especially in the use of nonbudgetary terminology and methodology. There are many factors and approaches that could be used for sources of information technology value, but four categories stand out as straightforward and usable:[21]

- *Cost efficiency,* in terms of IT infrastructure, IT operations, and IT R&D investment
- *Service to the business,* in terms of customer satisfaction with IT products and customer satisfaction with IT service
- *Business improvements,* in terms of IT support effectiveness
- *Direct revenue/profit generation,* in terms of IT profit generation and competitive edge

As already discussed, it is not always (and may be very seldom) that direct revenue or profit generation can be attributed to specific information technology investments. The advantage to the use of these four categories is that value to the investment will likely be attributable to one or more of the remaining areas if not to direct revenue/profit generation. Remembering the adage that "you get what you measure," there is a clear correlation between practicing good evaluation techniques and getting good results from information technology investments. These benefits come largely from creating clear focus, priorities, and understanding (often by forcing the conversations, debates, discussions, and explicit decisions required to get to this understanding) regarding the benefits of individual and overall information technology investments.

Given the benefits of evaluation and the evidence that not even half of companies formally practice evaluation of their information technology investments, the current situation can only remain because the barriers—real or perceived—are great to doing so. Risk, risk, risk. In a survey of U.S., U.K., and other European companies' senior IT management, the key barriers identified were:[22]

- Inability to identify intangible benefits
- Inappropriate measures
- Absence of satisfactory metrics
- Financial focus of the organization
- Poorly defined IT deliverables

Based on available research, publications, and the trade press, it is clear that the search is still on for the silver bullet for measuring IT effectiveness. Many companies are moving to two techniques: the Balanced Scorecard approach by Robert Kaplan and David Norton, adjusted for IT, and benchmarking.[23]

The Balanced Scorecard approach, with adjustments suggested to make it more specific to IT, includes:[24]

- Corporate financial perspective; for example, profit per employee
- Systems project perspective; for example, time, quality, and cost
- Business process perspective; for example, purchase invoices per employee
- Customer/user perspective; for example, on-time delivery rate
- Innovation/learning perspective; for example, rate of cost reduction for IT services
- Technical perspective; for example, development efficiency and capacity utilization[25]

In these studies, the researchers report that those who have integrated IT-based Balanced Scorecards have reported a clear benefit from their use, including the conversion of what were measurement processes into management processes, causing the IT organization to focus on customer service and customer delivery, alignment of the IT group, its investments with the business strategy and business as a whole, and focusing the management team and employees on common goals. As might be expected, the application of any relatively new technique or way of thinking and working has its challenges. For instance, it can be quite difficult to institute, measure, evaluate, and understand a full range of measures without making an equally significant investment in employee learning. Another challenge noted by the researchers was that the IT-based Balanced Scorecard was not always aligned with the overall company strategy. Finally, according to the results, as one of the most difficult challenges of any process that includes evaluation, there were frequently reported problems with actually *managing* and *doing something*. Of course, all of these problems can be overcome, but how easy or how difficult it will be to do so generally boils down to the buy-in of those who are responsible for "doing something" and the support, encouragement, and commitment of those executives who are key to such commitments: you, your peers, and your partners.

Benchmarking, in contrast, means many things to many people. As observed earlier, benchmarking focused on financial measures associated with IT performance may lead the executive team to increase investments where the investments end up being of little return, no return, or antireturn. While benchmarking may be new to those companies just starting to use it as a technique, it has been around for decades and used by other industries. Just how applicable it is to IT is still being debated. Certainly its applicability to IT *spending* is under great suspicion, as mentioned earlier, and is not advisable—unless used to benchmark against unsuccessful competitors to find out whether your own company is over- or underspending relative to its lack of success.[26]

Those who use benchmarking and believe they are receiving benefit from it generally cite several "usual suspect" benefits. Key among them is that they benefit from learning what others are doing and can therefore be in a position to make better decisions. Interestingly, they also cite that it demonstrates that IT costs are well controlled, and that they are able to show the benefits of IT investments to their company. These last two benefits should be considered in the light of either no correlation to investment levels or the inverse correlation of more spending to better returns on the investment; that is, they are tenuous benefits at best and are likely to be extremely difficult to justify. That said, the difficulties noted with benchmarking management justifications are mostly associated with lack of organizational support for the benchmarking process and time requirements, resource investments, and general buy-in for using the results of the benchmarking (this latter placed into the category of "political interference").

Ultimately, the vast majority of the contributions to company profitability come from the strategic choices made that result in improvements and leadership in customer quality, capital effectiveness, and market share. It may be very difficult to assess any relationship between information technology investments and improved business performance due to the complexity of most IT projects and their adoption by their target customers, along with any necessary coinciding business process and employee behavioral changes required.[27]

Aligning IT resources to company strategy is both *directional* (strategic) and *operational*. This look at the directional lays the groundwork for looking at the operational, that is, looking at the necessary linkages between the operational and the directional (or strategic). For any journey to be successful, the parties must be properly provisioned—the necessary resources must be appropriately allocated. IT is no exception.

PROPER PROVISIONING: RESOURCE ALLOCATION TO IT

So, just how does the CIO ensure proper provisioning? Clearly, the first and most essential step is to be in strategic alignment with the company, peers, and partners. Because this includes buy-in from those parties who are beneficiaries of the actions and accomplishments of the IT group, the party is ready to embark. Actually, no, it is not yet ready. Proper provisioning requires a clear destination, resources, a route, and a guide:

- *Destination*: Knowing which problem is being solved and what that solution looks like. This is derived from working with your peers and partners on alignment.

- *Resources*: People with the appropriate skills, expense and capital funds, equipment, and leadership. This is derived from proper provisioning.
- *Route*: The plan for getting from the present to the solution. This is derived from proper provisioning.
- *Guide*: The person who will be the lead for the journey from the resources through the route to the destination—the program manager.

Earlier chapters have concentrated on the destination. The next sections will cover the resources and the route; and the last section of this chapter will cover program management and the role of the program manager.

Resources and Route

Understanding which and how many resources are needed and how much time is required to accomplish your goals and meet your commitments to your peers and partners is key to a CIO's success and to the success of the IT organization. In order to get to the point at which you know the answers and requirements you will have to establish and use appropriate processes. Process should *not*, however, be confused with bureaucracy. Process and processes are used to provide a consistent, experience-based means by which a team of people can accomplish a goal or start and finish a project. Bureaucracy is the intentional use of process to slow down, stall, or completely derail an individual, team, organization, or company from achieving these goals or projects.

Sooner or later, if you have not heard it already, you will receive a series of complaints from some groups—or particularly vocal individuals—asserting that the process requirements that they have been mandated for planning, organizing, performing, and learning from the results of their endeavors is waste of time and resources and should not apply to them. Often, the rationalization provided is that they are experts in their work, and the effects of putting processes into place and expecting them (as opposed to others less experienced) to adhere to these processes:

- Does not take into account their level of experience, or
- Is disrespectful, or
- Is bureaucracy, or
- Will unduly slow down the development work, or
- Will make it impossible to complete the work on time, or
- Any number of other assertions.

As the senior IT executive, it is the CIO's responsibility to prevent his or her teams from using any significant resources or participating in any significant project without proper provisioning—without identifying and securing the necessary resources and, *especially,* without developing a plan for resource utilization according to a project plan with milestones along the way. Only a fool would go on a safari without first establishing a few basic survival tactics: the availability of sufficient resources; knowledgeable guides who know where they are going and how they are going to get you there; a map and timetable from the start to the finish with appropriate places to stop along the way. Why would any reasonable CIO agree to spending valuable and increasingly scarce IT resources on projects without adequate planning, progress milestones, endpoints that marked success, and of course, a project review to see what could be learned to improve or to avoid for future expenditures?

The type and amount of preparation and planning varies from expedition to expedition. Although projects may not be similar, the methods used to identify resources, milestones, endpoints, and lessons learned can be. One of the more common and successful means for making these assessments evolved from the Capability Maturity Model (CMM) developed under the stewardship of Carnegie Mellon University,[28] a method that has been tested by many evaluations, analyses, and comparisons of the other approaches to quality management and improvement.[29] The CMM was originally developed as a set of standards and criteria for a company to become a defense contractor. Over time, the methodology evolved to become applicable to many types of development efforts, and it is fully applicable to information technology projects.

The core principle of the CMM is to evaluate the *maturity* of an organization and its processes. The development spectrum ranges from no real process to continuous improvement in five total levels of achievement:[30]

- Level 1 is an organization's basic developmental process before attempts are made to standardize. It is often loose and chaotic.

- Level 2 includes initial project management processes, such as quality assurance, that keep tabs on cost, schedule, and functionality. The object of this level is to build on top of past application work for future projects.

- Level 3, the minimum requirement for Department of Defense contractors, documents and standardizes existing development processes. Some new methods brought to play include process definition, integrated software management, intergroup coordination, and peer reviews.

- Level 4 collects data about software quality and the development process. Businesses at this level hope to back up what they believe does or does not work with real numbers.

- Level 5 feeds that data back into the development process so that the development team can use it to prevent bugs, input new features, and streamline the development process.

A comparative look at the levels and requirements to achieve a specific level is shown in Exhibit 5.3. Note that the CMM process focuses on *what* needs to be done to achieve a specific *maturity level*; it says nothing about *how* to do what is necessary.

It is important to understand the maturity level of the IT organization in order to know how to allocate resources (outfit) for projects in alignment with your business goals and peers' and partners' needs and how to plan (map) the projects on time completion within budget (destination). This requires making an assessment of the maturity level of your IT organization. While it helps to have this done by outsiders—trained experts taking a fresh and uninvolved look—there is no reason the CIO cannot make his or her own assessment of their organization. And, there is every reason the CIO should do so! Professor Jerry Luftman[31] has outlined a straightforward means by which the CIO can assess the information technology organization's maturity level:[32]

1. *Form the assessment team.* Create a team of IT and business executives to perform the assessment. Depending on the size of the company, 10 to 30 executives should be chosen to participate, depending on whether the assessment is related to the IT organization and a single business unit or the IT organization and the entire enterprise.

2. *Gather information.* Team members should assess the relationships in terms of a set of alignment categories and practices within those categories and determine which maturity level (1 to 5) best matches the organization. Three approaches are recommended: (a) meet in a facilitated group setting; (b) have each member complete a survey and then meet to discuss the results; or (c) use a combination of the first two approaches if it is not reasonable for all group members to meet.

3. *Decide on individual scores.* Reach a team consensus on a score for each practice. The most valuable part of the assessment is not the score itself but the understanding of the implications for the entire IT organization and what needs to be done to improve.

4. *Decide on an overall score.* Reach a team consensus on which level to assign to the organization. One method is to average the individual practice scores; another is to weight the various practices and to calculate a weighted average.

Luftman reports that most Fortune 500 companies on their first assessment score themselves at level 2 with some practices at level 1.[33] The suggested alignment categories are shown in Exhibit 5.4.

Once a maturity assessment is completed and shared with the CIO and the IT staff, the IT organization is in a much better position to understand the risks and potential for projects and project teams in relation to those participating on the teams and to the business unit(s) for which the projects are being done. This input is important as the CIO and the senior IT staff "plot the route" or plan the

EXHIBIT 5.3   THE CAPABILITY MATURITY MODEL

Level		Description	Capability
1	Initial	Heroic Efforts	Without Process	Design, Develop, Integrate, Test
2	Repeatable	Individual Initiative	Beginning Process	Requirements Management, Project Planning, Project Tracking and Oversight, Subcontract Management, Quality Assurance, Configuration Management
3	Defined	Institutionalized Processes	Establishing Process	Organizational Process Focus, Organizational Process Definition, Training Program, Integrated Development Management, Product Engineering, Intergroup Coordination, Peer Reviews
4	Managed	Quantitative Management	Improved Process	Quantitative Process Management, Development Quality Management
5	Optimizing	Continuous Improvement	Optimal Process (Complete Alignment)	Defect Prevention, Technology Change Management, Process Change Management

Source: Adapted from Will, "Can Quality Management Systems Improve Your Software Development and Business Performance?" 2002; and Luftman, "Assessing I/T and Business Alignment," 2002.

EXHIBIT 5.4   ALIGNMENT CATEGORIES FOR IT ORGANIZATIONAL MATURITY ASSESSMENT

Alignment Category	Description
Communication	Understanding of business by IT
	Understanding of IT by business
	Organizational learning
	Style and ease of cross-organizational access
	Leveraging intellectual assets
	IT-to-business liaison staff
Metrics	Existence and types of IT metrics
	Existence and types of business metrics
	Linkages between IT and business metrics
	Service-level agreements
	Benchmarking, formal assessments of IT investments
	Continuous improvement practices
Governance	Formal business strategy practices
	Formal IT strategy planning
	Organizational structure
	Reporting relationships
	How IT is budgeted
	Rationale for IT spending
	Senior-level IT steering committee
	How projects are prioritized

Source: Adapted from Luftman, "A Tool to Help You Assess IT-Business Alignment," 2002.

projects to meet IT's commitments. Sharper focus; clearer priorities. This assumes, of course, that the IT organization actually plans its projects. Believe it or not, there are many who do not. Recent studies have shown that upwards of 30 percent of IT organizations do not undertake what should be considered minimally acceptable project planning actions:

- Feasibility studies and evaluations prior to project start
- Project evaluation during the IT development project

Astoundingly, only 50 percent actually undertake postimplementation project analyses.[34] While it should be obvious why each of these three project planning and analyses actions should be undertaken, the 30 to 50 percent of organizations that do not do so suggest that a brief look at the value these approaches bring is warranted.

In a perfect world, all projects that go into development are necessary, finish on time (or earlier), on budget (or under budget) and meet (or exceed) the customer's requirements. The reality is that at least 10 percent of projects that enter the development phase get dropped before completion. This number could be significantly lower if feasibility studies, in-progress evaluations, and postimplementation analyses were undertaken for all projects of size or importance.

Feasibility studies should be undertaken before starting a project of any size for business and technical reasons. These studies generally focus on understanding the level of effort, level of resources, types of skills, calendar time, the required outcome of the project (the requirements it is satisfying), the return on investment, the alignment with business objectives, and the actual *doability* of the project. There are, of course, any number of challenges when doing feasibility studies and the most difficult usually revolve around the identification and quantification of the benefits, costs, and required timing. Among the most significant benefits in evaluating feasibility studies clearly include:

- Ensuring management, peer, and partner buy-in and support.
- Ensuring and reinforcing common vision between IT and affected peers and partners.
- Clear identification of responsibilities and accountability.
- Establishing the identity of the project's customers.
- Focus and prioritization.

During the development phase, one study showed that 60 percent of companies had terminated in-process projects; and these companies reported terminating about 10 percent of their total projects. The reasons reported varied, but the most-often cited reason was that the user requirements changed. This situation can arise when insufficient work has been done in the feasibility stage to clearly identify and understand the requirements and the necessary time frame and to adequately involve the project's customer in each step—including continuous review through the development phases of the project.[35] Exhibit 5.5 lists additional reasons for project termination.

Interestingly, the most significant problems these companies encountered during the development phase of their projects was their inability to hold meaningful project evaluations and reviews (not the reasons for the termination of the projects). This matches the experiences of many seasoned CIOs and product development executives, including my own: (1) changing and/or misunderstood requirements through the life cycle of the projects, (2) management and end-user absence from and lack of buy-in to the evaluation and review process, and (3) a shortage of skilled resources to perform the evaluations and reviews. This last reason is disappointing but not at all unexpected given the views that many senior managers and IT developers and management have toward program and project managers; that is, that they are unnecessary overhead and seem to have a high cost-

EXHIBIT 5.5   REASONS FOR PROJECT TERMINATION

Reason for Termination	Percent Reporting This Reason
Change in user requirements	75%
Change in organizational needs	59%
Risk too high	43%
Budget exceeded	33%
Missed deadlines	18%

Source: Adapted from Seddon, et al., "Measuring Organizational IS Effectiveness," 2002.

to-benefit ratio. Coincidentally, the opportunity to discuss this situation with the CEO of a medical products start-up arose recently, and his experience was exactly the same. He had insisted on hiring a program manager over the objections of his board of directors. Over a very short period of time it became evident that he was right in his judgment. This person prevented a near-disaster in their product deliveries. The fact is that, when properly applied, these skilled resources are worth their weight in gold. They are independent viewers and analysts, and the best of them are able to address the reasons for termination *before* they become reasons for termination, indeed!

Terminating a project after it has begun not only wastes resources but also ties up those resources, preventing them from being applied to a project that may very well be more important to the company and to your peers and partners. The net effect is a double-whammy: resources wasted and needed projects starved (not to mention the demoralizing effects on the people and the organization caused by terminating a project). At the same time, the reputation of the entire IT organization suffers, while the business has objectives that do not get met and your partners and peers do not receive the expected support in meeting their business and organizational objectives.

Whether a project succeeds or fails (for whatever reason) it is *always* a good idea to have a postcompletion (or posttermination) review and analysis, because this is where the organizational learning happens. The CIO and the IT organization come to:

- Know what went well and can reinforce what went well so that it happens again.
- Know what did *not* go well and look at improvements and changes with the idea of learning from the mistakes.
- Apply what was learned to improve the skills of the project/program management and staff and management teams.

In fact, the study just cited reported that these were the most common reasons for holding reviews.[36] Given the significant value for doing so, why is it that only

50 percent of companies do formally review project performance? Many reasons are cited, but they all boil down to a general belief that the cost-to-benefit ratio is too high and that little or no value will come of doing so. In some cases, people believe the results would be used for negative purposes (for example, scapegoating). In my own experiences, and in those with whom I have worked who regularly perform these reviews, such reviews are the key to long-term success—for the CIO personally, for the IT organization, and, therefore, ultimately for the peers, partners, and company.

Given that slightly more than 30 percent of IT projects produce less than expected results or end in complete failure[37] the view that postcompletion reviews are unnecessary is unsupportable, and as the senior IT executive you should consider it unacceptable. In fact, it is highly likely that the failure rate is high enough to be the reason behind a reported 32 percent of companies that reported a gap between the expected and perceived delivered services. Any CIO with a significant gap is a CIO who should be focused on reducing the gap or preparing the way for his or her successor to do so. Why has this pattern not changed significantly for the past nearly 20 years? One potentially significant reason could easily be the entrenched company culture based in traditional accounting approaches to IT management:

> The switch from traditional bureaucratic accounting techniques to a benefits management and risk analysis culture represent(s) a significant change in the underlying concepts and values of evaluation. This [is] not just the introduction of some new techniques, it [is] a paradigm shift from a formal-rational conception to an entrepreneurial approach.[38]

So, back to the question of whether the CIO should allow significant resources to be used and/or significant projects be accepted without plans, milestones, and adequate program management to provide focus and priorities every step of the way: You absolutely *must not*. Insist on feasibility studies; insist on in-process project evaluations, reviews, and analyses; and insist on postcompletion reviews, analyses, and follow-up actions. Do not be taken in by those who would tempt, cajole, insist, belittle, or torture you into thinking otherwise. You must stand firm or you risk all—an entirely unacceptable risk profile.

ADAPTIVE SYSTEMS: IF WE HAVEN'T STARTED IT YET, IT COSTS NOTHING TO CHANGE IT!

As a successful senior manager and executive, it is necessary to be flexible and adaptive. At times, of course—we are human beings—it can be very difficult to force oneself to be flexible and adaptive. When such a situation arises, there are those who are truly unable to deal with it and end up defending a position or plan for originally good intentions (for example, organizational or plan stability); but after some time, the reasons for resisting are outweighed by the reasons for changing viewpoints. After a number of years at IBM, and having both encountered and perpetrated such situations, a phrase popped into my head: "If we haven't started working on it, yet, it costs us nothing to change it!" Of course, this sounds simple, even obvious. But as I think about it and observe people today, it does not appear to me to be obvious or simple to many, or even most, people. Perhaps a bit of the circumstances of this serendipitous clarity of thought might help explain how this impacts the focus and priorities of the CIO and the IT organization.

At the time of this serendipitous thought (the late 1980s/early 1990s), I had been working on iterative improvements to a software development process that I had defined and had used over a number of years (and projects) with varying degrees of success. The three greatest challenges at the time, in my view, were:

1. Adapting development plans throughout the development time line to new information gained through development, through marketing and sales, or through direct customer interactions.

2. Meeting growing expectations and needs by marketing and sales teams to see something working as soon as reasonably possible so they could both tell their customers they had seen something and that they could bring their customers in to see.

3. Having a good idea of actually how far along development was at any point in time—in contrast to where the development team *thought* they were.

During this period, I was refining a development process that went through various changes and incarnations. It started out as an interactive cascaded development process that had small groups working together and integrating their development results in small, manageable amounts in a successive or cascaded manner. Based on the lessons learned from working through this process, it was possible to make it a more sophisticated model that allowed for multiple subteams that together constituted a much larger team. By carefully timing the development and integration of the work from the subteams through synchronization preplanning, it was possible to run projects in a way that looked like a "small team project" and had a benefit of creating and maintaining an "always-executable" base. With an always-executable base, it was possible to incrementally develop, test, and deploy functions on a timely basis. This approach created considerable inertia with the management team to create the plans to execute the process, assign the resources, and then do their best to avoid making any changes to the plans and resource allocations.

In a perfect world, this idea of making no changes might be acceptable. In real life, this is neither reasonable nor rational if there is an expectation of being responsive and flexible and adaptable. So, after a review of what the development team had completed so far and what was yet to come, the marketing team brought in new information about a change in priority for particular features and functions based on a new survey they had completed of the most likely first customers for this new product.

As discussion and debate ensued, the volume level of those involved rose significantly. Both the engineering teams and the marketing teams were clearly "digging in their heels" to keep the current-order thinking that later, new information might cause the original order to be reinvoked. (This was the verbal rationale; the real reasons were more along the lines of not having to redo what they had already done or to insist that if the changes were made "the dog wouldn't hunt.") This is when the flash happened: From a practical point of view from a development perspective, if the work on those future requirements (current or new ordering) had not started, there was no real cost to change the order. Conversely, if work had started or had been completed, then there was a significant, real, and quantifiable cost to making the changes, and in that case change should be strongly resisted. What would be resisted is redoing or scrapping something already completed. So, once we got everyone calmed down, I put it before both groups:

> If we *haven't* started it, it costs us nothing to change it. If we *have* started it, we are going to be extremely resistant to changing it.

Surprisingly (at least to me), after a brief period of thought and discussion, this approach was accepted by all groups involved as in the best interests of everyone. Just plain amazing (I thought at the time). After that, we started projects with this concept explicitly stated, discussed, and understood by all. This was a quite reasonable compromise between those who need stability long enough to complete their project and the need to be flexible, adaptive, and manage through new information.

The CIO who can internalize especially the first portion ("if we haven't started it, it costs us nothing to change it") does the IT organization a significant service by being perceived as reasonable, flexible, and realistic, while encouraging the same characteristics from the IT organization and from peers and partners and their organizations. You will not regret doing so.

CHARTING THE JOURNEY MILESTONES: IT PROGRAM MANAGEMENT

It is now time to chart your journey's course. Continuing with the survival analogy, think of these situations:

- You are going to take a serious mountain climb of the Tibetan variety: Would you even consider this climb without a sherpa?

- You are going to sail around the world in a yacht: Would you even consider this without someone with serious ocean-going navigation skills?

- You are going to fly to the North Pole: Would you even consider this without someone with serious flight navigation skills and experience flying into that exotic (and dangerous) environment?

- You are going to navigate an oil tanker from the ocean byways into port: Would you even consider this without an experienced pilot?

With many more examples that can be suggested, why then do so many IT organizations and so many CIOs allow nonprofessionals to chart their journey milestones and allow these nonprofessionals to guide them and their teams from their point of departure to their destination? A major study in the United Kingdom validates that more than 30 percent of U.S. IT projects terminated before completion and compares it with only 5 percent of such terminations for U.K. IT projects.[39] The author insinuates that the United Kingdom's greater use of project and program managers for its IT projects has reduced the ratio of abandoned projects. For those involved in engineering and construction projects outside the IT industry, it would be unimaginable to run a project of any size or importance without a project or program manager; it is not a matter of debate—it is expected and used because experience has shown the value of doing so. The reasons that project and program management has been slow to catch on in the IT world has yet to be identified; but don't wait for the academicians to figure out why: Take it on faith (or basic common sense) that your use of good project and program managers will be paid back many times over.

It may well be that many CIOs do not really know what a project/program manager does, the expected qualifications for such a person, and how to tell a good one from a bad one. Let's take a look at each of these. The primary responsibilities of a program manager are to get the job done on time, within budget, and according to the specifications. A more formal definition reads as follows:

> An individual responsible for establishing the project infrastructure, acquiring and directing people internally and from contractors, leading and managing the project's tasks, supporting or leading tasks aimed at new or expanded project engagements; and measured on revenue, profit and client satisfaction.[40]

From a project point of view, your program managers are the CIO's and senior management's right hand. These professionals receive incentives to work toward the success of the CIO and the IT organization: This is their sole reason for existence. By this point you are probably thinking that this last description is much broader than the previous definition; and it is. The fact is that trained, professional program managers spend a significant amount of time on much more than just project management. When asked how they spend their time, the top three responses were development and implementation (15.5 percent of their time), client communications (15.1 percent of their time), and monitoring and control (13.7 percent of their time). In Exhibit 5.6 it is also interesting to note that they also spent a considerable portion of their time on stakeholder communication and unanticipated problems. In addition, about half of the program managers pay significant attention to team selection; in my view, this should be 100 percent especially given the discussion and recommendations from team selection and dynamics in earlier chapters.

Several other observations about where they pay close attention to detail suggest that you should expect this of the better program managers:

- Over two-thirds of the program managers ensure sign-offs at each stage of a project.
- Over two-thirds actively manage sponsor commitment.
- Almost three-fourths expect team members to be fully committed to the team and each other and actively work to build team commitment.

What are the characteristics of successful program managers? That is a very difficult question to answer specifically because projects can vary so widely. One answer (with tongue firmly planted in cheek) is that you will know a good one when you see him or her in action. That said, there are a number of characteristics that are key, and they are a blend of those listed in Exhibit 5.7. The first column represents what the program managers believe is necessary for them to be successful, whereas the second column represents the characteristics the program managers see exhibited in the best-known—to them—and successful program managers.
' There is no right answer to which characteristics are more important, but the

EXHIBIT 5.6   HOW PROGRAM MANAGERS SPEND THEIR TIME

Activity	Proportion of Time Spent
Development and implementation	15.5%
Client communications	15.1%
Monitoring and control	13.7%
Unanticipated problems	13.4%
Planning and replanning	12.3%
Stakeholder communication	11.8%
Team building	10.2%
Managing conflicts	8.0%

Source: Adapted from "IT Management: Project Management: Research Will Set Project Management Benchmark," 2002.

EXHIBIT 5.7 CHARACTERISTICS OF SUCCESSFUL PROJECT MANAGERS

Rank	Characteristics of Successful Project Managers	Characteristics of the Best-Known Project Managers
1	Commercial awareness	Confidence
2	Confidence	Goal orientation
3	Preparedness to take risks	Integrity
4	Understanding of IT	Enthusiasm
5	Integrity	Prior success in managing projects
6	Goal orientation	Energy
7	Written communication	Understanding business processes
8	Attention to detail	Ability to manage change
9	Problem solving	Leadership
10	Enthusiasm	Initiative
11	Preparedness to work in a team	Commercial awareness
12	Planning	Oral communications
13	Delegation	Problem solving
14	Prior success in managing projects	Preparedness to work in a team
15	Energy	Planning
16	Stakeholder management	Stakeholder management
17	Leadership	Understanding of IT
18	Conflict resolution	Perspective
19	Securing resources	Attention to detail
20	Time management	Delegation
21	Ability to manage change	Written communication
22	Initiative	Securing resources
23	Oral communication	Conflict resolution
24	Perspective	Time management
25	Understanding business processes	Preparedness to take risks

Source: Adapted from "IT Management: Project Management: Research Will Set Project Management Benchmark," 2002.

CIO must ensure that the program managers for specific projects are matched to the needs of the particular project, project team, development team, customers, and stakeholders. Also important, the experience level of the program manager should match or exceed the complexity level of the project. My own experience has been that the program managers have a way about them that makes it easy for them to be in the confidence of nearly everyone in the project, making them privy to significantly more information than any number of others combined on their project teams. As a result, they are good people to have a rapport with, and as CIO, you have an unofficial means by which to corroborate the information provided during normal staff and project updates.

Convinced? If not, consider this:

> Projects turn corporate strategy into reality, and in a sense, everything an IT manager does takes the form of a project. Yet too often, the concept of managing projects is poorly understood and executed. It's no wonder that many companies do a lousy job of prioritizing and allocating project resources. Worse, they fail to effectively implement their hard-won strategies. The results of this mismanagement can be devastating, with projects missing key deadlines, exceeding budgets, and failing to meet business goals.[41]

It might be tempting to believe that this is a dated view, but it is not; it is from late 2002. I was fortunate enough as an undergraduate to be encouraged to take a project management course, and it had a lasting effect—so much so that it would be difficult to imagine being responsible for any major project without the benefit of a qualified, professional, program manager at my side. I recommend that all CIOs consider the same for themselves.

TEN QUESTIONS THE CEO SHOULD ASK THE CIO FOR SUCCESSFUL ALIGNMENT

> *A strategic conversation is a carefully thought-out but loosely facilitated series of in-depth conversations for the key decision-makers throughout an organization. Strategic conversations don't exist in addition to existing planning efforts; they are effective ways of framing the planning efforts that already take place, to further illuminate the decisions that are already being made.*
> —Peter Schwartz, *The Art of the Long View*[42]

Previous 10 Questions sections looked at what the CIO must ask the CEO, peers, and partners. Now, it is time to turn the table and look at 10 important questions the CEO should ask the CIO so that together they can work to align IT and company strategy. If the CEO does not know enough to ask these questions, consider them as a basis for strategic communication with your CEO. These are 10 key pieces of information about the CIO and the IT organization's activities that guide practical implementation of the CEO's business strategy so that the company's investments in information technology can become complementary and fully leveraged. Given the opportunity, a potential CIO should work to answer these questions during the interviewing process with the CEO. If these or similar questions are not part of the interview process, an indirect approach can provide opportunities for discussing these 10 critical areas just as well. In the process, the CIO learns the CEO's level of relationship awareness, and the CEO learns about the CIO's comprehensive view of business/technology interrelationships as they apply to IT organization and company strategic alignment as a means to value creation.

As the senior executive, the CEO is responsible for the company's strategy, plans, and execution. Good CEOs are both leaders and followers, and they know when to be in each role. As a senior executive in the CEO's inner circle, the CIO also needs to be a good follower and good leader to both the CEO and the IT organization. Connecting the executive team and the operational team is one of the central responsibilities of the business unit senior executives and the CIO. As discussed throughout *The Guide*, the special relationship of the CIO in supporting the needs of all business unit executives means that he or she is a conduit of strategic understanding for the entire organization. This puts the CIO in a unique position of one who understands the strategic direction from the CEO and can interpret that strategic direction through the eyes of each peer and partner as they work to align themselves and their units with the company's strategic direction. Dialogs with the CEO are key to uncovering the value of this position.

Getting to know the CEO should be high on the new CIO's list of things to do. Throughout the year, the CEO calls on the CIO for advice and counsel, support, and to address problems within the organization. In light of the potential risk for an overly tactical focus on emergencies and the short-term solutions they generate, the CIO must have a true understanding of the CEO's business strategy to ensure that IT-related decisions are made in a context that advances the company toward strategic directions, whenever and wherever possible.

There are many reasons that a CEO and CIO fail to connect on the level of strategic alignment suggested by these questions. Because the CEO is generally a person with many demands and never enough time, the CIO should be ready to introduce the topics suggested by these questions at every opportunity. CEOs who lack a technology background often need some encouragement to participate in the dialog these questions suggest. In some cases, the CEO is simply unschooled or unaware of the value-creation opportunities inherent in the IT organization—especially those CEOs who see IT exclusively in terms of an expense used to solve short-term tactical and operational problems (i.e., as a necessary evil). In such cases, the CIO must use strategic discussions to demonstrate the ways IT can create value and ROI.

While there are many possible questions to ask to facilitate and strengthen this relationship, the following 10 point to key areas of IT value and performance that help the CEO work more effectively with the CIO to align IT and company strategies:

1. Do you view information technology as an expense or an investment?
2. Who is/are your customer(s)?

3. Why do you think I need a CIO?

4. Why do you think our company needs a CIO?

5. What risk profile do you favor?

6. Where do you spend more of your time: on strategy or operations?

7. Why should you report directly to me?

8. What books have you read to help improve the way you and your staff perform your jobs?

9. What professional publications do you read to stay current and learn about new leading-edge technology and business practices?

10. What do you believe is the proper alignment of business and technology for your job?

Number 1: Do You View Information Technology as an Expense or an Investment?

I recently had the opportunity to ask this question of a controller for a start-up company. He clearly saw investments in information technology and development as means to a profitable return. As the company's chief accountant, he was careful, of course, to emphasize that this did not mean that he believed in an open checkbook. He did, however, follow up immediately with the assertion that his experiences as both company accountant and local IT financial planning administrator gave him a healthy appreciation for the value of looking at information technology and development as investments. His practical experiences working both sides of the "Business/Technology Intelligence Quotient" (BTIQ) gave him the insight to see value creation from both the expense and value-creation perspectives. This enlightened view is becoming more common, but it is still so rare that some explanation is required.

As the *Guide* has repeatedly emphasized, information technology value creation stewardship is a balanced blend of business and technology understanding and experience. Nontechnology senior executives excel at business applications and often miss the ways the IT creates value for all stakeholders. Technology-specialized senior executives excel at tactical or operational hardware and software applications, but in the process often lose sight of valid strategic business applications. The BTIQ, a term coined by Joe and Catherine Stenzel, has been surreptitiously prefaced throughout the *Guide*. Readers who have made it this far deserve to know the foundation of this critical dynamic.

Consider the accountabilities of today's CEOs. ROI is the coin of their realm. In economies of regression or little movement, investment means cost. CEO responses to any external set of conditions depend on past history and investor pressures—it's a matter of maturity. Mature, experienced CEOs realize that investors are interested in short-term gain and that investor interests drive executive behavior. These same mature CEOs temper investor avarice for immediate ROI with the long-term advantages of sustainable, renewable ROI.

The most mature CEO should ask these questions of the CIO during the initial job interview. When not initiated by the CEO, it must be outlined by the prospective CIO, to gauge the maturity of this executive relationship for aligning company and IT strategies. If it was overlooked during the job interview, then it really must be one of the first strategic questions the CIO discusses at length and in depth with the CEO at the first available opportunity. Exhibit 5.8 shows the spectrum of two profiles: one for assessing CEO BTIQ and one for assessing CIO BTIQ. CEOs with low BTIQs have a limited awareness of the ways that information technology and the CIO can create value for the company. Likewise, CIOs with low BTIQs routinely bury their heads in the technology and never learn to understand the company's business.

As more businesses and their leaders come to the realization that product-based companies are fundamentally different from service-based companies, executive leadership learns to see information technology as a means for gaining and retaining a competitive edge through improved internal operations and management, manufacturing versus service efficiencies, appropriately designed reporting and analyses efficiencies, and information infrastructures. The CEOs of such companies carefully track their companies' investments in information technology and expect a genuine return on their strategic and capital investments. Understanding the CEO's expectations (and responsibilities) in this area encourages the CIO to take actions to meet those expectations by applying appropriate resources and direction to the information technology group, or correct the CEO's misguided BITQ. As always, the enabling CIO ensures that peers and partners are also onboard with these same priorities.

While it may be difficult to believe in this day and age that information technology would be viewed as a mere *expense*, it is all too often the case—ever more so in the "new economy of cost consciousness." The fuel for this belief is as simple as a lack of executive information or as complex as an executive backlash reaction. Regardless of the reasons, the CIO must actively work to understand, anticipate, mitigate, and correct the devaluation of information technology as a mere expense. Information technology is one of the primary ways for any organization to create value for all stakeholders.

When the CEO views IT as an expense (and probably a nonstrategic one at that), the CIO must first learn how the CEO understands the business contributions of IT in general, beyond the *expense* versus *investment* view, and learn why the CEO sees it in that way. Sometimes the CIO learns these answers early, during a discussion with the CEO on expected IT organization cost reductions and

EXHIBIT 5.8   BUSINESS/TECHNOLOGY INTELLIGENCE QUOTIENT PROFILES FOR CEOS AND CIOS

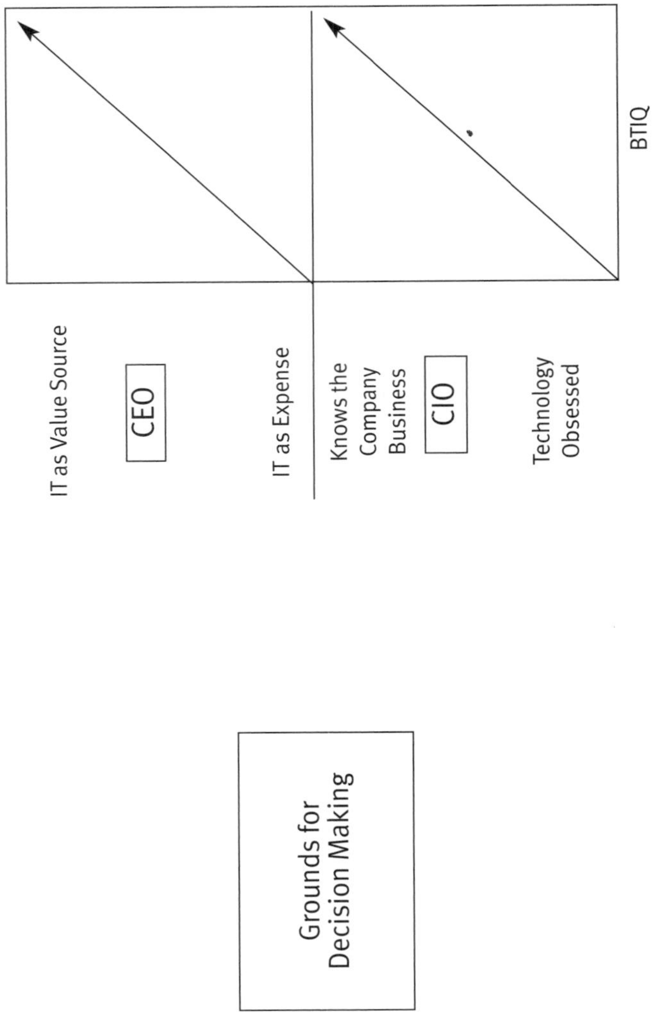

IT as Value Source

CEO

IT as Expense

Knows the Company Business

CIO

Technology Obsessed

BTIQ

Grounds for Decision Making

productivity efficiencies. These are usually code words for downsizing, which also suggests a focus on cost rather than value creation. Or the CIO might carefully and indirectly introduce the topic by pointing to companywide strategic value-creation success stories from past experience or successes by the company's competition. The reaction and/or follow-up questions from the CEO provide the clues to the most senior executive's BTIQ. CEOs with an above-average BTIQ expect to see similar or greater value-creating activities and decisions from their companies' CIO and IT organizations. CEOs with a low BTIQ need to be actively enlightened.

A lack of CEO interest in CIO experiences emanating from an earlier role the CEO had in a prior company could mean that the IT organization has been neither a significantly positive force in value creation nor a significantly negative force in wastefulness. In this case, the CIO's challenge is to set a course to demonstrate the ways that the IT organization creates value, and to do so by ensuring the buy-in of the CEO, peers, and partners. The CIO elevates such CEO and peer/partner BTIQs through regular strategy discussions in group settings and one-on-one interactions.

Neutral CEO reactions are not uncommon on the BTIQ spectrum. In these cases, the CEO has either not had the time to explore the value of investments in information technology or is simply not knowledgeable about how IT creates companywide value. In this situation, opening the strategic alignment dialog that focuses on discussions of strategic value creation hit the "sweet spot," where the CEO spends the most time: strategy, value creation, and how each of the company's business units participate, as seen by customers and investors alike.

When the CEO responds with nothing but negative verbal and postural responses, the CIO should suspect some event or series of events during which the CEO was burned by the information technology group, and should work to avoid a repetition at all costs. In such extreme cases, field work and research is required. The CIO can heal the damage by investigating past traumas and demonstrating how things might be different with a partnership approach between the CEO and CIO. When the CIO discovers that the CEO's business/technology circumstances represent similar past experiences, the CIO can more readily accept the CEO's hidden BTIQ experiences as valid. When the CIO discovers that the CEO generalizes each and every IT risk to past failures, the CIO knows that the CEO BTIQ needs to be heightened through patient guidance and gradually increasing IT ROI risk trials.

For example, the CIO should discover: Has the CEO experienced negative performance from an IT group that delivered overbudget with fewer-than-promised features on a key project? Does the CEO make decisions from a strictly financial cost-accounting background and lack the experience to believe that IT is a strategic business partner? Does this same CEO look at investment cost/benefit ratios with a bias against IT's ability to create value for the company? For most of these CEO BTIQ scenarios, the CIO will have a nearly full-time job trying to establish credibility for the IT organization and for himself/herself in terms of value creation. In fact, if the CEO's experience is overwhelmingly negative, it may never be possible for the CIO to overcome those views and move IT from the expense to value creation category. Again, this is why it is so important to have this frank discussion prior to accepting or taking a position. If the ultimate result is that the CEO's BTIQ cannot be improved in favor of IT as a means of creating company value, prudence suggests that the CIO with a high BTIQ begins to look for a new position or not accept the offered position. Sooner or later (probably sooner) the CIO's frustration level will grow to the point at which the position becomes, frankly, unbearable. Better to anticipate this Rubicon before it becomes an obstacle (remembering that each person's career is in his or her own hands and no one else's!).

Number 2: Who Is/Are Your Customer(s)?

If the CEO asks you this question, you are indeed fortunate. It is, however, a trick question, and one for which you should already have a clear answer: All current and potential users of IT's services and all current and potential customers of the company itself. As an enabler, it is clearly the CIO's role to enable all these information technology customers. If the CEO does not ask this question, the CIO must bring it up—and bring it up early—in the interview process or as early as possible in one-on-one strategic discussions. The CEO who asks this question is tacitly admitting that the IT organization exists to provide value to portions of the company, at the very least.

Conversely, CIOs who find themselves introducing this question into a strategic dialog with the CEO should proceed cautiously. The CIO can indirectly start this dialog by letting the CEO know that the entire IT organization is lined up behind the CEO's strategy for the company and that the IT organization is working with each group in terms of a customer partnership. At this point, the CIO pauses to gauge not only the CEO's BTIQ, but also the CEO's ability to learn as the CEO either affirms, explores, or rejects the customer-based approach. If the dialog stalls or remains open, the CIO can test the waters further by asserting that information technology investments should be used for the benefit of IT's customers as a means of creating value for them. This establishes that IT has internal customers and sets the tone for introducing the concept of IT's external customers. In the end, the CIO establishes the view that *value creation through investment* is the winning philosophy for information technology in the company.

At this point, the CIO again gauges the CEO's overall reactions in terms of voice, words, and body language. If the CEO is not thinking of IT in terms of providing value and services to the company's "customers," the CIO must attempt to enlighten the CEO to this approach on the assumption that the CEO may have a low BTIQ but is trainable. If, in the rare case, it turns out that the CEO is untrainable or uninterested in seeing the ways that IT provides services and creates value through a customer-style model, you, the CIO, should reexamine two questions: Is this company a good match for my talents? Does this company really need a CIO? Before giving up all hope, look to peers and partners who see the value of the customer relationship model and use a team effort in the attempt to enlighten the CEO.

One last time, who are the CIO's customers? The CIO's customers are all those in the company who can benefit from information technology as currently available or as available in the future. The CIO's customers are those peers and partners (inside and outside the company) who can benefit from the individual professional insights of the CIO relative to technology, information technology and investments, and value creation from both. It is difficult to imagine who is *not* a customer of the CIO.

Number 3: Why Do You Think I Need a CIO?

This particular question is not to be confused with the upcoming fourth question—why the *company* needs a CIO. This question focuses on the CEO's needs, specifically: Why do I, the CEO, need a CIO? If the CEO asks this question of his/her own accord, it could have several meanings depending on the particular situation:

- A job interview at a company where the position already exists or where it is a new position.
- The position already exists and the CIO has the position, but the CEO is not clear about the purpose of the position or about the value the CIO brings to the senior executive team and the company.
- The CEO's attempts to reaffirm the value of the CIO role.

When the CEO asks this question in a job interview, it is for two purposes: to confirm that the position is truly of value and to test the prospective CIO's views, convictions, and commitment to the value of the role. Being asked this question presents one of the greatest opportunities for the prospective CIO to make the case as a key contributor as an enabler, partner, and creator of value for the chief executive. An enlightened CEO will see the value in consolidating the interactions associated with information technology—both strategic and tactical—to one person, regardless whether the actual IT resources are consolidated. (Perhaps even more so if the resources are not consolidated, because the CIO then provides the single point of senior executive contact for all things IT. Without the CIO, the points of contact will be varied and, likely, disparate.) Additionally, the CIO is uniquely positioned to advise the CEO on the business value of the various information technology investments that create value for the company's businesses because the CIO works with all of the business unit peers and partners to define their business-specific information technology investments. And, of course, the CIO brings to one place and in one person the blend of business and technology for advising the CEO. Such advice supports decisions that are neither solely financially based nor technology-based but, rather, business-based.

If, during a job interview, the prospective CIO finds that verbal and body language suggest that the CEO does not value the business support a CIO can provide, the CIO has a choice: Ask the question directly or choose to close out discussions related to the position. Taking a position where the chief executive does not support your interests in the business is career stasis at best and career suicide at worst.

A CIO with a high BTIQ should expect the CEO with a well-matched BTIQ to use the CIO as a confidant and advisor, who always looks out for the best interests of the CEO and the company. The CIO/CEO team need a clear focus on IT's value creation and enabling activities. By definition, the CIO avoids increasing the budget or resources for IT independently of the needs, strategy, and direction as set forth by the CEO. With this approach, the CEO will clearly see the value the CIO brings.

Number 4: Why Do You Think Our Company Needs a CIO?

Though it might be difficult to see why the CEO would need a CIO but the company would not, it is not difficult to see why the company would need a CIO but the CEO would not. CEOs who ask this question during CIO interviews look for indications that the job applicant understands the information technology challenges faced by the company and its senior executives. Deployment and investment savvy earn high points with CEOs who possess high BTIQs. Even though the senior executive position has become a company commitment, experience suggests that the commitment is seldom unanimous. Sometimes the CEO lacks the commitment while a host of circumstances have forced everyone else in the company to recognize the need for a CIO. In such cases, the CEO and/or company are right on the cusp of an epiphany (just before or just after), brought on by an information technology crisis.

Interestingly, CIOs who begin working with a company well before such "crises of need" may even adopt an interview strategy to point out that it might be premature for the company to have a CIO based on the broad criteria and business responsibilities of the role. In this case, the applicant moves into the enviable position where the CEO tries to sell the prospective CIO on why the company needs a CIO. While you can name the key reasons why a company should have a CIO, if you are the one doing the selling, it will be much more convincing to link specifics about the company, its business units, senior executive team needs, and the external customer needs, and how the CIO and the IT organization can address them under your watch. Whether the CEO agrees with your approach or not, you establish yourself as a person with an understanding of the company's needs, the needs of your peers and partners, and a focus on value creation and information technology investment where it makes sense to do so.

Number 5: What Risk Profile Do You Favor?

An interesting question, indeed. Depending on the CEO's personality and preferences, this question either comes up naturally or it scares the CEO big-time. Ideally, the CEO and the CIO each feel more comfortable at opposite ends of the risk profile spectrum to provide a good balance of risks and benefits decisions. How far CIOs should work to accomplish their preferred end of the spectrum is probably best decided by balancing the expectations of the CIO's CEO and peers and partners. If they uniformly expect the CIO to produce major increases in value creation based on the information technology investments, then the CIO's profile needs to be more aggressive (read: higher risk profile). A slightly less aggressive CEO would be a good balance to such a CIO, especially when it comes to levels of risk associated with information technology investments. Similarly, if CEO responsibilities demand a high-risk profile, a complementary CIO should work with a lower risk profile to create the proper risk/benefit ratio balance, if this is not inconsistent with the genuine need of peers and partners. But remember that the other senior executives and their own risk profiles figure prominently into the dynamics of the overall risk equation. They form the third point in the triangle (see Exhibit 5.9).

Company strategic objectives dictate the proper balance of risk borne by each of the people in this dynamic triangle. Granted, risk profiles are more a matter of nature than nurture. However, over time, everyone demonstrates a risk profile that matches his or her inherent comfort zone. If the company and the CEO cannot tolerate high risk, then the CIO with a high-risk profile becomes a source of conflict. The converse is also true: If the company and the CEO tolerate high risk but the CIO is risk-averse, then conflict is inevitable. The risk profiles of peers and partners are no exception in this conflict equation, but because peers and partners are the only *group* in the risk profile triangle, the CEO looks to the CIO as a more manageable and expert "risk referee" for value creation and information technology investments. In short, CEOs with high BTIQs look for a more sophisticated approach to the company's overall IT risk profile management. Complementarity between the CEO and the CIO is the most important indicator of an intuitive but

EXHIBIT 5.9   COMPANY RISK PROFILE DYNAMICS

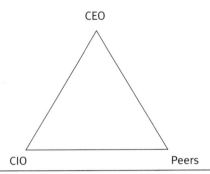

seldom-acknowledged risk equation, where overall risk includes value-creation expectations, actual IT investment dollars, a level of risk that all parties can accept, and the benefits that best information intuitively suggests for implementing the IT investment.

The successful CIO can master and employ multiple operational risk profiles while learning the CEO's *preferred* risk profile. If the CEO has a very low-risk profile, then the CIO profits from remembering that that any amount of risk seems large to such a CEO. The rationale behind the CIO's decisions must be meticulously thought through, not so much in terms of risk profile conflicts but in terms of sound business common sense. That is, if the CIO's natural risk profile is high, and the CEO's normal risk profile is extremely low, then a more relatively accurate relative description of risk profile for which the CIO should aim for would be "moderate." By the same token, if the CEO's normal risk profile is high, and the CIO's normal risk profile is extremely low, then a more relatively accurate description of risk profile for which the CIO should aim would be "neutral." Why is this? Because someone with a very high tolerance for risk is going to regard someone with even a low tolerance for risk as someone who probably has *no* tolerance for risk. While this may or may not be true, it is a matter of perception, and CEO perceptions carry more weight. People with a very low risk tolerance see others with a moderate tolerance of risk as the kind of people who decide from a very high tolerance of risk. In both cases, the exaggeration of risk tolerance occurs because that tolerance is evaluated relative to the *evaluator's* tolerance of risk.

Knowing your CEO's risk tolerance profile and your CEO's expectations of the risk tolerance level of his or her CIO is important to establishing a successful, functional relationship. The same awareness is essential for the CIO's relationship with peers and partners.

Number 6: Where Do You Spend More of Your Time: On Strategy or Operations?

This is a question that both you and the CEO need to ask and answer in terms of an appropriate alignment between IT and company strategies. The CEO should ask this question of the CIO to understand the balance that the CIO sees between tactical versus strategic activities demonstrated by the company's business objectives. With information technology investments and the IT group, there is always a mix of tactical and strategic priorities. Although the true role of all senior executives is, first and foremost, strategic, certain episodes emerge for which the business focus demands a tactical emphasis. Business conditions, the senior management team profile, the company culture, and the CIO's own natural proclivity determine *how* tactical, how *long* tactical, and how *often* tactically the CIO can depart from strategic responsibilities.

A few mileposts stand out in the many possible scenarios CIOs face with so many variables. Unless the company finds itself in a bonafide life-or-death business emergency, the primary focus for *all* senior executives is by default, strategic. Tactical management focus is the primary role and responsibility for line management. Therefore, if the CEO and other members of the senior management team rarely focus on strategic priorities, but instead micromanage tactical issues, the CIO probably focuses on tactical concerns more than any other executive due to the nature of the role and the expectations the company's top managers project on their information technology investments.

When the CEO is strategically focused but the rest of the senior management team is operationally focused, the CIO usually follows the focus of peers and partners—that is, tactical. Such CEOs are sole sovereigns of the strategic realm. Alternatively, when the CEO is operationally focused and the senior management team is strategically focused (this seems unlikely but, believe it or not, I have seen it, and it's not pretty), the CIO must meet the demands of a battle on two fronts and must readily provide enough operational information to satisfy the CEO. However, this expectation can be satisfied with a senior manager from the IT organization who serves as the necessary "fount of information" to the CEO on operational issues. While this takes mature executive experience on the part of the CIO, to recognize that the interactions of the CEO with someone on the CIO's staff is a reasonable approach, not everyone is comfortable with this approach. The successful CIO will find a way to become comfortable (perhaps through regular briefings by the senior manager on operational issues) and with not having to know everything at a minute level of detail.

That said, a prospective CIO should be very concerned about any company whose senior executives spend more time and attention on operational issues than they do on strategic issues. It's the equivalent of driving the freeway at night with only your parking lights. Or, for the more technically inclined, it's like a process under single or dual mode control whose behavior becomes unstable: When trend analysis fails to adjust the course, the result is that the process goes completely out of control. Either way, severe injuries and destruction are inevitable. In this context, the advice is a no-brainer: Do not hop into such a car; if you find yourself in such a car and you cannot see a means by which you can bring the car back under control (that is, get the senior management team focused strategically), then plan your exit before the car (and your career) crash!

Taking an inventory of the mix of strategic to operational priorities can be, of course, tricky. It should be *at least* 60/40, and it could be reasonably argued that the mix really should be more like 80/20 or 90/10. A CIO with a mix of 10/90 might be called a "chief information officer," but the truth is closer to a "DP manager." Conversely, if the true mix is 80/20 or 90/10, the CIO owns a true senior executive role where strategy and delivery both matter, with the emphasis on the strategic—as it should be.

Number 7: Why Should You Report Directly to Me?

This is a question every CEO should ask of each and every member of the senior executive staff. Having the right balance of direct reports—responsibilities, experience, skills, complementarity, developmental levels, and quantity—is an important survival issue for the CEO. Everyone wants to report to the CEO, just as everyone in the IT organization wants to report to the CIO. Consequently, whether the CEO or CIO raises this question, at least two issues come into play: Everyone wants to report directly; and there may be those who do not want the CIO to report directly to the CEO. In particular, if information technology investments are viewed as an expense, the CFO looks at the CIO as a direct report to ensure that the expense is managed in an accounting-based manner. Of course, a VP of operations thinks differently. Significant capital outlays necessary for information technology and concomitant operations activities and responsibilities (such as manufacturing) are so dependent on the information technology group that it is in the company's best interest for the IT organization to report through operations.

To complicate matters, the company may have a chief operating officer. Given the day-to-day nature of the operations side of IT, it may appear more appropriate for the CIO to report to the COO. With all these alternatives, any novice may wonder whether the CIO should even hope to report to the CEO. Practical experience with high-level positions demonstrates that some simple questions have no simple answers. This reporting conundrum is one of them. Remember, once a person achieves a certain level in most companies, the direct reporting structure tends to lose a bit of its hierarchy, giving way to an amorphous mass of senior executives.

Importantly for the CIO—an enabler of peers and partners—this amorphous mass becomes something for which he or she is expected to perform as a member, and at the same time, as an enabler. Regardless of reporting structure, the amorphous mass sees the CIO as reporting to each and every one of them individually and collectively. Yikes! This is a very strong reason that the CIO should seek to report to the CEO. There needs to be a balance and a reconciliation between the needs and requirements of the business unit executives and the overall needs and requirements of the company, to ensure that information technology investments, strategic plans, and overall execution align with the company's strategies. The need for a clear path of communication between the CIO and the CEO is essential to avoid aggrandizing the needs of particular business units to the level of strategic intent; the adage that "a group of local optimizations does not a global optimization make" applies in spades.[43]

An additional reason that the CIO should report directly to the CEO—and why you should want to—is so that the CIO can freely and readily engage in strategic conversations with the company's top strategic force: the chief executive officer. Don't expect that such dialogs happen between each and every executive who might just be able to schedule meetings on the CEO's calendar. Effective dialogs with the CEO occur with more effective approaches. Strategic discussions evolve over time in formal and informal sessions and often in conjunction with apparently nonstrategic events. Such events might pose a problem, an activity, a planned strategic session, or a serendipitous encounter.

Regardless of which path to a strategic encounter is taken, the successful CIO readily takes any appropriate opportunity to embark on a strategic discussion with the CEO. One of the most effective means by which these discussions give the CIO effective strategic input centers around specific scenarios, scenarios that allow the CIO to create a strategic context and then discuss the situations, alternatives, considerations, risks, and possible outcomes.

At the same time, discussion can and should include the rationale behind alternatives and views of both the CEO and the CIO. By sharing this level of thought and possible approaches, the CEO and CIO achieve a mutual understanding and better understand each other's thought patterns and preferences. In my experience, each party benefits enormously from invaluable insights into personal styles, preferences, and the commitment to the various parts of the overall business strategy. Let's not forget about the detailed knowledge and awareness of the "why" behind the "what." This common omission is absolutely necessary and invaluable to the CIO's ability to internalize that vision and use the resulting understanding to align information technology in a context that enables peers and partners to succeed in their strategies and plans.

For these reasons, it is highly desirable for the CIO to report directly to the CEO, and a prospective CIO is wise to have this conversation, during the interview process, before joining up. A wise CEO will see this and make it so. And, if you encounter a CEO who does not see this logic, and declines to see its merit, ask yourself if this is the direction you want to take for yourself and the people in your potential IT organization. Either way, it is a clear indicator as to how you will be viewed by the CEO and by your peers and partners, and consequently reflected by your entire IT organization.

Number 8: What Books Have You Read to Help Improve the Way You and Your Staff Perform Your Jobs?

This question should be an important one to the CEO as it relates to any prospective or current senior executive. When it relates to the CIO, the focus shifts to an integration of business and technology. Of course, many CIOs hear this question and wonder, "When would I have had enough time to read a book?" To be sure, finding the time to do so is always a challenge, but as for any evolving profession that requires continuing education, all senior managers and executives should be reading at least two books at any given time: a profession-related book and a personal entertainment book. CIOs who maintain good reading habits will be ready for this question.

The importance of continuing to be well-read professionally cannot be underestimated. The CIO's responsibilities encompass information technology, and this is an area of rapid continuous improvement, so the only way the senior IT executive can stay informed is to be well-read. Finding the time to read depends on one's work style and lifestyle and, to some degree on one's travel habits. Airplane travel is a perfect opportunity for some professional and some entertaining reading. For those who do not travel much, if necessary, schedule time into your day to ensure you have the time to read.

There are several books that each CIO or aspiring CIO should think of as critical reading resources in terms of career advice, technical enlightenment, business savvy, management skills, and for mental challenge and stimulation. I have referred to many of these already in the preceding chapters, but a few merit further mention here because I have found them truly worthy of good, serious reading for anyone with CIO-level responsibilities.

Career-oriented books come first on this reading list, and there are several very good books to help CIOs in the never-ending search for the best match between personal interests and professional capabilities. One of the most insightful career-oriented books in the past several years is Martha Beck's *Finding Your Own North Star.*[44] This book helps readers thoroughly examine and coordinate the work and leisure sides of life by focusing on the ways that aligning personal interests and professional talents can demonstrate best career paths. At the very least, this book helps challenge and validate personal goals and aspirations so that readers can make appropriate career decisions.

Another highly recommended career-oriented book is Mihaly Csikszentmihalyi's *Flow: The Psychology of Optimal Experience*.[45] "Flow" is a descriptive term that reflects the feeling when a person works, colloquially speaking, "in the zone." When work is performed in a flow mode, time seems to stop and focus and attention become very acute. In the author's own words: "[O]ptimal experience [is] based on the concept of *flow*—the state in which people are so involved in an activity that nothing else seems to matter; the experience itself is so enjoyable that people will do it even at great cost, for the sheer sake of doing it."[46] The focus of this book is to help the reader understand flow, how to practice the flow experiences, how to recognize the conditions of flow, how to get to flow-producing positions, and how to recognize patterns that can result in flow-inducing and flow-producing lives. Together, these two books are a powerful dynamic duo that address the outer and inner dimensions of career development and work. I cannot imagine anyone reading these two books and coming away unaffected. (In fact, I cannot help but wonder what life would be like if the ideas and suggestions in these two books were available 20 years ago.) Some CIOs or aspiring CIOs may wonder why such books would be important or of value to them. The answer is simple: You are at, or are approaching, a crossroads where you will be deciding the next direction to take on a path that requires a significant commitment.

The next level of detail for understanding one's personal and professional interests is addressed in Paul D. Tieger and Barbara Barron-Tieger's *Do What You Are: Discover the Perfect Career for You Through the Secrets of Personality Type*.[47] This book focuses on matching Myers-Briggs Type Indicator (MBTI) preferences to various career choices. The premise is that choosing the profession that best suits one's personality preference improves the probability of success and the pleasure that comes from performing work matched to one's natural gifts. This important reading makes for an interesting discussion between a prospective or current CIO and the CEO. Besides matching MBTI preferences with careers and jobs, the book profiles well-known people for each personality type and discusses how they perform their work and live their lives. These concrete examples help readers to find the best fit for their own lives while leveraging strengths and avoiding pitfalls along the way. When CIOs can discuss personality types with their CEOs, each person learns new ways to work together in a more complementary fashion.

For those new to the Myers-Briggs Type Indicator and personality types, David Keirsey and Marilyn Bates' *Please Understand Me: Character & Temperament Types* gives an excellent introduction.[48] This very accessible book carefully describes the types and temperaments and how personality types relate to our personal lives (including family) and leadership styles. For those who have not had the opportunity to learn their temperament through other means, a short questionnaire

provides an answer. As a senior executive, particularly as the leader of the IT organization that is likely to have a predilection toward two or three specific temperaments, the CIO needs to understand the material in this book. A better
understanding of how the IT organization works (as a group and as individuals)
helps bridge the gaps in behavioral differences among the CEO, senior executive
staff, and the IT organization.

Taking a critical, professional, and fresh look at technology, innovation, and corporate evolution is an exceptionally important focus for the CIO. One of the best
books on this key subject is Clayton Christensen's book, *The Innovator's Dilemma:
When New Technologies Cause Great Firms to Fail.*[49] The same author has recently
followed up with *The Innovator's Solution: Creating and Sustaining Successful Growth.*[50]
The first book, *The Innovator's Dilemma,* was truly a wake-up call for all companies.
The basic premise is that, regardless of seemingly good business approaches and solutions even outstanding companies tend to lose their leadership positions to companies that enter the market with a disruptive technology or market change. These
new companies introduce products that are initially underfeatured, but as they add
more features they hit the right feature-to-price ratio; in contrast, existing companies that listen only to their current customers focus only on *maintaining* their profits and customers. This leads the existing companies to overfeature and overprice
their products in the attempt to resist true disruptive product development that
might cannibalize their market position. Consequently, up-and-coming companies
steal the established companies' customers by eventually achieving the right mix of
features and cost while the established companies overshoot the needs and requirements of their customers. Products once rejected by mainstream customers as
underfeatured are embraced as being "right-featured" while the incumbent product is viewed as "old and tired," overfeatured, and overpriced.

The CEOs of product-based companies should understand these principles to
avoid falling into the traps identified by Christensen's book. These same CEOs
should expect their CIOs to understand these important principles—they are directly applicable, and many of the examples come from the computer industry. If
the subject does not come up, the well-read CIO should bring it up, offering insight about how the principles can be strategically applied to the company and its
use of information technology.

The recently published *Innovator's Solution* picks up where the *Innovator's
Dilemma* leaves off. It focuses on how to identify disruptive ideas, how to apply
them, how to find the right management team to bring them to market, and how
to avoid having the disruptive ideas smothered before they see the light of day. The
first book, published in 1997, has stood the test of time, and the second one is very
likely to also become a technology management classic. Any IT executives interested in taking charge of their own destiny, rather than having it take charge of
them, should read, understand, and make use of the experiences of these two books.

As the CIO incorporates change into a normal mode of information technology operations, John P. Kotter's book, *Leading Change* provides additional insights about the difficulties of change leadership.[51] The book gives a series of steps for effectively transforming the organization. Because many CEOs look to the CIO and their information technology investment as means of organizational change, it is important for the CEO to know that the CIO is knowledgeable and experienced in this area. Kotter's book is an excellent, concise, and experience-based recipe for managing change deliberately. His approach is based on a well-defined eight-stage process, beginning with establishing the need for urgency to change, and ending with ensuring the changes are strongly interleaved into the new culture.

In terms of understanding the real challenges of being a CIO—and understanding the expectations of those who are *not* CIOs—what is it going to take to be a successful CIO over the next 10 to 20 years? Paul A. Strassmann addresses this question better than anyone else. His book, *The Business Value of Computers: An Executive's Guide,* changed the landscape for evaluating CIO and IT investments.[52] Don't be fooled by the book's innocuous title; its core assertions are revolutionary. First, finding no correlation between level of spending on information technology and corporate profits or success, information technology success should be measured in terms of *return on management*. Strassmann defines return on management as the ratio of the value added by managerial activity to the company as a whole divided by the cost of that activity. Although return on management has not been widely adopted, the uproar caused by this book's assertions on IT investment has led to a significant investigation of IT spending over the past decade. The importance of this book is that it brings a *business-oriented* view to the management of information technology and, for all practical purposes, represents a business executive's handbook for CIOs and IT management. The CIO who is familiar with the topics and terminology in this book becomes an invaluable strategic business partner for the CEO. The content helps reinforce that the CIO truly recognizes that the role of senior technology executive does not only involve technology; it also involves business principles and value creation.

As a senior IT executive and a member of the senior staff, understanding customers needs, wants, and behaviors is key to long-term success. Stacey Hall and Jan Brogniez's *Attracting Perfect Customers* is required reading for every CIO serious about customer relationship management—both internal and external.[53] The most intriguing and universally applicable dimension of this book is that it has some very down-to-earth and practical ideas, observations, and actions that are natural follow-ons to market segmentation, in the spirit of *Crossing the Chasm* by Geoffrey Moore.[54] The basis for their customer approach is what they call "Creating Synchronicity with Perfect Customers and Clients," and they advocate replacing the thought "we need more customers" with the conviction "our business now attracts perfect customers only." One important lesson that executive teams seem to have to learn over and over is that some potential customers should not become customers. This subject may be a sensitive issue with some CEOs and some senior management peers, but it is essential to discover their attitudes early. A bad customer fit can handicap any company, and the CIO's awareness of working to find the best customers should sit very well with the CEO. If the CEO is not familiar with this concept, the CIO will perform a service for the company by making the CEO aware of it.

Looking to the future—and how to look *into* the future—two books are highly recommended. The first is a book edited by John Seely Brown, *Seeing Differently: Insights on Innovation*.[55] This excellent series of essays explores the changing business environment, new ways to look at innovations for competitive advantage, and the management of innovation. These very thought-provoking essays provide an almost endless amount of material that the CIO can use in strategic discussions with the CEO. The second future-oriented book is another of the most engaging books I have read: Peter Schwartz's *The Art of the Long View: Planning for the Future in an Uncertain World*.[56] A longtime friend who shares an interest in strategy and technology recommended this book to me. While we are two quite different people, we both appreciate the challenges and responsibilities of those who are burdened with taking a strategic view in a quickly evolving world of disruptive technological advances. A second subtitle for this book is "Paths to Strategic Insight for Yourself and Your Company." Schwartz takes the reader through the process of using scenarios for planning purposes and as a means of creating a strategic vision for the company. The book includes a "user's guide," a step-by-step description of a process that is intuitive, comfortable, tested, and effective.

As an example, Schwartz develops three scenarios for the world in the year 2005 that are broader, perhaps, than business scenarios, but effective in making the case. Discussing management principles from *The Art of the Long View* with the CEO should give the CIO great insights into the value that the CEO puts on strategic planning, and the appreciation the CEO has for the approach the CIO favors in developing such plans. The title itself will be useful for starting the discussion.

One final interesting and intriguing look at systems is enlightening, scary, and humorous: John Gall's *Systematics: How Systems Work and Especially How They Fail*.[57] This book focuses on the behavior of complex systems and complex organizations. Specifically, he discusses why they should be hugely successful rather than the resolute failures they often are. This engaging and very readable book introduces theorems into the systems (and computer systems) world that are well known in traditional engineering fields: "A Large System, Produced by Expanding the Dimensions of a Smaller System, Does Not Behave Like the Smaller System"[58] and "The Mode of Failure of a Complex System Cannot Ordinarily Be Predicted from Its Structure."[59] One of the benefits the reader gets from this book is a healthy respect for avoiding complexity when it comes to systems and to technology. This is a message that is worth ensuring that the CEO understands and that the CIO lives by. After discussing many of the problems raised by this book, the CEO will have a new appreciation for the value that the CIO brings to the company and the executive team.

Number 9: What Professional Publications Do You Read to Stay Current?

Whether your CEO is knowledgeable about the various appropriate magazines and journals an aspiring or a successful CIO reads is certainly the first question here. There are many business and management choices in the trade press and academic circles, but periodicals specifically targeted to the CIO are limited in number—although this number is increasing rapidly. Two that should be at the top of any CIO's list are *CIO Magazine*[60] and *CIO Insight*[61] magazine. A brief look at a recent table of contents (September 17, 2003) from *CIO Magazine* demonstrates why this is so (see Exhibit 5.10).

CIO Magazine also contains access to additional features through the magazine's Web page, such as issue archives; links to a series of electronic subscription newsletters; a listing of CIO conferences; an online store for purchasing studies and books; a section on career management; a section on research and polls; a section on expert viewpoints (which includes a very interesting section on performance metrics); a section on reports and guides; an online bulletin board for CIOs and IT executives; a special bulletin board for the Fortune 100 CIOs; and a research center that includes budgeting, executive considerations, emerging technology, IT value, leadership and management, outsourcing staffing and retention, supply chain management, and wireless topics. Similarly, a brief look at the *CIO Insight* Web page reveals the features listed in Exhibit 5.11. *CIO Insight* also includes additional online sections containing research, white papers, surveys; plus sections on management, strategy, technology, case studies, and an online bulletin board for discussions.

In the area of general information technology news magazines, the two at the top of the list are *Computerworld*[62] and *InformationWeek*.[63] Exhibit 5.12 is a brief look at a very relevant recent (September 17, 2003) table of contents for *Computerworld*.

One other trade resource, if you are interested in or involved with storage systems, is *InfoStor* magazine.[64] In the realm of refereed journals and magazines, there are a number of excellent choices—in fact, too many to list here. However, four that are worth regular attention include:

- *The Harvard Business Review*,[65] a publication of the Harvard University Business School, focuses on business, management, and leadership best practices.

EXHIBIT 5.10 SAMPLE *CIO MAGAZINE* TABLE OF CONTENTS

Cover Story: I.T. Outsourcing: Merrill Lynch's Billion Dollar Bet

Features:

Exclusive *CIO* Staffing Survey: What They're Saying about You

I.T. Staff Development: How to Launch a Leader

Business Intelligence: Business Intelligence Gets Smart(er)

CIO Priorities: Birth of a Salesman

Emerging Technology: E-Mail on the Cheap

Columns:

From the Publisher: Microprocessors Matter

Total Leadership: About Face!

Making I.T. Work: Don't Trust Your Code to Strangers

Reality Bytes: Why More Is Less

Career Counsel: How to Get to the Top

Sections:

Trendlines

Off the Shelf

Washington Watch

Under Development

Pundit

In Every Issue:

From the Editor: Leading Indicators

Inbox

Board of Advisors

Index

Executive Summary

Source: Adapted from *CIO Magazine* home page, www.cio.com, September 17, 2003.

- *MIS Quarterly*, a peer–reviewed scholarly journal that publishes research concerning both the management of information technology and the use of information technology for managerial and organizational purposes.[66]
- *Journal of Cost Management,* which addresses the relationship of managerial accounting and technology.[67]
- *IEEE Engineering Management Review,* which publishes reprints from other sources of interest to those actively involved in managing technical organizations.[68]

EXHIBIT 5.11 *CIO INSIGHT* **WEB PAGE CONTENTS**

Top Stories

    Case Study: Wal-Mart's Race for RFID

    Re-Engineering Security

    Sarbanes-Oxley: Comply with Me

    How to Improve Your IT Security Policy: A Six Sigma Approach

Research

    Research: Is E-Business Finally Starting to Deliver?

    C-Meter: CIO Confidence Rebounds

Opinion

    Tag, You're It!

    The Julius Caesar Syndrome

    The *CIO Insight* Reading Library

    Sites to See

Sidebar

    A *CIO Insight* Special Issue: The Alignment Gap

Source: Adapted from *CIO Insight* home page, www.cioinsight.com, September 17, 2003.

For the more technically minded, additional informative publications include *Computer Technology Review*,[69] *Storage Management Solutions*,[70] *Communications of the ACM*,[71] *Computer*,[72] and *IEEE Software*.[73] CIOs who are not technically inclined should find someone in the IT organization who subscribes to these periodicals and ask the person to be on the lookout for important articles. For instance, a recent edition of *Communications of the ACM*[74] contained an article entitled "How CIOs Manage Their Superiors' Expectations"; and a recent issue of *IEEE Software* published an article entitled "Trade-offs between Productivity and Quality in Selecting Software Development Practices."[75]

CIOs interested in looking into the future should enjoy *The Futurist* and *Technology Review: MIT's Magazine of Innovation*. For example, a recent issue of *The Futurist* featured these two articles: "The Future of the Book in the Digital Age"[76] and "World Trends & Forecasts—Technology: New System Reads Body Language." A recent issue of *Technology Review* published an article called "Where-Ware"[77] (software to help you figure out where you are, to provide appropriate location-contextual information automatically).

All this looks like a lot to read, and it would be if you were to read every article in every magazine or journal. The point here is that there are many sources of information, and the successful CIO keeps himself or herself informed about the experiences of others, current business and technology thinking, strategic planning, and technology and methodologies, and keeps an eye on the future of information

EXHIBIT 5.12 SAMPLE *COMPUTERWORLD* TABLE OF CONTENTS

Knowledge Center: Outsourcing
- Offshore Buyer's Guide
- IT's Global Itinerary

India	Canada
The Philippines	Mexico
Ireland	China
Singapore	Vietnam
Malaysia	Brazil
Russia	Opinion

- Special articles in online version
    - Offshore Security: Considering the Risks
    - Negotiating an International Outsourcing Contract
    - What Projects Should Be Outsourced Overseas?
    - Processes, QA Key to Successful Offshore IT
    - Outsourcing: Voices from the Front Lines

News
- Use of the H-1B Visa. . . .
- Extreme Networks. . . .
- Novell Plans. . . .
- Oracle Announces. . . .
- A Proposed California Privacy Law. . . .
- Power Companies. . . .
- The U.S. Marines. . . .

Online pointers to
- Breaking News
- Newsletter Subscriptions
- Knowledge Centers
- *Computerworld* Story

Source: Adapted from *Computerworld* home page, www.computerworld.com, September 17, 2003.

technology. Remember: CIO is chief information officer, the senior executive for information technology. You are expected to be *the* company IT expert.

Number 10: What Is the Proper Alignment of Business and Technology for Your Job?

Business and strategy alignment of the CIO's areas of responsibility is key to organizational and individual success. As the senior information technology executive, it is essential that the CIO align the IT organization with the business and strategic directions agreed upon by the executive team and implemented by the senior executives of the business units. These are the CIO's peers and partners; and the CIO and the IT organization enable those executives and their organizations to meet the agreed-upon objectives. You may very well be breaking new ground when you embark on the strategic discussions implied by these questions with the CEO. The number of strategic conversations that take place are usually small compared to those of a tactical nature; it is all too easy for the CEO and the senior executives to get wrapped up in the day-to-day operation of the company.

How serious a problem can this become? Let's look at an example. Say that some new problem demands a new capital-required IT project. What criteria will the executive team use to analyze the project for approval or denial? Most of the people involved in such a situation *believe* that they are considering the strategic ramifications, but often do not know what questions to ask. In this kind of project review, the discussion regarding merits generally focuses on the costs, how completely the problem can be solved, and perhaps even the return on investment. Is this a strategic discussion? Does this focus consider the long-term effects of doing the project, or not? Is there any discussion concerning the project's risk profile, its long-term effects after completion or failure to complete, or the impact of delays and unexpected costs? Is there any discussion about whether the project aligns in any way with IT's overall strategic directions based on alignment with the company and other business unit strategies? Is there any discussion about what other projects will not be done in a "zero-sum resource and capital" environment and their long-term effects? Is there any discussion about the effects of a change in environment that could disrupt this project?

The all-too-frequent pattern here is clear: Operational decisions—whether tactical or strategic—should be evaluated in terms of their strategic ramifications. This is not to say that individual project decisions will be different, but it becomes highly probable that, over a period of time, a discernable number of decisions *will* be made differently. When taken collectively, these decisions have a significant and lasting positive influence on the CIO's business and on all the people enabled by the CIO.

As with peers and partners, the CIO must keep in mind that strategic planning with the CEO is about the corporate strategic plan, the IT strategic plan, and the CEO's strategic plans: business and strategic alignment. The CIO's responsibilities are to enable the success of the other two strategic plans by implementation of a well-aligned IT strategic plan. When these plans are in alignment, the CEO's success is enabled, and in a closed-loop system, the CEO's success is the CIO's success.

You now have the 10 questions that you should expect from a CEO with a high BTIQ—or that you should insinuate into your strategic conversations with a CEO possessing a low BTIQ. If you are fortunate, your CEO will be an enlightened senior executive who works with a wise and balanced set of insights about the strategic value potential of information technology, as well as the value that the CIO brings to bear. If, however, the CEO is at the other end of the spectrum—financially focused and short-sighted—then it is likely that you must face the additional challenge of enlightening your CEO to IT's strategic value. Along the way, both the CEO and the CIO will benefit, if the CEO is trainable. A successful outcome will be beneficial to the CEO, the CIO, and the company. An unsuccessful outcome suggests that the CIO has managed to connect with an inappropriately appointed CEO; and if there is no change in sight, then it might well be time to move on to the next opportunity and remember to address these questions during the interview process for that next opportunity.

NOTES

1. Robert S. Kaplan and David P. Norton, *The Strategy-Focused Organization* (Boston: Harvard Business School Press, 2001): 8.
2. Kenneth I. Primozic, Edward A. Primozic, and Joe Leben, *Strategic Choices: Supremacy, Survival, or Sayonara* (New York: McGraw-Hill, 1991): 34.
3. H. Thomas Johnson and Anders Bröms, *Profit Beyond Measure: Extraordinary Results Through Attention to Work and People* (New York: The Free Press, 2000).
4. Catherine and Joe Stenzel, "The Reconciliation of Finance and Operations: A Conversation with Brian Maskell," *Journal of Strategic Performance Measurement*, vol. 3, no. 5 (October/November 1999): 23.
5. Roy W. Regel, "Change in the Controller's Role: Why Intuition Improves Operational and Strategic Decisions," *Journal of Cost Management*, vol. 17, no. 1 (January/February 2003): 31–38.
6. Ibid., p. 31.
7. Paul A. Strassmann, *The Squandered Computer: Evaluating the Business Alignment of Information Technologies* (New Canaan, CT: The Information Economics Press, 1997): 3.
8. Erik Brynjolfsson, "The Productivity Paradox of Information Technology," *Communications of the ACM*, vol. 36, no. 12 (December 1993): 67–68.
9. Ibid., p. 70.
10. Ibid.
11. Scott Leibs, "The Argument for Tech: Economist Erik Brynjolfsson Leads the Charge toward

a Greater Appreciation of IT," *CFO.com*, www.cfo.com/article/1,5309,7878 | | | 3,00.html (accessed September 6, 2003).

12. Ibid.

13. Bruce Caldwell, "A New Bible for MIS," *Information Week* (October 15, 1990): 36–40.

14. Ibid., p. 37.

15. Michael Pastore, *Global IT Spending Remains Robust*, http://cyberatlas.internet.com/big_picture/hardware/article/0,,5921_779671,00.html (accessed June 6, 2003).

16. Chip Gliedman, "Planning Assumptions: GigaWorld IT Value Program Poll—Still a Long Way to Go," *Giga Information Group*, Ver: 2 RPA-062000-00026 (June 26, 2000): 2, 3.

17. Ibid., pp. 4, 5.

18. Mark Anderson, Rajiv D. Banker, and Nan Hu, "Estimating the Business Value of Investments in Information Technology," White Paper published by the University of Texas at Dallas (December 9, 2002): 3.

19. Ibid., p. 15.

20. Ibid., pp. 15, 16.

21. Peter B. Seddon, Valerie Graeser, and Leslie P. Willcocks, "Measuring Organizational IS Effectiveness: An Overview and Update of Senior Management Perspectives," *The DATA BASE for Advances in Information Systems* 33, no. 2 (Spring 2002): 18.

22. Ibid., p. 19.

23. Robert S. Kaplan and David P. Norton, *The Balanced Scorecard: Translating Strategy into Action* (Boston: Harvard Business School Press, 1996).

24. V. Graeser, L. Willcocks, and N. Pisanias, *Developing the IT Scorecard*, (Wimbledon, London: Business Intelligence Ltd., 1998).

25. In those companies that have begun to look at outsourcing, it has also been observed that outsourcing appears to be a catalyst for improved practices related to the evaluation of IT, whether or not any IT functions are ultimately outsourced.

26. As noted earlier, Strassmann (as cited in Caldwell) reports a completely random correlation (i.e., no correlation at all) between investments in information technology and levels and/or improvements and/or degradation in company revenues, profits, and profitability.

27. Tom Pisello, "The CIO Makeover: From CTO to CFO of IT," *SearchCIO.com* (accessed August 28, 2003).

28. The Carnegie-Mellon University Web site is a treasure trove of information on the Capability Maturity Model: www.sei.cmu.edu/managing/managing.html.

29. For an example, see Brian A. Will, "Can Quality Management Systems Improve Your Software Development and Business Performance?" White Paper, Paroxys, LLC, Encinitas, CA 92024, available at www.paroxys.com (accessed September 14, 2003).

30. "What CMM Ratings Mean," *CSC Corporation Features*, www.csc.com/features/2002/19_sidebar.shtml (accessed September 13, 2003).

31. Professor Jerry Luftman is the executive director of the graduate information systems program at the Stevens Institute of Technology and Distinguished Professor in the Howe School of Technology Management; http://howe.stevens.edu/Faculty/JerryLuftman.html.

32. Jerry Luftman, "A Tool to Help You Assess IT-Business Alignment," *ABInsight*, IBM Advanced Business Institute, www-1.ibm.com/ibm/palisades/abinsight/issues/2002-May/article-2.html (accessed July 6, 2003).

33. Ibid.

34. Seddon, et al., "Measuring Organizational IS Effectiveness," p. 21.

35. Ibid., p. 22.

36. Ibid., p. 21.

37. Ibid., p. 23.

38. V. Serafeimidis and S. Smithson, "Information Systems Evaluation in Practice: A Case Study of Organizational Change," *Journal of Information Technology* 15 (2000): 101.

39. Cliff Saran, "IT Management: Project Management: Research Will Set Project Management Benchmark," *ComputerWeekly.com*, www.computerweekly.com/articles/article.asp?li ArticleID=117025&liArticleTypeID=1=&liCategoryID=2&liChannelID=105&liFlavourI D=1&sSearch=&nPage=1 (accessed September 14, 2003).

40. "Project Planning, Analysis, and Control Workshop for IBM," *Project Management Professional Development Program,* Educational Services Institute, in association with the George Washington University, Arlington, VA (1996): 286.

41. J. Kent Crawford and James S. Pennypacker, "Collaborative Strategies: Put an End to Project Mismanagement," *Optimize* 12 (October 2002): 1, available at www.optimizemag.com/printer/012/pr_collaborative.html.

42. Peter Schwartz, *The Art of the Long View* (New York: Doubleday, 1996): 221.

43. Someone might be asked whether reporting to the COO is as good as reporting to the CEO. The answer is, of course, no. However, given the choice of reporting to the COO or the CFO (or an otherwise-peer business unit executive), the COO is generally a better choice. Whereas the COO will have a more tactical focus than the CEO, the COO will also likely have significantly more operational experience and business-related experience in the trade-offs of product, development, customers, and risks.

44. Martha Beck, *Finding Your Own North Star* (New York: Three Rivers Press, 2001).

45. Mihaly Csikszentmihalyi, *Flow: The Psychology of Optimal Experience* (New York: Harper-Perennial, 1991).

46. Ibid., p. 4.

47. Paul D. Tieger and Barbara Barron-Tieger, *Do What You Are: Discover the Perfect Career for You Through the Secrets of Personality Type* (New York: Little, Brown & Company, 2001).

48. David Keirsey and Marilyn Bates, *Please Understand Me: Character & Temperament Types* (Del Mar, CA: Prometheus Nemesis Books, 1978).

49. Clayton M. Christensen, *The Innovator's Dilemma: When New Technologies Cause Great Firms to Fail,* (Boston: Harvard Business School Press, 1997).

50. Clayton M. Christensen and Michael E. Raynor, *The Innovator's Solution: Creating and Sustaining Successful Growth* (Boston: Harvard Business School Press, 2003).

51. John P. Kotter, *Leading Change,* (Boston: Harvard Business School Press, 1996).

52. Paul A. Strassmann, *The Business Value of Computers: An Executive's Guide,* (New Canaan, CT: The Information Economics Press, 1990).

53. Stacey Hall and Jan Brogniez, *Attracting Perfect Customers: The Power of Strategic Synchronicity* (San Francisco: Berrett-Koehler Publishers, 2001).

54. Geoffrey A. Moore, *Crossing the Chasm* (New York: HarperCollins, 1995).

55. John Seely Brown, ed., *Seeing Differently: Insights on Innovation* (Boston: Harvard Business Review Publishing, 1997).

56. Schwartz, *Art of the Long View.*

57. John Gall, *Systematics: How Systems Work and Especially How They Fail* (New York: Pocket Books, 1977).

58. Ibid., p. 45.

59. Ibid., p. 93.

60. *CIO Magazine* describes itself as "The Resource for Information Executives." It is published twice each month by CXO Media, Inc., a part of the International Data Group. The online version, www.cio.com, is updated daily. Subscriptions are free of charge to those qualified, and are most easily requested through the Web site, www.cio.com.

61. *CIO Insight* magazine describes itself as focused on "Strategies for IT Business Leaders." It is published twice per month by Ziff-Davis, Inc. The online version, www.cioinsight.com, is updated daily. Subscriptions are free of charge to those qualified, and are most easily requested through the Web site, www.cioinsight.com.

62. *Computerworld* describes itself as "The Voice of IT Management." It is published weekly by International Data Group. The online version, www.computerworld.com, is updated daily. Subscriptions are free of charge to those qualified, and are most easily requested through the Web site, www.computerworld.com.

63. *InformationWeek* says that it concentrates on "Business Innovation Powered by Technology." It is published weekly by CMP Media LLC. The online version, www.informationweek.com, is updated daily. Subscriptions are free of charge to those qualified, and are most easily requested through the Web site, www.informationweek.com.

64. *InfoStor* magazine calls itself "The Leading Source for Enterprise Storage Professionals." It is published monthly by PennWell. The online version is available at www.infostor.com and is updated daily. Subscriptions are free of charge to those qualified, and are most easily requested through the Web site, www.infostor.com.

65. The current issue (as of December 20, 2003) of the *Harvard Business Review* is available online at http://harvardbusinessonline.hbsp.harvard.edu/b01/en/hbr/hbr_current_issue.jhtml.

66. The current issue (as of December 20, 2003) of *MIS Quarterly* is available online at www.misq.org/archivist/home.html/current.

67. The current issue (as of December 20, 2003) of the *Journal of Cost Management* is available online at www.riahome.com/Estore/detail.asp?ID=ZMCM.

68. David J. Wells, ed., *IEEE Engineering Management Review*, vol. 31, no. 2 (Second Quarter 2003).

69. *Computer Technology Review*, vol. 23, no. 7 (July 2003), www.wwpi.com.

70. *Storage Management Solutions*, vol. 8, no. 3 (Third Quarter, 2003).

71. *Communications of the ACM*, vol. 46, no. 8 (August 2003).

72. *Computer*, vol. 36, no. 7 (July 2003).

73. *IEEE Software*, vol. 20, no. 5 (September/October 2003).

74. Richard E. Potter, "How CIOs Manage Their Superior's Expectations," *Communications of the ACM*, vol. 46, no. 8 (2003): 74–79.

75. Alan MacCormack, Chris F. Kemerer, Michael Cusumano, and Bill Crandall, "Trade-offs between Productivity and Quality in Selecting Software Development Practices," *IEEE Software*, vol. 20, no. 5 (2003): 78–85; available at http://computer.org.

76. David J. Staley, "The Future of the Book in a Digital Age," pp. 18–22; Hope Cristol, "New System Reads Body Language: The Truth Is in Your Eyes—and Mannerisms," p. 16; both in *The Futurist*, vol. 37, no. 5 (September–October 2003); available at http://www.wfs.org.

77. Eric W. Pfeiffer, "WhereWare," *Technology Review*, vol. 106, no. 7 (September 2003): 46–52; available at www.technologyreview.com.

CHAPTER 6

Final Preparations

As we fix our sight on the future and anticipate all the wonders yet in store for us, we should also reflect back and marvel at the journey we have taken so far. . . . We are all, each in our own way, seekers of the truth and we each long for an answer to why we are here. . . . And, as [we] marvel at our new view of the universe—our new way of asserting the world's coherence—we are fulfilling our part, contributing our rung to the human ladder reaching for the stars.

—Brian Greene[1]

U p to this point, the *Guide* has followed a distinct path. It began by urging the CIO or aspiring CIO to look inwardly and outwardly for what to expect and what is expected of the CIO. It then examined the differences between the CIO and the CTO in terms of the relationship of the business and technical aspects of the CIO's role, and indexed the key skills necessary for a CIO to perform successfully both personally and professionally. Next, it charted the key areas and means for the CIO to make the IT organization and the company successful by connecting information technology and the IT organization to companywide value creation. All the while the *Guide* urged you, the CIO, to keep in mind that what makes for success is true business alignment, achieved by working with your peers and partners as an *enabler* to help them achieve their goals.

With that groundwork, you are now ready to go forth as a cross-functional executive champion. To help you prepare to head out to do good, this chapter focuses on the necessary preparations for the journey by looking at the barriers and accelerators to success and some decisions the CIO should not make alone. Then the chapter takes a final look at your own skills and needs, and explains how to prepare and sharpen them. The well-prepared CIO is then fully equipped to make the technology trek that creates business value.

THE TREK INTO (UN)KNOWN TERRITORY: BARRIERS TO SUCCESS

> *Despite the fact that most of us are familiar with teams, we are imprecise in thinking about them. For that reason, gaining a clear understanding of what a team is and is not—and particularly how teams and performance depend on each other—can provide useful insights in how to strengthen the performance of your group. Imprecise thinking about teams, however, pales in comparison to the lack of discipline most of us bring to potential team situations. Teams do not spring up by magic. Nor does personal chemistry matter as much as most people believe. Rather, we believe that . . . most people can significantly enhance team perform-ance. And focusing on performance—not chemistry or togetherness or good com-munications or good feelings—shapes teams more than anything else.*
> —Jon R. Katzenback and Douglas K. Smith[2]

> *The primary role of top management is to focus on performance and the teams that will deliver it.*
> —Jon R. Katzenback and Douglas K. Smith[3]

There are many barriers to success—personal and professional—for the CIO and the IT organization, for the CIO's peers and partners, and for the company. Fortu-nately, many of these are within the CIO's reach and realm and can therefore be addressed and mitigated. Among the most challenging barriers are those that can affect the CIO alone, a group of senior executives, or an entire organization. For instance, inaccurate self-assessments have some CIOs believing that they are highly effective, fully supportive of peers and partners, and fully aligned with their busi-ness strategies, when the reality may well be that the peers and partners experience things differently. The same CIOs' actual performance records demonstrate that they are clueless about peer business strategies and how IT fits into those strategies. Thus, self-assessments need to be validated by someone else. Who better than the peers and partners who constitute the CIO's critical strategic customer base?

Another barrier regularly encountered by CIOs is the anti-IT bias. In many companies, the IT organization works under the burden of an unfavorable reputa-tion, deserved or not. It is up to the CIO to change this outlook, and the CIO can begin this change process in some very concrete ways. For example, the so-called Pollyanna Syndrome often gets the CIO and the IT organization into the prover-bial dog house when it comes to making commitments and then following through on them (more on this syndrome a little later). The reputations of almost all development organizations have been tainted by this problem. As a deliberate executive management response, the CIO must look for better ways to create and manage the project estimation process prior to commitment, and thereby ensure that commitment risks are balanced to produce on time, on schedule, and on budget. Another common internal barrier comes in the form of those who are afraid to try anything different either for fear of failure or fear of success. Watch phrases for the erection of these barriers include "But we've always done it this way" and "We've already tried that and it didn't work." Removing these barriers is tricky, and sometimes part of the solution will be to remove the barrier guards.

Finally, one additional barrier CIOs encounter is self-set: workload. Over time, many CIOs and other senior executives are tempted, encouraged, or intimidated into accepting unreasonable (read: irresponsible) workloads. Sooner or later, an excessive workload impairs the CIO's effectiveness in ways that ultimately spell disaster for the CIO, the IT organization, and sometimes the company.

Inaccurate Self-Assessments

> *Data: As you examine your life, do you find you have missed your humanity?*
> *Spock: I have no regrets.*
> *Data: "No regrets." That is a human expression.*
> *Spock: Yes. Fascinating!*[4]

How well do you know yourself? On the one hand, no one knows you better than you know yourself. On the other hand, everyone knows you better than you know yourself. How can this be true? Quite easily. As people mature, each forms a concrete mental and internal image of self: looks, behaviors, relationships, and the like. Generally, I know my motivations and intent for these aspects of myself better than any other person—alive or dead. However, the CIO and others in leadership position need another perspective. How are you viewed by those around you who must (directly or indirectly) follow your orders and work with you? There are a number of objective ways to validate your self-assessment of your performance.

As a first-time manager at IBM, I was sent to first-line managers' school in Armonk, New York, in the late 1980s. I truly looked forward to this experience because the school had a fantastic reputation, and I felt there was a lot I could learn. People did not attend this management school until they had worked as a manager for at least three months. (There was a local management school employees attended in their first month that taught management basics, associated paperwork, and legal requirements.) The process used an evaluation form as a part of the preparation for the corporate management school. It asked a number of questions about my style: How do I approach and solve problems? How do I interpret success and failure? What are some of the most important experiences that I have encountered in my interactions with peer managers, my boss, and those I have managed?

Besides my own version of this form, I was instructed to mail the same evaluation form (focusing on my performance) to some of my employees, a peer or two, and my manager. The results were then gathered together and presented to me at the corporate management school. This was done in such a way that I would not be able to identify who responded, and how. The various evaluations of how I approached and performed my work was similar in many areas, different in some areas, and significantly different in one or two areas. Each student in corporate management school also had the opportunity to see how others in the class evaluated themselves relative to their coworkers. These same opportunities were repeated in later levels of management school, and each exercise afforded a more detailed and focused look.

Eventually, in the mid-1990s, IBM integrated this into its general review and evaluation process for employees, calling it a "360-review"—meaning a full-circle or 360-degree look at the individual's work and approach. This approach is very informative, very direct, and, at times, very disturbing. It is informative to see yourself as others see you. Only then can a CIO or other leader correlate the two perspectives and learn what to do differently or what should be reinforced to ensure continuing performance excellence. The general anonymity of the process results in direct, straightforward observations and suggestions. Some of the most important (and very disturbing) feedback comes when the observations and suggestions are very contrary or diametrically opposed to your own view of yourself, your actions, and your intent performance. This addresses the core of the self-assessment dilemma: An inaccurate self-assessment only puts off the inevitable. An inaccurate external assessment might feel good (when it is a positive one), but if the CIO cannot candidly accept the results of a negative external assessment, that same CIO creates a self-established barrier that continues to undermine successful, effective work with fellow employees at all levels.

By the same token, some CIO personalities always maintain an overly negative self-assessment when coworkers at all levels see things positively. In any case, where your assessment and the assessment of those with whom and for whom you work are significantly different, there are barriers in place that will inhibit your ability to succeed in your leadership role. Subsequent external assessments determine which responses were effective and which were not. Consider the value of getting accurate assessments and opinions about your car or your health for routine maintenance or when a problem arises. Unless you are also a professional mechanic or a medical doctor, your assessments of problems may not be anywhere near the real problems—especially if the problems are complex. If you were to make decisions based solely on your information technology knowledge, you would likely damage a perfectly good car or cause yourself further suffering and disease. Both cases call for a trained professional. As a professional executive, seek the input and feedback of others in your full circle so you get an accurate self-assessment. Just how well *do* you know yourself? No matter what your answer, test it with several external, expert opinions.

Anti-IT Biases: Solution versus Problem

> *It's been my experience that the prejudices people feel about each other disappear when they get to know each other.*
>
> —James T. Kirk[5]

At one time or another, probably every CIO and senior IT executive has encountered the anti–IT bias—that look, the body language, the eyebrow, the grunt, the many other visual and verbal queues—communicating a lack of respect for anything IT. The anti–IT bias is especially common in companies with a product development group parallel to the IT organization's development group. While most local work groups naturally build a strong sense of tribal unity (and superiority), the anti–IT bias is a substantially different dynamic.

Most IT organizations have both information technology development and information technology operations groups integrated under the IT umbrella. From the perspective of their separate nontechnological fiefdoms, non–IT organization's business units primarily see IT in terms of its operations people. The local exposures and experiences of their day-to-day work create this erroneous perspective. Consequently, these same non–IT business units come to believe that the IT organization is staffed by people who are significantly less qualified than those in the non–IT organizations. Fortunately, some companies have found ways to demonstrate IT's development work.

For instance, Dell's IT organization has often been larger than its product development group—and significantly more sophisticated as well. Many companies see such a balance as a likely barrier to success, whereas Dell deliberately managed the arrangement so that it became a significant plus for the product development group and the company. By working together to identify needed, useful, and timely solutions, Dell's product group could pretty much guarantee a higher "hit" ratio of products for enterprise customers. Dell's IT organization had the benefit of influencing the next generation of products and solutions. This helped managers know which solutions they would be able to get from Dell (as a customer) and which solutions they would have to get elsewhere. Generally, the reason the product group might not be supplying all solutions that Dell IT needed was that there was not significant enough revenue for Dell's mainline (high-volume) customers. This allowed both groups to optimize their investment dollars.

The CIO must focus on becoming part of the solution at all levels of the company when employees demonstrate an anti-IT bias. Interacting with the business units on a regular basis, making use of assigned liaisons between the IT organization and the business units, and ensuring clear communications on the level of support that IT provides the business units' strategic and tactical plans undermine anti-IT bias by demonstrating how IT creates value. Through these means, people get to know each other, and the prejudices will disappear over time. Do you know your customers?

The Pollyanna Syndrome: Overcommit and Underproduce

The Pollyanna Syndrome takes its name from the character in the book of the same name, but in a less-than-positive light.[6] A person with this outlook is often referred to as wearing rose-colored glasses, with the implied if not explicitly stated message being to take off the glasses and see the world as it really is. Unfortunately, many IT organizations and their people suffer from the Pollyanna Syndrome—regularly overcommitting and underproducing. To a great degree, this mismatch between promises and results can be traced back to intent and ability to deliver. Malicious intent is very rare; perspectives on genuine intent and ability to deliver vary based on the time and place performance is measured. Very often, people remember and cling to the CIO's or IT staff member's original commitment even though the original working conditions and project requirements have changed, generally without a coincident adjustment of their expectations to align with current conditions. Most active CIOs have experienced this dynamic either by actively participating in it or by becoming a victim. Those same CIOs can probably provide a number of reasons for getting into the predicament. Among the most common reasons are:

- Politics
- Naïve promises made by marketing, senior executives, naïve project managers, and others
- The start-up mentality of fledging, entrepreneurial companies
- Intense competition caused by globalization of markets
- Intense competition caused by the appearance of new technologies
- Intense pressure caused by unexpected government regulations
- Unexpected and/or unplanned crises[7]

Politics might not seem to be a reason for overcommitment, but in my experience, it is probably the third most common reason behind just plain poor estimating and naïve promises. Politics covers a large area, but most mistakes boil down to well-meaning but self-focused intentions on the part of the "committer" to meet the commitments in an objective set by a senior executive. In doing so, the committer usually adjusts schedules, budgets, and/or resources to arrive at a proposal that is acceptable to the customer—in intent, that is. Politically motivated overcommitments end up one of two ways: underproducing and the subsequent search for and identification of the scapegoats, or a mandatory "death march." Neither of these options enhances the career of a CIO. The Pollyanna Syndrome is the most common reason for afflicted CIOs to adjust schedules, budgets, and resource estimates optimistically. In contrast to the Pollyanna belief that all or nearly all possible events will turn out well, experience suggests that Murphy's Law—anything that can go wrong will—provides a more realistic IT philosophy for planning commitments. For those very complex projects, go with Murphy.

Promises made with good but naïve intent by marketing, senior executives, naïve project managers, and others are more often than not made with the best interests of the company at heart and its current or potential customers in mind. For example, consider the marketing executive who firmly believes in the abilities of the IT organization and the CIO to deliver the needed features and functions in the desired time frame. Such a marketing executive has benefited previously from the CIO and the team meeting a very challenging deadline with flying colors. The marketing executive therefore feels emboldened to make similar risky commitments: You did it before so you can do it again.

The worst times for naïve behaviors is the electrically charged atmosphere of the "feeding frenzy" that follows a strategy and/or planning session during which everyone comes to believe they can take on the world and win. At such moments, realism has been temporarily suspended, and groupthink euphoria is in the air. While the equivalent regret of buyer's remorse may soon follow, people seldom back down from the promises they make in such inappropriately positive atmospheres. Activities and projects that in saner moments would have been estimated to take a year to accomplish—even with extraordinary efforts—have been committed to complete in six months, with at least a fourth fewer resources than really needed, to boot! These commitments set the CIO and the IT organization up for failure. The sooner the CIO reestablishes, the better for everyone. Though difficult from a personality and an ego point of view, it is essential for the health of the company, the well-being of his or her employees, and for his or her own professional and ethical well-being. It's part of the CIO role and its responsibilities to work with peers and partners to prepare the way for new information and potentially bad news so that they remain fully informed and can support (or at least understand) the CIO's position. Then the CIO can gather them together to formally reset expectations.

Perhaps the most common road to overcommitted underproduction is laid when the CIO makes estimates and establishes requirements based on what it will take to get takers. That is, the CIO pretty much knows that a given project or series of projects requires a certain amount of resources, time, and expenses. At the same time, the CIO knows that the informed, probable estimates will signal a no-go to the person who approves the project. This situation can arise from within the company or from an outsourcer or contractor bidding on a job. This "start-up mentality" is pushed and touted as "a new way of doing things," "the wave of the future," "doing more with less," and so on. Edward Yourdon describes this dynamic very well:

> [I]n general, start-up organizations are understaffed, underfinanced, under-managed, and outrageously optimistic about their chances of success. They have to be because a cautious, conservative manager would never dream of starting a new company without tons of careful planning and a large bank account to deal with unforeseen contingencies.[8]

This outlook applies to nonstart-up organizations, also; an IT organization that has overcommitted, for whatever reason, will have the same result: underproducing and failure. In the case of the start-up, the entrepreneurs continually increase their commitments to deliver, while decreasing their requirements for resources until those who would invest are accepting of the two. The mismatch created will, over time, make it very difficult for the entrepreneurs to succeed and for the investors to see the return on their investment they are expecting. Those that do succeed, start-ups and projects, are likely to have done so due to a resetting of the expectations or through a death march. Given the choice, resetting the expectations is much more reasonable and rational, as it is more likely done through more careful planning and analyses.

Unexpected or unplanned crises create a different challenge for the IT organization and for the CIO. Twenty or 30 years ago, it might have been that each organization had enough people and resources available to absorb the effects of such aimless practices. Today, that is rarely if ever the case. As a result, every person in the IT organization and every dollar in the IT budget is usually spoken for (and then some), and the CIO hopes and prays that nothing unexpected or unplanned arises. Of course, this is the Pollyanna Syndrome at its worst. Using the techniques outlined in the *Guide*, the CIO can prepare for inevitable crises. By aligning the IT strategy with the business strategies of the company and its business units, the knowledgeable CIO builds a proper foundation and avoids many common barriers to success. Inevitably, some projects must be slowed down, put on hold (temporarily or permanently), or readjusted with formal agreements for additional resources to deal with the crises. Working with peers and partners will result in acceptable solutions and outcomes for all. The CIO who uses these techniques does not please everyone all the time, but everyone comes to understand and appreciate the CIO's honest intentions, realistic commitments, and reliable follow-through.

Whatever the outcome, the CIO does well to avoid the Pollyanna Syndrome and, instead, to work realistically within the appropriate risk profile for everyone's benefit. Can the effects of the syndrome be severe? That depends on the situation, of course. Using Exhibit 6.1 as an example, the CIO's program management and development management teams can work through their options case by case. Prioritizing this table from highest to lowest risk adds an additional useful dimension; risk exposure is calculated by multiplying the size of loss by the probability of loss.

When it comes time to making major commitments designed to build the business, the wise CIO asks an important question to keep decisions and commitments properly structured: Am I succumbing to the Pollyanna Syndrome or am I being the realist I need to be for my organization and my company?"

"But We've Always Done It This Way"

Or, "We've already tried that way and it didn't work." These two phrases serve as whining mantras chanted by those who are resistant to change or who are not interested in looking at the same information in different ways. Basically, each is

EXHIBIT 6.1   PROJECT MANAGEMENT RISK ASSESSMENT

Risk	Probability of Loss	Size of Loss (Weeks)	Risk Exposure (Weeks)
Project approval slower than expected	75%	8	6
Schedule overly optimistic	50%	10	5
Additional features after project start	25%	5	1.25
Lab & testing environment not ready on time	25%	5	1.25
Program management reporting consumes more-than-planned developer time	20%	2	0.4

Source: Steve McConnell, *Rapid Development: Taming Wild Software Schedules* (Redmond, WA: Microsoft Press), 1996.

simply a longer and more passive-aggressive way to say no. The CIO must find a way to dismantle these roadblocks so that the organization can reach its next level of performance and quality delivery. The logic is not too challenging. If the "old ways" are completely successful, there is no need for new management (in most cases). Most methods in change-averse cultures were first established, and last challenged, a long time ago, therefore the original people and circumstances are no longer part of the equation. Thus, the astute CIO realizes that the people behind the change barricades need to learn how to objectively reevaluate their assumptions and helps them to do so. Ramming the barricades with a forceful full frontal assault should be considered only as a last resort. However, if this same group throws up several roadblocks and impairs the progress of the entire IT organization and the company, then the needs of the many outweigh the needs of the few.[9]

One last thing to remember: Be careful that you are not the one thinking and/or chanting these mantras. If you feel the urge to do so coming on, stop yourself in your own tracks and remember that this is exactly what you do not want to do. Remind yourself that these phrases are crutches used by the complacent, the unimaginative, and the frightened. To be successful you need to do better. When was the last time you thought or said either of these phrases yourself? With a think-twice speak-once approach you eventually train yourself to not think or talk this way at all. You also open yourself to the level of flexibility necessary for considering new approaches from your peers, partners, customers, and subordinates.

The Workload Monkey

> *Most of the challenges in life are the ones we create for ourselves.*[10]
> —Old Man to Janeway, *Star Trek Voyager*

Workload perennially stands as one of the CIO's greatest challenges as a significant barrier to business success. Many CIOs, and senior executives for that matter, have battled workload issues throughout their entire careers. When challenges arose, they would deal with those challenges from a standard repertoire of actions:

- Pour on extra coals.
- Work 20-hour days.
- Pull all-nighters.
- Work all weekend.

Before long, exceptional behaviors became the norm—and the expectations—of peers, employees, and the CEO. With the ability to be "connected" 24/7, expectations of the CIO grow each year. This need-to-be-connected and need-to-be-online at all times becomes a true addiction, and like any mood-altering substance or behavior, the "workload monkey" is a difficult habit to break. Even when productivity plummets, nerves get frayed, and personal life disappears. Sure, the behavior may appear and feel heroic, but burnout is the inevitable result. On the way to burnout, many bad decisions are made and many leadership faults rise to the surface, due to extreme exhaustion. Additional workload items usually accumulate slowly; they did not seem overburdening at the time they were accepted. Odds are good that the additional workload items are tactically oriented—a case where the odds are good but the goods are bad. As with all habits, practice makes perfect. The result is that the CIO gets better and better at identifying the trees, though lost in the forest.

Like any senior executive in this state, the CIO is in danger of personal burnout and professional crash-and-burn. The cycle is significantly worse for the CIO than virtually any other senior executive because he or she works to enable everyone else and therefore works on behalf of all company employees. A CIO meltdown impacts all parts of the business and many additional people. Therefore, it is truly a requirement for successful CIOs to balance their workloads and eliminate this major barrier to success. If this is a topic of significant difficulty—which it can be from time to time, regardless of your experience level—a brief refresher from any one of several helpful books or short courses on this subject might be helpful.[11]

Anticipation is the art of good healthcare maintenance. The problem with workload assessments and workload addictions is that they seem normal on the inside. This is where the successful CIO takes advantage of the peer and partnership network, by putting each network member on notice with a simple request: "Please work with my network to intervene when my behavior and performance suggest that I have unwittingly taken on too many responsibilities." Also remember that there is one common and virtually diagnostic statement for work overload. "That could never happen to me."

NIRVANA ACCELERATORS

Buddhists define *nirvana* as "the state of perfect bliss in which the self is freed from suffering and desire and is united with the creator of the universe" and "a time or condition of great peace and joy."[12] As a CIO, there is a lot to be gained by accelerating the achievement of the IT organization and the company with two-thirds of the meaning of nirvana (forgoing uniting with the creator of the universe for some later time, hopefully). The importance of successful cross-functional performance was reemphasized in the lead editorial of a recent *CIO Magazine* in which the editor-in-chief asked members of *CIO Magazine's* "CIO Best Practice Exchange" to describe the most effective thing they were doing to manage the challenge of greater need than resources to meet it. Each person gave the same answer: better strategic planning and alignment in the business and better governance of IT.[13]

The only way to do this effectively is to involve the business unit executives as participants who prioritize their needs and match their needs with the available IT resources—taking into account both the tactical and the strategic implications of their choices. The CIO is in a unique position where cross-functional thinking can help by accelerating the activities necessary to achieve this kind of success. The successful CIO nurtures his or her personal chemistry with fellow peers and partners and with those peoples' subordinates. By working together through all aspects of strategy, planning, and problem solving, the CIO forms personal strategic alliances that benefit all parties in accelerating understanding and support (and, therefore, progress and results).

Sometimes, it becomes necessary to break old, time-honored routines to gain a new perspective on where you are, where you need to go, how you can get there, and whose help you will need along the way. Sometimes, the current IT team will be right for current needs but will not be adequate for emerging needs. CIOs have to make some regular changes and improvements to anticipate personnel needs for rapidly emerging, new strategic directions. Along the way, the challenge of the naysayers is ever-present, and the wise CIO realizes that setting them free is a true "twofer": It helps the naysayers move on to a place and job where they really want to be successful, and it frees up you and your organization to take a positive attitude toward success. The sooner a CIO takes these first steps on the path to nirvana, the better everyone feels and performs.

Nurturing Personal Chemistry and Personal Strategic Alliances

As a senior executive, a CIO succeeds (or not) as much on *how* he or she does something as on *what* he or she does because the relationship aspects of the senior executive role are critical. Hand in hand with this goes the need for personal strategic alliances. Some of these alliances are visible and some of them are not; some of them are explicit and some are implicit; some of them are publicly acknowledged and some are not; and, some are internal while others are external.

Consider the important and contradictory relationship between the CIO and the CIO's peer in a key supplier or a key customer. The fact is that there first has to be a relationship, and that relationship must be nurtured, honest, forthright, and bidirectional. Suppliers need customers and customers need the support of their suppliers. It is not necessary to be liked, but it is necessary to be able to get what is needed from a supplier. Recently, I got together with a colleague with whom I worked in the mid-1980s. Our families have kept in touch over the years, and we spent a day in New York City catching up. Naturally, I brought up the subject of

CIOs. "CIOs are *snakes*," he said. "You have to watch out." I was quite surprised at the intensity with which he said this, particularly because his job over the past 20 years or so has been dominated by dealing with CIOs. He gave many reasons for his negative feelings, but he also said he believed CIOs played an important role in the companies. However, his observation was fueled by his own experiences and observations: He believes that most CIOs are not knowledgeable enough and too closely aligned with the CFOs-as-accountants to be able to see the opportunity of information technology and its potential for value creation with correct application. Clearly, most of the CIOs with whom he has dealt have not worked to cultivate him (and his team) as partners; these CIOs are missing significant opportunities for strategic alliances and are not nurturing personal chemistry where they should. (Besides, who wants to be thought of as a "snake," especially when ". . . in the grass" cannot be far behind!)

In addition to the official, publicly known organizational alliances, most companies have a "functional underground," the unofficial channels and communications paths that exist within every organization. If you are not familiar with the functional underground, then you probably have not been as aware of your surroundings as you should be. Making use of this valuable resource for information gathering and for information dissemination is a key skill for senior executives. It is especially important for the CIO because of the high level of interaction within the IT organization and with each and every business unit and its infrastructure. Let's take a look at each of these.

CFO: Friend or Foe?   If the CFO is friend, then it is highly likely that the CIO effectively creates business value for the company and its business units by having the necessary resources to do so. This does not mean, of course, that the CFO supports each and every request made by the CIO. It means that the CFO understands (or is willing to learn) the key dynamics of value creation and value management, in addition to performing the more traditional cost accounting and management responsibilities that come with the role of chief financial officer. The astute CIO needs to make an assessment of the CFO to understand that person's background and modus operandi. As discussed earlier in the treatment of personality types, it is important to deal with the CFO in that person's preferred manner. However, if the CFO is the quintessential "bean counter," then the CIO must decide whether to work with that CFO cooperatively to achieve the value creation objectives of peers, partners, and company.

Working from the standpoint of important opinions wherein the CIO's firsthand experience is the priority opinion, relationships with the CEO and the functional underground come in handy as second and third opinions as to whether the CFO has the appropriate value creation mind-set. If the opinions of the CEO and the functional underground support the opinions of the bean-counter CFO, the company has little to offer or receive from a CIO dedicated to strategic value creation from the IT organization. Conversely, if the opinions of the CEO and the functional underground support the opinions of the CIO, it becomes worth the CIO's effort to nurture the personal chemistry and create a personal strategic alliance with the CFO. At the very least, the CIO seeks to reach a point at which most of the difficult work with the CFO happens off-line to avoid public and publicized conflicts. After all, the CFO also works as a companywide enabler. A good-chemistry strategic alliance between the CIO and the CFO enables both people to work through short-term challenges related to the IT organization and the business groups working with IT.

If, instead, the CFO is foe, you face an interesting challenge, indeed. CFOs who see themselves as the crusaders for cost control and who work to get all expenses to zero (or as close to zero as they can possibly manage) are generally motivated by control rather than value creation. Given the choice, join a company with a more mature CFO. Ferret out this type of CFO during the interviewing process. Remember that CFOs traditionally and consistently possess a different type personality than a CIO, so the actual personality preference might suggest something different from the CFO's actual approach. Discuss mutual modus operandi with your CFO, the CEO, peers and partners, and the functional underground before accepting a CIO position. Personal chemistry and personal strategic alliances can be formed with the traditional CFO types; they just have to be approached and nurtured in a way that is meaningful to them.

Identifying the CFO as friend or foe is important. Words and deeds must be evaluated. Which is your CFO: friend or foe?

CEO: Your Most Important Ally   Why is the CEO your most important ally? In the end, the CEO is the person to whom the CIO is accountable for the company's information management and technology. As a member of the senior executive staff, the CIO has the same need as the other senior executives: to nurture the personal chemistry between herself or himself and the CEO and to develop a healthy, mutual trust and respect through a personal strategic alliance. There are times when peers and partners need more than the CIO can provide, and the CIO who has a good personal relationship with the CEO can make that case comfortably. In such cases, the feedback is honest and helpful, whether it is positive or negative. When the inevitable challenge to balance resources across conflicting priorities and differing business units arises, the CEO can be advisor and, if necessary, adjudicator, to ensure a timely solution with full consensus. This can certainly accelerate business decisions with respect to IT resource utilization.

In the end, the CIO is accountable to all business units and the CEO for effective deployment and use of information technology resources, thus the CEO becomes an important CIO ally at the highest level of strategic decision making and implementation support. CIOs inevitably take actions and apply resources according to company strategic objectives and tactical requirements that are not in line with the objectives and needs of one or more peers or partners. The CIO who is in synch with the CEO knows that these disagreements are unavoidable but that they will not derail established strategies and plans from being executed on behalf of the company. This backing is important when dealing with peers, partners, and the CFO (especially if the CFO is a foe). A knowledgeable and supportive CEO knows the challenges involved with information technology—either innately or because the CIO has been careful to nurture this—and supports the CIO's strategically aligned information technology decisions as necessary. Is your CEO an ally?

The Functional Underground   In olden times, the functional underground was both underground and aboveground, just specially camouflaged. Consider the fool in the Middle Ages. Today, we see the fool as a buffoon, an imbecile, or a simple jokester, but medieval villages respected the fool, who employed these façades to remain the one person who could tell the truth to anyone, any time—even to royalty. The fool's dress and demeanor camouflaged uncomfortable truths within a cloak of absurdity. "Many a thing's said in jest . . ." and so on. The functional underground operates in a similar fashion, but generally not as openly. The functional underground is a series of communications lines within and across a company's organizations (even potentially involving people outside the company) that can be, and usually are, outside the normal organizational, hierarchical, and official informational channels. Another name for this underground is "back channel." Regardless what it is called, the functional underground is generally so effective in companies that senior executives do well to afford themselves of the advantages of its existence and information. A CIO looking to accelerate a project, a strategy, a plan, or personal career taps into the information flow of the functional underground.

If there is any doubt about the functional underground, consider the workings of the U.S. government and how information is made available to the American people on various subjects—particularly from the Executive and the Legislative branches. Each day the media reports from news agencies refer to "unnamed sources inside the Senate" or "sources inside the Department of Defense, on the condition of anonymity" or "an unnamed White House source." These organizations make use of the informal underground to get information out to the populace in order to gradually prepare it for something more profound (or otherwise shocking). This allows the organization to better prepare for making the information available "officially" and for gathering information about the types of questions that are likely to be asked.

The functional underground in a company can be (and is) used in a similar manner. For instance, consider the situation where a company's senior management decides that personal computers are just too expensive for every employee. Instead, nearly everyone will be given a terminal (a dumbed-down personal computer) that is connected to a server. Most employees would reject such a proposal.

Mature executives and managers use the functional underground to gauge resistance, look for options, discuss the implications, get feedback, and anticipate key questions. Based on the particular feedback, the CIO and the senior management team could decide whether to pursue the strategy, modify it (and recirculate it through the functional underground), or abandon it for the time being.

As the senior information technology executive, the CIO must be aware of and nurture the functional underground relative to information technology topics and the key people in the business units of peers and partners. Knowing how to make use of this candid information resource can be truly accelerating—and can prevent a real deceleration. Do you know about the functional underground in your company? Do you know how to put a question into it and how to get the feedback?

Breaking Routines

> *Everyone here has been so good to me. . . . I don't want you to think I'm ungrateful . . . I've just been thinking that maybe—there's more. I don't know what that means . . . but I know I'm changing, and I know that there are things that I'm not satisfied with. I want—complication in my life.*[14]
>
> —Kes to Janeway, *Star Trek Voyager*

One of the best pieces of advice I received 20 years ago or so was to remember to stand back occasionally—especially when it came to big, important, dangerous, or critical decisions—and take a look from another perspective. The same advisor suggested that one way to help this along is by breaking a routine, taking a different route into work, performing morning routines in a different order, taking the stairs rather than the elevator, walking backward from the car to the office door (carefully, of course!). All of these suggestions are intended to create openings for looking at things differently by changing the thought and behavior patterns, to make way for new ones. This is especially important for senior executives and their staffs. Such people may be viewed as a part of a counterculture; at IBM they even had a name: wild ducks.

> In IBM we frequently refer to our need for "wild ducks." The moral is drawn from a story by the Danish philosopher, Soren Kierkegaard. He told of a man on the coast of Zealand who liked to watch the wild ducks fly south in great flocks each fall. Out of charity, he took to putting feed for them in a nearby pond. After a while some of the ducks no longer bothered to fly south; they wintered in Denmark on what he fed them.
>
> In time they flew less and less. When the wild ducks returned, the others would circle up to greet them but then head back to their feeding grounds on the pond. After three or four years they grew so lazy and fat that they found difficulty in flying at all.

Kierkegaard drew his point—you can make wild ducks tame, but you can never make tame ducks wild again. One might also add that the duck that is tamed will never go anywhere any more.

We are convinced that any business needs its wild ducks. And in IBM we try not to tame them.[15]

The IT organization is particularly susceptible to wanting to follow the same routine over, and over, and over. On the tactical horizon, this can be a very good practice; with iterative improvement it is even better. However, maintaining the same approach over a strategic time frame could really be just a matter of comfort: We've always (as far back as we can remember) done it this way; therefore, we should continue doing it this way forever. Perhaps, perhaps not. The best way to find out is to look at the task from a different perspective, to approach it differently, to perhaps even solve it differently. The result may be to go back to the original method, but it may well not be. A better way may be found. Finding that better way may be possible only through breaking routines.

Have you ever tried varying how you do things yourself, personally? For instance, have you tried getting ready for work in the morning in a different order? Have you ever tried putting your clothes on in a different sequence? Have you ever purposely driven to work using an alternate route? The point behind breaking routines is to see things differently, add a new perspective, go down a fresh path. Consider this: Military and airline pilots tend to develop severe hearing loss in the particular frequencies their engines produce. The phenomenon is so predictable that people testing their hearing can tell which planes they flew by the location of the dip in their hearing in a specific area across the hearing spectrum. Why wouldn't the same apply to you in what you do and how you do it?

Future and Present Tense and Team

> *Exactly. For that one fraction of a second, you were open to options you had never considered. THAT is the exploration that awaits you: not mapping stars and studying nebulae, but charting the unknown possibilities of existence.*[16]
> —Q to Picard, *Star Trek: TNG*

Management across time is really quite simple. A good leader simply looks at the past, present, and future and makes decisions based on what can be known from each. The astute senior executive realizes that the current, present-tense team has a certain set of characteristics and experience levels. At some time in the future, the same team would have many of the same characteristics but its level of experience would be different; and there might have been some team member change-outs. The key point here is that those team member change-outs may be instigated by management or by employee instigation or happen as the result of a natural act (such as death or other event). Focusing on teamwork, trust, and what a team can be or can evolve into is an important skill for senior executives, including the CIO.

As the senior information technology executive, the CIO must look at the IT team in terms of its present makeup and the potential for its future makeup. "The car will go where you look—that's the way it works," say driving school instructors. As the leader of this team, it is the CIO's responsibility to provide the leadership for proper development and evolution of the IT team. The one thing the CIO must ensure he or she does not become is "missing in action" when it comes to leadership. Have you considered where your team is and where it needs to be? Are you "missing in action" from a leadership and team-building point of view?

DECISIONS A CIO SHOULD NOT MAKE ALONE

As a peer, partner, and enabler, it might be argued that there are *no* decisions the CIO should make alone. Given the fact that the CIO is a senior executive, though, that is not practical. All senior executives are expected to make decisions, take the necessary initiatives, and consult and partner with their peers to achieve the company's objectives. The CIO's situation is simply more consultative and more of a relationship partner. The CIO is expected to take any and all responsible actions within the range of the role's delegated responsibility and authority to enable his or her peers' and partners' success. This is a tall order given the range of the role's potential responsibilities and authority. Given the potential for significant capital expenses and significant effects on the business as a whole, there are some decisions the CIO would be wise to not make alone.

Strategic IS/IT Initiatives

By their very nature, strategic initiatives are directional, long-term, and designed to have a significant impact throughout the company. To be effective in a positive manner, strategic initiatives need a commitment longevity that matches their implementation time horizon. Research shows that the decision to make a strategic investment is much more likely to succeed if it is made through a portfolio management approach.[17] Such an approach necessarily involves the entire senior management team.

Consider a scenario where the CIO has independently sponsored and initiated a conversion from one type of technology to another, and three-fourths of the way through the conversion the indications are that the expected benefits will not be achieved. If the decision to make this strategic investment did not include an effective mix of decision makers, the opportunity to weigh and advise the CIO on the benefits of that investment versus several other potential strategic investments is lost. Not only might these other strategic investments have a higher benefit for the time, resources, and costs, but they might also address more critical needs within the CIO's partners' and peers' business units and the company, overall.

It is never too late to get onto the right track, however, so the CIO in this situation can proactively initiate a strategic planning group to evaluate the project and recommend an appropriate project disposition and redistribution of strategic resources.

Outsourcing

Because outsourcing is the current management rage, it might appear to be the right bandwagon to which the CIO should unilaterally hitch the company horses. Maybe and maybe not. Earlier chapters examined the many reasons for outsourcing, and the reason(s) for outsourcing a particular project must be able to stand up to the scrutiny of advantages and disadvantages from many perspectives. If it appears that the advantages outweigh the disadvantages, the successful CIO takes the time to engage the appropriate peers, partners, and superiors to fully discuss the rationale, advantages, and risks. The CIO also needs responsible representatives from within the IT organization and their business unit counterparts onboard, because without their support the project(s) end up failing.[18] This kind of stakeholder participation improves the likelihood of success because everyone is aware of and signed up for the same overall project outcome/project objective. In addition, should things not work out quite the way they were envisioned, participation reduces the likelihood of scapegoating.

The first outsourcing projects are the trickiest, and it is worth the effort to ensure that the stakeholders understand the risks and the key risk mitigation plans. Remember, projects can always be brought back in-house, and it is worthwhile ahead of time to agree on the criteria for how that decision will be made and then implemented. Outsourcing has several dimensions, also, and there are often separate and potentially overlapping groups that can participate in the decision-making process. For example, there is the "what" that is being outsourced, the "how" it should be outsourced (full or partial), the "where" it can be outsourced (domestically, internationally or both), and the "when" it will be outsourced. Let's not forget such factors as whether there are already people currently doing those jobs and their disposition as a consequence of the outsourcing.[19] Importantly, the astute CIO approaches this complicated, involved, and charged topic with direct stakeholders participating in all aspects of outsource decision making.

Leasing versus Buying

The decision to lease or buy information technology is a challenging one. There are times when one is more appropriate than the other—regardless of what the apparent accounting answers say. The decision rationales can be different for software versus hardware in terms of their intended use and business needs. With large-ticket items (usually hardware-based), leasing makes sense when the capital costs are high and the technology is changing faster than the depreciation period and salvage value of the hardware would justify buying. On the other end of the spectrum, personal computers may also make more sense to lease rather than buy—depending on company size and number of systems—not because of single capital expense, but because their two- to three-year lifespan is shorter than the typical capital depreciation period.[20] However, if it is important to reduce ongoing cash outlay commitments, then leasing may not be the right solution.

Though leasing may cost more, it may also allow for more frequent equipment upgrades to match users' changing applications profiles. Additionally, IT leases generally include the service contract costs, whereas purchased equipment generally requires an additional-services contract. The lease-versus-buy decision must be examined for each business unit to match its business budget and expense management model. For corporate-based equipment (and particularly that which will not be apportioned back to business units specifically) the key partners to consider are the CFO and the CEO, while keeping peers informed as appropriate.

The lease-versus-buy consideration for software, in contrast, is in an evolutionary state—although it could be argued that it is in a *Back to the Future* state. Mainframe software was generally leased with some initial start-up one-time charges, a monthly licensing fee, and an additional monthly service and support fee for greater-than-warranty support. The advent of the personal computer resulted in the evolution of the generalized software procurement model being one of purchase rather than lease, sometimes with the addition of service and support fees and sometimes not. Recent moves toward application service or solution providers (ASPs) and Web-based or network-based application and services software have reintroduced the concept of leasing, but, with a twist. The twist is that the applications would be paid for on a per-use or a standard usage fee basis and would actually reside in computer systems under an ASP's control.[21]

As with hardware leasing, there are certain advantages to leasing versus buying, including lower up-front capital (expense, really) expenditures and freedom from maintenance and service update issues. However, a major downside of this new model is that the application is located off-premises (at the ASP's facilities); therefore, if the network connections are down or the ASP is having other problems, the application(s) are not available. In the other situation, where the software is on local systems or on local personal computers, the application can still run when networks are down. So, unless there are significant cost advantages, the off-site approach is likely to have a slow "take rate." Because of these cost and availability issues (risk), it is critical that the CIO work with his or her peers and partners to be certain that the right cost-to-benefit ratios are maintained and that the most informed decisions—including more than just initial costs—are considered. Keep in mind the adage that you can only rent (lease) beer.

Proprietary versus Open Systems

An astute CIO recognizes this is as much a "religious discussion" as it is a technical discussion. There are reasons why choosing one over the other for a particular application or specific environment is indicated. That said, making this decision alone or in a vacuum is not advised. Even (perhaps especially) within the IT organization this is a highly charged topic. There are implications related to costs, skills, stability, availability, service and support, and many other areas of consideration. The decision-making process is not as simple as asking, "Does it cost less (or anything at all) to buy, or is it supported by a commercial company?" The astute CIO knows that the up-front costs for something are rarely the greatest expenses incurred and that just because something is paid for does not mean it will receive exemplary service. It is clearly a very complicated set of questions.

Because these questions have very long-term affects, and are difficult, costly, and disruptive to change once implemented, it is important to avoid making this decision alone. Gather the affected peers and partners, the cost analysts, the technical advisors, and the users' representatives to talk it through and reach consensus. Would you convert to a new religion without talking with a significant number of people and considering the effects on you and your family?

Expense Center versus Profit Center versus Value Creation Center

The value of the IT organization being a *value creation center* was the main topic of Chapter 4 in the *Guide*. The CIO must be the first person to commit to this approach. But, the transformation does not happen overnight or without a significant amount of effort. Determining whether this is within the realm of possibilities is important, and doing so during a job interview is ideal as a way of establishing up-front agreement for moving to this more effective model. Current CIOs need to use a combination of persuasive powers, cold, hard business facts, and firm commitment to demonstrate that it is the right approach to enable the business strategies and plans. As CIO, do you want to be an expense, a profiteer, or a value creator?

Line versus Staff

Obviously, the CIO cannot unilaterally transform herself or himself from line management to staff or from staff to line management. Deciding which is better is a kind of "you have to be there to know" issue. The health of the organization and the CIO's risk profile and threshold come into play. Given a choice, having direct management responsibilities for the IT organization is preferable to being in a staff position. The value of being responsible for the strategy and the implementation is highly desirable. The CIO who currently works in a staff role can carefully discuss the advantages and disadvantages with the CEO in their one-on-one time—and, should! Is it reasonable to be responsible for managing what you cannot control?

Centralized versus Distributed

Interestingly, this could be taken either as an organizational or an implementation consideration. That is, as an organizational consideration, it is a discussion of whether all IT resources reside in the IT organization or if some reside in the company's business units. As an implementation consideration, it is a discussion of whether the IT systems are located centrally or are distributed geographically, whether located with business units or where people are congregated. In both cases, it is essential that the decision of resource placement (people and/or equipment) be discussed, argued, and decided on by those who have to make it happen, those who have to maintain it, and those who make use of it.

Organizationally, if the CIO believes that the IT resources should be consolidated into one group, it is going to be necessary to convince the business unit heads—the CIO's peers and partners—that giving up control of their internal IT resources is going to be to their advantage. This is almost always a difficult sell. Conversely, from an implementation point of view, especially where hardware and capital are involved, many business unit executives would be more than pleased to have such heavy budget-hitters consolidated (i.e., in someone else's budget) as someone else's worry. This is not so hard to sell.

Before jumping into doing either or both of these approaches, understand what you are getting yourself into. That is, if the personnel resources-related consolidation is strongly advocated by a particular business unit executive, it could be that he or she has a problem he or she is looking to unload. True, this could be an excellent opportunity to shine, but you, as the CIO, need to know that the problem exists, along with its associated challenges. Taking an albatross off someone's back and taking it the way of the phoenix could be a great success for you and your company, and be a great teamwork and trust builder for you and the business unit executive.

Similarly, if the business units are looking to consolidate their hardware into one CIO IT budget, it could be that the hardware is out of date and its residual value is significantly less than the remaining payments. Again, knowing what you are undertaking, accepting an albatross and taking it the way of the phoenix can have the same positive effect as it might have with the personnel-resource case. Not that these actions are risk-free; however, removing the risk from a business unit executive and handling the need competently could have a significantly positive effect and certainly put a large deposit into your "favor bank." Are you, as the senior information technology executive, willing to accept risks because you see it as the right course of action?

Prioritization

Consider the old saw: Lack of planning on your part does not constitute an emergency on mine. It's a small jump to the corollary that one person's priorities may not match another's. The only way to be certain that you agree on—or at least understand—each other's priorities is to work together to set them. A clear understanding of priorities, even as they change due to changes in business conditions, reinforces that the CIO is focused on enabling success rather than personal advancement or a private agenda. A prioritization with the full awareness and participation of the other senior executives and the CEO is important not only at budget time, but also when unexpected and unplanned problems or critical situations arise.

Clear prioritization allows the new news to be prioritized into the other commitments, and the new priority list can be used to determine how resources can be realigned, if necessary. As a peer, partner, and enabler, the CIO's and the IT organization's priorities should be the business priorities of the senior management team and should also reflect the company's commitment to strategic initiatives. Do you have your strategic commitments and your tactical commitments prioritized such that you can ensure that your peers and partners are fully aware of what they are, they can explain them to their organizations, and they can endorse them?

Career Decisions

This should go without saying, but experience suggests that it does need to be said: Senior executives should make use of their professional networks, mentors, and closest confidants (e.g., spouse, significant other, etc.) when facing major career decisions. It is just too easy to overlook something obvious when considering changes, and having your support network "onboard" with your decision-making process and your ultimate decisions proves invaluable over time. It gives you peace of mind that you are less likely to have overlooked some key element in making your decision. Should things go wrong, your network is there to help you find your way back to a path that makes sense for you. Would you rather travel a path with people along to help (or at least close by in case of trouble) or would you like to go your own way with no safety net? The choice is yours.

There are many more specific topics that could be included in this section, but the key point is that there are decisions the CIO should not make alone. The list of what these decisions are varies by company, by CIO, by senior executive team, and by CEO. Regardless of the final makeup of the list for a particular set of circumstances, it is important that it be created, distributed, acknowledged, and used to focus the solutions on the problems and to ensure that those who are served are engaged and participate. To be successful at this, the CIO has to be aware of methods for getting the commitment of his or her peers and partners for the key elements of IS/IT strategy, plans, and implementations. Research shows that:

> [T]he top IS/T executives have not been very influential with respect to initiation and implementation of IS/T projects. Reasons for this include the relatively new position (CIOs) hold in the top echelons of management . . . [and] many have suggested that CIOs have failed to deliver on projects, which weakens their ability to influence organizational members with respect to new projects . . . and many CIOs have been viewed as too technically oriented and still have trouble relating to managers with different backgrounds than theirs.[22]

The same research found that there has been a recent uptick in the influence of *some* CIOs, and that increase is attributed to their business acumen, industry-specific knowledge, strategic relationships with their peers, and increasing reliance on information technology for improving the business performance of companies. The results of these findings were quite enlightening:

- CIOs in industries where information technology is more crucial to the success of the business are more influential.
- CIOs whose vision is to transform and whose organizations are not seen as cost centers are more influential than those whose vision is to automate and whose organizations are seen as cost centers.
- CIOs with a technical background are preferred for situations where automation and cost cutting are key elements of the role, and this is especially the case in processing and manufacturing organizations.
- CIOs in decentralized organizations had a more difficult time convincing all stakeholders to be onboard with strategic projects.

- CIOs proposing strategic initiatives that were aligned with current company business strategies were more effective.

- CIOs proposing strategic initiatives with incorrect and invalid original project assumptions faired poorly, and they were viewed as not having done their "homework."

- CIOs who built relationships and partnerships with their peers were more successful at requesting and obtaining these executives' support for strategic initiatives.

- CIOs who successfully build partnerships can effect a change in the IT organization, from being managed as a cost center to being managed as an investment center.

- CIOs who adjusted their strategic proposals language to match the technical background (or lack thereof) of those whose support they were working to get were more effective than those who did not.

- CIOs who were able to relate their strategic proposals and initiatives to the business needs and value creation of their peers were more likely to gain their peers' support.

- CIOs who adjusted their behavior to one more familiar to those peers faired better than those who did not.

- CIOs who used a consultative and/or ingratiating approach(es) with their peers were more successful in gaining support for strategic initiatives when the peers were less technical than the CIO, and received greater resistance to these approaches from more technical peers.

- CIOs without sufficiently strong working relationships with their peers suffered more unsuccessful project implementations.

- CIOs who did not also ensure the support of the next-layer down of management support (below their peers *and* below themselves) also suffered more unsuccessful project implementations; it was observed that the difference between compliance and commitment is important to understand.

- CIOs who had good working relationships with their peers, who assigned qualified people, and who kept stakeholders informed about progress were rewarded with successful projects and the continued involvement and support of the stakeholders.[23]

Are you going it alone, or do you have a list of decisions that you should not make alone? Have you engaged those who should be party to these decisions to do so? Are you working sufficiently with your peers and partners, and have you adjusted to their level of experience and need relative to information technology, to gain and maintain support for the appropriate and needed-for-value-creation strategic initiatives and projects—so you are not standing out there alone doing so?

Problem Children

> *Nothing makes them happy. They are dedicated to being unhappy and to spreading that unhappiness wherever they go . . . they are the Ambassadors of Unhappy.*
>
> —Bashir to Sisko, *Star Trek: Deep Space Nine*[24]

There are going to be those on any team or in any company who are not happy. They can include peers and partners, superiors, subordinates, even you. There are many reasons for someone to be unhappy, and many of them can affect a person's work profile regardless of whether the source of unhappiness comes from work, his or her personal life, or both. Levels and expressions of personal unhappiness vary, but the result is the same: Productivity, teamwork, and even leadership can suffer tremendously. For an organization and team that is in the business of enabling others, this can be disastrous. It might be tempting to confuse the unhappy workers with the wild ducks, but resist the temptation and test the premise. Wild ducks may express unhappiness, but their unhappiness is predictably directed at areas where they see that things can be done better.

Sometimes the management team and/or technical leadership can address those job elements that are making employees unhappy and sometimes they can't. Within the IT organization itself, good management techniques like one-on-one and career counseling and mentoring increase the likelihood that the CIO and the management team can tell the difference and address employee unhappiness at the source. Above all else, the CIO must work with the IT staff to avoid including a true "Ambassador of Unhappy" on the team. These ambassadors can spread their negativism to such a point that entire teams become poisoned. As the senior executive for the IT organization, the CIO sets the tone for the organization and has responsibility for ensuring such poisons do not spread. This does not mean that the CIO is responsible for specific actions to be taken with each and every individual; it does mean that the CIO is responsible for fostering an environment to prevent Ambassadors of Unhappy from taking root.

Another common class of problem children is the naysayer. The naysayer differs from the Ambassador of Unhappy in that he or she is more likely to be someone who is not unhappy but demonstrates a predilection for believing that whatever it is that others are proposing will not work. The naysayer takes a contrarian's view on nearly everything—not because this individual believes or feels strongly about the position he or she is taking; rather, the naysayer takes this position because he or she feels compelled to do so. The "Dr. No" in Chapter 5 is an example of a naysayer. Depending on the level of influence and the scope of communications within the IT organization, a naysayer can be just as disruptive as someone who is significantly unhappy—even though his or her approach is different. The naysayer can stall new ideas and bring forward progress to a complete standstill.

Even worse, naysayers can cause significant regression from progress already made in an organization that is in the process of transition. Several years ago, a start-up was bought by a company with the intent of accelerating entry into a new and larger market segment. There appeared to be a good match between the management and technical teams, and both companies were under their own pressures to do something different than they already were. The start-up was running out of money and was either going to need to raise more (which would have been its fourth or fifth round of capital) or would need to merge with or be acquired by another company. The acquiring company was under pressure to find a new product base for the market it was looking to enter because a potentially hostile company was acquiring its current supplier. So, the two companies reached an agreement for acquisition.[25]

Before long, the CEO of the acquired company left and one of the senior executives from the acquiring company was asked to run the acquired company. As time slipped by, it was clear that a focus on delivery was needed. As it turns out, this was the first indication of a cultural clash between the two companies: The start-up was created with a familial culture, whereas the established company was created (and was still run) as a delivery culture. Time and economic pressures magnified this cultural difference. As a result, several key people from the acquired company emerged in the forms of both naysayers and Ambassadors of Unhappy.

The naysayers appeared to be mostly made up of those who were inexperienced at product development or had lost some level of influence and control as a result of the acquisition. The unhappy appeared to be those who realized and felt the difference between the familial culture and the delivery culture. The majority of the employees, though, were neither naysayers nor unhappy; in fact, there were as many extremely happy employees as there were unhappy employees. These tended to be people who had spent more time in companies with delivery-based cultures and had found it difficult to adjust to the familial-based culture.

In combination, the effects of the naysayers and the unhappy employees on the organization and team as a whole were tremendous—tremendously detrimental. Information gathered through the functional underground verified these observations. The next question for the management team and the senior executive was what to do. Basically, the answer and approach were very straightforward: Liberate the naysayers and unhappy employees. That is, empower them to either address what was making them unhappy and causing them to be wholesale naysayers or look at an alternative: Liberate themselves from that which they were not willing to deal with. "If you are not happy where you are or with what you are doing, and you are not able to find a way to make it better, then please look to find your happiness elsewhere so that you can work to provide the *positive* support your team needs."

The management team floated this message through the functional underground and received significant feedback: The majority favored the approach. The results were good news to the senior management team, but the challenge remained of helping move the naysayers to their "next opportunity." The idea was verbalized at the next available all-organizational meeting, just as one of the naysayers attempted to hijack the proceedings. The proposal created a combination of applause and gasps. Those who had become tired of the unhappy and the naysayers were pleased and surprised to hear it become public; the unhappy and the naysayers felt blindsided by the suggestion.

Over the next month or so, the proposal generated a significant amount of discussion, and the naysayers and unhappy engaged in a series of antiorganizational activities that significantly damaged teamwork and morale. Ultimately, a number of the malcontents left, and morale and productivity eventually improved significantly. It continued to be necessary to encourage some lingering naysayers and Ambassadors of Unhappy who would not leave voluntarily, but in the end, they were either liberated or liberated themselves. Certainly, encouraging liberation opens difficult conversation, but it is far better than having the naysayers reduce the value-creation potential for the organization and for the company.

Liberating the naysayers has a compounded positive effect: It eliminates the highly negative people while freeing up those who want to produce and succeed, which improves their morale and their productivity. The successful CIO does what needs to be done to liberate the naysayers, help the unhappy transition to where they can be happier, and, as a result, liberate those who are really the key to his or her success and the success of the company.

One more person who may covertly be unhappy (perhaps even approaching being an Ambassador of Unhappy) and/or a naysayer is you, the senior information technology executive or the aspiring one. If the person at the top has these characteristics, then he or she has two choices: Decide to live with it or do something about it. If you decide to live with it, it is essential that you do just that. Do not externalize your unhappiness or naysayer approach to anyone. Doing otherwise results, sooner or later (and probably sooner), with a CIO who works under the label of either hypocrite or malcontent. So, are there naysayers and unhappy people in your organization who should be liberated? Should you be liberated or should you liberate yourself?

DISTANT HORIZON

Locating the horizon is one thing; figuring out how far you can see is another. Plotting a course to a specific point on the horizon and figuring out how long it will take to get to the final destination—the distant horizon—presents other challenges. Before that course can be laid, it is necessary to know the point of origin as precisely as possible; and, for the CIO, the point of origin starts with an assessment of professional strengths and needs. The value in making this assessment lies in part in whether the CIO is contemplating a position, is new in a position, or already owns a position. A recent "Leadership Agenda" column in *CIO Magazine* makes the point quite well:

> Great leaders understand how to renew their leadership agenda. . . . Now more than ever, given the weak economy and aging demographics, the ability to renew your focus and energy and regain your purposeful footing is important.[26]

After making and considering the professional strengths and needs assessment, the next appropriate action is to examine one's overall career path. A major consideration is whether that career path includes personal strategies and plans to continue upward movement, lateral movement, or some deliberate combination over time. An on-the-rise executive with his or her eye on the CIO position might be wondering about the prudence of lateral moves. Given the requirements on and expectations for CIOs from their peers and partners, a well-rounded background of business and technical acumen is critical. In order to get the breadth of experience needed in an area outside one's predominant career path, CIOs who conscientiously develop their careers frequently take lateral steps or even slight demotions to gain new experiences and strengthen areas of professional weakness. Such a practice is not career-limiting; it is career-enhancing—if you keep one eye on the distant horizon and know it to be on your true path.

Many roads lead to the same destination, but rarely is there a direct, straight-line route. It is often necessary to take a circuitous route—in fact, the circuitous route may paradoxically end up being the fastest route when all is said and done. Consider the options that users are given when looking for Web-based directions (such as Mapquest or YahooMaps): Do you want the shortest way, the fastest way, or to avoid freeways or make the most use of them. The fastest can often prove to be the longest and, perhaps, even more circuitous than the shortest route. Many factors affect the speed at which any career moves from origin to destination, and actual distance is only one of them. Give some thought to the others; can you relate that to a career path?

Professional Strengths and Needs Assessment

As a member of the senior executive team, you have reached a point in your career when no one else is looking out for you—besides you. That means that any self-analyses, improvement plans, or strengths and needs assessments are your responsibility. This has been a constant theme throughout in the *Guide*: Your career is in your own hands. True, some very fine companies make active investments in the professional development of their senior executives, but you cannot count on finding such programs everywhere, which, in any case, often direct your development according to the way the company interprets what it needs from you. The point is, a CIO who is not regularly performing a thorough professional self-assessment at some reasonable interval can expect to be looking for a new and less fulfilling job, over and over again. Unfortunately, this is the way many senior managers learn about their inadequacies: They find out there is a problem when they are given their walking papers. This is especially likely in a company that has a dysfunctional senior management team. Thus, it is essential to explore this part of the company culture when interviewing for a potential position. (And, of course, ask why your predecessor is being replaced.)

Exhibits 6.2 and 6.3 show two approaches that work well for making a quick first pass at personal strengths and needs:

- Make two simple lists, one for strengths and one for needs.
- Conduct a personal SWOT, the marketing tool approach used for evaluating competitive strengths, weaknesses, opportunities, and threats.

EXHIBIT 6.2   PROFESSIONAL ATTRIBUTE SELF-ASSESSMENT

Attribute	Strength	Need
Vision		
Leadership		
Business acumen		
Technical expertise		
Matched risk profile		
Executive presence		
Ambition and competitiveness		
Professional integrity		
Comfort in enabler / peer and partner role		
Life balance		

**EXHIBIT 6.3   PROFESSIONAL SWOT
SELF-ASSESSMENT**

Strengths (Internal/Controllable)	Weaknesses (Internal/Controllable)
Strengths (Internal/Controllable)	**Weaknesses** (Internal/Controllable)
Opportunities (External/Uncontrollable)	**Threats** (External/Uncontrollable)

When completing the SWOT assessment, the opportunities and threats are external to you personally and are things that you cannot control; the strengths and weaknesses are internal to you and are controllable. Key attributes to consider for both approaches should include those listed and any others that may be specific to the current or future situation or environment.

An overall assessment emerges by honestly checking the appropriate boxes or filling in the quadrants. These deceptively simple techniques demonstrate where an executive is in good shape, those areas that require minor attention, and those areas that need significant attention. Areas of need do not necessarily point to a mismatch with the role or position; they are typically a by-product of the specific path that brought each potential CIO to the point of being an interested, viable candidate. The same is true for the existing CIO, who is interested in reaffirming strengths, identifying needs, and taking appropriate actions to improve effectiveness (and *keep* the job).

After performing a simple strengths and needs assessment, it is worthwhile to give it a bit of time to settle in to the subconscious—to internalize it—before going into deeper, more refined detail. The assessments in the exhibits work like a stake in the ground, a reference point for the next level of in-depth professional self-assessment. There are two professional strengths and needs methodologies that can be very effective for a more detailed analysis of professional strengths and need. One, the Myers-Briggs Type Indicator, was introduced earlier in the *Guide*. Any senior executive—and especially the CIO with a broad range of required skills and types of customers—can benefit from the MBTI assessment and analyses.

The second methodology is the "Executive EQ."[27] The approach used in this methodology adds the dimension of emotional intelligence to understand what separates successful and unsuccessful executives, and provides a path to the successful group. Robert Cooper and Ayman Sawaf define "emotional intelligence" as "the ability to sense, understand, and effectively apply the power and acumen of emotions as a source of human energy, information, connection, and influence."[28]

Executives increase the probability for long-term strategic success in their work by reintegrating emotional considerations into business decisions. Emotional intelligence improves judgment and reasoning that have obvious links to company profitability and personal and professional success. In their book, Cooper and Sawaf include an introductory version of their EQ Map™ that identifies an individual's strengths and vulnerabilities as they relate to the key attributes of emotional intelligence. Their aim is to bring the second part of the equation—emotion—in balance with rationality, to help create more successful and fulfilled senior executives:

> I think about many of my corporate colleagues, most of whom, during business school, crunched at least a million numbers and analyzed a thousand balance sheets. But not one of them had 30 seconds' worth of counsel about the ABCs of building deep, trusting relationships, or about respecting and expressing the truth of deeply felt human values and creative intuition—the combined intelligence of the heart *and* head—or holding to credibility and integrity while flowing *with* problems instead of getting overwhelmed or derailed by them.[29]

As illustrated in Exhibit 6.4, the EQ approach is based on four premises, or "cornerstones." Each cornerstone has attributes with which an executive should actively manage for continuous improvement.

The EQ Map™ approach starts with a self-scoring questionnaire. The results are then transferred to a visual map. The questionnaire covers a thorough set of emotionally related topics:

- Current personal and professional environment (life events, work pressures, personal pressures)
- Emotional literacy (emotional self-awareness, emotional expression, emotional awareness of others)
- Emotional quotient competencies (intentionality, creativity, resilience, interpersonal connections, constructive discontent)
- Emotional quotient values and beliefs (compassion, outlook, intuition, trust radius, personal power, integrity)
- Emotional quotient outcomes (general health, quality of life, relationship quotient, optimal performance)

Of course, about this time, some CIOs are getting a bit queasy thinking about the emotional side of their being and life in contrast to their rational or technical side. However, as has been discussed throughout *The Guide*, being an enabler and partner who builds strategic relationships requires more than just the rational abilities. Therefore, successful CIOs have learned to develop and tap into their EQ.

EXHIBIT 6.4   FOUR CORNERSTONES OF EMOTIONAL INTELLIGENCE

Cornerstone	Attribute
1. Emotional Literacy	
	Emotional honesty
	Emotional energy
	Emotional feedback
	Practical intuition
2. Emotional Fitness	
	Authentic presence
	Trust radius
	Constructive discontent
	Resilience and renewal
3. Emotional Depth	
	Unique potential and purpose
	Commitment, accountability, and conscience
	Applied integrity
	Influence without authority
4. Emotional Alchemy	
	Intuitive flow
	Reflective time-shifting
	Opportunity sensing
	Creating the future

Source: Cooper and Sawaf, Executive EQ, 1997.

Is Up Always the Right Direction?
Determining Fit in Career Choices

Just where is the horizon? Well, it depends. In an airplane flying upside down, the relative up is not the right direction; down is. To many, the thought of not continuing in the up direction is akin to flat–lining, or, more politely, career stagnation. Alternatively, it may represent a sense of lack of ambition, a sign of old age; it may feel like a loss of status; or manifest as the challenge of avoiding the "Peter Principle."[30]

So, when is up not the right direction? Up is the right direction as long as the person who is asking the question believes that up is the right direction, because he or she is the only person who calls the shots. Everyone gets a lot of advice along the way—some solicited and some not, some welcomed and some not—and much of that advice focuses on moving up, stabilizing, stepping aside, or backing off. Up is not the right direction when the person asking the question truly believes that up is not the right direction. This type of decision, of course, is not irreversible and is not permanent. Hard as it may be to believe, a respite from the climb might just be what it takes to prepare for the next ascent.

Consider an analogy. Those hardy souls who climb the highest and most challenging mountains do so in stages with camps set up along the way that allow them to contemplate the day's success and to rest up for the next-day's challenging ascent. No mountain-climbing party would start at the base and climb to the top of Mt. Everest in one continuous climb (well, Sisyphus, maybe). They would just not be able to do so, due to stamina, hunger, stress, weather, acclimation to altitude, leaving parts of the team without the same fortitude behind, and so on. The reasons include things they can control and things they cannot. Why, then, would a person attempt the equivalent with his or her career? Burnout, stress, acclimation to new environment, reduced or no teamwork due to insufficient teamwork and team integration, and so on.

For quite awhile, IBM has had a program for early identification and mentoring of people the executive team felt had high technical or managerial potential. Those identified were mentored, monitored, and given assignments and promotions designed to provide a varied and rounded experience in the company's business. The idea was to "fast-track" these potential executives in such as way that within five to seven years they would be ready for the executive ranks and could then be positioned to make major contributions to the business. The "chosen" were young enough to move their way very high in the company with many years of potential contribution at the executive level.

Notably, a significant number of the fast-trackers were successful; however, many managers involved in the process observed that more of them "flamed out" before reaching the executive level than made it all the way through. Very few moved much beyond the director level. Why would that be? One possibility lies in the difference between being in a job and doing a job. In the fast-track approach, the person was given a job assignment, and often it was more important that he or she understood what the job was about rather than becoming proficient or successful. There were those who, simply, became overwhelmed by the continual pressure to succeed and climb, fail but continue to climb, or just to move to the next (climb) job assignment. Would these fast-trackers be better served by having a rotation of climb, acclimate and reinforce, climb, acclimate and reinforce? Regardless of what others may want for you, what you do is truly up to you.

In my own experience, I have found alternating job types and responsibilities to be rewarding and restorative. In a smaller company, the potential is there for assuming more roles and having more varied responsibilities without moving to another job assignment or position. In a larger company, it may be necessary to be mobile (at least virtually if not physically) in order to achieve the same rewarding (personally and professionally) career. It might appear that it takes longer to achieve a career objective, but it is far more likely that you will actually achieve that objective and maintain that objective with this approach. What is the point of making the climb if you are not comfortable being there, are not good at being there because the proper groundwork has not been laid, or if you "flame out" before achieving your objective?

Each senior executive must locate the horizon, relate the horizon to his or her own location, and continually reevaluate both location and relative direction, all the while remembering that up is relative. Do you know where your horizon is? Do you know which direction you should be going today and which one you should be going tomorrow? Have you taken into consideration just how near or how far away that horizon is?

CREATING THE HORIZON

In the end, your career is in your own hands. There are those who believe in the saying that "the future is what you make it" and there are those who do not. Regardless, it is hard to argue that the future is affected by what you do. As a member of the senior management team, the CIO is expected to be an active participant in creating the future for the company. In this value-creation activity, the CIO's role is to enable his or her peers and partners to achieve their business strategies, objectives, and plans. Unfortunately, the CIO works with a lot of horizons; it would not be difficult for the CIO to lose a bearing on the *true horizon*. The true horizon has to be your own: the one you create, maintain, and evolve by yourself for yourself. For long-term success, personally and professionally, senior executives need to have their lives in balance; at any point in time, that balance is affected by many factors. Having a plan for maintaining personal and professional balance is important to ensure that key opportunities are not lost.

A very effective sounding board for balancing and managing your horizon is to create your own informal "board of directors" or "advisory board." Getting involved with peers groups and participating in professional conferences where other CIOs congregate provide excellent opportunities for keeping yourself focused. The science of physics says that a body at rest tends to stay at rest; and it takes more energy to start a body moving than it does to maintain the movement once started.

Mentors and Peer Groups

Once at the senior management level, mentoring becomes both more important and trickier. As the senior information technology executive, the CIO typically has no direct like-job peers in the company, and it may be necessary to go outside the company to find an appropriate mentor relationship. If there do not appear to be any candidates, examine business cards or e-mail contacts for sources. Mentoring does not have to be an official relationship; it can start simply, by calling an acquaintance in a standard networking mode and then "innocently" asking whether this person has encountered some current active challenge, question, or problem. Give some thought, also, to finding mentoring candidates who are of differing personality type (a different Myers-Briggs Type Indicator), so that when looking at challenging issues there can be another, potentially quite orthogonal, set of observations from which to benefit. A good friend or significant other can serve as a mentor, as long as the person can often provide valuable insights and different ways of seeing your work. In addition to mentors, peer groups are another excellent means to broaden personal and professional outlooks and to see what is possible. For example, *CIO Magazine* sponsors regular conferences targeted to CIOs from industry and government. The focus for a recent conference:

> [T]he nation's leading CIOs and IT executives will take a hard look ahead at the trends and issues that will significantly impact the CIO role in the next 12–24 months. We'll examine and forge solutions to issues such as: jobs and IT people, probing into the complexities of preparing the next generation of IT leaders when the baby boomers retire, the economy—what's the outlook? Especially for the hard-hit tech sector and the future of IT and the CIO— some gurus claim IT is no longer strategic and can't provide a competitive edge, should the CIO be worried? These and other challenging issues will be discussed amongst top CIOs and IT executives as they try to figure out what the future holds for their organization and their IT roles, and how to position themselves as leaders and minimize their vulnerabilities. Join us in Phoenix to see how your plans for the future stack up against your peers and competitors. Are you ready for the challenge?[31]

This is one of several conferences sponsored annually by *CIO Magazine*, *CIO Insight,* and *Computerworld;* as the senior information technology executive for your company, attend at least one of these per year. The contacts, the discussions of problems and solutions, and sharing leadership insights with your peers can repay many times over the one-time expenses. Are you ready for the challenge of sharing—giving and getting help?

Serious Intentions: Personal Transition Plan

If you have made it this far through the *Guide,* it is reasonable to assume that you have serious intentions to make changes and improvements to yourself, your work, your career goals and horizon, and your life balance. This is best done through a personal transition plan—not unlike a technology transition plan, an application transition plan, or a business transition plan. Such a plan can start out as simply as writing on a piece of paper the headings "1 year," "2 years," "5 years," "10 years," "15 years," and "Retire As," with spaces in between to note specific goals and end points for both career and quality of life. Or it can be a combination of goal focuses with the results and subsequent planning from an MBTI assessment and an EQ assessment. These plans come from knowing where you are and creating the horizon for where you want to be. Survival to this point demonstrates interest. It is now time to use the same executive leadership and planning skills that made it possible for you to get to this point, grow them, and use them to get to where *you* want to be. Shouldn't you put as much thought and effort into creating the future *you* want as you do creating the future *others* want?

How serious are your intentions? Find yourself five 3 x 5 note cards and write down something you intend to focus on over the next week on each one of the cards. Put four of the cards in your top dresser drawer. Take the fifth one with you everywhere you go for a full week and refer to it constantly. Stay with that first one until you have mastered it or until one week is up—whichever is longer. Then get a second one from your top dresser drawer. Repeat the process, continuing to look at both cards; the first one to avoid regressing and the second one to make that transition. Continue on for the first month or until all five card transitions have completed. Are you serious enough about your intentions to transition from where you are to where you want to be so you can reach the horizon you created?

TEN QUESTIONS THE CIO MUST ASK ABOUT FUTURE HORIZONS

> *A man either lives life as it happens to him, meets it head on and licks it, or he turns his back on it and starts to wither away.*
> —Dr. Philip Boyce to Captain Christopher Pike, *Star Trek*[32]

In proportion to the development of his individuality, each person becomes more valuable to himself, and is therefore capable of being more valuable to others.

—John Stuart Mill[33]

People often say that this or that person has not yet found himself. But the self is not something that one finds. It is something that one creates.

—Thomas Szasz[34]

Earlier, 10 Questions sections explored what the CIO must ask the CEO or peers and partners, and what the CEO should be asking the CIO so that together they can work to align IT and company strategy. Now it's time for the CIO to look inward and consider 10 questions to ask of himself or herself. These questions represent 10 key pieces of information and considerations about the CIO for the CIO and of the CIO in contemplating the future horizons for personal, career, and organizational needs. We are by nature an inquisitive species with a tendency to ask ourselves questions and seek answers. Our search for knowledge is both internal and external, and the process of searching is continuous. CIOs are presented with regular opportunities to reconsider life balance across three areas: personal, career, and organizational. Do I have the correct proportions today? Am I getting them aligned properly for tomorrow? Have I considered how they need to be aligned at the horizon as I see it and as I will be creating it?

As CIO, many people help create the priorities for the organizational side of your life and its work. The challenge comes in reconciling those many views and inputs to achieve the ideal balance for your personal and career interests. Fewer people provide input from a career point of view: mentors, peers and peer groups, and close family members. Apart from the assistance of a significant other, most of us are alone when it comes to input on balance regarding areas of personal interest, which is as it should be—your life and your career are in your own hands.

The *Guide* has mapped the rapidly changing, challenging business landscape of the CIO. This landscape contains many hazards for those who would approach the roles and responsibilities of the CIO as predictable and uniform from job to job, company to company, or sector to sector. As an enabler, by the very nature of the work, the CIO always runs the risk of losing sight of the big picture, and how IT figures in that picture, by becoming lost in the priorities of peers and partners.

In the IT world, today, it is fair to say that "it's a jungle out there"; and the odds are that the jungle is only going to get rougher and tougher for the CIO. Recent anecdotes suggest that CIOs are staying in their jobs longer, but who knows what the future holds. Jungle rules will apply—cleaned up for business—for the foreseeable future. The CIO who has properly provisioned, prepared for the unknown, and has a successful frame of mind comes back a survivor. Final preparations occur over and over for CIOs with expert survival skills because no other senior executive position is so new and in such constant flux. Ten questions help create structure and personal balance while contemplating the future career-related horizons. Unlike other 10 question installments, this one suggests no answers or guidance. Those come from the heart of the one who asks these questions.

One last word of advice: Articulate an answer to each of these questions on a regular basis. Search parties are notoriously unsuccessful when it comes to finding someone lost enough to ignore them.

1. Do I know who I am and what I find rewarding?
2. Do I know my next life goal?
3. Am I on a path to achieve the next life goal?
4. Do I know my next career goal?
5. Am I on a path to achieve my next career goal?
6. Is my "board of directors" effective for me?
7. Am I in the right job?
8. Do I have the relationships I want with my peers and partners?
9. Am I leading my organization to effectively create value?
10. Is my life in balance?

NOTES

1. Brian Greene, *The Elegant Universe* (New York: W.W. Norton & Company, 1999): 387.
2. Jon R. Katzenbach and Douglas K. Smith, *The Wisdom of Teams: Creating the High-Performance Organization* (New York: HarperBusiness, 1994): 61.
3. Ibid., p. 174.
4. Jill Sherwin, *Quotable Star Trek* (New York: Pocket Books, 1999): 16.
5. Ibid., p. 223.
6. Eleanor H. Porter, *Pollyanna* (London: Puffin Classics, 1994).
7. Edward Yourdon, *Death March: The Complete Software Developer's Guide to Surviving "Mission Impossible" Projects* (Upper Saddle River, NJ: Prentice-Hall PTR, 1999): 8.
8. Ibid., p. 13.
9. Mr. Spock to James Kirk, "The needs of the many outweigh the needs of the few—or the one," from *Star Trek II: The Wrath of Khan.*
10. Old Man 2 to Janeway, *Star Trek: Voyager,* "Sacred Ground" episode, in Sherwin, *Quotable Star Trek,* p. 220.
11. Several books helpful on the subject of burnout are: Stephen R. Covey, *The 7 Habits of Highly Effective People: Restoring the Character Ethic* (New York: Fireside, 1990); Stephanie Winston, *The Organized Executive—A Program for Productivity: New Ways to Manage Time, Paper, and People* (New York: Warner Books, 1983); Alec Mackenzie, *The Time Trap* (New York: MJF Books, 1997); and William Oncken, Jr., *Managing Management Time: Who's Got the Monkey?* (Englewood Cliffs, NJ: Prentice-Hall, 1984).
12. *Webster's II: New Riverside Dictionary* (New York: Berkley Books, 1984): 476.
13. Abbie Lundberg, "From the Editor: The Greatest Threat to CIO Success," *CIO Magazine* (October 1, 2003): 16.

14. Kes to Janeway, *Star Trek Voyager,* "Darkling" episode, Sherwin, *Quotable Star Trek,* p. 220.

15. Thomas J. Watson, Jr., *A Business and Its Beliefs: The Ideas That Helped Build IBM,* (New York: McGraw-Hill, 1963): 27–28. It might be argued that IBM (despite its founders' efforts) has fallen victim to what it was trying to prevent; nevertheless, the point is still valid: Each business and each company needs its "wild ducks" to ensure that it does not miss an opportunity due to lack of viewpoint—or, colloquially, falling prey to "groupthink."

16. Q to Picard from *Star Trek: The Next Generation* Episodes Web site www.ugcs.caltach.edu/st-tng/episodes.html, aired June 5, 1994, 7th Season Final Series episode, www.ugcs.caltech.edu/st-tng/episodes/747.html.

17. Meredith Levinson, "Q&A with Dan Ariely: Why Good CIOs Make Bad Decisions," *CIO Magazine* (May 1, 2003): 86.

18. An appropriate analogy is that of looking where you want your car to go because it will certainly follow your vision.

19. They may be redeployed in other positions, laid off, transferred to the outsourcer as part of the deal, or a combination of these dispositions. Of course, depending on the number of people affected, there may be local, state, or federal regulations involved, such as the plant closing laws.

20. Adam Stone, "The Lease-Versus-Buy Equation," www.smallbusinesscomputing.com/testdrive/article.php/2184701 (accessed October 10, 2003).

21. The University of Pennsylvania, "Should You Buy Your Software or Lease It?" *Research at Penn: Advances in Knowledge from the University of Pennsylvania* (September 13, 2001), available at www.upenn.edu/researchatpenn/article.php?226&bus.

22. H.G. Enns, S.L. Huff, and B.R. Golden, "How CIOs Obtain Peer Commitment to Stratgic IS Proposals: Barriers and Facilitators," *Journal of Strategic Information Systems* 10 (2001): 85.

23. Ibid., pp. 87–90.

24. Bashir to Sisko on hosting several visiting federation ambassadors, *Star Trek: Deep Space 9,* "The Forsaken" episode. Sherwin, *Quotable Star Trek,* p. 343.

25. A number of significant challenges and problems arose during and after the acquisition, too many to chronicle here. However, one piece of advice: Before acquiring, ensure a true cultural fit evaluation is done as part of the due diligence. A highly recommended book is by Philip H. Mirvis and Mitchell Lee Marks, *Managing the Merger: Making It Work* (Englewood Cliffs, NJ: Prentice-Hall, 1992).

26. Susan H. Cramm, "Leadership Agenda: The M.I.A. CIO: Five Ways to Regain Your Focus—and Retain Your Job," *CIO Magazine* (October 1, 2003): 105.

27. Robert K. Cooper, Ph.D., and Ayman Sawaf, *Executive EQ: Emotional Intelligence in Leadership and Organizations* (New York: Berkley Publishing Group, 1997).

28. Ibid., p. xiii.

29. Ibid., p. xxv.

30. Laurence J. Peter and Raymond Hull, *The Peter Principle: Why Things Always Go Wrong* (New York: William Morrow, 1969).

31. Abstract for *CIO Magazine* 4, JW Marriott Desert Ridge Resort & Spa, Phoenix, AZ November 2–4, 2003; available at www.cio.com/conferences/.

32. Dr. Philip Boyce to Captain Christopher Pike, *Star Trek,* the original series, "The Cage" episode. Sherwin, *Quotable Star Trek,* p. 2.

33. In Ashton Applewhite, William R. Evans III, and Andrew Frothingham, *And I Quote* (New York: St. Martin's Press, 1992): 155.

34. Ibid., p. 155.

Glossary

ADSL (Asymmetric Digital Subscriber Line) *n.*—Often shortened to DSL, this is a telecommunications connectivity technology that is generally advocated by phone companies for relatively high-speed connections. "Asymmetric" refers to there being a difference in uplink (from your computer to the Internet) and downlink (from the Internet to your computer) speeds. Uplink speeds in the hundreds of kilobits per second and downlink speeds in the low megabits per second are common.

AIT (Advanced Intelligent Tape) *n.*—A technology used to store computer data on magnetic tape. AIT uses 8mm magnetic tapes and a drive and head mechanism that is similar to that used in digital camcorders (helical scanning).

AIX (Advanced Interactive eXecutive) *n.*—IBM's proprietary Unix operating system, originally for its RISC-based computers.

ARM (Advanced RISC Machine) *n.*—An efficient, low-power, low-cost RISC microprocessor by Advanced RISC Machines, Ltd. These processors are often used in embedded systems for host bus adapters and microcontrollers.

ATA (Advanced Technology Attachment) *n.*—A more generic acronym for IDE and EIDE, ATA got its name from being the disk drive attachment technology for the IBM PC/AT, as in IBM PC/Advanced Technology Attachment.

ATM (Asynchronous Transfer Mode) *n.*—The predominate internal data transfer methodology for telecommunications networks. This technology has been optimized for voice data and has been adapted to data and video. ATM uses small fixed-size data packets.

B/R (Backup/Recovery) *n.*—*Backup* refers to making copies of existing data in case there are problems with the data media, or the data are deleted. *Recovery* refers to restoring data when necessary due to media problems, data deletion, or corruption problems.

CIFS (Common Internet File System) *n.*—The file system format used by Microsoft in its Windows products for remotely accessing files on file servers. CIFS is a proposed standard but remains under the development control of Microsoft.

CRM (Customer Relationship Management) *n.*—Generally used when talking about the software and processes associated with storage and retrieving information related to a company's customer interactions and needs and wants.

DASD (Direct Access Storage Device) *n.*—Generally pronounced "DAZ-dee" (the "a" is pronounced as the first "a" in "Indiana"). The "direct access" portion refers to being able to directly get to any data without having to go sequentially through all data before it as you would with a tape drive. Usually, DASD is used when referring to mainframe-based storage.

DLT (Digital Linear Tape) *n.*—A technology used to store computer data on magnetic tape. DLT differs from other technologies (which are similar to the way VCRs or camcorder tapes work) in that the data are written linearly along multiple tracks. Typical tape cartridges can store more than 100 gigabytes and transfer through tape drives at more than 10 megabytes per second. LTO and AIT are the primary competing tape technologies. DLT was originally developed by a group that is now part of Quantum.

DNS (Domain Name System) *n.*—The service through which Internet names are translated into IP addresses.

DR (Disaster Recovery) *n.*—Represents the set of actions, following a disaster recovery plan, that an IT organization takes to recover data and data processing capabilities after some type of serious problem has occurred with a set of computer systems or a data processing site.

EIDE (Enhanced Integrated Drive Electronics or Enhanced Intelligent Drive Electronics) *n.*—An enhancement to the original specification for IDE drives. The primary improvements were the support of larger-capacity drives, more efficient data transfer methods and rates,

and support for removable IDE drives. These drives are also often referred to as *ATA drives.*

ERP (Enterprise Resource Planning) *n.*—Generally refers to the software systems that are associated with managing the operations side of a business, such as procurement, inventory, supplier management, order management, and customer service. Products that are generally considered to be in this category include SAP, PeopleSoft, and J.D. Edwards.

FC (Fibre Channel) *n.*—A hardware technology generally used in high-performance computer systems to connect data storage devices and subsystems to servers. Current technologies support up to 1 or 2 gigabits per second bidirectional data transfers; 10 gigabits-per-second rates will be commonly available in the not-too-distant future. The physical hardware connection can be via optical or copper cabling, with optical cabling providing for a significantly longer distance between connection points (at correspondingly higher costs). The SCSI commands are encapsulated into IP packets at the source side and are unencapsulated at the destination side. *See also:* SCSI.

FTP (File Transfer Protocol) *n.*—An Internet-based protocol for exchanging files between computers connected through a network.

GBIC (GigaBit Interface Converter) *n.*—A plug-in module that allows changing the connection type on Ethernet and Fibre Channel switches and host bus adapters (HBAs). For example, a 1-gigabit-per-second GBIC could be replaced with a 2-gigabit-per-second GBIC by popping out the first one and popping in the second one. Switches and HBAs using GBICs are more expensive, and inside industry reliability data have shown them to have higher error rates than fixed-interface switches or HBAs.

GUI (Graphical User Interface) *n.*—The generalized interface that most personal computer users (whether IBM PC-based, Apple-based, or RISC/Unix-based) use when they are interacting with their computer. Features include pointing devices such as a computer mouse or a touch-screen, drag-and-drop capability, and the like. The original GUI was developed by researchers at Xerox's PARC (Palo Alto Research Center) in the early 1970s. Usually pronounced "GOO-ee."

HBA (Host Bus Adapter) *n.*—The plug-in cards that allow you to connect external devices to the computer. The device adapts the protocols and connectivity of the external devices to the protocol of the computer bus and the computer itself so data and control information can be passed to and from the device(s) from and to the computer(s).

HP-UX (HewlettPackard-UniX) *n.*—HP's proprietary Unix operating system developed for its HP 9000 series of RISC-based computers.

HTTP (HyperText Transfer Protocol) *n.*— The primary means by which data is transferred across the Internet; the vehicle is usually through a Web browser. The term *hypertext* refers to the capability to have characters that represent references to other information located elsewhere; the hypertext provides the link to that data.

IDE (Integrated Drive Electronics or Enhanced Intelligent Drive Electronics) *n.*—Because the original disk drives had drive electronics that were separated from the mechanical aspects of the drives, it became a big deal when the electronics were integrated into the disk drive assembly. Besides eliminating op-

erational issues, it improved manufacturability and reduced overall cost. Also commonly referred to as *ATA.*

IETF (Internet Engineering Task Force) *n.*—The standards group that defines and ratifies the Internet operating protocols such as TCP/IP. The group is supervised by the Internet Society Internet Architecture Board and is composed of individuals and organizational member representatives. Standards are published as Requests for Comments (RFCs).

IM (Instant Message or Instant Messaging) *n., v.*—A means by which one can send text messages back and forth directly, for instance from computer to computer or phone to phone or combinations of both.

IMS (Information Management System) *n.*—High-speed database management system for IBM's mainframe systems, introduced in the early 1960s.

I/O (Input/Output) *n.*—Refers to the transfer into or out from a computer from or to something else. For instance, keyboards are input devices and displays are output devices, whereas tape drives and disk drives are both input and output devices. Pronounced "EYE-oh."

ISCSI (Internet Small Computer System Interface) *n.*—An emerging technology to allow storage devices and subsystems to be connected to servers using Internet Protocol (IP) as the higher-level communications protocol to carry the SCSI commands that actually control the storage devices and subsystems. The SCSI commands are encapsulated into IP packets at the source side and are unencapsulated at the destination side. Current uses are predominantly for long-distance connections and requirements such as remote mirroring. This technology is likely to become more popular when its costs are more commoditylike.

ISDN (Integrated Services Digital Network) *n.*—A telecommunications-based standard for digital transmission over standard copper telephone lines. (Voice transmission over regular phone lines is usually analog-based.) Speeds of up to 128 kilobits per second are achievable. ISDN is very popular in Europe, but it has not achieved a following of any size in the United States, primarily due to its metered approach and its high cost to the user.

ISP (Internet Service Provider) *n.*—A company that provides gateways to the Internet and that also hosts Web sites. Some also host actual hardware for customers on which the customer maintain their own Web sites and Internet services.

LAN (Local Area Network) *n.*—A hardware and software combination that allows computers, through the use of cabled connections or wireless connections, to communicate and share applications and data in a reliable and safe manner. (The level of reliability and safety are dependent on prudence and a good IT staff following accepted security practices.)

LED (Light-Emitting Diode) *n.*—A very low-power electronic device that lights up when electricity is passed through it. LEDs are generally a single color.

LTO (Linear Tape Open) *n.*—A technology used to store computer data on magnetic tape. LTO was jointly developed by Hewlett-Packard, IBM, and Seagate. Like DLT, LTO stores the information linearly. The Accelis format uses 8mm tapes that load at their midpoint for faster access to read-intensive applications. The Ultrium format uses half-inch tape. DLT and LTO are considered directly competing tape technologies, each of which has its adherents.

LUN (Logical Unit Number) *n.*—Originally, a term related to IBM's Storage Network Architecture (SNA). Primarily in today's usage, Logical Unit Number refers to a specific logical address for a device associated with the Small Computer System Interface (SCSI) and is related to either an initiator or a target. There can be a maximum of 16 devices, or LUNs, on a SCSI bus, of which one is usually an initiator and the remaining 15 are targets. There can be sub-LUNs, but they are rarely used. Because Fibre Channel architecture and technology, as used in Storage Area Networks (SANs) are based on encapsulated SCSI, LUNs are relevant in a Fibre Channel environment, also. Most commonly, a LUN corresponds to a tape drive or a disk volume.

MAC (Media Access Control) *n.*—The electronic component that identifies computers on a network; it is a unique hardware address number, hence there is one for each network adapter on a computer. Typically, there is one per computer, but with workstations and servers, there may be multiple MACs; still, each address number is unique. This acronym is usually used in the form of "MAC address" to refer to that unique number; on an Ethernet LAN, it is the Ethernet address and is mapped to a corresponding IP address for IP-based networks.

MAN (Metropolitan Area Network) *n.*—A network that connects users across an area that is larger than a Local Area Network (LAN) but smaller than a Wide Area Network (WAN). In large metropolitan areas, there is often a MAN ring that goes around that area and provides high-speed interconnects for LANs.

MS-SQL (Microsoft-Structured Query Language) *n.*—Microsoft's relational database product. Usually pronounced as "emm ess SEE quell."

MVS (Multiple Virtual Storage) *n.*— IBM's flagship operating system for its System/360, System/370, and System/390 mainframe systems.

MySQL (My Structured Query Language) *n.*—An open source relational database management system that uses Structured Query Language (SQL) for entering, using, and managing the in-formation in the database. It is available on Linux-based, Unix-based, and Windows-based systems and is popular with small companies and start-ups because there are no license fees associated with it. Support is available through the general user community. Usually pronounced as "my ess cue ELL."

NAS (Network Attached Storage) *n.*— Refers to a storage subsystem architecture that allows data to be available across networks through file system protocols. A computer would access a NAS through, for example, a TCP/IP network, and the data would look as if it were in a networked file system. This is in contrast to direct-attached storage, in which the storage subsystem is directly attached to the server through fibre channel, for example, and the data would be accessed by the computer in record and block mode. NAS has been gaining popularity in recent years for its ease of deployment, management, and use. Usually pronounced as "nass," where the "ah" is as in the first "a" in Indiana.

NFS (Network File System) *n.*—The predominant file system for Unix-based and Linux-based systems. NFS is based on a client/server architecture and provides remote access to files by a client computer to a host or server computer. Standard access to an NFS file system is over TCP/IP in more recent versions of NFS, whereas earlier versions used User Datagram Protocol (UDP), a less reliable delivery protocol. NFS was developed by Sun Microsystems and has subsequently been standardized, and there are user communities and standards groups associated with its evolution.

NIC (Network Interface Card) n.—A specialized Host Bus Adapter (HBA) whose external connection is designed for communications/networking. Today, the most common NICs are Ethernet LAN adapters (wired or wireless).

OLTP (OnLine Transaction Processing) *n.*—The predominant computer application approach for companies involved in commerce such as airlines, supermarkets, banking, and such. The *online* portion means that when information is put in, used, changed, or removed, it is done immediately (in real time), as opposed to being done later as part of a series or "batch" of updates. The *transaction processing* portion means that all the actions are split into one-at-a-time operations, or transactions, that can be managed to ensure that complex operations are completed correctly or not at all (they can be restarted if they do not complete). This is important particularly where lives and money are at stake.

Open Source *n.*—When used in general terms, refers to software programs or applications for which the original source code (what the programmers created or wrote) is made available for use without charge and to encourage public collaboration. When used in association with the Open Source Initiative, it refers to an official certification by that group, and can be used by software developers and companies if they agree to a certain set of rules and approaches. The Open Source Initiative's Web site is www.opensource.org.

PDA (Personal Digital Assistant) *n.*— Small, handheld computers that are approximately the size of a notepad and can be synchronized with a personal computer. The most common uses are for calendar and contact management. The original PDA was the Apple Newton introduced prematurely in 1993. The bane of every CIO, this is user anarchy at its best and the support team's worst nightmare. Because they are popular holiday gifts, combined with their many hardware and software variations—to say nothing of the security challenges—the use of PDAs is a calamity of horrific proportions for the IT organization. Then again, they are hard to live without, aren't they?

PEAP (Protected Extensible Authentication Protocol) *n.*—A certificate-based authentication scheme for wireless networks developed jointly by RSA Security, Cisco, and Microsoft. PEAP is a standards-based approach, although the standard has not yet been ratified (as of this writing). It is considered a follow-on improvement to Cisco's proprietary lightweight extensible authentication protocol (LEAP).

PPPoE (Point-to-Point Protocol over Ethernet) *n.*—A protocol to allow multiple computers to connect to an Ethernet-based LAN through dial-up modems and DSL (aka ADSL).

RAID (originally, Redundant Array of Inexpensive Disks; currently Redundant Array of Independent Disks) *n.*—An approach to storing data on disk drives, generally, by mirroring the data, striping the data across multiple drives, and using a parity scheme to manage through drive or data faults, or through the use of a combination of both these approaches. The original approach was to get groups of inexpensive disks, stripe data across them, and create parity information for each stripe and store it. The idea was that smaller, cheaper drives could be put together to form larger storage capacity systems at a significantly lower cost than the computer manufacturers were selling disk subsystem for. But because more drives were needed, and they were less robust drives, the view was that you would have a greater number of failures and therefore needed to be able to recover from data errors brought about by drive problems. One side benefit was that, by using multiple disks at the same time, the data transfers to and from the disk subsystem could overlap and, therefore, an overall higher rate of sustained data transfer could take place. A set of RAID stripes looks like a single disk to a computer server, making the use of RAID close to transparent.

RFID (Radio Frequency IDentification) *n.*—An emerging technology that could replace bar codes as a means of tagging objects (animate or not). One clear advantage is that no touch is required (e.g., no bar-code scanning) and there is no requirement for line-of-sight. A major disadvantage being raised in the retail industry is a concern about personal privacy. However, as an equipment inventory or stock management approach, for example, this could develop into a major applications breakthrough.

RISC (Reduced Instruction Set Computer) *n.*—In contrast to a CISC, or Complex Instruction Set Computer, a RISC architecture uses very few processor instructions and does complex combinations of actions by putting these instructions in specific sequences. Early on, the thinking was that RISC computers would execute one processor instruction per clock cycle (ignoring pipelining, look-ahead, and other optimization techniques). Whereas with

CISC architectures, a single instruction may take multiple or many clock cycles to complete. RISC-based systems have generally become associated with proprietary Unix-based (such as IBM's AIX or HP's HP-UX) and Linux-based operating systems, while CISC-based systems have generally become associated with proprietary operating systems such as Microsoft's Windows and IBM's MVS. The debates will rage on over whether RISC or CISC is better.

RSS (RDF Site Summary) *n.*—Also known as Rich Site Summary, RSS is a way to describe Web content that has been published by an online service. RDF (Resource Description Framework) is a World Wide Web consortium standard for defining the material published. RSS was originally developed by Netscape.

RYO (Roll Your Own) *n.*—Generally used when talking about whether a company is going to develop its own products (particularly software) or buy them from someone else. Developing your own products is referred to as RYO. Generally, this term, when used by companies that produce a product that could do the function, is considered as somewhat derogatory.

SAN (Storage Area Network) *n.*—A high-speed data network designed for the connection of storage devices and subsystems to servers for midrange and enterprise-class systems. Generally, SANs today are based on fibre channel interconnection using switches and host bus adapters. An emerging technology in this area is iSCSI.

SATA (Serial ATA) *n.*—The next-generation evolution for ATA (or IDE) device attachment. One of the key differences is that this is a serial-signaling technology-based approach, in contrast to ATA, which is a parallel-signaling technology-based approach. Among several key improvements are that the connection cables are much smaller (parallel ribbon cables are large and flat) and the signal voltage is significantly lower in the cable.

SCSI (Small Computer System Interface) *n.*—Usually pronounced "skuzzy," this is a standardized set of interfaces used to connect devices to personal and other small (generally nonmainframe) computers. Apple Computer was the first to ship peripherals using SCSI interconnect. SCSI is a parallel-based protocol, and various improved versions allow for increased data transfer rates of up to 160 megabytes per second and attachment of up to 15 devices (in addition to the host connection) on the interface. It is highly likely that SCSI will become less important as Serial ATA (SATA) becomes more predominant.

SDK (Software Development Kit) *n.*—A set of programs, algorithms, subroutines, and functions that can be used by a software developer to write computer programs. Also referred to as Software Developer's Kit.

SDLT (Super DLT) *n.*—A higher-capacity, faster data transfer version of DLT. SDLT tape drives can read but cannot write DLT format.

SIP (Session Initiation Protocol) *n.*—A standard protocol for starting an interaction between a computer and a server that involves multimedia. Transfers can be across multiple types of communication protocols. This protocol is managed through the IETF.

SMB (Server Message Block or Small and Medium Business) *n.*—In the technical community, SMB refers to the Server Message Block protocol, a client/server approach that enables computer users to get to data on servers. SMB was developed by Microsoft and has evolved over time to be replaced in

Windows by CIFS. Unix-based and Linux-based systems provide access through a shareware program called SAMBA (www.samba.org). In the business world, SMB refers to small and medium businesses.

SMS (Short Message Service) *n.*—Allows Global System for Mobile (GSM) phone users to send text messages to each other. The receiving phone does not have to be turned on at the time the text message is sent; the message will be queued for a later time when the phone is turned on.

SNA (Systems Network Architecture) *n.*—IBM's proprietary networking architecture generally deployed through IBM's VTAM product and primarily used with IBM mainframes. This architecture is being superceded by TCP/IP in most applications.

SNIA (Storage Networking Industry Association) *n.*—*The* storage industry association. SNIA is focused on the advancement and interoperability of storage systems and software for trusted and reliable storage networks. More information is available at www.snia.org.

SNMP (Simple Network Management Protocol) *n.*—The standards-based means by which computer and networking equipment is monitored, sends alerts of problems, and is managed. SMNP is not tied to any particular networking protocol (e.g., TCP/IP) contrary to common belief.

SNTP (Simple Network Time Protocol) *n.*—A standards-based means by which to get the correct, synchronized time so all computers in your network can be set to the same time.

SQL (Structured Query Language) *n.*— The predominant programming language for dealing with database products; it was developed around the use of relational databases.

SRM (Supplier Relationship Management or Storage Resource Management) *n.*—In the Customer Relationship Management environment, SRM refers to Supplier Relationship Management as a series of products and processes to manage the interactions a company has with those companies that provide services and goods. In the IT storage world, SRM refers to Storage Resource Management as a series of products and processes to manage digital data and the devices on which the data are stored.

SSD (Solid State Disk) *n.*—A memory-based device that emulates a disk drive. It is significantly more expensive (by an order of magnitude or two) than a regular disk drive but operates at memory speeds. While seemingly a great idea, SSD has generally not caught on (although it did achieve some interest in high-performance mainframes in the 1980s as a fast virtual storage device).

SSID (Service Set IDentifier) *n.*—A set of characters used to uniquely name (or identify) a wireless LAN. This is not a security feature, as the SSID is knowable by all; WEP (Wired Equivalent Privacy), MAC access lists, and other evolving techniques are being developed to provide wireless LAN security. Multiple wireless LANs can operate in overlapping areas by having different SSIDs so the appropriate people who would be connecting to a particular LAN could do based on the SSID they are set up to use.

SSL (Secure Sockets Layer) *n.*—A standardized protocol for managing the security of information transferred to and from a computer across the Internet. This protocol uses the private and public key encryption system developed by RSA. When a padlock is shown in the bottom right corner of a Web browser, that's a sign that SSL is in use.

TCP/IP (Transmission Control Protocol/ Internet Protocol) *n.*—The primary protocols used for Internet and intranet traffic. TCP is concerned with packaging messages and data for transmission, and IP is concerned with routing the messages and data to their correct destinations.

UDP (User Datagram Protocol) *n.*—A communications protocol designed for computer-to-computer communication through an Internet Protocol (IP) network. UDP does not sequence packets (whereas TCP does); it does provide optional checksum capability. It is generally regarded as less reliable than TCP, although of higher net performance when the communications lines are of high quality. Generally, use of UDP is being phased out in favor of TCP over IP.

UPS (Uninterruptible Power Supply) *n.*—A piece of hardware that provides power via battery to devices plugged into it when the electrical line power goes out. Additionally, UPSs usually also condition power, protect against power surges or spikes, and can electrically isolate pieces of equipment from each other.

URL (Uniform Resource Locator) *n.*—The address of something located on the Internet. Pronounced yew-r-ell, the URL is specified either through a name (such as www.wiley.com/WileyCDA/), which is subsequently translated to a network address via DNS, or directly as a network address (such as http://192.168.0.1).

UWB (Ultra WideBand) *n.*—A preemerging technology designed to have high data-transfer rates with very low power over short distances; UWB can also go through doors, windows, and other physical obstacles. Also referred to as *digital pulse wireless.*

VLAN (Virtual Local Area Network) *n.*—When a series of computers are mapped to a logical, rather than a physical, LAN, they have been connected to each other via a virtual LAN. Generally, this is done when the computers are not physically close to each other (most LANs are based on physical proximity).

VM (Virtual Machine) *n.*—An IBM proprietary mainframe operating system that is designed to host multiple other heterogeneous operating systems (such as MVS, CMS, Linux, or VM itself). Each hosted system gets its own "virtual machine." Most of IBM's mainframe operating systems and database and transaction processing programs were developed in the VM environment.

VoIP (Voice over Internet Protocol) *n.*—Describes use of the IP network to send and receive voice transmissions. Practically, the intent is to use the IP network rather than the standard telephone network for telephone-type voice calls. This is an emerging technology.

VPN (Virtual Private Network) *n.*—An architecture and implementation that allows remote users and offices to connect through a public network in a secure manner with their company's internal computer systems and networks. VPNs encrypt data at both ends of the connection when sending, and decrypt when receiving; in addition, the sending and receiving network addresses are encrypted for extra security.

VTAM (Virtual Telecommunications Access Method) *n.*—IBM's implementation of SNA that gave developers the ability to deal with telecommunications devices from a logical, rather than a physical, point of view. VTAM is most commonly linked with IBM's 3270 family of displays.

WAN (Wide Area Network) *n.*—Generally, refers to public shared user networks over a large geographic region.

WEP (Wired Equivalent Privacy) *n.*—A security protocol for wireless networking, defined as part of the Institute of Electrical and Electronics Engineers (IEEE) Wireless Fidelity (Wi-Fi) 802.11b standard. This is done by en-crypting the data at point of transmission and decrypting it at the wireless access point.

WLAN (Wireless Local Area Network) *n.*—A means for connecting a computer to a network through radio frequency transmission that conforms to the IEEE 802.11 standard.

Index

360-review at IBM, 238

Accelerating decisions with the CEO, 248
Accelerators and barriers, 235–236
Accelerators, Nirvana, 245–252
Accomplishment, creating an atmosphere of, 126
Accountancy and information technology, 9, 10
Accounting and value creation, 177
Acquisitions:
    cultural clashes, 261–262
    cultural compatibility, 274
    problem children, 261–262
Active listening/active listener, 30
Activity-based costing, 90
Adapting, as a communication style, 42
Adaptive IT posture, 200–202
Advanced technical skills:
    project planning and cost estimates, 77–79
    drawing-up your own approach, 81–83
    environment-specific, 76–77
    key technologies evolution, 79–81
    outsourcing and insourcing, 77
Airplanes and career choices, 267
Albatross, organizational, 256
Aligning IT:
    organization strategy, 184–192
    company strategic resources, 152
    strategic plans, 154–156
Alignment:
    IT maturity assessment, 197
    business, strategy, technology, 229–230
Alliances, personal strategic, 246–250
Alternating job types, 269
Alternative perspectives on routines, 250
Always-executable base, IBM, 201–202
Ambassadors of Unhappy, 260–262
American Airlines:
    CIO Monte Ford, 12
    former CEO Don Carty, 12
Anarchy, PDA(s), 4
Andriole, Stephen J., 102
Answer-first:
    approach to communication, 37–38
    outsourcing service provider, 105
Anti-IT bias, 236–237, 239–240

Application service or solution providers, 254
Armstrong, Neil, A., 127
Art of the Long View, The, 224
ASPs. *See* application solution providers
Assessment:
    IT organization maturity, 195–196
    leadership vision, 100
    project management risk, 243
ATMs, 186, 187
Auspex, innovator's dilemma, 145

Back to the Future, 254
Bacon, Francis, 79
Balanced scorecard for IT, 190–192
Baldridge Award, 177
Bandwagon, outsource, 253
Barricades, 244
Barriers and accelerators, 235–236, 237
Barron-Tieger, Barbara and Paul D. Tieger, 221
Bates, Marilyn and David Keirsey, 221–222
Bean counter, CFO as, 247
Beck, Martha, 24, 101, 220–221
Bellmen, Geoffrey M., 94–95, 100
Benchmarking IT, 191–192
Berra, Yogi, 26
Best Buy, 101–102, 167
Biases, anti-IT, 239–240
Bleeding-edge risk profile, 179
Blind spots, personal and professional, 53
Board of advisors, personal, 269–270
Board of directors and IT, 9
Braniff Airlines, 79
Breaking routines, 250–251
Brennan, Jack, 12
Brogniez, Jan and Stacy Hall, 122, 223
Brooks, David, 151–152
Brown, John Seely, 224
Brynjolfsson, Erik, 186–187
BTIQ. *See* Business/Technology Intelligence
    Quotient
Buckley, John, 130–131
Budget management and the IT staff, 88–89
    focus on variances and exceptions, 88
    open-book management, 88
    business acumen, 86–89

Budget versus actual, CIO performance, 188
Building future technology evaluation team, 138–141
BUNCH, The, 146
Bureaucracy versus process, 193
Burnout:
  career choices, and 268
  personal, 245
  recommended reading, 273
Business acumen, 83–93
  budget management, 86–89
  defined and characteristics, 83–84
  financial management, 89–91
  information technology management, 93
  operations management, 92–93
  personnel staffing and management, 84–86
  procurement and contract management, 91–92
Business or technology, 25–26
  fork in the road, 21–63
Business success metrics, choosing effective, 126
Business Value of Computers, The, 223
Business value of information technology model, 189–190
Business/Technology Intelligence Quotient (BTIQ), 208–212
  profiles for CIOs and CEOs, 210, 230
Businologist or Technologist, 45–49
But we've always done it this way, 237, 243–244
Buyer's remorse, strategic planning, 157, 241–242

Call center, 12
Capability Maturity Model (CMM), 194–198
Capital equipment, 91–92
Career:
  decisions, 257–260
  flat-lining, 267–268
  stagnation, 267–268
Carpenter's rule, think twice/speak once, 30
Cascaded development process, IBM, 201–202
Centralization, operations and management, 4
Centralized versus distributed, 255–256
CEO:
  business/technology intelligence quotient, 210
  CIO reporting to, 218–220
  CIO reports to, 6–8
  inner circle, 207
  most important ally, 248–249
  preferred risk profile, 216
  strategically focused, 217
  what they really want from their CIOs, 10–19
  who does not want a CIO, 214
  why needs a CIO, 213–214
CFO:
  accountant, 247
  bean counter, 247

CIO reports to, 6–8
  friend or foe, 247–248
  member of the executive team, 177
Champion, cross-functional executive, 235
Change, IT cultural resistance, 130–132
Charting journey milestones, 202–206
Chemical companies, 9
Chemistry, nurturing personal, 246–250
Chicken versus the pig, 43
Christensen, Clayton, 146, 147, 222
CIO:
  business/technology intelligence quotient, 210
  competent, criteria for visions, 97
  creating custom-designed role, 22–24
  CTO as, 50–51
  Dell, Randy Mott on ideal CIO, 65
  desirability of the role, 101–102
  emphasis on business, 9
  evolving expectations, 45–49
  ideal, Pete DeLisi on, 65
  influencing decisions, 258–259
  innovation priorities, 145–148
  innovation focuses, 148–149
  job and role, 46, 47, 59–63
  key network relationship groups, 27
  left-brain activities, 128–129
  liberating yourself, 262
  important skills for success, 68
  organizational authority and structure, 6, 8
  corporate-level strategic planning, 152–153
  personal comfortability, 24
  personal innovation philosophy, 145–149
  practical strategic planning beyond IT, 135–138
  primary focus, 115
  professional publications, 225–229
  relationships with CTO, 49–51
  reporting structure, 6–10, 16–17, 218–220, 232
  right-brain activities, 128–129
  risk-averse, 215–216
  risk profile assessment, 177–184
  Roles, 6, 15–16, 21, 23, 43, 52, 53–54, 116, 127, 163
  self-improvement, 220–225
  skills required, Darwin, 67
  state of the profession, 5–10
  successful CIOs, 46–47, 97
  successful, *Financial Executive*, 46–47
  Sun Microsystems' Bill Howard, 12
  The Reluctant, 100–101
  value creation, 47–48
  views on responsibilities, 12–13
  versus DP manager, 218
  why the CEO needs one, 213–214
  why the company needs one, 214–215
CIO Insight, 225, 227, 233

Ciulla, John J., 12
Closed-loop system, 230
CMI Group, The, 59–63
CMM (Capability Maturity Model), 194–198
Collaborating, 44, 124–125
Collins, Jim, 152
Commercial off-the-shelf products, 79
Communications of the ACM, 227, 233
Company risk profile dynamics, 216
Competence:
   leadership competence and vision, 94–95
   leadership competence and vision, defined, 94
   unified profile, 65–114
Competitive strategies, 167–168
Computer Technology Review, 227, 233
Computer, 227, 233
Computerworld, 225, 228, 233
Connecting the executive and operational teams, 207
Consolidated organization effects, 255
Continuous process improvement:
   discontinuous process improvement, 130–135
   executive EQ, 266
Contract and procurement management, 91–92
COO managing the CIO, 6–7, 218, 232
Cooper, Robert and Ayman Sawaf, 265–266
Coopers & Lybrand, 46
Cornerstones:
   emotional intelligence, 267
   executive EQ, 266
Correlating IT investments and profits, 188, 189
Cost or profit or value center poll, 149–150
Cost versus price, 149
Cost-to-benefit ratio(s), 255
   projects, 198–199
Counterbalancing the engineering team, 143
Cramm, Susan H., 157–158
Crash-and-burn, 245
Creating:
   custom-designed CIO role, 22–24
   the horizon, 269–271
Credible threat:
   Dell CTOs, 8, 9
   future technology evaluation team, 143
Creeping elegance, 111
Crises of need, 214
CRM. *See* Customer Relationship Management
Cross-functional executive champion, 235
Crossing the Chasm, 223–224
Csikszentmihalyi, Mihaly, 25, 221
CTO(s), 8, 9, 49–51
Culture:
   Clashes, 261–262
   Compatibility, 274
   resistance to change, 131–132
   start-up, 261–262

Customer Relationship Management, 275–276
Customer relationships, 121–122, 149
Customer(s):
   attracting perfect, 223
   finding "perfect" customers, example, 119–120
   firing less-than-perfect, 121
   managing customer relationship value, 118–127
   primary points of contact, 12
   start-ups and customers, 119–120, 121
   strategic customer relationship postures,
      122–127
   strategic relationship management, 120–122
   resisting "more-is-better" temptation, 121
   why not to employ discounts and gimmicks, 124
Customer-chasing, 125–126

Darwin effect, 131
Data center 3
   manager, 3
Data processing center, 3
Death marches and Pollyanna Syndrome, 242
DEC, innovator's dilemma, 145
Decentralization, 4
Decisions a CIO should not make alone, 252–262
   career decisions, 257–260
   centralized versus distributed, 255–256
   expense versus profit versus value creation, 255
   leasing versus buying, 254–255
   line versus staff, 256
   outsourcing, 253
   prioritization, 257
   problem children, 260–262
   proprietary versus Open Systems, 255
   strategic IS/IT initiatives, 252–253
DeLisi, Pete, 65
Delivery culture, 261–262
Dell:
   CIO Randy Mott, on ideal CIO, 65
   CTOs roles, responsibilities, and expertise, 8, 9
   former CIO, Gregoire, Jerry, 12
   future technology evaluation team, 138–144
   innovation and new technology, 146–148
   innovator's dilemma philosophy, 8, 9
   IT as a key core competency, 8
   online order taking and risk profile, 180
   product group CTOs, 8, 9, 145–148
   Valente, John, former Dell executive, 101–102
DeMarco, Tom, 77
Development:
   contrasted with research, 79–81
   difficult project problems, 198–199
   iterative improvement, 201–202
Discontinuous and continuous improvement,
   130–135
Discounts and gimmicks, why to resist, 124

Disruptive:
    ideas, 222
    technology, 222
    technology shifts, 146–147
Distant horizon, 263–269
Doability of projects, 198
DP manager, 3
    versus CIO, 218
Dr. No, 261
        risk profiles, 183–184
Dysfunctional:
    IT organization, taking over, 133
    senior management team, 264

Early adoption strategy and innovation, 148
Early citations of the CIO title, 5
EMC, 145
Emotional intelligence, 21–22, 265–266
Enabler(s):
    CIO and IT, 40
    inhibitors for IT, 128–129
Enterprise Resource Planning, defined, 276
Enterprisewide strategic planning, 127–129
    CIO's role, 127
Entrepreneurial accounting approaches, 200
Entrepreneurs and Pollyanna Syndrome, 242
EQ assessments and personal transition plans, 271
EQ Map™, 266
EQ, Executive, 265–266
ERP. *See* Enterprise Resource Planning
Evolution:
    CFO's role, 177
    visionary leadership competency, 96
Evolutionary and revolutionary improvement,
        130–135
Executive:
    champion, cross-functional, 235
    clarity as a measure of strategic success, 159
    EQ, 265–266
    agendas and interests, 45
Expectations of IT, asked of CEO, 14–15
Expense versus profit versus value creation, 255
Exploration, 251

Familial culture:
    transformation to delivery culture, 262
    clash, 261–262
Fast-trackers, IBM, 268–269
Favor bank, 52, 257
Feeding frenzy from strategic planning, 241–242
Final preparations for the journey, 235–273
Financial management:
    activity-based costing, 90
    budget management, versus, 89–90
    business acumen, 89–91

Financial planning and analysis (FP&A), 86, 88
Finding Your Own North Star, 220–221
Finney, Stephen C., 155
Firing less-than-perfect customers, 121
First law of performance measurement, 110
First time:
    manager experience at IBM, 237–238
    outsourcing, 253
Flame-out and IBM fast-trackers, 268–269
Flat-lining, career, 267–268
Flow, 25, 221
Focus and prioritization, 173–230
Ford, Henry, 130
Ford, Monte, 12
Fork in the road, 25–26
Fortune 500 companies maturity assessments, 195
FP&A, 86, 88
Friend or foe CFO, 247–248
Functional underground, 247, 249–250
Future and present tense and team, 251–252
Future technology evaluation team, 138–145
Future:
    planning, 145–148
    planning without disruption, 138–149
Future-based intentions, 169
Futurist, The, 227, 233

Gall, John, 224–225
Genealogy:
    information technology, 3
    IT profession, 1
Gerstner, Lou:
    IBM's lackluster leadership, 175
    "the vision thing", 96–97
Goleman, Daniel, 21–22
Goodman, Richard A. and Michael W. Lawless, 150
Greene, Brian, 235
Gregoire, Jerry, 12
    time spent on strategy versus operations, 93
Groupthink:
    among executives, 165
    IBM, 274
Gutenberg, Johannes, 1

Half-life of relevant knowledge, 10, 11
Hall, Stacy and Jan Brogniez, 122, 223
Hammitt, John, 46
Harvard Business Review, The, 225–226, 233
Highbarger, John, 46
Hijacking of meetings by naysayers, 262
Hippocrates, 101
History of the IT profession, 1–10
Hollerith, Herman, 2
Horizon:
    creating the, 269–271

distant, 263–269
true, 269
How Systems Work and Especially How They Fail, 224–225
Howard, Bill, 12

IBM:
360–review, 238
adaptive posture, 201–202
always-executable base, 201–202
cascaded development process, 201–202
CEO Lou Gerstner on strategy and vision, 96–97
fast-trackers and flame-out, 268–269
first-time manager experience, 237–238
formation/creation of, 2
groupthink, 274
innovator's dilemma, 145
iterative development process, 201–202
JES3, 79
mainframe executives and their successors, 175
near bankruptcy, 175
small-team project, 201–202
toady up and bully down, 175
wild ducks, 250–251, 260, 274
IEEE Engineering Management Review, 226, 233
IEEE Software, 227, 233
Implementation, centralized versus distributed, 255–256
Inaccurate self-assessments, 237–239
Incremental planning and realized strategies, 169
Incrementalizing, 169
Information technology:
board of directors-level interest, 9
business acumen, 93
culture and resistance to change, 130–132
business units' strategic planning, 154–155
financial/business perspective, 149–150, 208–212
financial planning and analysis administrator, 88, 89
innovation awareness, 82
investment and value to bottom line, 187–188
maturity assessment, 195–197
operations management business acumen. *See* operations management
organization, 8, 9, 239–240
perfect supplier, 122
performance measures, lab technician example, 162
performance and strategic goals and initiatives, 158
posture as adaptive, 200–202
profession genealogy, 1–3
profit or cost center, 18
program management, 202–206

resources and strategic alignment, 184–192
strategic plans, 154–155, 167–168
strategic planning, 9
strategy input to the strategic plan, 155–156
success enablers and inhibitors, 128–129
value, sources of 190
Information Week, 225, 233
InfoStor, 225, 233
Innovation:
focuses for the CIO, 148–149
management dynamics, 147
planning for the future, 145–149
priorities for the CIO, 145–148
Innovator's dilemma, 8, 9
key foundations, 145
Innovator's Dilemma, The, 222
Innovator's Solution, The, 222
Insight into strategic paths, 224
Insourcing, 73–75
Intelligence, emotional, 265–266
Interception points requiring new skills, 85–86
Internal partnership network, creating, 26–32
International Business Machines. *See* IBM
Interview, questions the CIO should ask, 219–220
Investments:
CIO as final signature on IT-related, 16
resources to execute the strategic plan, 157–158
return on from IT, 17–18
IT. *See* Information technology
Iterative:
continuous process improvement, 132–133
improvement, 31
development process, IBM, 201–202
process, strategic planning as, 152
IT-related investments, CIO as final signature, 16

Job description, IT executive, 60–62
Johnson, H. Thomas, 174–177
Journal of Cost Management, 226, 233
Journey, final preparations, 235–273
Jungle rules and career planning, 272

Kaplan, Robert and David Norton:
balanced scorecard for IT, 190–192
on focus and prioritization, 173
Katzenback, Jon R. and Douglas K. Smith, 236
Kavan, C. Bruce, 160–161
Keirsey, David and Marilyn Bates, 221–222
Kelly-Bootle, Stanley, 138
Key technologies evolution, what and when, 81
Kierkegaard, Soren, 250–251
Kirk, James T., 149, 239
Knowledge age, paradox, 11
Kotter, John P., 223
Kraft Foods North America, 155

Language of the Industry, 116–118
Lateral moves, 263
Lawless, Michael W. and Richard A. Goodman, 150
Leadership and management differences, 100
Leadership:
  competence and vision, unified competency profile, 94–101
  competence and vision, 95–100
  competencies, business reality, 96
  intangibles, 21–22
  missing in action, 252
  vision assessment, 100
Leading Change, 223
Leading the witness, 165
Leading-edge risk profile, 179
Leasing versus buying, 254–255
Left-brain CIO activities, 128–129
Liberating yourself, 262
Line executive, CIO as, 15–16
Line versus staff, 256
Lower-level executives, CIO reports to, 6–7
Luftman, Jerry, 195–196
Lunatic fringe risk profile, 179

Management:
  by business reality, 95
  by means, 174–177
  by means, and how living systems work, 176
  focus derailment, 174–175
  team, senior, dysfunctional, 264
  versus leadership, 65
Manager, 3, 237–238
Managing and doing as a difficult challenge, 191
Many-worlds interpretation, 47
Market segmentation, 137–138
Marketing requirements document, innovation planning, 149
Maskell, Brian, 176
Matching higher risk with lower failure severity, 181
Maturity of the organization, 194–198
Maximizing, partner network, 32–45
MBTI. *See* Myers-Briggs Type Indicator
McNealy, Scott, 12
Measurement:
  IT value poll, 150, 151
  linkage, 162
  methods, strategic performance, 161
  realistic project plans and, 77–79
  Schubert's first law of performance, 110, 158
  validating execution against the strategic plan, 158–162
Meltdown, CIO, 245
Mentoring and mentors, 270–271
Mill, John Stuart, 272

Mind-set, value creation, 247–248
Minimally acceptable project planning actions for IT, 197–200
MIS Quarterly, 226, 233
Missing in action on leadership, 252
Money as a measure of executive commitment, 159
Monkey, workload, 244–245
Moore, Geoffrey, 223–224
Mott, Randy, 65
Moves, lateral, 263
MTBF, 117–118
MttlTFEDBS, 117–118
MTTR, 117–118
Multiverses hypothesis, 64
Murphy's Law, 241
Myers-Briggs Type Indicator, 32–25
  mentoring and peer groups, 270
  pacing process improvement, 135
  personal transition plans, 271
  personality types, 34
  self-improvement reading list, 221
  senior executive team example, 33–45
  strengths and needs assessment, 265

Naysayer(s), 260–262
Needs and strengths assessment, 263, 264–267
Network:
  concentric zones of influence, 28–29, 30
  cultivating, concentric zones and hierarchical, 28–30
  cultivating, first contact attempts, 30
  cultivating a broad, 28–32
  hierarchical, 29, 30
  maximizing the partner, 32–45
  relationship groups, 27
Networking partners perspectives:
  awareness of IT strategic plan, 153–155
  balancing tactical versus strategic issues, 56–57
  balancing business versus technical issues, 56–57
  CEO expectations of CIO, 58–59
  CIO role and job, 55–56
  IT as an expense or investment, 58
  IT reporting structure, 57–58
  strategic planning, 155
New information technology, reasons for adopting, 141
Nirvana:
  accelerators, 245–252
  defined, 245
Non-computer technology companies, 9
North Pole expedition, 203
Norton, David and Robert Kaplan:
  balanced scorecard for IT, 190–192
  on focus and prioritization, 173

Not-on-the-edge risk profile, 179
Nurturing personal chemistry and alliances, 246–250

Objectives, timeline from CEO, 18–19
Office of Personnel Management, United States, business acumen definition, 83–84
Oil tanker, 203
Onboard for career decisions, 257–258
Open versus proprietary system religious discussions, 255
Operational logic as applied to focus and prioritization, 176
Operations:
    management, business acumen, 92–93
    management, successful approaches, 92–93
    time spent on strategy or, 217–218
Optimizations, local versus global, 219
Organizational:
    albatross, 256
    centralized versus distributed, 255–256
    maturity, 194–198
    phoenix, 256
Organizations looking to IT for solutions, 164–165
Outsourcing:
    additional areas to consider, 107–108
    Andriole, Stephen J., thoughts on, 102
    candidates, 73
    common themes to success, 73
    decision a CIO should not make alone, 253
    effects on overcommitting and underproducing, 242
    expectations, 74
    flexibility in changing service providers, 109–110
    handling risky technologies and companies, 112–113
    help desk and problem management, 74–76
    insourcing viability, 72–74
    measuring quality of delivery, 110–111
    needed of service provider, 105–106
    procurement and contract management, 91–92
    projects, the first, 253
    service provider key drivers, 104–105
    successful regular performance reviews, 111–112
    successful service provider relationships, 106–107
    what not to outsource, 109
Overcommit and underproduce, Pollyanna Syndrome, 240–243
Overengineering because it's cool, 148

Pacing process improvement, 133, 135
    Myers-Briggs Type Indicators, 135

Paradox:
    executive perceptions of strategy, 151–152
    information technology, productivity of, 186–189
    knowledge age, 11
    strategy, 151
Parallel universes hypothesis, 47, 64
Partner network, maximizing, 32–45
Passing on less-than-perfect customers, 120
Personal Digital Assistant(s), 4
Peeling the productivity paradox onion, 186
Peer groups and mentors, 270–271
Perfect customer:
    attracting, 119–120, 125–126, 223
    embracing the (external), 118–127
    introduced, 116
    not captive customer, 127
    profile and innovation, 148
    revisited, 126–127
Perfect supplier, IT as, 122
Performance management, key questions, 160
Personal:
    burnout, 245
    risk profile, 174
    skills and leadership, cultivating, 27–28, 264–265, 271
Personality types and temperaments, 221–222
Personnel and management, business acumen, 84–86
Peter Principle and career choices, 268
Phoenix, organizational, 256
Pillsbury, 46
Pilots, military and airline and routine, 251
Planning for the future, 145–148
    without disrupting the present, 138–149
Plotting the route to meet commitments, 195, 197
Political interference in the benchmarking process, 192
Pollyanna Syndrome, 236, 240–243
Postimplementation project analyses, 197, 199–200
Power politics, 115
Price versus cost, 149
Primal leadership, emotional intelligence and, 21–22
Primozic, Primozic, and Leben, 173
Prioritization, 257
Proactive alignment of strategic plans, 154–155
Problem children:
    decision a CIO should not make alone, 260–262
    start-up company, 261–262
Process improvement:
    continuous and discontinuous, 130–135
    continuous, iterative approach, 132–133
    evolutionary and revolutionary, 130–135
    pacing, 133, 135
    selecting, management perspectives, 132–133

Process versus bureaucracy, 193
Procurement and contract management, business acumen, 91–92
Product-based versus service-based companies, 209
Productivity paradox, information technology, 186–189
Professional crash-and-burn, 245
Professional publication suggestions, 225–229
Profile of success:
    Dr. C. Bruce Kavan, 59–60
    John Valente, 101–102
Profit or cost center, IT as, 18
Profit or cost or value center poll, 149–150
Program management:
    avoiding Pollyanna Syndrome, 243
    IT, 202–206
Program manager:
    characteristics of success, 204–205
    defined, 203
    how they spend their time, 203–205
    involvement in team selection, 204
Project:
    analyses, postimplementation, 197, 199–200
    complexity, 205
    development phase, most difficult problems, 198–199
    doability, 198
    life cycles, 198
    management risk assessment, 243
    mismanagement, 206
    planning actions for IT, minimally acceptable, 197–200
    plans, measuring estimates realistically, 77–79
    termination reasons, 199–200
    terminated before completion, 203–206
Proper provisioning, 192–200
Proprietary versus open systems:
    decision a CIO should not make alone, 255
    religious parallels, 255
Punched cards, invention of, 2

Quantifying risk, 182
Quantity as an indicator of commitment, 185
Queasiness and executive EQ assessments, 266

R&D investment, 79–81
    effects of minimizing, 176–177
Reading suggestions for self-improvement, 220–225
Realist versus Pollyanna, 243
Reasons for terminating projects, 199–200
Recommended professional publications, 225
Regis McKenna, 12
Relationship executive, CIO as, 116

Relationship(s):
    actively preserving, 42–43
    CIO and CTO, 49–51
    strategic customer, postures, 122–127
Religious parallels, proprietary versus open systems, 255
Reluctant CIO, 100–101
Removing obstacles, 54–55
Reporting structure, 16–17
Research contrasted with development, 79–81
Resistance to change and the IT culture, 130–132
Resource(s):
    allocation as aligning resources to strategy, 185
    allocation to IT, proper provisioning, 192–200
    path to proper IT resource allocation, 193–200
    resources to execute the strategic plan, 157–158
Return on management, context of self-improvement reading list, 223
Revolutionary and evolutionary process improvement, 130–135
Right-brain CIO activities, 128–129
Right-featured products, 222
Right-sizing based on company's strategic plan, 156
Risk assessment, project management, 243
Risk management with strategic management equals explicit strategy, 133, 134
Risk profile(s), 177–184
    dynamics, 216
    favored, asked of CIO by CEO, 215–216
    personal, 174
Risk referee, 215
Risk-averse CIO, 215–216
Roadblocks, 244
ROI and IT, 211
Roll Your Own (RYO), defined, 281
    versus shrink-wrapped software, 71

Sabotage of strategic goals by employees, 136
Sawaf, Ayman and Robert Cooper, 265–266
Sawhney, Mohanbir, 116, 126
Scapegoating, outsourcing, 253
Schubert's first law of performance measurement, 110, 158
Schwartz, Peter, 224
    strategic conversations, 206
Search parties and career management, 273
Seeing Differently, 224
Self, essential and social defined, 24–25
Self-assessment:
    inaccurate, 237–239
    personal attributes 264
    professional SWOT, 265
Self-awareness, importance of, 24–25
Service-based versus product-based companies, 209

Service-level agreement(s), 117
  acronyms, 118
  innovation, 148
Seven catastrophes of computing, 138
Skills, most important for CIO success, 68
Small-team project, IBM example, 201–202
Smith, Douglas K. and Jon R. Katzenback, 236
Software development process iterative
    improvement, 201–202
Software project, controlling, 77–79
Sources of IT value, 190
Spending time, strategy or operations, 217–218
Spock, Mr., 237
SRM. *See* Supplier Relationship Management
Staff executive, CIO as, 15–16
Staffing assessment and IT future visions, 85–86
Stagnation, career, 267–268
Start-up(s):
  company controller and expense or investment,
    208
  choosing collaboration not competition,
    124–125
  cultural clash, 261–262
  strategic challenges, 135–138
  market segmentation, 137–138
  pacing process improvements, 135
  "perfect" customers, 119–120, 121
  Pollyanna Syndrome, 242
  problem children, 261–262
  sabotaging of strategic goals by employees, 136
Stealing competitors "good customers" can be
    hazardous, 125–126
Stenzel, Joe and Catherine, on BTIQ, 208
Storage Management Solutions, 227, 233
Strassmann, Paul A., 223
  CIO & IRM acronyms, 13
  executive "agendas", 45
  investment in IT and intrinsic value, 187–188
  IT as a primary strategic resource, 185
  job versus role, 46
  thoughts on primary focus of CIO, 115
Strategic:
  alliances, personal, 246–250
  communication for strategic alignment, 160
  customer relationship management, 120–122
  customer relationship postures, 122–127
  enabler, CIO as, aligning IT resources strategy,
    163
  horizon, and IT shadows across plans, 162–165
  insight paths for you and your company, 224
  inventory, 167
  IS/IT initiatives, 252–253
  performance measurements methods, 161
  resources, blending methods, 137–138

success, executive clarity as a measure of, 159
synchronicity, related to "perfect" customers
    120–122
thinking, adding risk management factor, 133,
    134
vision understanding, 159–160
Strategic plan:
  dependency on successful execution of, 165–166
  IT strategy as input to, 155–156
  proper resources invested to execute, 157–158
  validating execution against, 158–162
Strategic planning:
  team, CIO as member, 15
  enterprisewide, 127–129
  information technology as a key element of, 9
  positive and negative organizational descriptors,
    170
  paying for executing the plans, 157–158
Strategic reprioritizations:
  accounting for fixed computing resources,
    163–164
  managing fixed computing resources, 164
  organizations looking to IT for solutions,
    164–165
  solution scope to actual requirements and needs,
    164
Strategies:
  competitive: defender, prospector, analyzer,
    reactor, 167–168
  risk profiles matched to, 180–182
  translating into actionable business plans, 174
Strategy:
  aligning your IT resources to the organizations,
    184–192
  difference between intended and realized,
    169–170
  explicit, as combination of strategy and risk, 133,
    134
  paradox of executive perception, 151–152
  time spent on operations or, 217–218
Strengths and needs assessment, 263, 264–267
Success enablers and inhibitors for IT, 128–129
Successful strategies, 65
Sun Microsystems, CEO Scott McNealy, 12
Supplier Relationship Management, defined, 282
SWOT:
  IT portfolio based on corporate strategy,
    168–169
  personal, 264–265
  professional, 265
Symbiotic relationship of company and IT
    strategic plans, 156
Synchronicity, strategic, related to "perfect"
    customers, 120–122

System/360 and System/370, 3
Szasz, Thomas, on finding one's self, 272

Taco Bell, 157–158
Team, future and present tense and, 251–252
Technical skills:
    advanced, in context, 76–83
    basic technical fundamentals, 69–76
Technobabble, 75–76
Technology Review: MIT's Magazine of Innovation,
    227, 233
Temperament and personality types, 221–222
Temperament Theory, 33, 35
    Myers-Briggs matrix, 35
Ten Questions:
    BTIQ for the CEO, 230
    CIO must ask the CEO, 13–19
    CIO should ask entire executive team during
        strategic planning, 150–170
    CIO should ask network partners, 51–59
    CIO should ask outsourced service providers,
        102–113
    CIO should ask himself/herself regularly, 273
    expectations of CEOs from their CIOs, 10–19
Terminating projects before completion, 203–206
Texas Instruments, 145
Think twice/speak once, Carpenter's rule, 30
Tibetan climb, 202
Tieger, Paul D. and Barbara Barron-Tieger, 221
Tolerance of risk, 216
Trailing-edge risk profile, 179
Transformation to value creation center, 255
Transition plans, personal, 271
Troublemaker, 165
True horizon, 269
Turing, Alan, 2
Twofer on the way to nirvana, 246

Underground, functional, 247, 249–250
Underproduce and overcommit, Pollyanna
    Syndrome, 240–243
Unhappy employees and naysayers, liberating,
    261–262
Unhappy, ambassadors of, 260–262
Unified competency profile, 65–114
    business acumen, 66
    leadership competence and vision, 67
    management expertise, 66–67,
    technical skills, 66, 67–83
Up as the only career direction, 267–268

Valente, John, VP of operations & engineering (IS),
    Best Buy:

profiles of success, 101–102
on linkage to company's competitive strategy,
    167
Value center, 149–150
Value creation:
    center, transformation to, 255
    connecting IT to, 115–170
    enabling via changes in accounting-based
        measures, 177
    external customer relationships, 149
    mind-set, 247–248
    ROI, discussion with CEO, 207
    "sweet spot", 211
    through investment, 212
    transformation to delivery culture, 262
Vanguard Group, Chairman and CEO Jack
    Brennan on wants from CIO, 12
Vignette, CIO John J. Ciulla, 12
Vision:
    alignment with superior and subordinates,
        97–99
    evolution of leadership competency, 96
    leadership assessment, 100
    leadership competence and vision, 95–100
    scenarios, onboard, 99
    scenarios, rudderless, 99–100
Vocabulary, building an expanded 117–118
Volunteering for business units' strategic planning,
    154–155

Wall Street, 175
Wal-Mart's EDI history as bleeding edge risk
    profile, 180
Want versus need, CEOs from CIO, 11–12
Water runs downhill, 174
We've already tried that and it didn't work, 237,
    243
We've always done it this way, 243–244
"What edge?" risk profile, 178–179
What the customer really wanted, 44
When up is not the right direction, 268
Wild ducks at IBM, 250–251, 260, 274
Workforce diversity, importance of, 86
Workload:
    barrier to CIO success, 237, 244–245
    monkey, 244–245
WorldCom, 175

Yachting, 203
Your career is in your own hands, 264, 269, 272
Yourdon, Edward, 242

Zero-sum resource and capital, 229